Crisis and Change Today

Crisis and Change Today

Basic Questions of Marxist Sociology

Second Edition

Peter Knapp and Alan J. Spector

ROWMAN & LITTLEFIELD PUBLISHERS, INC.
Lanham • Boulder • New York • Toronto • Plymouth, UK

Published by Rowman & Littlefield Publishers, Inc.
A wholly owned subsidary of The Rowman & Littlefield Publishing Group, Inc.
4501 Forbes Boulevard, Suite 200, Lanham, Maryland 20706
http://www.rowmanlittlefield.com

Estover Road, Plymouth PL6 7PY, United Kingdom

British Library Cataloguing in Publication Information Available

Library of Congress Cataloging-in-Publication Data
Knapp, Peter, 1944-
  [Crisis & change]
  Crisis and change today : basic questions of Marxist sociology / Peter Knapp and Alan J. Spector. -- 2nd ed.
      p. cm.
  Includes index.
  ISBN 978-0-7425-2043-1 (cloth : alk. paper) -- ISBN 978-0-7425-2044-8 (pbk. : alk. paper) -- ISBN 978-1-4422-0823-0 (electronic)
  1. Communism and society. 2. Marxian school of sociology. 3. Communism. 4. Marx, Karl, 1818-1883. I. Spector, Alan J. II. Title.
  HX542.K532 2011
  301--dc22

                                                                    2010032346

♾™ The paper used in this publication meets the minimum requirements of American National Standard for Information Sciences—Permanence of Paper for Printed Library Materials, ANSI/NISO Z39.48-1992. Printed in the United States of America

Contents

List of Figures and Tables   ix

Preface to the Second Edition   xi

Introduction   1

1 Base and Superstructure: Marx's Theory of History   13
Introduction: Sociology Confronts History—Class as the Basis
                of Social Structure and the Backbone of History   13
Section 1.1:   Is There a Logic to History? If So, What Is It?   17
Section 1.2:   What Is the Basis of Social Structure?   25
Section 1.3:   Have States Always Existed?   35
Section 1.4:   Have Classes Always Existed?   42
Section 1.5:   What Is Feudalism? What Is Liberalism?   52
Section 1.6:   What Causes Social Movements and Social Change?   65
Section 1.7:   Are Events Inevitable? Was the French Revolution
                Inevitable?   71
Section 1.8:   What Are the Dynamics of the Modern World?   78
Section 1.9:   What Are the Fundamental Problems of the
                Modern World?   84
Section 1.10:   Are Classes in the United States Based on Exploitation?   93
Summary and Conclusions: History, Historical Sociology, and
Comparative History   102

2 Surplus Value: Marx's Economics   107
Introduction: Marxist Economics and the Science of Social Change   107

Section 2.1:   What Is a Commodity? What Is the Labor
                Theory of Value?   112
Section 2.2:   What Is Surplus Value?   118
Section 2.3:   What Is Overproduction? How Can There Be
                Too Much Food, Housing, or Health Care?   122
Section 2.4:   What Are the Dynamics of Production for Profit?   129
Section 2.5:   Why Is There Unemployment?   135
Section 2.6:   Who Benefits from Racism and Sexism?   143
Section 2.7:   How Much Misery Is There in the United States?   154
Section 2.8:   Is the United States a Land of Exceptional
                Mobility? Does It Matter?   162
Section 2.9:   Why Are There Economic Depressions?   169
Section 2.10:   Why Has the United States Been "Number 1"?   180
Summary and Conclusions: Economics and Political Economy   189

3   Class Struggle: Class, Party, and Political Theory   193
Introduction: Economic Determinism Versus Political
                Processes and Ideas—A False Debate   193
Section 3.1:   What Is the Basis of a Truly Free Society?   195
Section 3.2:   What Are Capitalists' Political Resources
                under Capitalism?   203
Section 3.3:   What Are the Crucial Political Changes in
                the World Today?   212
Section 3.4:   How Does Capitalist Politics Change?   219
Section 3.5:   What Is Fascism?   226
Section 3.6:   What Determines Different Degrees of
                Destructiveness of Fascism?   235
Section 3.7:   What Is a "Dictatorship of the Proletariat"?   243
Section 3.8:   What Are the Main Varieties of Marxism?   251
Section 3.9:   Why Did Socialism Collapse in the USSR and China?   256
Section 3.10:   What Does the Collapse of Socialist World
                Powers Mean for Change?   267
Summary and Conclusions: Marxist Political Theory   275

4   Applying Dialectics: Some Issues in the Philosophy of Science   279
Introduction: Dialectics—A Way of Looking at the World,
                or the Way the World Works?   279
Section 4.1:   Is a Science of Society Possible?   284
Section 4.2:   What Are the Main Sources of Error in Social Theory? 292
Section 4.3:   Are Attempts at Neutrality a Guarantee of Objectivity? 299
Section 4.4:   Crisis and Change   306
Section 4.5:   Can Social Science Be Value-Neutral? Should It Be? 317
Section 4.6:   Is Society Based on the Thoughts of Its Members?   324

Section 4.7:   What Are Ideologies?   331
Section 4.8:   What Contradictions Exist in Society?   339
Section 4.9:   Can One Find Laws of Change in History?   344
Section 4.10:   What Possibilities Are Open to Human Society?   350
Summary and Conclusions: Contradictions, Dialectics, and Science   359

Index   363

About the Authors   373

List of Figures and Tables

CHAPTER 1

Table   1.1 Epochal Changes in Modes of Production   27
Figure 1.1 Marx's Model of Base and Superstructure   29
Table   1.2 Cross-tabulation of Type of Economy with Stratification   36
Table   1.3 Cross-tabulation of Stratification with Form of the State   37
Figure 1.2 Class Polarization   49
Figure 1.3 Representation of Status Gradation   50
Table   1.4 Claimed Optima of Liberal Theory   54
Table   1.5 Outcomes of Liberalism in the Presence of Classes   56
Figure 1.4 Images of Change of American Stratification   59
Figure 1.5 Trends in Ownership of Means of Production in
            the United States   62
Figure 1.6 Distribution of Income in the United States   64
Figure 1.7 Types of Alienation   88
Figure 1.8 Tower of Income   95
Table   1.6 Income by Type and Size, 1982   95
Table   1.7 Influences on AFDC Caseloads at Time t 100

CHAPTER 2

Table 2.1 Contradictions of Capitalism   111
Table 2.2 Correlates of Occupation   140
Table 2.3 Effects of Race Inequality on Income Inequality   147

Figure 2.1 Spendable Average Weekly Earnings   157
Figure 2.2 U.S. Number in Poverty and Poverty Rate, 1959 to 2008   158
Table 2.4 Occupational Mobility in the United States in 1972   164
Table 2.5 Occupational Mobility in the United States in 2006   164
Figure 2.3 The Dot-com and Housing Bubbles   174
Table 2.6 Partial List of Possible Causes of Variation
            in Military Spending, 1949 to 1976   176
Table 2.7 Sector-specific Determinants of U.S. Military Spending   177
Table 2.8 Regression of Income Inequality of Investment
            Dependence, Size of Tertiary Sector, and
            Per Capita GDP   186

CHAPTER 3

Figure 3.1 Fundamental Positions in Political Theory   198
Figure 3.2 Kinds of Alienation   204
Figure 3.3 The Policy Formation Network   208
Figure 3.4 Krugman's Four Periods of Twentieth-Century Politics   215
Table 3.1 Kondratieff Cycles and Restructuring   218
Table 3.2 Party Realignments   221
Table 3.3 Violence and the Outcomes of Social Movements   243

CHAPTER 4

Table 4.1 Chains of Acquaintances   342
Figure 4.1 Wright's Model of Class and Class Struggle   354

Preface to the Second Edition

We wrote the first edition of this work in the wake of the fall of the Berlin Wall and the collapse of the Soviet Union. In the United States, politicians, the media, and many academics proclaimed, "Marxism is dead; capitalism has won!" However, like most Marxists, we had argued for decades that the Soviet politics, culture, job structure, and class structure had become essentially capitalist. The collapse of two decades ago was the outcome of a long development of institutions and culture based on inequality, individualism, selfishness, and visibly corrupt oligarchic rule.

Nor did the failure of those regimes prove that capitalism had solved its problems. It had not, and we suggested that "the world economy rests on interconnected debts like a house of cards. Worldwide crises continue to worsen. Economic crises become political crises, and political crises lead to military action" (P. Knapp and A. Spector 1991, xi). We see little reason to change our assessment, and below, at the end of the Introduction, we shall essentially repeat the end of our 1991 Introduction, that argues that "a Marxist perspective suggests a broad historical crisis at the end of the twentieth century, involving the economy and the political system of the whole world." Indeed, throughout this edition, we have tried to retain the outline of the form and content of the first edition, which we have made available online, to maintain continuity.

But of course, much has changed. While a Marxist perspective allowed us to glimpse some of the shapes of crises and changes on the horizon, their concrete form is now manifest. In some cases, we may not have embraced our own perspective radically enough. We could see that the prosperity of the world capitalist economy was often illusory, built on speculation, but we did not see how far the cascade of breakdown would reach. We could see cruel, quasi-fascist rationales of the United States' preparations for the military occupation of an oil rich country that had nothing to do with 9/11. We could not know, for example, that even a subsequent Democratic administration of Barack Obama would carry out similar policies; we did not entertain—for example—that Mohammed Jawad, a twelve-year-old boy, would be captured, tortured, held for nearly a decade, and then released, August 2009, without charges, apology, or indemnity, to a country hostile to him, even though there was no evidence against him except the self-incrimination produced by torture. Like others, we could anticipate the growth of Marxian theory and debate generated by the Soviet collapse, but we could not see its details.

In 1990, Michael Burawoy argued that the demise of the Soviet Union, far from spelling the demise of Marxism, would lead to its liberation from apologetics and further development (see the Suggestions for Further Reading at the end of the Introduction). Burawoy correctly suggested that capitalism showed no signs of solving its own irrationalities so that there would be a wider search for socialist solutions of many different kinds. This second edition attempts to summarize some of these developments within Marxist thought, within the broader debates of critical, humanist, and radical thought, and within mainstream sociology. We could see that Burawoy was probably correct, but we could not know that in the wake of his presidency of the American Sociological Association, his proposal for a "Public Sociology" aiming to contest the dominant assumptions of United States policy would be debated as the main stream of sociological argument, within many of the major journals.

The destructiveness and irrationality of late capitalism is visible to many people. As we write, the war in Afghanistan edges toward its second decade, and the destruction of the United States' third largest port by lack of preparation for Hurricane Katrina under President Bush has been followed by the destruction of much of the Gulf Coast ecology by a catastrophic BP oil spill under President Obama. By May of 2010, it was evident that the awesome technology to accomplish deep-sea drilling off Louisiana had been harnessed to the profit motive, not to social needs or to safety. There was no back-up plan, and so the technological development was a human and environmental catastrophe rather than a blessing. What is less visible to observers is the possibility of a different society and the political struggles that would bring us to it.

Marxian positions are of many different kinds, and there are many other radical and critical positions that they engage in discussion. One of the authors of this work has argued that the core of Marxian analysis is class analysis, although that class analysis is seen differently by different groups of sociologists (Spector 2002). For example, "critical theorists" often stress cultural, psychological, and value aspects of domination. "Neo-Marxists" and "analytical Marxists" often stress the use of methods of analysis and theory construction similar to rational choice models in economic theory. "Postmodernists" often stress parallel forms of oppression stemming from gender, race, nationality, and religion. The crucial insight to seeing the contribution that Marx can make to those discussions is that Marx understood "class" in a way that is much broader than amount of wealth, and this understanding addresses other historical, political, philosophical, and social conditions of human creativity and well-being.

Introduction

Marxism, when it appears within an academic discipline like sociology or economics, is somewhat like a beached whale among a flock of seagulls. For one thing, it does not fit into any of the academic disciplines. Parts of it belong in several different ones. If you go to the library to read the books on "Marxism," you find one big section devoted exclusively to history and theory of Marxism. But other books on Marxism are scattered throughout the library, especially under sociology, history, economics, politics, and philosophy. Marxism is not one topic, but a whole system of knowledge, parallel to the one dominant in the United States. Moreover, Marxism is not a purely academic discipline. Rather, it is in its true element in human history, where it has been a powerful force.

Marx's ideas constitute one of the most powerful developments in Western thought. In one way or another they have touched everything important that has happened in the last century. The central idea of Marx's sociology is that is it possible and desirable to eliminate classes and nation states. In his time, there was an epic battle to get rid of certain forms of class (titled, landed aristocracies in Europe and slavery in the United States) and certain forms of states (monarchies, empires, and their smaller equivalents). Marx saw that even after aristocracy was abolished, enormous class inequalities would remain. In this he was surely right. Three decades of free market policy in the United States has qualitatively increased inequality. Moreover, Marx saw that even after monarchy was abolished, political inequalities and structures of political domination would remain. And in this he was also right. Every contemporary sociologist recognizes that modern societies have huge structures of police, prisons, and military coercion. Two world wars have been fought since Marx's time, and the last two decades have seen increased military actions and increased insecurity.

Marx believed that classes and states are connected to each other, that they are the basis of social structure, and that they constantly change through history with changes in production. The fundamental attraction of Marxism is that it suggests that these structures of inequality and coercion can be eliminated. Marx believed that a classless and stateless society, which he called "communism," was possible and indeed inevitable. All sociologists would agree with Marx that inequalities and the structures for maintaining them are very important factors in human life. All social institutions are influenced by them—cultural ideas and values, deviance and social contacts, religion and education, science and art. Not all sociologists would agree that these phenomena are basic, and not all sociologists would agree that it is possible to construct a classless, stateless society. But even when they reject Marx's answers, they recognize the importance of his questions.

How classes and states are related to each other and whether it is possible to eliminate them are difficult questions. They are bound up with the analysis of the rest of social structure. It will take the rest of this book to present some basic parts of the evidence and arguments relevant to the questions. At the very least, questions of historical change, of economics, of politics, and of value are involved.

States and classes—the structures of inequality and coercion in the modern world—are immensely powerful. We read about millions of people starving, about billionaires, about a trillion dollars worth of weapons (the equivalent of a million dollars a day from the birth of Christ to the present). Even when such structures of inequality and power strike us as obscene, as they often do, the idea of a transformation that could sweep them away is such a big idea that many find it frightening. Many people in the United States see that change is happening, and they feel that things are crumbling. They are afraid when they get in an airplane; they are afraid when they drive through a strange part of the city and see people sleeping in the streets; they are afraid of new diseases; they are afraid of losing their homes or jobs. Because they are afraid, some people try to resist change. Marx's ideas were an attempt to understand the transformations of the nineteenth century and to grasp the positive opportunities in those changes.

Marxism is often described as a synthesis of three complex, independent systems of knowledge: German philosophy, British economics, and French political theory. From German philosophy Marx took dialectics (a way of describing the nature of change), which he combined with philosophical materialism. From British economics he took the labor theory of value, and he developed the theory of surplus value. From French social, historical, and political thought he took analyses of class struggle and socialism, and he developed the theory of a workers' revolution leading to a workers' state. Philosophical dialectics, economics, and French political thought are diverse. What constitutes their unity? What do they have in common? One way of seeing the unity of Marxism is to look at Marx himself and his life. Marx lived in a time of change and transformation. An older form of society was crumbling. The Marxist synthesis was a way of understanding those transformations and allowing people to get a hold on them.

MARX'S LIFE AND WORKS

Marx was a European revolutionary who lived in the middle of the nineteenth century. He was born in Trier, a part of Germany close to France, in 1818. The turning points of his life were the main revolutionary episodes of the nineteenth century: he was born after the French Revolution and the Napoleonic wars. He reached thirty at about the time of the revolutions of 1848, in which he participated and for which he drafted *The Communist Manifesto*. He reached fifty around the time of the Paris Commune (1871). He died in London in 1883, thirty-four years before the Russian Revolution.

In many ways, the French Revolution at the end of the eighteenth century was the beginning of the modern era. Even more than the American Revolution at about the same time, it marked the crisis resulting from the rise of democratic, anti-aristocratic, urban, industrial, secular, capitalist society. These developments form the background of Marx's writings, just as they form the background for the development of sociology.

In the generation before Marx, armies and mass movements had battled all over Europe. Before that time, most countries were monarchies. Indeed, most European countries were not even nation states. Eastern Europe was within the amorphous Turkish, Romanov, and Austro-Hungarian empires. Germany and Italy were patchwork quilts of duchies, bishoprics, principalities, and kingdoms. The Napoleonic armies and the Napoleonic Code destroyed the old regimes of many European countries, and doomed the rest. But with Napoleon's defeat, monarchies were restored and creaked along under threat of rebellion through the nineteenth century, until they were finally demolished in the twentieth century. For example, in Marx's birthplace, Trier, the liberal Napoleonic regime was replaced by a conservative one under the absolute monarchy. Marx's father, descended from a rabbinical Jewish family, converted the whole family to Protestantism to escape discrimination. In the 1830s, Marx studied philosophy for five years at the University of Berlin and wrote a doctoral dissertation on the ancient materialist philosophers Democritus and Epicurus.

In the early 1840s, as a journalist and editor of a newspaper called the *Rheinische Zeitung*, Marx became a radical democrat for a time. He defended freedom of the press. He exposed the economic and political actions of landlords against their workers and tenants. And he began to develop a political philosophy. When the government closed down his newspaper, Marx moved to Paris. He became an active revolutionary, working within and learning from the secret societies of German workers there. He met the main socialist and communist theorists in Europe, and began his lifelong collaboration with Friedrich Engels, author of *The Condition of the Working Class in England*. While Engels and Marx did not have identical views, they were both so influenced by each other that the term "Marxism" could properly be called the product of both men. They jumped into the heated philosophical arguments of the day, and together they wrote a criticism of the young Hegelians, *The Holy Family*.

In 1845, Marx left Paris for Brussels, as a result of pressure from the Prussian government. There he wrote *The Poverty of Philosophy* and he and Engels collaborated on *The German Ideology* and published a little book that has probably influenced more people than any other ever published: *The Communist Manifesto*. In early 1848, there was mass insurgency and rebellion against the monarchies of France, Austria, and the German states. Marx went back to Germany and worked to promote the revolutions, publishing some 300 issues of the *Neue Rheinische Zeitung* in his effort to influence the struggle. The revolutions of 1848 were defeated, but Marx and other revolutionaries had learned a great deal. Marx was only thirty years old, but he had already written extensively about history, politics, and current affairs, both in Europe and in the rest of the world. He had recognized the importance of economics, and especially of class, to politics and indeed to all of society; these were to be the theme of his intellectual work.

In 1849, Marx moved to London. His life was hard. In exile, the Marx family lived in grinding poverty, especially during the first seven years. Marx made a meager living as a journalist, writing hundreds of newspaper articles. But since he was paid only a few dollars apiece for them, the Marx family often had no money for rent, food, or medicine. They pawned books and other possessions, even clothing. Four of the six children died. Unlike the other figures who founded sociology—reasonably comfortable and secure university professors—Marx showed no tendency to buy into the comfortable illusions of his society, and he built a working class party (the First International) to unite the often illegal unions and parties of different countries.

Under these circumstances, it is not surprising that Marx was unable to complete many of the most important books he had planned to write, which in turn has contributed to disputes about his theories. Nevertheless, Marx was able to write an enormous amount. Three books on French politics, *The Class Struggles in France* (1850), *The Eighteenth Brumaire of Louis Bonaparte* (1852), and *The Civil War in France* (1871), form the core of his political writings. Marx also wrote some 500 articles as European correspondent of the *New York Daily Tribune*, focusing on the coming of the American Civil War. Marx played a dominant role in founding the International Working Men's Association, and he wrote the inaugural address and the provisional rules of the International. Two other books written during this period are the core of Marx's economics. He published the *Critique of Political Economy* in 1859 and the first volume of *Capital* in 1867. During this period he also wrote the popular introductions to his economics, *Wage Labor and Capital* and *Value Price and Profit*, as well as the large manuscript usually called the *Grundrisse* (1858) and the manuscript from which the volumes of *Theories of Surplus Value* were later extracted.

In the last twelve years of his life, Marx worked on the second and third volumes of *Capital*, although he was not able to complete them. He also wrote a number of important political analyses such as the analysis of the Paris Commune, *The Civil War in France* (1871). For example, the *Critique of the Gotha Program*, written in 1875, was a commentary on the program on the basis of which the two socialist parties of Germany merged.

Thus, there are four main roads into Marxist social theory. The clearest road—the one that Marx and Engels themselves usually recommended—was through political writings: the *Manifesto*, the books on France, and some of Marx's articles. A second related route follows Marx's analysis of history from the *German Ideology* to the historical parts of *Capital*. Third, many people approach Marxism through the philosophical criticism of Hegel in Marx's early manuscripts, books, and articles, comparing them to the later works, especially by Engels, such as *Anti-Duhring* and *Ludwig Feuerbach and the End of German Idealism*. Fourth, probably the most challenging road, but one every student of Marxism will want to follow sooner or later, is the economic writings, starting with the popular introductions and moving to the *Critique*, *Capital*, and *Theories of Surplus Value*. Of course, all four roads lead to the same place. One of the reasons the Marxist synthesis is so important is that it powerfully connects these disciplines in a way that transforms the social sciences. The four chapters of this book will introduce contemporary sociological work relevant to each of these four strands of analysis.

One way of understanding the unity of Marxism is to note that Marx saw that human labor contains the key to four distinct problems central to the development of Western thought. **In history**, people had wondered what was the fundamental logic of historical development. Marx's answer is that by human physical and mental labor—the labor of millions and millions of people through the centuries—people make themselves what they are. This stress on human labor leads to the concept of the real foundation or economic base of the society. In history, human labor takes the form of the economic base as the foundation of historical materialism. **In economics**, people had wondered what was the source of wealth and of the increase in wealth. Marx's answer is that labor is the source of wealth. The reason that inedible green paper is sought after is that you don't have to grow cabbages if you have it; you can pay someone else to do whatever you want. In economics, the labor theory of value views labor as the source of wealth. **In politics**, people had wondered what were the sources of political change and political movements. Marx argued that class is the basis of political movements, and the working class is the basis of any progressive transformation of society. In politics, Marx's stress on labor leads to his theory of a workers' revolution leading to a workers' state. **In philosophy**, people had wondered for centuries how we learn that true statements are true. The fundamental Marxist answer is practice doing something and learning the consequences. Ultimately, differences between systems of knowledge boil down to practical differences. One theory says or implies that if you do this, one thing will result, and if you do that, another thing will result. A different theory disagrees. Ultimately (but not always), people decide which theory is true by doing this or that and finding out what happens. In philosophy, the form that human labor takes is practice. It is the basis of materialist dialectics. Thus, human labor takes four forms: labor as the economic base, labor as economic value, labor as the working class running the country, and labor as practice.

What do these ideas in history, politics, economics, and philosophy have to do with sociology? The answer depends, in part, on how you look at sociology. If you consider sociology as a narrow academic discipline, these concerns in history, economics, political science, and philosophy are extraneous to it. They are still very important because they are connected to Marxist theories within sociology. Moreover, they are very important for the connections between sociology and the other social sciences. But from a narrow standpoint, these ideas are nonsociological.

Many standpoints in sociology are non-Marxist, developed in explicit opposition to Marx, and define society so that economics, politics, and history lie mainly outside it. It would be convenient if the real world were divided into discrete compartments that could be studied by different academic disciplines. But it is not. The real puzzles and problems of this world, whether theoretical or practical, have interrelated aspects. To understand them, one needs to consider history and economics and philosophy and politics. Think of the problems of the war, racism, AIDS, toxic wastes, new religious movements, urban decay, drugs, unemployment, and a thousand others. We cannot usefully analyze these problems independently of politics, economics, history, and broad philosophical questions of method and value. When we ignore power, money, social change, and value, our analysis becomes narrow, weak, and untestable. This is true both of topical questions like the Afghan war and the BP oil spill—questions which involve the continuation of the human race—and of specialized issues about education, family structures, or birth rates. These are often linked to larger historical, economic, or political structures. The attempt to divide the world into compartments has merely led to academic fragmentation and many of the important theoretical and practical problems get lost in the cracks between the disciplines.

When one chooses to ignore the big structures of politics and economics in favor of looking at smaller face-to-face processes in families, small groups, and communities, one is usually treating those big processes as given, as basically static the way they are. If the smaller processes are influenced by big structures, then even if those big structures do not change, the analysis will be incomplete and misleading. It can be a useful simplification to assume that causes are separate from effects, and that effects are unconditional and invariant, or to assume that there are no systemic feedbacks or interactions. However, at other times, those simplifying assumptions distort essential features of the reality. In practice, contemporary developments in mathematics, physics, chemistry, and other fields are exploring the chaotic, turbulent, and discontinuous processes that violate those assumptions. Dialectical analysis is sensitive to these complex forms of causality.

Marxism often appears to be an academic white elephant or, to use our earlier analogy, a beached whale. It is not as neat, as light, as pretty as many academic disciplines. And there have always been academics who announced that it is a dead whale. In the 1950s, as today, campuses were quiet, conservatives were active, and many people announced the end of Marxism. But reports of Marxism's death are greatly exaggerated. As soon as one tries to understand events in the world, particularly changes in the huge structures of power or inequality, one needs to deal with history, economics, politics, and philosophy. Then Marxist synthesis slips into its element and proves to be very much alive. Anyone who tries to change any of these structures finds that they have a struggle on their hands. In such struggles, Marxism turns out to be not only alive but an awesome force.

THE STRUCTURE OF THIS WORK

This broad conception of sociology determines the structure of this work. In sociology, as in each of the other social sciences, there has been a flowering of neo-Marxist theorizing in the last few years. Many journal articles represent an application of Marxist theory, and even more articles attempt to address the big questions raised by Marx. To understand the main research traditions which operate from a Marxist perspective, it is necessary to see their common foundation. To give an exposition of this foundation we have subdivided this book into units dealing with the historical, economic, political, and methodological (philosophical) foundation blocks of Marxist sociology.

We believe that going from the specific to the general is best, but readers are, of course, free to start with chapter 4 and proceed to chapters 1, 2, and 3 should they wish to examine the work from its most general assumptions to its specific conclusions. This work, like research, is a circle which can be started at many points.

Each unit is divided into ten short sections. Each section has a dialogic or dialectical structure in that it begins with an issue or question. These questions are real issues; in posing them, we have tried to avoid meaningless rhetorical questions. Many of the questions do not allow cut-and-dried answers. If you cannot understand how anyone but a fool could maintain the positions being put forward, look again. Each of these positions has been maintained by sophisticated minds. At the same time, we have tried to take clear and definite positions on each question.

We cover a large amount of ground. Accordingly, we believe that we owe our readers a large-scale preliminary map of crucial concepts, even though the anticipation of data or arguments not yet presented may seem simplistic and dogmatic. These four sets of six propositions are discussed at the end of each chapter as a summary of the material.

The historical ideas in chapter 1:

1. Human life is social and historical.
2. We live in an era of class societies.
3. In class societies, some control the labor power of others.
4. Class struggle has been the motor of history.
5. In capitalism, owners buy the labor power of workers.
6. This process creates conflicts, poverty, and misery.

The economic ideas in chapter 2:

7. The value of commodities is determined by labor.
8. The owning classes exploit laborers to accumulate wealth.
9. Overproduction and a falling rate of profit are endemic to capitalism and cause crises.
10. Private credit and Keynesianism are only temporary solutions to crises.
11. Imperialist foreign investment is also a temporary solution.
12. As temporary remedies falter, economic crisis intensifies.

The political ideas in chapter 3:

13. Even liberal capitalism does not mean real freedom; the capitalist state generally serves the capitalist class.
14. In severe crises, liberal capitalism turns into fascism.
15. The danger of fascism can be defeated only by eliminating capitalism.

16. The USSR initially defeated capitalism but then moved from Marxist socialism back to a kind of state capitalism.
17. Opportunism has severely weakened Marxist movements.
18. The struggle for egalitarianism needs principled, anti-opportunist, organized leadership.

The philosophical ideas in chapter 4:

19. The world exists outside of our consciousnesses.
20. Everything changes in qualitative, irreversible ways.
21. There are no absolute truths, but there are concrete truths.
22. Humans change; there is no fixed human nature.
23. Social structure and history can be studied scientifically.
24. In order to do that, one must examine the contradictory forces, the contradictions that lie within everything, especially social phenomena.

These twenty-four points should be viewed in the context of two important characteristics of this book. First of all, while these points define, in a fairly abstract way, what we see as the skeleton of Marxist thought today, the chapter headings and subheadings of the text do not mechanically follow these points. The text consists of theory, data, examples, and illustrations woven around the points rather than of essays on each point.

Second, Marxist sociology strives to be a living science. It tries to get a better understanding of the world, with the realization that conclusions will eventually have to be revised because of the incomplete nature of science and the ever-changing nature of the world. As a result, there are many different interpretations within Marxist social thought. On a whole range of questions, one can find most of the same debates within Marxist social thought that go on within the traditional academic disciplines, including the relationship between free will and determinism, the amount of explanatory emphasis that should be given to individual acts versus institutional structures, politics and historical culture versus economics in defining class, quantitative change versus qualitative change, the importance of classical theory versus new data and methods of data analysis, and many others. This is not bad; it means that, as in other sciences, many investigators are working on trying to understand. Without that, we would have dogma, not science.

One book cannot possibly support, or even examine, all the conclusions of all the thousands of social scientists working in the Marxist tradition. There are doubtless many such sociologists, for example, who would strongly disagree with some of the conclusions in this text. We hope we have done a thorough job explicating the fundamental tenets of Marxist sociology. On the more controversial questions within Marxist sociology, we have tried to lay out the major positions, with some references for further examination, even as we put forward our own interpretations. We encourage comments from readers on both the form and content of this book. There is always room for improvement, and comments from readers can be especially helpful.

Labor, work, and human accomplishment are central to Marxism. What you get out of this book will depend on what you put into it. That insight is one of the reasons for the exercises at the end of each section: thought-experiments, textual analyses, games, analyses of data, field work investigations. We hope that the work of doing the exercises will be interesting. In any case, we believe that it will determine how much you learn. We have tried to design them so that they pose challenging problems.

At the end of each section is a brief essay giving Suggestions for Further Reading. Even a superficial bibliography on Marxism would be much longer than this whole book, and so we have not tried to be exhaustive. The suggestions for further reading comprise an annotated bibliography of some 200 contemporary Marxist sociological works.

The flowering of neo-Marxist theory, though it has intellectual and theoretical sources, has significant social and political roots. A generation of students matured believing that positive social change is possible. They believed that the oppression of women, of racial and ethnic minorities, of people of the Third World, and of the working class as a whole was not a minor aberration but rather was built into the capitalist system. We believed this because we took part in trying to change the system and we saw how powerfully the system reacted against change. The movement against the Vietnam War of the 1960s was, along with the Civil Rights movement and the women's movement, the main root of the revival of neo-Marxist theory in the United States in the 1980s. The outcome of free-market policies, global capitalism and military adventures, producing war and economic, social, and ecological crisis, feeds Marxian practice today.

This work is meant for a wide audience, from introductory students to those with considerable background in social science. It is both a thematic work, with an integrated train of thought and some strong assumptions and conclusions, as well as a survey that introduces readers to contemporary Marxist writings.

Furthermore, any work that aspires to be scientific rather than dogmatic must be open to change as changes in the world take place. Even as there has been a revival of Marxist theory in Western countries, there has been a crisis among political movements calling themselves Marxist. Yet, even as procapitalist writers declare that these developments disprove Marxism, the capitalist world, too, is wracked by turmoil. Brushfire wars sweep over Asia, Africa, Latin America, and the Middle East. There are forebodings of crisis in Asia, Europe, and North America. As the United States spends trillions of dollars on arms, the environment is degraded and millions starve in the Third World, while people pay trillions of dollars to shore up and pay interest to U.S. banks on debt that places the world financial system on an increasingly shaky foundation.

By themselves, these millions and billions and trillions daze us. They connote no crisis—no possibility of real change. But, from a Marxist perspective, they suggest a broad historical crisis at the beginning of the twenty-first century, involving the economy and political system of the whole world. Our purpose is to write a book that would be as useful in provoking questions as in pointing in the direction of answers. We believe that whatever this book has of value comes from its connection to the battle of working class people throughout the world for a better world for all.

Suggestions for Further Reading

There are many good introductions to Marxism, to sociology, and to Marxist sociology. The most useful resource on the life and writings of Marx and Engels is the *Marx-Engels Cyclopedia*, in three volumes, by H. Draper (Schocken, 1985). Two good biographies of Marx's life and work are *Karl Marx* by Franz Mehring (London, 1936), an activist who knew some of Marx's contemporaries, and *Marx's Politics*, by Alan Gilbert (Rutgers University Press, 1982). Also useful are the eulogy given by Engels at Marx's funeral and a short pamphlet by V. I. Lenin, "The Three Sources and Component Parts of Marxism" in *Selected Works of Marx and Engels* (International Publishers, 1977). Michael Burawoy's "Marxism as Science: Historical Challenges and Theoretical Growth" was in *American Sociological Review* 55:775–793 (1990), and his presidential address proposing a "Public Sociology" was in *American Sociological Review* 70 (2005). A. Spector, "Marxist Sociology and Humanist Sociology: Diversity, Intersections and Convergence" appeared in *American Sociologist* (2002).

1

Base and Superstructure

Marx's Theory of History

INTRODUCTION: SOCIOLOGY CONFRONTS HISTORY—CLASS AS THE BASIS OF SOCIAL STRUCTURE AND THE BACKBONE OF HISTORY

Marx spent much time investigating and writing history, using it even in his most theoretical books, such as *Capital*. Many students do not see any reason that they should be interested in history. The glories of Greece? The agonies of the French Revolution? John Brown's raid? The rise of Mussolini? What does it matter? Some people view history as the story of dead people. They say that history is interested in the past for itself—to find out how it really was. Others define history as the story of famous people: princes and politicians, popes and poets, painters and philosophers. Famous dead people can be the topic of sociological theory, just as anyone else can. But history is not just stories about famous dead people. True, history studies the past, and the past can't ever be changed. But history is important to sociology for three reasons: (1) it shows how social institutions are interconnected; (2) it shows how choices and tensions are embedded in social structure; and (3) it shows how change is pervasive in society.

Interconnection of Social Institutions

Marx pioneered an approach to history which concentrates on social history, the history of the social situation of ordinary people. His approach looks at society as a constantly changing whole. Some important parts of social structure, such as classes and nation-states, seem to have always been there, independent of the rest of social structure. Even smaller pieces of social structure like romantic love, family structure, crime, education, or medicine often seem that way. But a look at history shows that these institutions are very closely tied to each other and more changeable than they seem.

Most organizations, such as schools or firms, are younger than many people. If we ask why they are the way they are, a large part of the answer is that they are part of a system of organizations such as the American educational system or the American economy. And if we then ask why *that* is the way it is, we find that the different institutions are connected to each other and that they are deeply influenced by big structures, especially classes and states. Even these big structures change. They only assumed their present form in the last century or so. In Marx's day, few contemporary nation-states had been created. Many people are older than most nations are, today. In Marx's day, most of the population was self-employed. Marx was virtually the only theorist of the nineteenth century who could see the importance of the process which would virtually eliminate self-employed farmers, peasants, and artisans, expanding the number of people working for someone else. These economic changes would also change families, churches, governments, neighborhoods, and the rest of social structure.

All social structures change. In the 1990s, when the Soviet bloc collapsed, a concept of Fukuyama's, called "the end of history," became popular. He predicted that the United States' capitalist system was the final stage and end point of world history, with its invulnerable military force and all-powerful economy. However, after 9/11, two wars, the rise of China, and the near economic collapse of 2009, such views seem pathetic. All social structures change, but not by magic. If we take a longer view, to include preliterate societies, we see that humankind spent most of its existence in societies which were not even remotely like contemporary ones, especially in terms of classes and states. Thus, the first reason that history is important is that without a sense of history one cannot see how the different parts of society fit together.

Choices and Tensions

History is not the history of beings on another planet. It is the way we have become who we are. Institutions such as monarchy, slavery, or Nazism expanded, declined, and then were eliminated. Their defeat is how the present world was created. Understanding that process is important for understanding the present. It is like knowing a person. All people have gone through many changes to become who they are. A person may not even remember those changes. But often these changes left tensions lying beneath the surface, which are important for understanding how that person will behave in the future. The same is true of society. Just as you have made choices which have made you who you are, society has made choices which have made it the way it is.

Human beings are social, historical beings. All people are born into a society, and the society into which they are born affects them. Every society comes from a previous society. History not only shows the interconnection of the different parts of social structure, it also shows the choices and dynamics embedded in social structure. People did not just "happen" to fall into different nations, races, or religious groups. It took an enormous amount of action and organization and violence to divide people into the groups which exist today. Native Americans didn't just "happen" to die out in North America. They were largely exterminated and their descendants corralled by European settlers. This history is important for understanding the present.

Another reason that it is important to know your own history is that if you don't, you will have to adopt a history which someone else has created. Often that other history is a censored history, an ideological history, a history that reflects particular standpoints and interests in a way that makes it an *inaccurate* history. Western movies give a particular view of how North America came to be as it is. Elementary school histories show Squanto, the friendly Indian, helping the Pilgrims plant corn. This also gives a particular view. Many students react to history as something that does not concern them. But it is important to retrieve history because if someone controls your view of history, they control your self-conception; if they control your self-conception, they control your future.

Historical Change

There is a third reason that history is important for the social sciences. If everything stayed the same, then it would not be so important that institutions interconnect or that choices and tensions are embedded in the present. But things do change. Sometimes it appears that nothing ever changes and nothing will ever change. But it is more correct to say that nothing ever stays the same. Change is pervasive.

If a person confines his or her view to the present and to the surface, change may not be visible. In 1948, just before the final success of the Chinese Revolution, the most massive transformation of the largest society in world history, it appeared that in China nothing changed and that nothing would ever change. As far as one could tell from published reports, the Communists were an isolated bunch of bandits, off in the hills, without popular support or program. According to those who controlled information in China, they could not possibly succeed. Similarly, the day before the French Revolution, it appeared to most contemporaries that there was and there would be no change. The same could be said about other societies on the verge of change—Vietnam in the 1950s, Iran in 1979, or the Soviet Union in 1989. However, hidden changes had accumulated so that those societies were about to go through great, discontinuous, catastrophic transformations.

The transformation of social structure was very visible in Marx's lifetime. The idea of a scientific study of social structure can only arise when people are familiar with different social structures. But in the nineteenth century, the remnants of feudal society and the growing capitalistic society were often sitting right next to each other. That helped show how different components of social structure can fit or fail to fit with each other. A rural community, farming as a way of life, obedience to church and king, inherited family position, and strong local and kinship ties all fit together. Industry, commerce, democracy, education, secularism, individualism, and social-political equality fit together in an opposed system, which was tearing the first one apart. People's deepest loyalties were engaged. And the battles over freedom, equality, and progress swept armies and mass movements back and forth all over Europe. Many people believed that changes of world historical importance were taking place, and they tried to understand these changes. Their attempt to understand these changes produced classical sociology.

All the early sociologists produced historical theories of the changes which were going on, which gradually separated off from philosophies of history. In the United States, sociological theory was somewhat less historical. And during the first half of the twentieth century, some sociologists in the United States began to pull back from general theories of history and social change, dismissing them as "grand theory." More recently, there has been a surge of historical studies in sociology. Marxism has always maintained that the analyses of structure and of change have to proceed simultaneously; it has always maintained that there is an important historical dimension of the present. Thus historical sociology has been promoted by and has promoted the increase in Marxist analyses in sociology.

During the 1950s and 1960s, the leading journals in sociology almost completely neglected history. The data and the theories with which they dealt were largely cross-sectional within a given society and period. However, since the late 1960s and 1970s, there has been an explosion of historical and comparative-historical research in sociology. The world today is changing very rapidly. Political and religious movements which no one had heard of twenty years ago have swept over some countries, transforming them. A financial crisis or economic change in Iraq, Brazil, or Hong Kong can quickly transform the lives of people in Ohio or California. Under these circumstances, an historical approach to social structure which looks at its change and interconnection is very important.

Suggestions for Further Reading

Three theorists are especially central to the explosion of historical sociology: Barrington Moore, Charles Tilly, and Immanuel Wallerstein. Each of them spans the disciplines of sociology, political science, and history. Each has produced analyses which revolutionized many subdisciplines in sociology. Each has been profoundly influenced by Marx and by the ongoing traditions of Marxist history. For overviews of their historical sociology, see T. Skocpol (editor), *Vision and Method in Historical Sociology* (Cambridge University Press, 1984).

SECTION 1.1: IS THERE A LOGIC TO HISTORY? IF SO, WHAT IS IT?

Prior to Marx, the division of labor in social theory tended to leave the empirical analysis of the past to historians, while theories and explanations were produced by philosophers of history. Thus the philosophy of history was one of the main building blocks of the modern social sciences. Philosophies of history maintain that the course of human history is not a random, static, accidental jumble of brute facts, but rather that history has an intelligible structure and movement. Different philosophies analyzed that movement in different ways, and contemporary accounts of social change still recollect those theories. One of the main building blocks of Marxism is an account of the pattern of history. And the other sociological paradigms were, in large part, a response to Marx and to philosophers of history such as Hegel. If we see how Marx transformed the philosophy of history, we shall see the sociological basis of his theory of history.

These philosophers mainly stressed ideal, cultural forces behind social change, changes in people's ideas or religious values or political views. Against them, Marx stressed that *people's ideas and ideals change when their practice—their social actions and relationships and way of life—changes*. These debates introduced the main theories of social change still important in sociology.

1. *The growth of knowledge*. One of the main forces that Enlightenment philosophers, such as **Kant**, believed was driving history was the growth of knowledge. They saw reason as the driving force of history and human progress, using the term "reason" to include the development of science and technology, the spread of education and literacy, the decline of superstition, and the increase of knowledge.

Some kinds of knowledge *can* be powerful and fairly irreversible forces, especially in the long run. But whether that knowledge grows, and whether it is diffused through society depends mainly on other things. Often people who are in the knowledge business overestimate how powerful it is.

2. *The change in people's values.* During the nineteenth century, another German philosopher, **Hegel,** took Kantian ideas of the growth of reason and freedom, and applied them to the history of politics and law, art and literature, religion and ethics, philosophy and science. In one sphere after another, Hegel attempted to find progressions based on scientific-type laws. Often he spoke in a somewhat mystical way of this lawfulness, as the "cunning of reason." But he developed a very large number of insights about how social and historical developments did follow "law-like" patterns, and these insights were of immense importance to Marx and to sociology.

Often Hegel spoke as though religion and religious values were the driving force behind social change. (He linked this idea to the popular notion that history was preordained by Divine Providence.) In the first generation after Marx, several social theorists developed forms of sociological analysis in explicit contrast to Marx. The most important of these theorists were **Emile Durkheim** in France and **Max Weber** in Germany. Against Marx, they stressed the importance of cultural forces of religion and law. Some modern sociologists believe that cultural values are the fundamental bases of social structure and social change. Their theories are usually derived from Durkheim, who developed a **functionalist** analysis which treats **norms** and **culture** as the basis of social structure and social change. (**Norms** are rules, laws, values, ideals, obligations, and duties.) These analyses recall one strand of Hegel's ideas.

3. *Changes in law and politics.* Kant and Hegel wrote just as the French Revolution was destroying the feudal regime. Hegel's whole philosophy makes history—particularly political history and law—very important. He believed that any systematic analysis of law, religion, art, philosophy, custom, property, or social institutions had to be historical. He believed that there was a scientifically lawful development underneath political events. He believed that history is the history of the growth of human freedom, especially political freedom. From a situation where there was no freedom and no history, the human race first managed to achieve the freedom of *one*, then to achieve the freedom of *some*, and finally to achieve the freedom of *all*. For Hegel, the period of freedom of *one* was the empires of Egypt and the Middle East, where absolute rulers were "god-kings." The period of freedom of *some* was the Greco-Roman ancient world of democracies and law where slavery permitted the freedom of citizens. The modern period, Hegel said, is the only one when humans, as humans, are recognized as free. Hegel believed that the growth of freedom is the march of reason. One thing this means is that the growth of science and knowledge and literacy and enlightenment roots out irrational exploitation and domination. Thus **spirit**, the collective product of culture and of human history, is the basis of freedom and reason.

Within sociology, the stress on law and politics characterized another very important sociologist, Max Weber, who developed a classification of organizational and political forms. He viewed the development of reason and of structures of domination as linked to each other, and he founded an organizational analysis which treats organization, law, and the meanings and intentions of individuals as the center of social structure.

Hegel was important for Marx (and for the rest of sociology) because he developed more fully than anyone had before the idea that human life is social and historical. We transform ourselves. At the same time there is a tragic and static component of Hegel's analysis. For Hegel, this march of spirit and reason to freedom was also butchery, the triumph of selfish passions, of evil, and of private interests. Humans are free creators, but the movement of history is also **objectification** and **alienation**. Our impulses and feelings are translated into objects which are outside of us. Every act irrevocably freezes behind us into objectified structures which rule the present. Our acts and the consequences of our acts slip out of our control.

According to Hegel, this *objectification* is the way that humankind becomes itself. Humans are not unchanging. We have a collective essence or *"species being."* If you've seen one kangaroo, you've seen them all. But if you have seen one human or one society, you have not seen them all because humans *make themselves* into what they are. For Hegel, this objectification, by which we become ourselves and become free, is also a process of *alienation*—loss of freedom. *Alienation* is powerlessness, and Hegel viewed history as a tragic process in which we become free by losing freedom. Perhaps the clearest case is when one makes a commitment, as in marriage. One gives up freedom in marriage (or any other commitment), but commitments are the basis of all institutions and human freedoms. Hegel valued such commitments (law, religion, culture, community) as the way humans become human.

For Hegel, the driving force of human history is the realization of human freedom in its loss. Every situation in the present is based upon the past and is in the grips of the past. Every freedom is based upon and contains within it the forms of previous domination. Slavery was the basis of Greek freedom. In Hegel's philosophy, alienation and species being are the basis of our freedom to realize our possibilities. And so Hegel's analysis of freedom and reason concluded that the movement of history can only be understood, not changed; it concluded that the political arrangements of the Prussian monarchy were "freedom."

4. *Change in the economy and classes.* Marx believed that Hegel confused alienation with objectification. Not all objective consequences are out of our control. Some degree of objectification is inevitable, but Hegel managed to confuse avoidable alienation with unavoidable objectification.

While Hegel's analyses of alienation and history were important and profound, Hegel's philosophy of history was always retrospective: history was
what led to the present. This meant that the present was justified as the end
of history, the end of structural change. And so Hegel's radical philosophy
of freedom and incessant change treated the present as the end of history.
Hegel ended up celebrating the Prussian monarchy and the property relations within the Prussian state, and his philosophy proposed the end of
history with its own creation.

Marx believed that historical, structural fundamental change lies in the
future as well as the past. Marx says that Hegel's method is the method
of modern political economy; it is a structural method. Modern political economy (economics) was the sphere of the "invisible hand," where
people pursue their private interests, but in fact accomplish something
quite different. In Adam Smith's classical eighteenth century economics,
there was one "invisible hand" (the market); in Hegel's analyses there were
literally hundreds of them. Throughout history, in economics and law, in
philosophy and art, in religion and science, what happened was not what
people thought they were accomplishing; but it is what we need them to
have accomplished. For Hegel, the effects of people's actions are almost
never what they expect, but they accomplish more general, necessary, universal outcomes. Marx regarded these analyses as important, profound,
and often correct. But at the same time, they were mystified. They end in a
kind of functionalist analysis which says that "everything has a reason and
therefore, in a sense, is justified." Hegel obscured the actual mechanisms at
work. And so Hegel's philosophy became a kind of theology and justification of the way things are.

Marx agreed with Hegel that there was an interrelation of all of the elements of society—that the art and the freedom of the Greeks were bound
up with their possession of slaves. He also agreed that the progress of humankind is a blocked progress, full of contradictions. But while Hegel saw
the main motor driving that progress in philosophy and law, Marx saw it in
the life of the masses, and in the rise of new class forces. While Hegel saw
history as ending in the rational reality of the Prussian state, Marx saw the
processes of change continuing in a way that would transform the societies he saw around him. Thus, Marx argued, the starting point and guiding
thread of his studies was to see the real basis of the ideal changes which
Hegel had described in mystified form.

> My investigation led to the result that legal relations as well as forms of the
> state are to be grasped neither from themselves nor from the so-called general
> development of the human mind, but rather have their roots in the material
> conditions of life, the sum total of which Hegel, following the example of the
> Englishmen and Frenchmen of the eighteenth century, combines under the

name of "civil society," that, however, the anatomy of civil society is to be sought in political economy. (*Selected Works*, p. 182)

"Civil society" is, roughly, the economy, the ordinary day-to-day work of most people. "Political economy" is, roughly, economics, the study of the relationships of work. In Marx, history is a blocked progress in freedom. Many viewed both the development of alienation and the possibility of freedom as very important. But their interest is not the experience of philosophers but of the masses.

The social structures ("collective structures") which Hegel recognized when he talked about "spirits" are real enough. But Hegel talked as though spirits were huge invisible butterflies. Many contemporary sociologists and historians, who feel immensely superior to Hegel with his theological overtones, still treat most cultural and common attitudes as given—as though they dropped out of the sky. For Marx, the only scientific way to proceed was to find the solid, empirical, real, "material" situations and relations which produced those attitudes. In many ways, Marx's criticisms of Hegel are still fundamental disagreements between Marxists and Durkheimian or Weberian approaches to sociology.

Marx begins the analysis of culture from the analysis of ideology, from the analysis of the social dynamic of ideas and the influence of dominant groups which Marx called "ruling classes."

> If now in considering the course of history we detach the ideas of the ruling class from the ruling class itself and attribute to them an independent existence, if we confine ourselves to saying that these or those ideas were dominant at a given time, without bothering ourselves about the conditions of production and the producers of these ideas, if we thus ignore the individuals and world conditions which are the source of the ideas, then we can say, for instance, that during the time the aristocracy was dominant, the concepts honor, loyalty, etc. were dominant, during the dominance of the bourgeoisie, the concepts of freedom, equality, etc. (*German Ideology*. Complete Works 5, p. 60)

Some standpoints in sociology, derived from Durkheim and Weber, treat changes in certain ideas as the ultimate sources of change. Marxism operates on the working hypothesis that all really fundamental changes in attitudes, ideas, or values are never adequately explained until they have been related to changes in production, power, and real, material social relationships. Marx founded social history, the history of the masses, of the way of life of ordinary people, and the means by which that way of life radically changes over the course of time. Sociology developed out of social history. Marx believed that sudden political changes do not drop out of the sky. Rather, he saw them as scientifically lawful phenomena in relation to the ups and downs and the transformations of economic relations—in contrast to the purely political history of ruling groups. Political sociology continues to analyze political movements in terms of the impact of social forces like class, organization, and a host of other groups and relationships.

For example, many American sociologists have treated the Soviet Union and Eastern Europe as evidence that politics rules independent of economics—that political structures channel or freeze development irrespective of class, economic, and international forces. And popular American analyses of the transformations of the Eastern bloc often treat the political dynamic as an unmoved mover, but when the world economy changed, and when the Soviet system no longer served the purposes of the Soviet elite, it was abolished. For a time, the Soviet system represented the aspirations of the mass of people in those countries, even though it frustrated those aspirations in favor of the interests of the elite. Its collapse has given a boost to positions, such as postmodernism, that say that nothing ever really changes. However, what we see in the world is massive structural change, as the world arrives at a series of decision forks. In all these decisions the gains and losses of different classes remain the most potent driving force of historical change.

Exercise 1.1: Package Deals

Take a sheet of paper and write down at least one thing about the structure of society or of government policy today that seems to you a "good," something desirable in itself. Then write down at least one thing that seems to you a "bad," something undesirable in itself. Beneath the "good" write down some possible reasons that someone else might oppose it. Possibly they believe that the good has some side effects or preconditions or costs which are not so nice. Similarly, beneath the "bad" write down some possible reasons other people might not want to get rid of it.

We have said that the different parts of society are interconnected. One job of sociology is to analyze the connections. This first exercise is a thought-experiment about some of the problems of that analysis. It concerns the relation of "fact" and "value" in that what you like or dislike about things is often related to how they connect with other things.

In a restaurant, sometimes the items on the menu are sold separately ("a la carte") so that you can get any items in any order. Sometimes the food is in combinations or dinners so that you are faced with package deals which allow no substitutions. The combinations are often for several people, so that you have to agree with others what to order. But even if you have to agree with several other people on ordering a combination dinner, the problem of ordering is not too difficult. For one thing, you only have to eat what you like. For another thing, at least there is a menu so that you know what you are getting and what it will cost.

Unfortunately, social structure is almost never "a la carte," and people rarely know what they are getting and what it costs. Almost any piece of social structure has a number of different effects and preconditions in other parts of social structure. Some parts of social structure have very powerful effects on almost everything else, so that having one rather than another is like ordering a whole dinner. And the connections are not obvious, so that you are rarely sure what you are ordering. For example, you may decide to "order" a society that attempts to fight crime by reducing civilian authority over police officers or the military. Suppose you say, "Let's get the courts off the backs of the police, and let's deregulate the financial institutions and get Congress off the backs of the CIA." But you may get more than you ask for. You may find these changes go along with various other things that you don't like, including a rise in police corruption, police violence against innocent suspects, imprisonment of innocent suspects (and therefore free-dom for the ones who really committed the crime), and the possibility of a tremendous amount of political and military power being concentrated in the hands of a small dictatorial group. If that were to be the case, it would do no good to say, "No one told me that was part of the deal." Most major arguments in social theory concern what the deals are.

Ordering is hard because the connections are not obvious; social struc-ture comes with no menu. And besides, the final order depends on the joint actions of millions of people. No wonder that some people are apathetic and order "whatever everyone else is having." No wonder other people prefer to act as though there were no connections at all and say, "Well, all that I know is that I want plum pudding." For example, some people say, "I don't know why there are people sleeping in the streets or why there are people starving in Africa and Latin America. But it doesn't have anything to do with me. It's their tough luck. I'm not sleeping in the street; and because I have a good education, I never will. I don't need to be concerned with what causes or what would cure other people's starvation or homelessness. It's probably their own fault." There are tens of thousands of families in the United States who could not locate Iraq or Iran on a map but who are now dealing with a dead or damaged family member and there are many mil-lions more dealing with the economic crisis partly caused by overspending in Iraq. Now, when everyone has finished ordering, the waitress is going to plop something in front of us. It may not be too appetizing. History often has a nasty surprise for people who think things are going to stay the way they are. Remember what the past generations got: the Great Depression, world economic collapse, the rise of fascist governments practicing geno-cide (the extermination of "racial enemies" to the last man, woman, and child), and world war. We wouldn't want to order that again. Yet there are deep disagreements about whether that combination is still on the menu and, if so, which of the dinners includes that as the final course.

Class structures and political systems are the bases of some of the most intractable disagreements. They are part of package deals that connect many different things, often in unexpected ways. No serious Marxist believes that every village in every region of the world went through an identical set of stages of economic and social change, but every part of the world has been powerfully affected by the development of different, complex forms of accumulation of wealth. The world would be simplified if each thing could be changed independently, leaving everything else the same. But if you look at any real debate, like those on pollution, poverty, or pornography, it is evident that change is usually a package deal. Sociology looks at the causes and consequences of things; it tries to clarify what's in the package deals we are being offered.

If the "good" and "bad" you chose to write down were such that other people might disagree with your evaluations, then the problematic linkages of social arrangements were probably evident. Sometimes it seems that people evaluate things differently because they have different values—they agree about consequences, but they have a different evaluation of such things as equality, or human dignity, or violence, or cruelty to animals. But more commonly, different evaluations stem from different conceptions of what the package deal is. People disagree about side effects or preconditions or costs. Similarly, people who dislike something in itself might not want to get rid of it because they think it has positive side effects or because it is the result of other things that are themselves desirable, or because eliminating it would have other costs.

Merely thinking about the "bads" that may be connected to some "goods" and the "goods" that may be connected to some "bads" in social structure is a useful introduction to sociology and social theory. But there is one other thing which it may be useful to think about, even though it cannot be resolved right now. Take your first example. Suppose that there was a disagreement. Suppose that you think a particular "good" is not connected to the "bad" that you listed, but someone else disagrees. How might you resolve that disagreement? Of course, there is trial and error. You could order the "good" and then see what else the waitress brings. But trial and error is not very efficient in some situations. How else might you resolve the disagreement? You may want to look at Exercise 4.4 to pursue this question.

Suggestions for Further Reading

An immense amount literature deals with Marx's relation to Hegel. We shall return to it in chapter 4. One of the more useful analyses of Hegel's conception of alienation is J. Torrence, *Estrangement, Alienation and Exploitation* (Columbia, 1977). B. Ollman's *Alienation: Marx's Concept of Man in Capitalist Society* (Cambridge, 1971) is still a classic, as is Lenin's *Conspectus of Hegel's Logic*, Complete Works, vol. 38 (International Publishers, 1967). McCarney's *Hegel on History* (Routledge, 2000) and his *Hegel's Philosophy of History* (forthcoming) gives a lucid account of the importance of Hegel's concept of "spirit" in formulating concepts relevant to human collective action in history. Spirit is "an I that is a we, and a we that is an I," in contrast to asocial conceptions of action as the free choices of atomistic individuals. James Loewen gives a short justification and introduction to critical history in *Teaching What Really Happened* (Columbia Teachers College Press, 2010). Callinicos, *Social Theory* (New York University Press, 1999) gives an accessible introduction to the relation of Marx, Durkheim, and Weber to each other, to other nineteenth century theorists, and to contemporary debates such as those involving Habermas, Derrida, Beck, Giddens, and Bourdieu. Engels, *Anti-Duhring*, especially the chapter "Socialism—Utopian and Scientific," often published separately, gives the classic introduction to those issues.

SECTION 1.2: WHAT IS THE BASIS OF SOCIAL STRUCTURE?

For Hegel, the engine of history and the basis of human existence was "spirit." Sometimes "spirit" seems to refer mainly to culture, especially social norms. Hegel's influential lectures on religion and on history often treated norms and values, enshrined in the religious system, as the basis of social structure. In this he seems rather like modern functionalists. Sometimes the concept of spirit involves a general focus on knowledge and philosophy. At other times, spirit involves a more specific focus on political culture. In his influential works on law, Hegel treats the political and legal system as the basic structures of history and social change (sounding rather like Weber). But Hegel also touched on other views, which Marx developed.

Marx's fundamental theory of social structure and social change is called **historical materialism.** While this theory is sometimes caricatured as a narrow "economic determinism," it actually incorporates a belief in the importance of political and cultural structures, but disagrees that these are fundamental. Rather, Marx believes that economic structures are basic for understanding either norms or politics. Anti-Marxists (and some Marxists) mistakenly mischaracterize Marx's theory as starting from a narrow, shallow view of economics and so-called "human nature," as if the only things that motivate humans are food, comfort, or money. Marx was foremost concerned with what makes us human. Marx looked to the material world, including social relations, rather than the spiritual or metaphysical world, for an explanation. Our "humanness" is our ability to act in the world. Acting in the world means producing as well as consuming, and therefore, we are most free to be humans when we are free to produce in concert with the rest of humanity. So understanding the economic processes that enhance or block that activity gets to the core of understanding human society. Keep in mind that economic structures are not static, determined formulas; they are social structures based on the collective physical and mental labor of people. Marx gives a particularly cogent summary of historical materialism:

> In the social production of their life, men enter into definite relations which are indispensable and independent of their will, **relations of production** which correspond to a definite stage of the development of their material **productive forces.** The sum total of these relations of production constitutes the economic structure of society, the real foundation, on which rises **legal and political superstructure,** and to which correspond definite **forms of social consciousness.** The **mode of production** of material life conditions the social, political, and intellectual life process in general. It is not the consciousness of men that determines their being, but, on the contrary, their social being that determines their consciousness. At a certain stage of their development, the material productive forces of society come into conflict with the existing relations of production, or what is but a legal expression for the same thing with the property relations within which they have been at work hitherto. From forms of development of productive forces these relations turn into their fetters. Then begins an epoch of social revolution. With the change of the economic foundation the entire immense superstructure is more or less rapidly transformed. . . . In broad outlines the Asiatic, ancient, feudal, and modern bourgeois modes of production can be designated as progressive epochs in the economic formation of society. The bourgeois relations of production are the last antagonistic form of the social process of production. (Selected works [SW] of Mark and Engles: 182, emphasis added)

This outlines the bare bones of the Marxist view of history and the special importance that Marxists give to classes and production. Debates among Marxists are often centered around these institutions and over the relative emphasis that should be given to economics, politics, ideology, and culture. Many books and articles have explored this; a number of them are cited below. It is important not to overemphasize this passage. After all, it is only a comment in a biographical sketch in a preface which Marx allowed to go out of print. When asked to state the essence of historical materialism, Marx and Engels always referred to other works. Nevertheless, the passage states some ideas which are of considerable importance for the foundations of sociological theory.

Stages of History

Let's start at the end of the passage, briefly sketching Marxist notions about the stages of human history. Marx says the "Asiatic," ancient, feudal, and bourgeois modes of production form progressive epochs in history. What does he mean? Early humans lived for millions of years without any formal class structure. There were families and there was violence between humans, but there was not a formalized class structure with a system of laws to enforce private ownership. This stage is sometimes called **primitive communism**—communism in the sense that it was not a system with private appropriation of significant means of production. Hence, it was a social formation without classes or states.

According to Marxist theory, the earliest developed civilizations were the **Asiatic** theocratic, priestly, and military empires of Egypt, Persia, Syria, China, India, and South America. An apparatus of armies and temples extracted goods from peasant communities to build pyramids and more armies. These huge but stagnant empires were replaced in the West by varieties of **ancient slave systems.** The ancient city-states of Athens and Sparta and the Roman Empire are examples of these. There were several classes, but the economic structure was based largely on the labor of slaves. The most powerful class, usually a very small fraction of the population, owned, controlled, and consumed a disproportionately high percentage of the products and the means of production.

Table 1.1 Epochal Changes in Modes of Production

Epoch	Time	Means of Production	Forces of Production	Relations of Production
PRIMITIVE COMMUNISM	2,000,000 BCE to 1000 BCE	Land and Hand Tools	Land and Labor	Kinship No Classes
ASIATIC	8000 BCE to 1000 CE	Above plus Irrigation, Mines	Above plus Agriculture, Animals	Pharaohs, ** Priests, Soldiers, Merchants, Peasants*
ANCIENT	400 BCE to 700 CE	Above plus Aqueducts, Roads	Above plus Science	Slaveholding Citizens,** Soldiers, Merchants, Slaves*
FEUDAL	500 CE to 1800 CE	Above plus Waterways	Above plus Geared Machines and more Science	Aristocrats,** Priests, Merchants, Serfs*
CAPITALIST	1700 CE to Present	Above plus Factories	Above plus Power Plants and more Science	Capitalists,** Petty Capitalists, Managers, Workers*
SOCIALIST	1917 CE (temporary)	Above	Above	Workers
COMMUNIST	(future)	Above	Above	No Classes

* Surplus producing class.
** Ruling class.

Ancient slavery eventually gave way to varieties of **feudalism.** The main laboring class under feudalism in Europe was the **serfs.** The serfs owed labor services and part of their crops to the aristocracy and were not free to leave the land they tilled. On the other hand, they were not slaves; technically, the landlords did not own the bodies of the serfs. Feudalism, in turn, gave way to **capitalism,** which itself has gone through several stages and political forms. Capitalism is based on the two class system of the working class and the capitalist class, although, as we shall see, it is not always easy to determine a particular person's class. Table 1.1 is a schematic representation of the developments we shall survey in this chapter.

This view of history, like Hegel's, shows an intelligible development of human freedom. But that development is not one of law, ethics, or philosophy in themselves. Marx believed that the basic productive arrangements create class and social relations which place fundamental limits on the rest of social structure. The important point here is that while there are similarities among the different types of class societies, there are certain fundamental differences that not only made life different, but also laid the basis for the eventual transformation of those societies. For example, slavery in ancient Rome in 50 B.C. and in Georgia in 1850 were both forms of slavery, but the needs of the different ruling classes and the political economic systems made these two forms of slavery vastly different. Sometimes people say that capitalism will last forever, because human nature is basically "greedy," and we always have had capitalism and always will. The reality is that capitalism is a relatively new system, having become dominant only in the past two or three centuries. Many of the aspects of capitalism, including certain philosophies of selfishness, aggression, patriotism, and racism, simply did not always have the influence that they sometimes have today.

Base and Superstructure

To understand how Marx explained movement between these stages, let us start with six concepts, diagrammed in figure 1.1. Political and legal ideas and arrangements may seem to come out of thin air, but Marxism does not believe that they come from nothing or change by themselves. Rather, it says that certain relations of production such as slavery or serfdom make particular political arrangements possible and necessary. The overall society, or **social formation,** is divided into two parts, a **mode of production,** which Marx calls the "real foundation," and a **superstructure,** which he calls "ideological," and which he divided into political and legal arrangements and forms of social consciousness, of which he listed five: law, politics, art, religion, and philosophy.

What is involved is an overall causal model. Fundamental changes in the mode of production will cause fundamental changes in the superstructure,

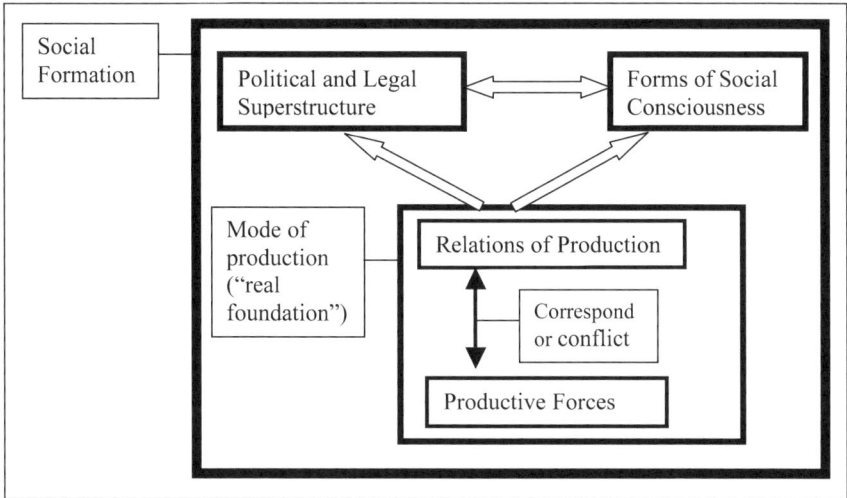

Figure 1.1   Marx's Model of Base and Superstructure

but not vice versa. Opponents of Marx have argued that this is all that Marx meant, that he presented a reductionist, economic determinist analysis which ignored such things as political movements, racism, and war. We can evaluate these ideas only after we have considered economic contradictions in chapter 2, political conflicts in chapter 3, and the concept of contradiction in chapter 4. However, most Marxists believe that those criticisms are directed against a caricature of Marx. Marx's analysis deals with the great, fundamental historical changes in social structure (**social formation**). Marx believed that political and intellectual sources of such changes are always bound up with class forces and changes in the **mode of production.** To define a change in the mode of production, Marx gave a list of the main kinds of modes of production which he perceived in human history. For Marx, changes in modes of production were the backbone of history.

Perhaps the easiest way to get a feel for the substance of these concepts is to make a rough estimate of the number of people who compose them in the United States today. The political and legal superstructure of the United States today is fairly clear. The legal structure consists of the Supreme Court and the hierarchy of other courts down to the local traffic court, an apparatus of many thousands. With prisons, probation departments, and the like, this structure includes millions. The political structure consists of the president, the administration, and the Congress at the federal level, the governors and the statehouses at the state level, and the mayors and the various kinds of city councils at the local level. The top levels of this structure include only a few thousand people, but if one includes all of the full-time jobs of people in it, it includes millions more. Nevertheless, with all its millions of members, this state apparatus includes only a few percent of the population.

It controls a much larger apparatus of civilian, military, and police. The military includes the regular Armed Forces and National Guard, includes several million more people, and the police includes even more. The court system controls the apparatus that incarcerates millions. Civilian government employees, depending who is included, is a larger group, and the whole includes somewhere between 5 and 10 percent of the population. The political and legal structure is large and important. Indeed, when one looks at all its members and powers, it may seem to include everyone and to be all-powerful. Many people have considered it to be the whole of the ruling class and to be all-powerful, determining the fundamental character of the society. Other considerations suggest that this is not so.

First, while the political and legal superstructure includes millions of people, this is only a tiny fraction of the population. If everyone in the political and legal structures could be counted on to do as they were told, and if opposition were always disorganized, then it might be all-powerful. But many of the people in this structure are not unconditionally loyal to it. Furthermore, the relatively small political and legal superstructure is dependent on the rest of the social structure. We may not see anything of ancient Egypt but the crypts of the pharaohs, but we may be quite sure that the pharaohs did not build their own pyramids. If we want to understand them, we need to know about more than their lives and times and that of their armies. We need to know their relationships to those other people.

Marx says that the superstructure corresponds to forms of **social consciousness**, and he lists religion, art, and philosophy as three of these. He also says that these are the ideological forms in which people become aware of their conflicts. How big is the apparatus of people that produces religion and art, newspapers and novels, sociology and mathematics? It is hard to say, because it is a more diffuse structure than, say, government. Certainly education is one of the largest industries in the United States, and organized religion is a structure which commands vast resources. On the other hand, the viewpoint which says that the structure which produces forms of social consciousness is just "everyone"—that we all have an equal say about what picture of the world becomes dominant—is also not accurate. There is a dominant set of structures which encompasses perhaps 10 percent of the population (35 million people). In analyzing history, you want to know about those structures. Moreover, despite the often grandiose views of teachers, preachers, talk show hosts, and others who work with words, this apparatus is neither unified nor independent of owners, any more than is the political apparatus.

However, we shall argue that these resources are, in fact, largely controlled by those who control the economy. Indeed, they constitute only a fraction of the resources those people control. But if you look at history, the fundamental fact that jumps out at you is that, *despite all those powers, there are times when the whole apparatus is overturned.* Marx devoted much of his energy to finding out when such crises, leading to fundamental changes, occurred. Those times mark the transitions between different types of social systems. He says that it is when there are contradictions within the mode of production, such as conflicts between the **forces of production** and **relations of production,** that all these other apparatuses become vulnerable to massive, structural, radical change. The **forces of production** are the means of production (factories, farms, mines, tools, waterways, machines, etc.) combined with science, technology, and the laborers themselves (skills and education, etc.). The **relations of production** make up the class structure of economic and political control and subordination in a society. Marx says that the forces and relations of production sometimes correspond to each other, in which cases the relations of production are forms of development of the forces of production. At other times they conflict with or contradict each other, in which cases the relations of production act as fetters on the forces of production. This can cause economic collapse and major crises that can lead to war.

There has been an explosion of historical research analyzing trade, wealth, and political/military power around the world over the past thousand years. Much of this research seems to indicate that the twists and turns and contingencies of social development were more complex than the way that many people understood in the mid-1900s. In particular, some of the Asian societies and parts of North Africa may have had more developed political-economic systems in "medieval" times than Marx and others may have realized. Some anti-Marxists have seized on this to assert that Marx and Engels were "Eurocentric" or even racist against non-European societies. But Marx and Engels could only evaluate information that was available to them. This newer research, while indicating that Marx and Engels may have been inaccurate in some of the specifics of their historical analysis, does not undermine the core of Marxist analysis of how class societies function on the basis of exploitation of labor. Marx and Engels clearly understood that all social theory should be subject to evaluation and critique, which is why their understanding of the social world also evolved over time.

Exercise 1.2: Diagnosing Problems of Modern Society

Think about and write your best answer to three questions: What are some of the things that are wrong with the United States? What is wrong with your school? "*What is wrong with the world?*" In each case, what is the main—the most important—problem? Why? Why does the problem persist?

Racism or sexism, poverty or war, hunger or violence. Virtually everyone is "against" them the way everyone is against "evil." But if you try to do anything about any one of them, you get disagreements about what causes them and what could change them. With regard to every major problem in modern society, the Marxist analysis represents a distinctive and often very powerful analysis of the sources of the problem and the conditions of its solution.

The question of what is "basic" has powerful *practical* implications. To say that something is "basic" is to say that a change in the base will bring about a change in the structure. For example, if racism is based upon (or rooted in) people's values, then it can only be changed by changing the values. But if racism is rooted mainly in the class structure of capitalism, then it can be changed only by abolishing capitalism. Trying to change people's ideas and values without changing those structures would be like pulling the leaves off dandelions. They grow right back. Thus, there are powerful practical implications in disagreements about what is "basic."

Different people view different things as problems. If you have three lists—things wrong with your school, with your society, and with the world—and your neighbor has another, partly overlapping one, how do you get together to do anything about the wrongs? How do you come to enough agreement to act? The view that something is wrong is partly a matter of value judgments, but those have a complex ("dialectical") relation with what one believes the causes, consequences, and possibilities are. Obviously a big world or country or school could have several problems, but there are links between problems, between solutions, and between different conceptions of the basis of social structure. People differ in who they know, in experiences, interests, and values. And different views of how social structure works affect what they believe is possible or impossible. Marxian analyses of society provide different answers of whether a society without many social problems could exist, and how to get there. If social structure is interconnected so that it often offers us "package deals" and if different people have different views of what deals are available, they will usually make different choices. And so the main views of the "basis" of social structure often determine the main overarching diagnoses and solutions to social problems.

In chapter 4 we shall see that there are three main views of the basis of social structure, and they are related to three main diagnoses of the fundamental problems of modern society. Marx views production and class inequality as the basis of society, and so he regards **alienation**, inequality, and powerlessness as the main source of social problems. Durkheim views norms and values as the basis of society, and so he regards **anomie,** *the breakdown of norms and values,* as the main source of social problems. And Weber regards organization as the main basis of social structure, so he regards **bureaucracy and technology** as forming an iron cage in which individuality is stifled and many modern social problems are created.

Each of these views of social problems (alienation, anomie, or the iron cage of bureaucracy) may focus either on how people subjectively feel or on *objective* social arrangements. Sometimes people's feelings of being alienated and powerless, of being without norms, or of being stifled are taken to be important in themselves, like the painful feeling of having a headache. At other times, the feeling is only a symptom of situations or objective conditions of powerlessness, normlessness, or bureaucracy. The concept of **alienation** (powerlessness) is a good example of this. One may or may not feel alienated. But the main thing is whether, as a matter of fact, one *can* control one's life. Many people, including many social theorists, describe alienation as some sort of general kind of sadness or resentment; it is often posed as a personal, subjective feeling or a psychological problem. But we can see that the discontent often stems from real powerlessness or from relationships of unequal power.

For example, consider someone who buys a parking permit to park a car on campus—it takes a long time to find a parking space, and then the person has to walk a quarter mile from the car to the classroom. The hassle of parking and walking is perfectly real. It can ruin someone's mood, create actual physical stress, elevated blood pressure, etc. Yet the same person who is angry about losing ten minutes in traffic might come home and waste twenty minutes rereading a newspaper ad. The same student who complains about that walk might go out that afternoon and jog three miles. What makes something *alienating* is not the degree of physical discomfort, or the amount of money or time involved, by itself. What makes it feel alienating is the feeling of being *robbed* of money and time, of being *compelled* to buy something that is worthless, and thus be *cheated*. If there are differences in power, control, and influence, then it is possible that some people are really being cheated to give other people privileges. On the other hand, if the parking arrangements are what people would agree to, if the prices are fair and everyone is being treated equally, then the feeling of alienation may be merely "subjective."

The concepts of a "sick" or "unhealthy" society have been developed to explore and explain why people in a rich society like the United States do not feel better and do not live longer. Rather, they are subject to elevated rates of a host of problems such as hypertension, heart attack, obesity, anxiety, mistrust, alcohol and drug use, crime, violence, homicide, academic failure, gangs, racism, social immobility, and poverty traps. These ailments are not "subjective," and the main explanations of them have centered on the effects of living in an unequal society. Indeed, if the arrangements really are exploitative, unnecessary, or unfair, it might be bad if people did *not* feel alienated. One can conceive of people being dutifully fleeced: paying fat fees for nothing; spending long hours standing in line; choking down resentment when privileged groups speed past; marching off to fight someone else's wars, or otherwise wasting their lives.

Of course, it is possible that the parking rules are functional, fair, and necessary. What alternatives one thinks are possible often affect how one analyzes the arrangements that exist. Durkheim might analyze the parking dissatisfaction in terms of a breakdown of rules and respect for authority. Weber might analyze it in terms of bureaucracy. Implicit in these diagnoses is a very different view of what possibilities there are from those in Marx's analysis in terms of alienation (robbery, privilege, and power).

This concept of alienation as being involuntarily separated from one's own productive activity, one's own labor, is a central aspect of Marxist social theory. The Marxist critique of capitalism is not simply that there are inequalities, but also that the *political-economic arrangements are stifling the creative, productive potential of humankind.* This stifling occurs in major ways such as war, racism, poor education, unemployment, misdirected scientific research, or fascist dictatorship. But it can also occur in more personal ways, such as the types of interpersonal relationships we have. In either case, there is a connection between the political-economic-social structure and our consciousness.

Whatever you suggested were the main problems in the country, the school, and the world, an implicit theory of how the social structure works made those things problematic for you. And your experiences and your relationships with other people helped shape that theory.

Suggestions for Further Reading

The concept of unequal societies as sick societies is presented, among others, by R. Wilkinson and K. Pickett, *The Spirit Level* (Bloomsburg Press, 2009). A group of academic, "analytical Marxists" have attempted to separate Marxist theory from any dialectical method which differs significantly from regular social science theory. One of these attempts was Cohen's interpretation of Marx's theory of history as asserting a functional relation between the forces and the relations of production, combined with autonomous growth of the forces of production. For a critique, see R. Miller, *Analyzing Marx* (Princeton University Press, 1984). A well-known criticism of Marx as reductionist and economic determinist is A. Giddens, *A Contemporary Critique of Historical Materialism* (Macmillan, 1982). For a contrary view, see E. Wright, "Is Marxism Really Functionalist, Class Reductionist, and Teleological?" *American Journal of Sociology* 89:452 (1983).

In chapter 4 we shall suggest that the different portions of dialectic reinvented by the analytical Marxists are a little bit like some of the pieces of three different watches spread out on a table. They are interesting, but they do not work very well.

SECTION 1.3: HAVE STATES ALWAYS EXISTED?

Marxism aims for a world without states. Non-Marxists think this is utopian. Have states always existed? Will they always exist? Have there always been nations and patriotism? Will there always be leaders and led? Does there always have to be a state with police, courts, laws, prisons, and armies? Whenever states and patriotism have existed, so also have wars. Will there always be wars? If wars continue, will the human race survive?

Hegel argued that it was essential to have states because the law was the basis of freedom. He also argued that it was essential to have war and to have monarchies. But he did not think we had always had states; rather, they are a product of history. What was fundamental and visible for Hegel, but is often ignored today, was that the human race spent perhaps 99 percent of its existence in stateless societies. The nation-state is a product of recent history. But for Hegel, that history is necessary and rational. You can see that there is enormous tension between Hegel's stress on the historical character of the state and his stress on the necessity of present arrangements, such as states. He was forced to argue that the present is the end of history. He believed that past history was a story of constant change, but in the rational arrangements of modern states all fundamental change and development come to an end.

Marxism and socialism are commonly portrayed as involving mainly an increase in government and celebration of the state. But in fact, the starting point and the most striking characteristics of Marx's analysis are just the reverse of this. Marx's most fundamental disagreement with Hegel and with most contemporary social theorists was that he detested nations, nationalism, government, and bureaucracy. Marx viewed class societies as systems of alienation and powerlessness. He viewed the state as the capstone of that doomed, destructive, oppressive structure. This was his main disagreement with the other paradigms. Weber and Durkheim were patriots. They believed in their states, and they believed there would always be states. There is not as much tension in their view of the states as there was in Hegel's, because they defined and analyzed the state in ways which downplayed the fact that it is an historical product.

Obviously, the question whether nations have always existed (like the question whether classes, religion, racism, families, exchange, science, or any other institution has always existed) is partly a matter of definition. It is always possible to define something like a "state" in a way which makes it more general or more historically particular. But that definition, or any other definition, does not solve the real questions about what will happen and what can happen. **Conceptual issues** about how general one's concepts should be may be confused with **empirical issues** about which structures are necessary. In chapter 4, we shall see that this is an issue about how history connects to methodological questions of how to make our social concepts sensitive to change.

For the moment, we face a simpler problem. Marx says that states are not always necessary, that they are a temporary blight or disease that occurs in human history. When society is divided into classes, it needs a state. If we create a society without classes, we can eliminate states. Is he right? How could you determine whether he is right or not? The category "state" is much broader than "nation"; the category "leaders" is very broad and vague. Both functionalists and organization theorists often define the state in terms of a much more general phenomenon which appears in societies that do not have nation-states. When people argue there have always been "leaders," claims to a monopoly of violence, or authoritative centers of social norms, they believe they have demonstrated that the apparatus of coercion and authority in the United States and other countries today—or something very like this apparatus—has always existed. But this is not true at all.

Certainly there is some anthropological evidence that societies with different kinds of economic systems have different class systems; and societies with different class systems have different political structures.

Preliterate hunting and gathering societies—the kinds of societies where humankind spent more than 99 percent of its history—have nothing remotely resembling the modern state. In general, they do not have political parties, police, parliaments, politicians, courts, prisons, armies, legal systems, executives, wars, monopoly of legitimate violence, uniform territory, or any of the other things we associate with states. Most of that apparatus developed in the absolute monarchies, during capitalist industrialization. When pre-agrarian societies have had leaders or councils of elders, those are not full-time jobs and they do not dispose of coercion and authority in the sense that a judge or general does. Hunting and gathering societies also do not have stratification systems which are like those in modern society. Table 1.2 shows the relation between economic arrangements and stratification.

Table 1.2 Cross-tabulation of Type of Economy with Stratification

Type of Economy	Degree of Stratification				Total	N
	Not Stratified	Wealth Distinctions Important	Nobility Present	Complex Class System		
Hunting and gathering	69%	20%	11%	1%	100%	101
Horticultural	56%	11%	24%	10%	100%	255
Pastoral	26%	30%	33%	11%	100%	76
Plow agriculture	9%	17%	17%	59%	100%	115

Table 1.2 is a cross-tabulation. Of the 101 hunting and gathering societ-ies examined, only 1 percent had complex class systems; of the 115 societies with plow agriculture, 59 percent had complex class systems. Even though not every plow society had a complex class system, and one hunting and gathering society had such a system, the overall relation is that economic development is very highly associated with the form of the stratification system. With increased economic development we find increasingly elabo-rate class systems. There are issues about how best to measure differences in the economy or in stratification. Here, we have used the usual anthropo-logical classifications. Classifications geared to Marxist theory would prob-ably allow the relations to appear more clearly. In any case, just by knowing the economic technology of a society, we cannot know for sure what is the degree of stratification of the society. But there is a very powerful relation between the type of economy and the degree of stratification.

It would be simplistic to try to account for stratification *without* knowing the economic arrangements. The economy is the first thing one will ordi-narily look at in trying to explain the class and stratification arrangements. The great majority of hunting and gathering societies have no developed stratification system at all. The great majority of societies based on plow agriculture have complex class systems. The economy is certainly a major source of variation in stratification. Historical and sociological theories which do not deal with this relation almost certainly fail.

But how are these economic arrangements related to the state and political coercion? Table 1.3 shows the powerful relation which exists between strati-fication and forms of the state. Once again, the relation is less than perfect, and there are problems of conceptualization. Nevertheless, the relation is very strong. In fact, it is even stronger than that between the economy and

Table 1.3   Cross-tabulation of Stratification with Form of the State

Degree of Stratification	Form of the State				Total	N
	No Political Integration	Local Com-munities and Peace Groups	Minimal and Little States	Full States Present		
No stratifica-tion	13%	66%	21%	1%	100%	236
Wealth dis-tinctions	6%	11%	30%	1%	100%	80
Nobility present	0%	27%	62%	11%	100%	110
Complex class system	0%	2%	26%	71%	100%	91

the degree of stratification. A substantial fraction of the societies without distinguishable strata also lacks *any* recognizable political authority. Most of the rest only have local communities and peaceful groups. Only among the societies with a nobility or a complex class system is a state of any kind common. Only societies with a complex class system have full states, large independent political units averaging 100,000 or more in population. When many people first consider Marx's theory, their first impulse is to say, "You can't abolish states; all societies have states." But this contradicts reality. You could define whatever organization people have as a "state," but if you give the concept of a state real content, it is by no means true that all societies have them.

A second impulse is to say, "Whether states exist doesn't depend on class; states do lots of things besides reinforcing inequality." Possibly. But these data suggest very powerfully that the stratification system is the single most important variable for explaining which societies have states and which do not. Marx's theory of class and state cannot be definitively tested using this kind of data. Nevertheless, the striking, obvious, fundamental fact which shows through these data is the linkage of class to economic relations and of political forms to class.

These data are consistent with Marxist theory but, alone, do not prove that states either can or will be abolished. The sample is cross-sectional and thus it is subject to diffusion and other forms of contamination. Some theorists would say that classes and states both responded to technology, and without going back to stone-age technology, we can't get rid of them. Others would say that states are produced by class differences, but we can never get rid of classes. By contrast, the Marxist interpretation of such data is that the development of agriculture and an agricultural surplus led to a class structure and a social structure different from the earlier, more primitive societies in three important ways.

First of all, there were now rulers who lived in part by expropriating (taking for themselves) some of the goods produced by the labor of the working classes in the group. That is, one part of the labor of the societies went merely to sustain the lives of the people in the society. But another part, which Marx called the **surplus** over and above what was necessary to sustain life, went for other things: for culture, luxuries, philosophy, and armies. When a group could expropriate some surplus, *they could use it to develop a structure to protect what they had, and get still more.*

Second, the fact that some people were living off the labor of others meant that maintaining the law required a centralized apparatus of coercion, terror, and violence. There are societies in which customary and conventional norms are maintained without an apparatus of prisons, police, armies, etc. But when there is a leisure class living next to the workers who produce the means of that leisure, some such apparatus always appears. *We live in an era of class societies.* That places limits on what the social structure can be like—limits which sometimes falsely appear to be laid down by human nature.

Third, along with the splitting of society into classes and the development of states over them, it became possible for the labor of the society to be organized more efficiently. But the view that the human race has always been organized in nation-states is false. Tilly has shown that in the last 500 years, the structure of states grew up and changed in response to the concentrations of capital and of coercion. Some 500 years ago, in the commercial areas of Europe, such as the low countries and northern Italy, there were high concentrations of capital, and those areas developed a set of relatively democratic city-states that could hire professional armies. In the agrarian areas of Europe, such as Russia and the Austro-Hungarian empires, there was a high concentration of coercion, based on landed aristocratic control of estates, and those areas developed empires based on the aristocracies. Then, the French Revolution and the Napoleonic wars created the nation-state, as a kind of hybrid, based on giving the mass of the population citizenship rights and instituting a mass draft and nation-in-arms army. That system of competing nation-states has produced an almost constant state of war, which threatens the human race with annihilation.

From the development of nuclear weapons in World War II until 1989, the major argument was that we needed them because "they," the USSR, had them. Now as the "they" becomes more countries, immersed in conflict, such as Pakistan, Iran, and Israel, often sitting right next to countries with huge stockpiles, our government says that it wants everyone to get rid of them and the vast military apparatus for delivering them, but we can't. "They" won't let us. But, as with most other destructive and coercive aspects of the state, Marxists believe that the problem of how to achieve peace is insoluble within, but only within, class-divided societies.

Exercise 1.3: Giving Aristotle a Lesson on Ethics

Aristotle thought slavery was natural and good. Write a brief dialogue in which you try to convince him that he is wrong.

Does change come about mainly through the growth of knowledge, change in values, and preaching at people? We saw that this was a main issue between different philosophies of history. Some saw knowledge, philosophy, and technology as the basis of historical change; others saw religion, values, and ideas as the basis of change; while still others saw law, politics, and freedom as the basis of change. Against all of these positions, Marx argued that economic and class changes (changes in people's relationships and material interests) were the basis of historical change, and this set of issues then reappeared as disagreements between different sociological theories.

Both in one's own experience and in history, it sometimes seems that the growth of knowledge is an inexorable process of development. While there are times when one goes around in circles or when one hardly moves at all, over the long term there is a definite, nearly irreversible development. Sometimes it seems as though knowledge is the only thing that is needed to produce change. It is especially likely to seem that way to people in the knowledge business. It seems as though one could go back in history and dump an encyclopedia in Greece, and make it unnecessary to go through the thousands of years it took to develop that encyclopedia.

Similarly, everything that one does, one does in part because one's values are what they are. Different people have different values. If one looks at the full range of societies and the real differences in history, it seems obvious that the values, like the ideas, of different societies and periods are different. If the values differ, and if different values produce different behaviors, it seems that one could cause different behaviors by changing the values. For example, many religious fundamentalists believe that if everyone would accept a set of religious values, many social problems would disappear.

Explore this question in a thought-experiment. Aristotle believed that slavery was natural, inevitable, and good. What would convince him that he is wrong? Keep in mind the fact that Aristotle was no fool. He was a great naturalist and scientist; he was a towering ethical theorist whose philosophy and ethics became the foundation of Christian philosophy.

Your dialogue should keep in mind the fact that information is only assimilated when it is tied to other information and practice. It would not be possible for the particular elements of an encyclopedia to be accepted piecemeal; one cannot accept an answer until one has asked the question. Knowledge is always tied to the rest of social life. Aristotle was a practical man. If you tell him that something is good, he is going to see if he can convince his friends and students to do it. Slavery was the basis of ancient civilization, making possible plays and sculptures, somewhat democratic institutions, and urban civilizations. You couldn't abolish it without destroying the society. If you ask Aristotle to destroy the whole society, he is going to want to know why that is a good thing to do.

At the same time, don't make your task harder than it is. In the first place, it is fair to do a certain amount of "Monday morning quarterbacking" from the standpoint of the present. We know that alternatives to slavery are possible. And if various preconditions are necessary for any movement which would abolish slavery and move to a different social system based on different principles, assume that Aristotle was in a favorable position to accomplish them. He was a persuasive teacher to a generation of students; he was the tutor of the conqueror of the known world (Alexander the Great); he was in a position to see, if not to understand, what is especially visible from our vantage point. The *polis* was based on slavery.

Therefore it had to expand, bringing it into conflict with others, producing a supply of plunder and slaves. Immediately prior to Aristotle's lifetime, this structure had just produced that ultimate disaster and bloodletting for Greece, the Peloponnesian War. Both victor and vanquished were bled white; the society was prostrate. Whatever arguments may arise about the good, you should be able to convince him that in that way lies only disaster, destruction, death, and despair.

This thought-experiment deals with the sources of social change. Our view of how social change comes about also influences how we look at social structure. This exercise allows you to work out the implications of your own intuitions about social change. Working out those intuitions does not prove them right or wrong, but it is a necessary first step.

We do not know whether you decided that Aristotle's fundamental views were changeable; if you did, we don't know what you thought were the crucial arguments to change them. But we suspect that at the very least, you have thought about the resistance that Aristotle would have had to changing his views *because he was part of the society*; he was related to other people who had ideas about what is good or bad, sensible or crazy; and his ideas fit into an overall system. You may have found that it is hard to produce modern ethics, social theories, or ideas without a modern social system to underpin them. It isn't impossible to build social structure. But making the changes in the social system as a whole might require changing the labor process, and if you need to change the labor process itself, you may find that Aristotle isn't the guy to do it.

Who is? Erik Wright utilizes the Li'l Abner cartoons by Al Capp from the 1940s to illustrate the different interests with respect to the general interest of different groups. He suggests that some groups have an interest in there being pools of poor, vulnerable, dependent groups; specifically capitalist employers have that oppressing interest. Other groups have an interest in everyone being as developed and self-sufficient as possible; specifically workers have that liberating interest. In Li'l Abner the issue is posed by an imaginary benevolent creature, the "Shmoo," who can and will provide people with necessities for free. Shmoos do not provide luxuries, just necessities, and so they eliminate slavery and people being trapped by ignorance and living hand-to-mouth rather than being able to improve themselves and their lives. Thus Shmoos are a kind of garden of Eden, like the existence of the basic subsistence that was true when land was widely distributed, or like a subsistence floor of basic food, shelter, health, and education for everyone. In other respects, Shmoos are like the elimination of pools of race, gender, national, or regional poverty and like the expansion of productivity due to education and technology.

Most of the people in the poor community of Dogpatch are delighted with Shmoos, and their lives begin to change for the better, but the factory owner and his manager think that free food and housing is an awful idea, "a communist plot." Why would people work long hours for a pittance, if they have resources to improve themselves? Who will work as a maid or chauffer for a dollar a day? Who will buy overpriced poor quality food, if they have enough to eat? Why will a lady-friend go out with a sleazy two-timer if she does not want a steak dinner?

Wright argues that people do not always act in their self-interest, and certainly the factory owner is going to talk as though he was in favor of self-sufficiency. But, Wright says, we must look at what happens to his income and his social position when there is cheap labor and when there isn't. Similarly, the poor people in Dogpatch may be convinced that Shmoos are evil, but we have to analyze what happens to them with and without Shmoos. Wright argues that the self-interest of owners leads them to promote the existence of poor and vulnerable groups, while the self-interest of workers is in the elimination of poverty and vulnerability. Thus Shmoos represent what Hegel would have called a "universal class."

Suggestions for Further Reading

On the anthropology of the state: a good starting place is G. Childe, *What Happened in History?* (Penguin, 1942). Debates are summarized in R. Cohen and E. Service, *Origins of the State* (ISHI, 1978) and J. Haas, *The Evolution of the Pre-Historic State* (Columbia University Press, 1982). There are obviously both similarities and differences between the kinds of political organizations that emerged in precapitalist societies and the nation-state which gradually crystallized out of feudalism at the time of the birth of capitalism. P. Anderson, *Lineages of the Absolute State* (NLB, 1974) and *Passages from Antiquity* (NLB, 1974), analyzes these differences and shows how forms of state, religion, and culture (which theories like Weber's treat as determining the development of capitalism) may be historically explained by a Marxist analysis. Tilly's analysis of the nation-state is outlined in *Coercion, Capital and Nation States AD990–1990* (B. Blackwell, 1990) as well as in works such as *European Revolutions* (B. Blackwell, 1993). A powerful account of ancient slavery is G. E. M. de Ste. Croix, *The Class Struggle in the Ancient World* (Duckworth, 1981), discussed below. Wright's parable of the Shmoo appears in *Class Counts: Comparative Studies in Class Analysis* (Macmillan, 1999).

SECTION 1.4: HAVE CLASSES ALWAYS EXISTED?

Hegel argued that it was essential to make property a central part of law and morals because he believed that passing property on to one's children helped make one social. As with the state, he did not believe that property had always existed. Rather, he believed that it was *necessary* to make humans fully human and social, but that it was a *product of history*. By contrast, he believed that slavery was a stage which had only been necessary in the past, but was necessary no longer. As with his theory of the state, we can see that a historical analysis of this kind invites one to ask what is so indispensable about *property*. Marx saw private property as historically variable, and he believed that private ownership of the means of production (private control of factories, land, and raw materials) generates inequality, unfairness, greed, misery, and alienation. He believed that it was historically doomed, like ancient slavery.

As in the case of nations and the state, conceptual issues about the generality of one's concepts can be confused with empirical questions about what can be changed. If one defines concepts very generally and very vaguely, the concepts so defined will explain very little, but they can give the impression that the particular social arrangements which occur are very general and cannot be changed. In sociology, during the 1950s and 1960s, debate on class and stratification was dominated by the **functionalist** account of stratification. Functionalists maintained that inequality was unavoidable because inequality was necessary and functional. They maintained that inequality was necessary to motivate people (especially the most talented) to obtain enough education and training to fill the most important positions in the society. They argued that inequality is a functional universal of all societies. A generation of students right after World War II, who were going to school to get better jobs, embraced the belief that the higher pay of those better jobs was a necessary reward of talent and effort.

But against this belief, others raised many points. (1) The whole theory ignores property income, picturing the top of the system as being occupied not by stockholders but by physicians. (2) It presents no real evidence that the highly paid positions in the society are, in fact, performing important functions. People at the top have the opportunity to convince others that top jobs are important, but some people doubt that such jobs (such as advertising executives, the publisher of *Playboy*, or tobacco company executives) perform functions which are *useful at all*. (3) The stratification system as a whole, far from calling forth the maximum of talent and education, stifles and wastes massive human resources. (4) Money, far from being the only possible motivator in all times and places, is only one motivator among many, even in capitalist society, which is very individualistic and materialistic. Many people would rather be famous than rich; many people would make enormous sacrifices for a group they really cared about, such as their families. (5) Moreover, even if the arguments of functionalists were entirely correct, they say absolutely nothing about *how much* inequality is necessary. By arguing that inequality in general is functional, functionalists seemed to legitimate the actual extreme inequality that exists.

Marxists regard inequality as a blight. It is a blight abundantly produced by capitalism. But far from dealing with inequality in the abstract, the Marxist analysis focuses on historical differences between the processes producing classes and inequality in different modes of production. Some kinds of social arrangements have been true of every organized group; others have been true of every class society but not of relatively classless primitive communities; still others have been true only of certain kinds of production, like slavery. A focus on production allows you to sort these out.

To illustrate the pervasive impact of a mode of production, consider the example of ancient slavery. Marxists believe that slavery was the basis of ancient civilization. It produced the flowering of Athens, the Hellenistic conquest of the known world, and the Roman Empire. Within that social structure slavery was necessary; it was part of a "package deal" which could not be changed. At the same time, slavery also set tight limits on that development, causing the decay and dissolution of these ancient civilizations, the catastrophic bloodletting of the Peloponnesian War, and the agonizing decline and fall of Rome. Ancient slavery produced urban, cultured, leisured citizens. Slaves rarely constituted a majority of the population and did not perform most of the production, but slavery supported the ruling group—the group that produced law and philosophy and art and literature. Every other relationship in society was affected and degraded by tensions and contradictions produced by the relationship between slaves and slave owners.

Is the existence of classes bound up with particular historical phases of production? Table 1.1 shows one way in which classes seem to be bound up with production. Consideration of the laws and other social arrangements which are needed to *make slavery work* suggests others. Slavery exists when one person can own another person. Marx defined classes as groups of people related to each other by their distinctive relations to means of production. Capitalist bosses (the bourgeoisie), wageworkers, slaves, self-employed artisans, landed aristocrats, and smallholding peasants are examples of classes. The historian G. E. M. de Ste. Croix argues that Marxist classes and class struggle are defined by the *process* of exploitation, not by common consciousness, political action, legal status, or anything else. Marx clearly regarded slaves as a class, yet slaves were not a political group that could function in their own interest. They were captured from different areas and had no common language. Thus, slave revolts were rare and political action was usually impossible. But despite the lack of political consciousness, action, or unity, Marx viewed slaves as a class, indeed as the crucial class for understanding ancient society.

Ste. Croix shows in what respect ancient society was based upon slavery. Even when slaves performed a small portion of the total production, *they were the main source of surplus*. Thus they were the main source of leisure, which produced politics, philosophy, and cities. And maintaining slavery was a struggle that marked every other social arrangement. To say that history is the history of class struggle does not say that it is only classes that act in history. Rather, it says that *the actions of the groups that act in history cannot be understood or explained without analyzing the process of exploitation and its relation to the rest of social structure.* It was not that the political system opposed slave owners to slaves. It was that all the opposed groups within the political system were slave owners or linked to them.

Classes, so defined, are obviously bound up with modes of production. You can have landed aristocrats under feudalism, where there is a place for them. Under capitalism, you cannot have landed aristocrats and you cannot have slaves in the sense that ancient society did.

In ancient society, slaveowners were not just one group among others. Any important political, religious, legal, or artistic tendency was tied to slavery. If this was true, how could it change? Why did ancient slavery destroy itself? There were many ways that the slave economy began to strangle. When labor is done by slaves, all labor is degraded, technological change is retarded, and social change is led into a blind alley. In 500 A.D. the Eastern Roman Empire looked much more viable than the Western. It was more secure. It had many developed cities (cities which are still in the news in Lebanon and Turkey) with a brilliant Hellenistic culture. But it was all like a Hollywood stage front. Behind that set of cities there was no urban economy. The city was not sustained by urban industry or crafts, but based on the extraction from the countryside. This process of extraction placed sharp limits on the possibility of transformation. The rural economy could sustain the cities, but it could not sustain change. Technologically, the feudal system was infinitely more dynamic and progressive than the ancient economy. The Eastern Empire was not conquered so much as it rotted.

Moreover, ancient slavery, like slavery in the United States, had to expand or die. In ancient times, slaves were derived mainly from war and conquest. The rulers needed conquests to keep the system going. Because of this, there was constant war. And if the society was not wrecked by war once a slave system had conquered the world and was not expanding, it was forced to undergo transformations which led to its decay. No serious Marxist believes that every village in every region of the world went though and must go through a rigid set of stages, including slavery, in a rigid pattern. But the spread and then the contraction of slavery reflects the development of more complex and efficient forms of wealth accumulation and classes.

Slavery as a mode of production has been abolished. Is it possible to abolish classes of all kinds? Most people say that it is not, but Marxists argue that it is. It is impossible to grow up in a class society without having a "gut sense" that it is impossible to abolish classes. Who would give the orders? Who would collect the garbage? But of course, that gut sense does not prove anything one way or the other. It was impossible to grow up under slavery without a gut sense that some people were born slaves, and it was impossible to grow up under feudalism without a gut sense that some people were born nobler than others. We live in an era of class societies. We have never seen a classless society; there has never been a technologically advanced classless society. But there was never an airplane to see until one was built.

Marxism asserts that a classless society can be built. One kind of evidence for this is that in the past fundamental changes in the relations of production always transformed everything else in the social structure. And fundamental changes in the social structure have always accompanied changes in the mode of production. *All precapitalist relations of production looked eternal to people in those societies, but they eventually came to an end.*

Exercise 1.4: What Is the Class Structure of the United States?

Class divisions are all around you; everywhere you look you see people in different social positions. Go out and identify a class. Itemize some examples of living people you know who might be shaped by their class position. Discuss whether you think they are.
The idea that inequalities of class, stratification, and background have powerful effects on people is not an idea which is held only by Marxist sociologists. Many sociologists who are not Marxists also believe that the analysis of social classes is the backbone of the discipline. In looking at social institutions such as medicine, law, politics, or religion many people believe that the single most important thing to look at is the way in which different people's class positions or resources affect what they want, who they know, what they do, what they can do, and how they think.

At the same time, the analysis of class and stratification is still one of the most disputed and heated areas of disagreement in sociology. Simple and basic questions are the subject of powerful disagreements. How is class defined? What is "class struggle?" What difference does it make whether we focus on relationships to means of production, to wealth, or to income? How much inequality of various kinds is there? Is it increasing or decreasing? It is very difficult to look at class and power except through ideological spectacles, and it is difficult to see what kind of spectacles one is wearing. We will be analyzing class and inequality over and over in this book. But as a first approximation, why don't you see what appears if you merely try to look at society with new eyes, as though you had just stepped off a spaceship. Where might you find them? Well, you might try the bus, your neighborhood, the TV, or your school. Write down on a piece of paper *where* you looked, what *kinds* of people you found, how you think *they are influenced* by their class position, and how you think that *society is influenced* by having those class positions. What are the classes that exist? That is, find some people in different positions in production, wealth, income, social position, or power, etc. How are these people influenced by being in those different positions? How is society affected by having those different class positions?

Today, you can use Google Earth to use satellite imaging technology to look at the buildings and activities anywhere on the planet, and for most cities in the United States, you can view 360-degree pictures that are detailed enough to show people, activities, cars, trash, or cracks in the sidewalk. Your experience allows you to make an estimate of how people live, and from hundreds of indicators such as the size and nature of their houses and cars to the trash or cracks on the sidewalks, you get one window on class. And you do not have to depend on those estimates. For many cities, websites allow you to map the rate of poverty, crime, or thousands of other things for each neighborhood. If you Google down to neighborhoods in Chicago, you can find not only indicators of class, but also evidence about its effects on every kind of behavior you can imagine. You can also zoom in to places like Beverly Park Terrace in Beverly Hills, California, and contrast that to some of the neighborhoods in Chicago, Detroit, or your own hometown.

First, on what you found:

You probably did find classes. They are hard to miss. If you walk across virtually any major city in this country, you will pass some people with millions of dollars, and you will pass other people sleeping in the street. Bill Gates owns some $54 billion; if he were to merely collect property income at around 5 percent, that would give him a *daily* income around $7 million. Less than 1 percent of Americans have that income in five years. The people with millions can jet around, they can live in crystal palaces, and they can buy the services of thousands of other people. This gives them a certain lifestyle, interests, and ways of looking at the world. Conversely, the people sleeping in the streets have different ways of life, different interests, and different ways of looking at the world.

We have drawn this picture in black and white, concentrating on the extremes. Most people are neither millionaires, nor so poor that they sleep in the street. But when we analyze the middle, it is important not to forget the range. Sometimes people, especially upper middle income people, do forget the extremes. Paradoxically, it is just because class is so powerful and pervasive that it is sometimes easy to overlook it. A given neighborhood or school is almost certain to be segregated by social class. Rich people don't like to associate with poor people, and they make arrangements that keep poor people at a distance. In a given neighborhood, you do not find people from the extremes, and if you only find a narrow selection of the middle, you may forget the extremes.

Some people don't take the bus because they can't afford it. And some people don't take the bus because they can afford to pay someone $50,000 per year to drive them around in a $150,000 car. And different classes of people take the bus at 6:30 A.M. and at 9:00 A.M. The range of people that you find on a bus is much more narrow than the range in the whole society.

Not only do we think that you did find classes, but we think that you found certain kinds of classes. We don't live in Egypt in 1000 B.C., so you didn't find peasants, pharaohs, or their apparatus of priests and military. Nor do we live in Greco-Roman or feudal society, so you won't find slave owners, titled, landed aristocrats, etc. (The titled aristocrats in places like England today acquire their wealth today as capitalists, whatever their title.) The fact that those pre-capitalist societies had those classes had a powerful effect on them. The fact that our society doesn't have those classes has a powerful effect on it. And the fact that our society has the kinds of classes it does, has a powerful effect on it. Without some knowledge of history, that effect will be difficult to see, but it is powerful just the same.

Second, on the different ways to look at what you found: there are two main views of class in American sociology. Marxists have tended to conceive of classes as *opposed groups*, related to each other in production. Others have developed Weber's ideas to conceive of classes as a set of gradations, in which people feel more or less distant from each other in terms of wealth, occupation, social status, political power, etc.

Many Marxists analyze class in different ways for different purposes, but the general outline of classes within Marxist theory is fairly simple. According to Marx, there are two really important classes in modern society: *workers* and *capitalists*. Groups characteristic of other kinds of society, such as aristocrats and peasants, disappear. Workers, **proletarians**, propertyless employees, stand opposed to owners, the **bourgeoisie**, bosses. Marx certainly did not think that these are the only two classes under capitalism. But while Marx did not think that workers and capitalists were the only classes worth distinguishing, he thought that they were the most important ones. He argued that processes of proletarianization and concentration of wealth were making the capitalists a small, shrinking portion of the population while workers made up a large and growing part. *For Marx the key thing was not how many toothbrushes one owned but how one's work was controlled.* In Marx's time, ownership of means of production was relatively widely diffused. Most farmers or artisans were self-employed. But Marx could see the dynamic process which would eventually strip the overwhelming majority of the population of their means of production and create a very small owning class and a very large class of employees without means of production.

Marx's analysis of the dynamic of change between modes of production argued that the interests of different classes were often in conflict. The growth of urban manufacture, based on the relation of workers and owners, had undermined the position of the landed aristocracy, and was leading to its replacement. Marx believed that the position and power of capitalist

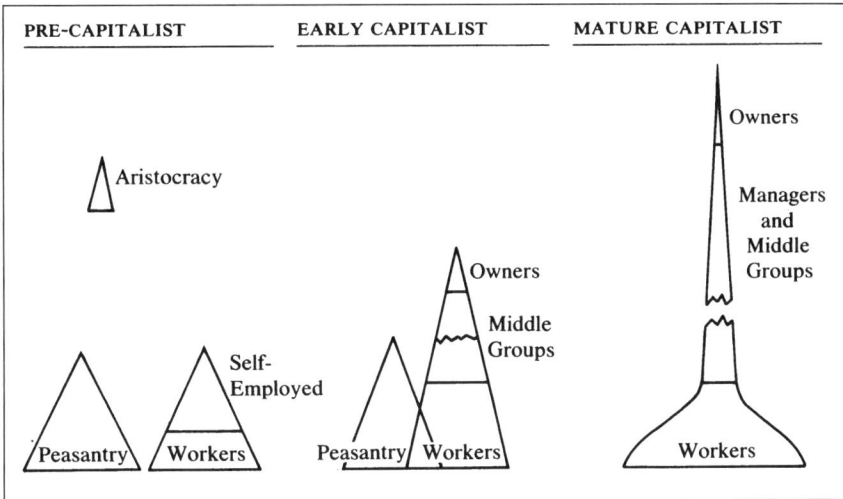

Figure 1.2 Class Polarization

owners would ultimately be undermined in a similar way, and would lead to their replacement, as pictured in figure 1.2.

In contrast to Marx, others focused on people's *conceptions* of social position. These conceptions show a larger "middle class," although it is often less than half the population. Both **functionalist** theorists, developing some of Durkheim's ideas, and **status** theorists, developing Weber's ideas, emphasize social status or prestige rather than class. They believed that "everyone," or "many people," or "increasing numbers of people" have capital. Or, at the very least, they said, "we have an affluent society, a middle class society, a society where almost everyone is comfortable and well-off." Some factual disagreements are involved, but the main disagreements concern concepts rather than facts. American sociology has concentrated on gradations of social status as perceived by participants rather than relations of production. Figures 1.2 and 1.3 try to contrast the two images. Figure 1.2 portrays a class society based on production relations. Classes other than owners and workers diminish. The aristocracy is destroyed, and capitalist society polarizes; the small landowning class gets smaller and the large working class gets larger. The distance between the top and the bottom grows. Figure 1.3 portrays a stratified society with a great middle class bulge. For a generation, sociology students were taught that figure 1.3 was descriptively accurate and theoretically more sophisticated than Marx's.

The "multidimensional" view of stratification, developed by Max Weber, argued that class (based on how much money one has), status (based on

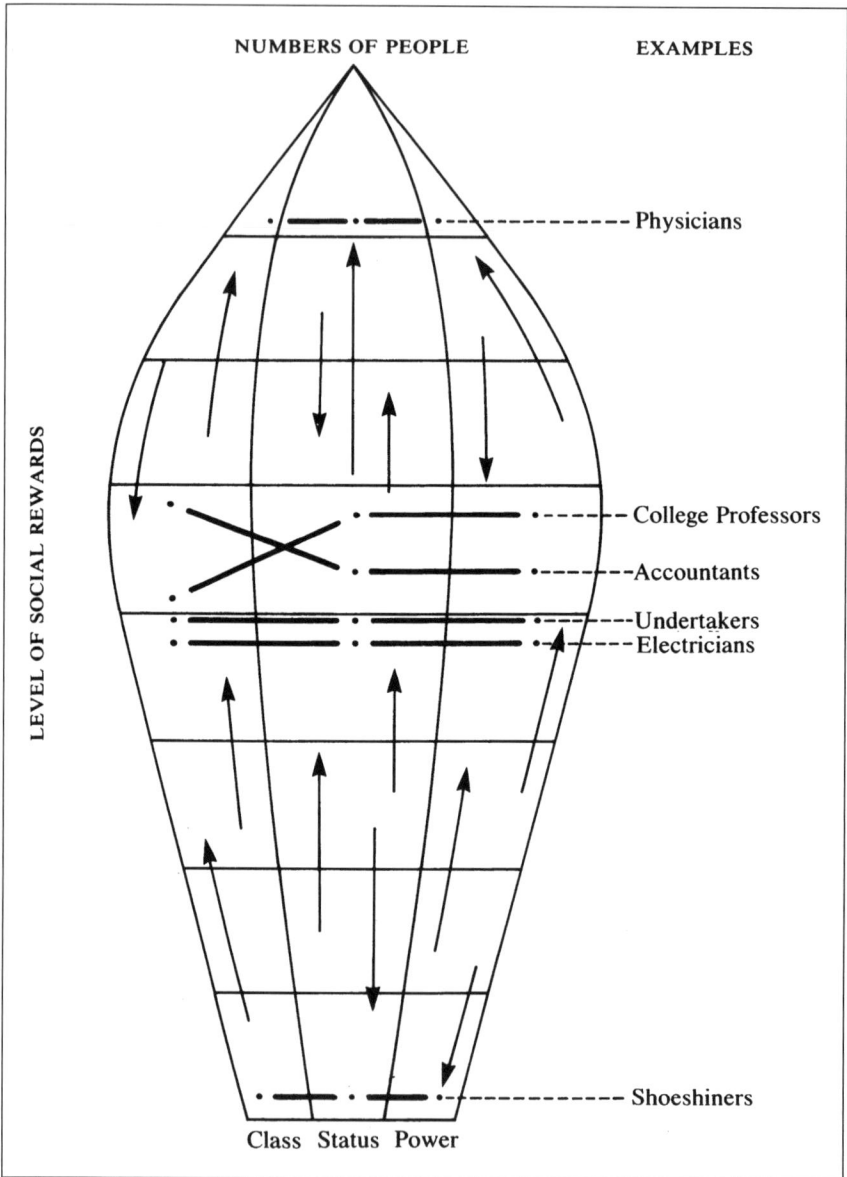

Figure 1.3   Representation of Status Gradation

how much prestige one has), and power (based on how much influence one has) can be quite independent of each other. Thus, someone in the Mafia can have lots of money but not much prestige. For Weber, even class was defined not in terms of production but rather as a market relation, based on one's bank account. It appeared that jobs were very important. To deal with jobs, American sociologists concentrated on occupational status. They devised ways of ranking the population from top to bottom, by reputational methods, by asking people whether such-and-such an oc- cupation or such-and-such a kind of person is "above" or "below" another. In general, they found a fairly high degree of consensus among different observers: ranks were similar in different countries and relatively stable over time. The ranking of individuals this way occupied much of the time and energy of American sociology. It gives a quantitative measure which is not associated with the idea of exploitation, allowing one to look at the effects of **status inconsistency**—of being at different levels with respect to differ- ent components of stratification.

In figure 1.3, people in different occupations have different amounts of income, prestige, and power, but the figure portrays the great mass of people in the middle, so that there is a small (professional) elite, a large middle class, and a small lower class. Actually, in figure 1.3, there aren't classes. The boundaries are arbitrary. What you have is a series of grada- tions (strata) with a loose relation between one gradation and another. It portrays a society in which there is a large bulge of people in the middle (specifically the upper middle).

Which picture is most accurate, figure 1.2 or 1.3? Even though figure 1.3 corresponds to popular perceptions, most Marxists think that it is both less useful and less accurate as a description of stratification. The actual distri- bution of power, income, and wealth will be examined later. Of course, you cannot just see these distributions because that requires both theory and data. But Marxists believe that the evidence shows structures far more polarized even than figure 1.2. Moreover, we think that twenty years of research has shown that the *main* determinant of status is money, the *main* source of money is production relations, and that no significant social be- havior is explained by status inconsistency. The Marxist concepts connect more powerfully to dynamic issues in history, economics, and political science. The main empirical belief on which the status picture rests is the belief that wealth, income, and means of production are becoming more widely distributed.

Suggestions for Further Reading

On classlessness: the functionalist account of stratification was articulated in K. Davis and W. Moore, "Some Principles of Social Stratification," *American Sociological Review* 10:242 (1945). References to the ensuing debate are given in J. Cullen and S. Novick, "The Davis-Moore Theory of Stratification" *American Journal of Sociology* 84:1424 (1979). On ancient slavery: P. Anderson, *Passages from Antiquity* (NLB, 1974) and G. E. M. de Ste. Croix, *The Class Struggle in the Ancient Greek World* (Cornell, 1981). For those who would like a shorter introduction to this 700-page work, Ste. Croix has provided it in "Class in Marx's Conception of History," *Monthly Review* 36:10 (1985). The idea that ancient civilization was based upon, driven by, and doomed by the dynamics of slavery was voiced by Hegel, and it is also the basis of Weber's *Ancient Civilization* (NLB, 1976), the conclusion of which provides an interesting introduction to Weber's work as a whole. Paul Gomberg, *How to Make Opportunity Equal: Race and Contributive Justice* (Blackwell, 2008) argues that unless all labor is valued equally, attempts to make society fair for everyone, including black people, will fail.

SECTION 1.5: WHAT IS FEUDALISM? WHAT IS LIBERALISM?

With the stagnation, decline, and fall of ancient society, a kind of social system arose in the West which was unique in some ways, although it resembled many other social systems. Why and how did it arise in the West? What is the relationship between it and the Industrial Revolution? How did it come to be replaced by the form of society we have now?

The new system developed over a period of hundreds of years and eventually evolved into **feudalism.** Feudal society was based on agriculture; the main laboring class was the **serfs.** It was similar to the slave system in that serfs were not free. They were obligated by law to work a certain period for their liege lord. The political system and law were controlled by the aristocracy who also benefited from it. Serfdom was different from slavery in that serfs were not owned as property and could not be sold. It was different from capitalism in that serfs were not free to decide whom to work for but bound by obligations of personal dependence. There were fewer markets. Buying labor was rare. Much of production was for subsistence. Feudalism was a more productive system than ancient slavery. Larger populations could be sustained. However, feudalism also contained the seeds of its own transformation and death.

The kings, landlords, and aristocrats ruled. They controlled the land, the military system, and the idea system, which was predominantly religious and justified their right to rule. The aristocracy dominated the sources of power and influence under feudalism, so much so that it seemed impossible that any other group might ever replace them. The origin of the essential dynamic which would destroy the whole social system was in the growth of production and exchange. Eventually the power of the throne, backed by the church, and the power of money and production began to come into conflict with each other.

Cities grew up dominated by merchants, businessmen, and bankers who were not part of the titled aristocracy. These urban groups—"burghers" or the **bourgeoisie**—were a middle class between the aristocracy and manual laborers. They constantly grew in wealth and influence and they sponsored new kinds of philosophical ideas, social theories, religious practices, and scientific ideas. The kings and the church feared and opposed much scientific investigation because it could produce evidence that the kings were not chosen by God to be the rulers of the world. On the other hand, the kings and the church both needed money. They often had to increase the productive and scientific capacities of their societies. A society which failed to develop found itself in a backwater, and gradually became subject to societies which did. The growth of science also accompanied the growth of trade. Since the entire legal and intellectual apparatus was in the hands of people committed to a continuation of feudalism, it seemed that change was impossible; but the various tradespeople and merchants began to develop new ideas, organizations, and institutions. Political or economic arrangements that benefited the aristocracy often stifled the urban middle class. Moral arguments and ideas which made sense to landed aristocrats often made little sense to urban groups. There were any number of other conflicts between the worldviews of the aristocracy and the rising bourgeoisie—in religion, culture, and leisure, for example. Sometimes the crucial battles took on a religious form. The battles between the Catholic and the Protestant churches were often tied to the conflict between the rising merchant-capitalist and the old landlord/aristocratic classes. Sometimes they were principally legal and political. Other times they were carried out within the confines of a given nation or through international relations, colonies, and wars. But underlying all of these conflicts of history was the rise of certain groups and the fall of others.

Earlier, we suggested that this conflict between two kinds of social systems—one feudal, agrarian, monarchical, religious, aristocratic, traditional, and rural and the other capitalist, industrial, more democratic, secular, dynamic, and urban—was a fundamental inspiration for sociology as a discipline. One can conceive of "society" only when different kinds of social structure can be observed. Marxists believe that different economic arrangements and especially different relations of production are the key to these two social structures. Specifically, we shall see that the two sets of policies and forms of labor were not just different but contradictory. Of course, groups did not "merely" fight for their self-interest. What was at stake was a whole way of life. Groups fought over what was fair or unfair, just or oppressive, sacred or blasphemous, good or evil. But they differed in their views of what was fair or good because they had different experiences, different connections to other people, and different interests. Rules, laws, and ideals which made sense in the rural countryside conflicted with opposed rules, laws, and ideals which made sense in the city.

One of the ways of seeing the organizing principle of the new social system is to analyze its basic **ideology**. In chapter 4 ideology is discussed as a set of ideas which is rooted in the experience and interests of a particular group and which justifies certain social arrangements. The ideology supported by the rising middle class was called **liberalism** (classical liberalism). It is the ideology dominant among all mainstream political groups in the United States today. Here, we use the term **liberalism** or **classical liberalism** in a broad sense that includes both those considered "liberals" (i.e., "social welfare oriented" liberals) and "conservatives" in the United States. Classical liberals opposed the economic, political, social, religious, and educational monopolies of the aristocracy, and they supported free competition. They accept the general outline of free enterprise and parliamentary democracy. From a Marxist perspective, in all class societies, some control the labor power of others. What is distinctive about capitalism is that *owners buy the labor power of workers*. For the system to operate, both owners and workers have to be free to dispose of their goods and services. And the market serves as a model for other institutions in the society.

Classical liberalism justified a more open system—more open toward scientific investigation, different religious groups, "democracy"—in contrast to the authoritarianism of the pre-capitalist world, where rulers had more control over the economy, political structure, religion, science, and culture. (In the United States, someone who supports moderate reform of inequality within the present capitalist system is called a "liberal" in contrast to conservative. Today's liberals are liberals in the broad sense we use here, but modern conservatives are also "liberals" in the broad meaning of the word, often supporting "free market" policies similar to the classical liberals and their adoration of a mythical "pure" capitalism. Classical liberalism was the fundamental ideology of the rising capitalist middle class.) Classical liberalism has been the fundamental paradigm of Western economic, political, and social thought for the past 200 years.

In its most general, theoretical sense, classical liberalism advocates free competition. Competition is not valued in and of itself. Rather, classical liberal analysis says that in one sphere after another (science, economics,

Table 1.4   Claimed Optima of Liberal Theory

Sphere	Policy	Claimed Optimum
Economics	Laissez-faire	General equilibrium
Politics	Pluralism	Responsive
Philosophy	Libertarianism	Truth
Ethics	Individualism	Individual self-development
Art and culture	Art-for-art's sake	Rich artistic variety

politics, culture, etc.) free competition leads to the optimum position that all people are as well off as they can be. Table 1.4 shows the common logic of a number of classical liberal arguments. Free competition, based on the limitation of government monopoly, is supposed to yield various kinds of optima. In fact, we shall argue, what occurs is actually not those optima but something very different.

In economics, classical liberals advocate **laissez-fare**, letting the economy run itself. They say that government is best when it governs least. They contrast markets, where everyone with a nickel has a nickel's say, with government monopoly and bureaucracy. If we can eliminate government interference, then the economy will move in the direction of a general equilibrium in which labor and other resources are used in the most efficient possible ways to produce the goods and services that are most needed and desired. Milton Friedman, a leading laissez-faire economist, argues that leaving all social arrangements to the market (even education, medicine, or highways) is the best protection of freedom. Does the operation of markets produce a general equilibrium in which the most needed goods are most efficiently produced?

In the political sphere, classical liberals advocate **pluralism** in which constitutional guarantees (the Bill of Rights) allow different interest groups to compete with each other to influence government policy. Liberals say that "only your feet can tell whether your shoes are pinching," and therefore the main thing in achieving the common good is to unblock communication from below to the government. Liberals believe that is achieved by freedom of speech and a multiparty system. They think that if there is a competitive alternation by two parties, then whatever needs are not being met by one party will be used by the other party to gather support. For example, the American Civil Liberties Union argues that the protection of the right to organize of groups like the Ku Klux Klan and the American Nazi Party is the best protection for everyone else. Is this true? Does the alternation of parties and the Bill of Rights achieve responsive government? Why do you agree or disagree with this?

Linked to the political sphere is the sphere of ideas. Classical liberals believe that if everybody has their say and different positions are allowed to compete freely, the outcome will be the truth. J. S. Mill argued that allowing free competition of different positions maximizes the chance of reaching the truth. Is this true? Does the free competition of ideas maximize the chance of reaching the truth? If not, why not? This position does not only imply political libertarianism. In the sphere of ethics, the rise of the middle class was accompanied by the growth of forms of individualism. Both utilitarianism and the Protestant Reformation can be related to this central theme. Other strands of modern theology and ethics are individualistic in other ways. Society is ultimately only the individuals who compose it, individualist positions argue, and therefore the good and the wishes of individuals have to be primary.

In the sphere of culture and art, the classical liberal position was especially associated with the rise of romanticism. In many different ways it was argued that there was no ultimate criterion and no ultimate tribunal of art, and therefore each creator should follow his or her own lights, maximizing artistic variety, innovation, and popular appeal. Do we have a flowering of the arts and a maximum of variety in the United States today? If not, why not?

More generally, does the maximizing of "free" competition achieve any of the optima which liberals claim? During the eighteenth and nineteenth centuries, the guiding thread of social development was the rise of liberalism and of its representatives and beneficiaries—the middle class and the capitalists. In one sphere after another the economic, political, intellectual, and religious monopolies of the aristocracy were dismantled. Marx considered much of this real progress and a necessary step forward for humankind. But, in general, it achieved none of the optima which liberalism had claimed. Moreover, there is no theoretical or empirical reason to suppose that it should have done so.

Liberal competition and markets naturally create enormous class inequalities. **These inequalities produce *new* forms of monopoly and oppression, analogous to those of the aristocracies.** There is a crucial blind spot to classical liberal analyses—a blindness to classes and class concentration. Only in the absence of classes would you ever expect classical liberal policies to produce liberal optima. In the presence of classes, diametrically opposed outcomes result, schematized in table 1.5.

One can define an efficient general equilibrium as what occurs under market competition. One can define responsive democracy as representative government with competing parties, etc. One can take the liberal analysis and make it something that follows from the definition of words, regardless of the nature of the world. This is a nonscientific way of proceeding. The issue is not how to define words, but whether liberal arrangements live up to liberal claims. Liberalism in the philosophical sense, as a set of

Table 1.5   Outcomes of Liberalism in the Presence of Classes

Sphere	Policy	Empirical Optimum
Economics	Laissez-faire	Concentration, waste, stagnation
Politics	Pluralism	Intense bourgeois domination, fascist thought
Philosophy	Libertarianism	Ideology; a marketplace of ideas
Ethics	Individualism	Selfish, predatory isolation
Art and culture	Art-for-art's sake	Sexploitation, homogeneity, wasteland

doctrines, could be contrasted with autocratic feudalism, totalitarian fascism, and Marxism. But in the practical sense of an ongoing movement, liberalism is quite unstable and often sacrifices the personal freedoms of the many to protect the economic freedoms of the few.

Some people say that liberal arrangements are not perfect, but they still are better than any alternative. They say that even if liberal arrangements don't reach optima, they still get as close to them as human arrangements can. But the Marxist criticism of liberalism is not that there are imperfections—minor problems that need to be reformed. The Marxist critic says that liberalism ultimately gives rise to arrangements of unparalleled inequality, inequity, brutality, bigotry, and human degradation. Far from producing heaven on earth, it produces living hells.

Liberalism's Instabilities

Competition devours itself; the free play of interests in a system of immense inequality leads to increasingly distorted solutions. That this is true, and why it is true, is the burden of much of chapters 2 and 3. For the moment consider television, among the most popular forms of culture today. The notion that creators should not be subject to censorship is certainly reasonable. The notion that free competition should lead to variety is not silly. But, for example, consider television in capitalist society, supposedly the highest stage of human freedom. Does television really display such a flowering of the arts, compared to, say, sixteenth-century Elizabethan culture or ancient Greek drama? In fact, television often degrades humanity with violence for its own sake, racism, sexism, and crude nationalism. Why? An answer to this question will tell us a certain amount about the free market.

Measuring any optimum, like government responsiveness or artistic variety, is a profoundly difficult sociological problem. It requires a general theory of what is causing various kinds of degradation and what would happen under different arrangements. We cannot solve all of these problems, which many liberal sociologists and Marxists might handle in different ways. But the question of excellence in art is an interesting one, one that Marx returned to several times.

Some people say that if television gives people trash, that is because people want and deserve trash. If they wouldn't watch it, then the businesses who pay for television time wouldn't fund it. But this oversimplifies both what goes on in front of the TV set and what goes on behind it.

In front of the TV set, people who are brutalized, miseducated, and exhausted just "happen along." We find ourselves watching superheroes make flamethrowers out of old Pepsi cans, or comedies based on one constantly repeated joke—people humiliating and insulting each other—or "reality shows" where we watch other people's lives mainly so we can feel superior to them.

We don't turn it off because there is nothing better. If one treats the schooling, jobs, and relationships of society as fixed and given, then one can say that that is how consumers "just happen to be." But even Marx's great liberal opponent, Adam Smith, agreed that profit-oriented businessmen will design jobs in a way that degrades and dulls workers. The profit made from the workers in the automobile plant or brewery that funds that TV show is one of the main reasons why we can often do no more than just watch the show.

Moreover, behind the TV set there is a huge bureaucratic structure that decides what to show us. There are a number of reasons that it does not show us "whatever we want to see." For one thing, there is a lowest common denominator, so that if there are ten different audiences and stations, each of the stations may aim for the largest audience, satisfying no one very well. Or they may try to appeal to that group of viewers targeted by the particular set of sponsors. For another thing, the executives of that apparatus have definite ideas of what we want to see. Fox is merely the most obvious example of the truism that "freedom of the press belongs to the person who owns one." This sometimes leads them to show us superheroes using flamethrowers on villains with foreign accents. And sometimes it leads to more or less well-disguised propaganda; the executives and the funders of that apparatus may have definite ideas about what they want us to see; certain things appeal to them personally. When there is enormous concentration of control, authority, power, and influence, the idea that the controllers are executing the popular will is often a pious hope. Even relatively recently, popular shows have disappeared and popular authors have been blacklisted as a result of such pressures.

Whether TV is a wasteland or a flowering of the arts, what is important is to see that there is a family resemblance among liberal institutions and a common logic to the analyses and justifications of most of the social arrangements that exist. Those analyses and justifications first appeared with the rise of the bourgeoisie. But the analyses systematically ignore the creation of classes and the effects of class concentration. There are logical and empirical reasons to suppose that, in the presence of classes, these competitive systems will produce less than ideal outcomes.

Exercise 1.5: The Change in Stratification of the United States

How is the class structure of the United States changing? Do you think the gap between the bottom and the top is growing or shrinking? Why? On what evidence do you base your impressions? How do you think further major financial collapses or major wars will affect the trends? Work out your best answer to these questions before going on.

During the rise of capitalism, the middle class was in the middle between the aristocracy and manual laborers. Once the aristocracy was abolished, the capitalist class was on top. A very important question is: what happens to the groups between them and the bottom? Does the middle class portion of the society grow or shrink? Does the gap between the top and bottom grow or shrink? In many respects, the most important question about the class system is not what it looks like at any point, but how it tends to change.

During the 1950s and 1960s many students and professors believed that the United States was a middle class, affluent society. Right now, more people are aware of the millions of people living below the poverty line and the increasing gap between rich and poor. One cannot live in any major American city without seeing people sleeping in the streets. When you look at the distribution of means of production, of wealth, or of income, what you find is not a great middle class bulge but rather inequality forming a grotesquely elongated pyramid, or tower of inequality. But concentrating on the distribution of income or wealth ignores what the essence of the matter was for Marx—the historical process. It is not the static distribution of income, means of production, wealth, or anything else that is important. **Rather, it is the process of change.** How is the distribution of wealth, income, and means of production changing? For example, what were the effects of the New Deal? Did the progressive income tax offset inequality? Have class differences in the United States disappeared, stayed constant, or increased? What long-term trend with regard to class differences can we expect? A sociologist named Leon Blumberg discusses four models or general pictures of the American stratification system and its changes, pictured in figure 1.4.

In the first model, *convergence*, the position of the upper group is seen as improving relatively slowly compared to that of the lower income group, so that class divisions are moderating or disappearing. This was the standard picture within sociology during the 1950s, promoted by theorists who announced the obsolescence of Marx, the end of ideology, and the arrival of an affluent, postindustrial society. According to that picture, back in the

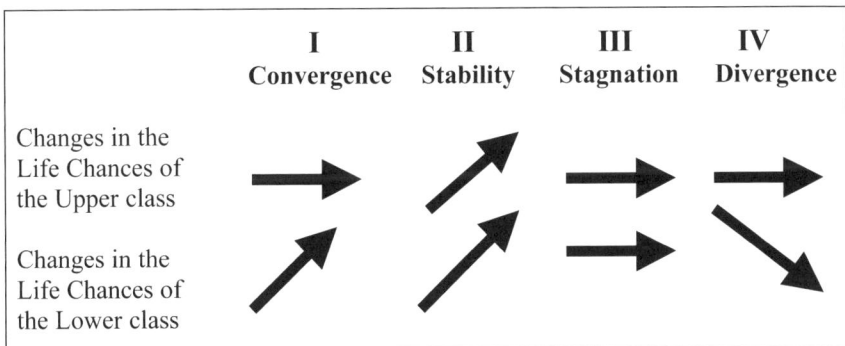

Figure 1.4   Images of Change of American Stratification

bad old days of the Industrial Revolution, the robber barons, or slavery, inequality, and class divisions were very important in America. But, they said, class divisions had disappeared or were disappearing. This view of an affluent, classless (or one class—the middle class) society was the picture dominant in the popular media and in *Fortune* magazine. It came to dominate sociology in the 1950s.

According to the second model, *stability*, the lifestyle of everyone is improving at about the same rate. Thus, while the first model saw class differences as disappearing, the second model suggested that the lifestyle of everyone was improving, but the divisions and relative differences were remaining constant. More people had cars, but there was the same gap between Cadillacs and clunkers as there had been between horsemen and footmen.

According to the third model, *stagnation*, not only relative position but also everyone's lifestyle is staying about the same. People may have more income, possibly even more income after controlling inflation, but does this improve the quality of their lives? Some sociologists came to question whether it did. Much of the increase came from having two-income families, but that involved additional costs as well. In the last generation there has been an increase in the number of people with automobiles. But having an automobile doesn't improve your ability to compete with someone who now has a plane. If the location of your job changes, it may not even get you to work faster. It may not even improve one's absolute well-being. If jobs used to be located where you could walk to them, or if public transportation used to exist, then, when these conditions change, getting a car may be a way of merely standing still rather than improving. If all the exhaust fumes require that you then get an air conditioner to breathe and your income does not increase enough to cover that, this may actively lower the quality of life. Critics of the convergence theorists emphasized aspects of class which did not seem to change, not only relatively, but also absolutely.

Finally, a fourth model, *divergence*, argues that the long-term tendency is for the position of the lower groups to be eroded more and faster than the position of the upper group, so that there is increasing polarization and a larger gap. Indeed, there are three different kinds of divergence, depending whether it is caused by deterioration of the position of those at the bottom, windfalls for those at the top, or both. At particular points in time, the overall processes undermining the situation of the lower half may not be visible. Ups and downs may obscure the overall movement for a time. But, even before the crash of 2008, an increasing number of theorists came to argue that the class structure was, in fact, diverging over the long run. They suggested that far from classes disappearing, class divisions were growing. Today, it is hard for anyone to argue that the pattern, not only of the recent past, but even of the last generation is anything other than divergence.

Marx had suggested that capitalism, like Monopoly, produce polarization, concentration, and the accumulation of opulence at one pole and misery and degradation at the other. That is certainly the tendency built into the rules of the game of Monopoly. Marx argued that while there are temporary countertendencies that result from historical circumstance and the political organization of the working class, the tendency built into the rules of the game of capitalism is also divergence. For example, in *Capital*, Marx summarized the historical tendency of capitalism in terms of a process of exploitation and polarization. We have already seen one part of the process. From a situation where most producers own their own means of production, those means (land, tools, factories, and raw materials) are gradually expropriated; they are concentrated into fewer and fewer hands. For Marx, *in class societies some control the labor of others*. What this means will become clearer in chapter 2. But within the system of capitalism, the control of means of production allows owners to control others' labor power. Although any particular capital enterprise may fail, capital as a whole constantly expands and constantly becomes more concentrated.

> [E]xpropriation is accomplished by the immanent laws of capitalistic production itself, by the centralization of capital. One capitalist always kills many. Hand in hand with this centralization or this expropriation of many capitalists by few, develop, on an ever extending scale the cooperative form of the labor process, the conscious technical application of science, . . . the entanglement of all peoples in the net of the world market, and with this, the international character of the capitalistic regime. Along with the constantly diminishing number of the magnates of capital, who usurp and monopolize all advantages of this process of transformation, grows the mass of misery, oppression, slavery, degradation, exploitation; but with this too grows the revolt of the working class, a class always increasing in numbers and disciplined, united, organized by the very mechanism of the process of capitalistic production itself. (*Capital*, vol. I, chapter 32)

There are many important ideas in this passage which will be discussed later. The world market and the international character of capitalism will also be discussed in the next two chapters. Discussed in chapter 3 is the question whether (and when) an effect of the process is that the working class becomes increasingly disciplined or increasingly in revolt. But for the moment the main thing is the overall picture of the change in the class structure. Marx says that the development of capitalism opposes a diminishing number of magnates to an increasingly miserable, exploited mass.

The central issue of the analysis is the change in people's relation to production, the ability of some people to control the labor power of others, and the set of relationships by which that control is exercised. As shown in figure 1.5, during the late nineteenth and twentieth centuries, the self-

Chapter 1

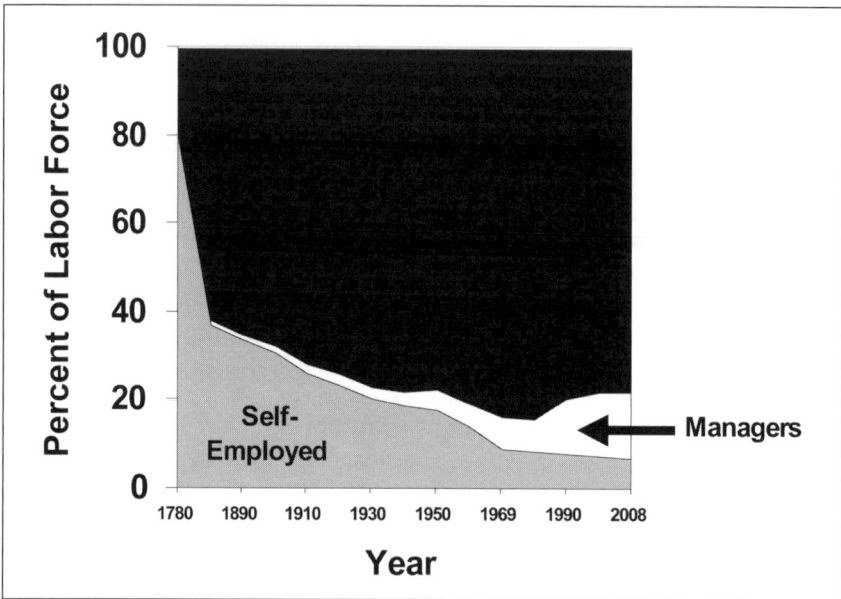

Figure 1.5   Trends in Ownership of Means of Production in the United States

employed fraction of the population was essentially eliminated. We are now a society of employees. There was a growth of managerial strata, but the relationships to production have changed as Marx predicted.

However, in terms of size of payment, many people's intuitions tell them that polarization has not taken place and is not taking place in countries like the United States. There are complex questions involved, about which some Marxists disagree. Long-term trends are entangled and obscured by short-term crises. Much of the importance of Marx's analysis involves accumulation on a world scale, rather than differences within a given country like the United States. And it is possible that the misery Marx is speaking of is mainly relative rather than absolute; few people interpret him to mean that the absolute standard of living of the working class always declines. But don't underestimate the number of things people cannot afford which their parents could. Even before the great financial melt-down and recession of 2009, there were enormous populations of homeless, hungry, and insecure people, and much of the supposed prosperity of others was based on an insubstantial bubble. Therefore, we must not underestimate the amount of misery that a society may conceal, out of sight now or around the bend of the future. Moreover, this fourth alternative, in distinction from the others, is notably unstable. Divergence and polarization can only continue so long, before an explosive situation is produced.

Which of these models seems most accurate to you in describing the last couple of years? Which seems most accurate in describing the present decade? Which seems most accurate in describing the long-term tendencies of the class structure? Why? Above all, how would you describe the *changes* in the distributions of means of production, income, and wealth? How will a major financial collapse or war affect these trends?

For Marx, the fundamental divergence of capitalist society was the disappearance of self-employment. Whether one is "one's own boss" is not just something that is important and gratifying in itself; it is a question whether, during the bulk of one's waking hours, one is free. The distribution of *money* is not the whole story. The question is what money buys. If one is comparing incomes, then inflation hits all people. (However, it has been shown that the price of necessities has increased faster than the price of luxuries. Think of how the prices of gasoline, utilities, college tuition, and food have increased while the prices of big televisions, fancy cameras, and computers have fallen. This means that poorer people with the same relative income lose ground with respect to the actual purchases they can make.) More important, money income only includes those things that pass through the market as money transactions. If one spends forty hours growing a bushel of turnips which one then eats, then that does not show up as one's money income. On the other hand, if one works for the same forty hours to get the money to buy that same bushel of turnips, then that shows up as money income. One's real income has increased, but one is still working the same hours and one is still eating the same turnips.

One of the striking phenomena of the last generation is the huge increase in inequality in all the developed, capitalist economies, and particularly in the United States. Figure 1.6 shows that whether one is considering inequality in terms of the fraction of income received by the top 20 percent or by the top 5 percent, there was a sharp increase in inequality during the 1980s that wiped out the gains in reducing extreme inequality that had been made during the period of the New Deal.

During the 1990s (the Clinton era), income inequality grew somewhat more slowly than it had during the Reagan era, but it continued to grow, and from 2000 until 2008 the gap widened more quickly again. That growth of inequality seems to be largely a function of a structural change in the U.S. economy and in the world economy. This has led to an overall, long-term dynamic of divergence, which, in turn, has generated a host of further, intractable social ills.

As we will discuss in a more general way in chapter 4, every process has limits and when a process reaches its limits it will change. Sometimes the change happens in direct ways but often there is stagnation, decay, collapse, and then major turbulent change. When the ruling classes of societies seek to invest their wealth less in productive projects and more in short-

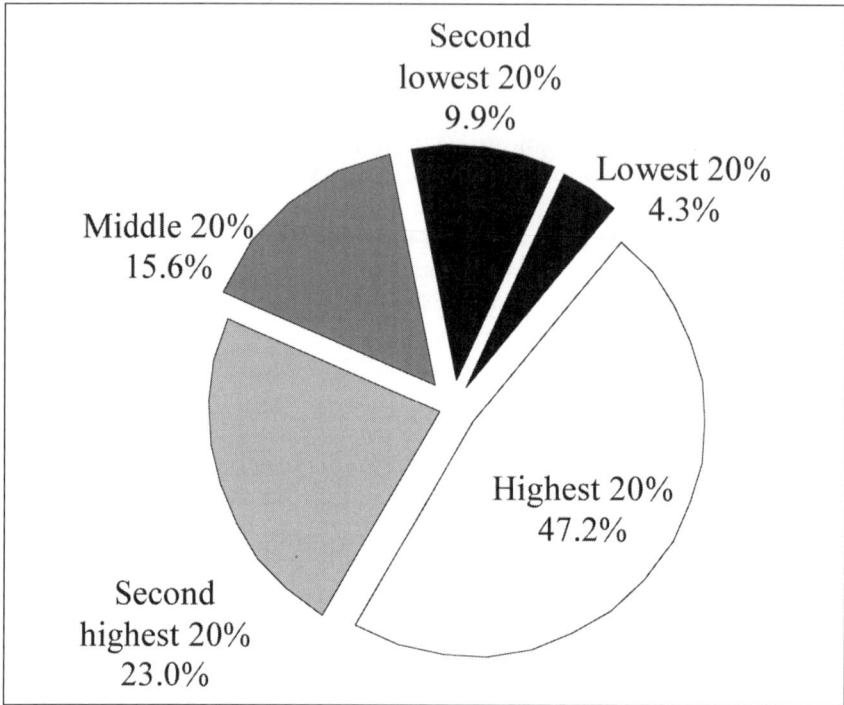

Figure 1.6   Distribution of Income in the United States

term, higher immediate return projects that are not productive, including wasteful consumption and high military expenses, we see stagnation, decay, erosion of the middle layers of society, and movement toward collapse . . . along with increased material and cultural alienation of much of the population. This was true in ancient Rome, in sixteenth century Spain, and in the United States and Europe in the 1920s. Can we see any similar developments today in the United States and Europe? But beyond this, what is important about the development of capitalism is not just that the good things do not trickle down from the top to the bottom. It is not even that capitalism poisons workers so that owners can afford to buy clean air and good food. There are times, periods, and countries when some can get a better existence at the expense of others or the future. But this better existence cannot be for all, and it is fundamentally unstable. The development of capitalism can only provide a good life for some at a cost to others and to the future. Slavery also allowed a cultured, leisured existence for some, but it was a vicious, self-destructive system of terror and degradation that led to war, stagnation, and collapse. So is capitalism.

Suggestions for Further Reading

In a number of works such as *Uneven Tides: Rising Inequality in America* (Russell Sage Foundation, 1993), S. Danziger and P. Gottschalk have shown that earlier in the century, it was basically true that "a rising tide would lift all boats." During that period, economic expansion would produce a tight labor market, raising wages at the bottom. However, that is no longer true. In the late twentieth and twenty-first centuries, economic expansion does not reach those near the bottom. The end of feudalism and the origins of liberal society is a topic which could fill several libraries. One of the best introductions to the neoconservative form of liberal analysis is still M. Friedman, *Capitalism and Freedom* (Chicago, 1962). A systematic critique is E. Rayack, *Not So Free to Choose* (Praeger, 1987). On class process in the modern world: the four models of class process are adapted from L. Blumberg, *Inequality in an Age of Decline* (Oxford, 1980). A recent elementary treatment of the rationales and ideologies created by and for polarizing structures of privilege is M. Schwalbe, *Rigging the Game* (Oxford, 2008).

SECTION 1.6: WHAT CAUSES SOCIAL MOVEMENTS AND SOCIAL CHANGE?

Theories of social change are the main link between sociology and history. In the last generation, when sociology was dominated by functionalism, it often treated the problem of analyzing social structure as separate from and prior to the problem of analyzing social change. Thus, theories of social change were a kind of afterthought, tacked onto the end of theories of structure. The main conception of social structure was a kind of liberal view that different groups' values are averaged out to form a general set of social values which shape the society. Most general theories of change were actually recollections of the classical philosophies of history. There were also fragmentary theories of particular sources of change: one theory for science and the diffusion of knowledge, another for law and its change, one theory of politics, a different theory of social movements, etc. Many of these had something useful to say, but they did not amount to a theory of social change. The topic of "social change" remained undeveloped, and theories of change were largely sterile, because unless one has made the task of accounting for change a major part of one's fundamental theory, one will never be able to develop it separately.

Moreover, when the analysis of social change is divorced from the real tensions, conflicts, and contradictions in the society, it becomes shallow. Perhaps the best example of this is the theory of social movements and social revolutions which was developed by the **functionalists.** Functionalists believed that social structures are functional and legitimated by the value system. They tried to account for social movements in general, irrespective of the particular kind of social movement or the particular kind of society within which it developed. Under these assumptions, how could they explain the rise of groups of people attempting to change society? Most functionalists viewed social movements, and especially violent social movements, as irrational. Social movements were classified with crazes, panics, fads, or any other kind of social behavior which was "non-institutionalized." To account for them, functionalists developed a catchall category of "strain." To say that social movements resulted from "strain" often said no more than that some people in society thought that some aspects of social arrangements were unsatisfactory. No doubt they did, but since strain in this sense is pervasive, it hardly constitutes a very powerful or predictive theory of social movements.

Other people do not go so far as to dismiss all movements for social change as the reactions to strain, but they say that Marx had too narrow a view of the causes of such movements. Marx argued that **class struggle** has been the motor of history. Other theorists have argued that conflicts are important, but class conflicts are not central to what historical sociologists and theorists concerned with social movements should analyze. People come into conflict with each other for all kinds of reasons because they differ in values, color, or customs. It is too narrow a view that class struggle is the only source of change.

If you look around the world, you see people fighting each other on the basis of race and religion in Sudan, religion in Israel, India, and Pakistan, ethnicity, religion, and politics. That is also what Marx saw in the last century. He did not say that we should ignore such issues. He did say that we can only understand them if we analyze the class issues that are involved. At the very least, all of these conflicts involve some group of people having means of production, land, jobs, or other resources which other people want. And so all of the situations lead to disputes about the fundamental questions concerning the socioeconomic structure of society. Since those disputes always concern related issues and involve neighboring disputes, this gives them all a familial resemblance. In fact, racial conflicts in South Africa and the United States, and religious conflicts in Ireland and Israel, etc., have profound similarities which are only visible if one focuses on their relation to class, production, and control of means of production.

In contrast to the view of social movements as unusual, unstructured, and irrational, historical sociologists such as Charles Tilly and his collaborators have developed extensive, fine-grained analyses of social protest and social conflict. The process by which identities, organizations, and conflicts with others reinforce each other is complex, but Tilly et al. found the key to social movements over the last century not in the breakdown of social values or processes of "differentiation," but in the expansion and concentration of capital and the formation of nation-states which resulted from that. To a considerable degree, they have rediscovered the fact that

> . . . the history of all hitherto existing society is the history of class struggles. Freeman and slave, patrician and plebian, lord and serf, guild-master and jour-neyman, in a word, oppressor and oppressed, stood in constant opposition to one another, carried on an uninterrupted, now hidden, now open fight, a fight that each time ended, either in a revolutionary re-constitution of society at large, or in the common ruin of the contending classes. (*Communist Manifesto*, SW, p. 35–63)

In the first place, contemporary historical sociology has confirmed the pervasiveness of protest. There is variation in the forms, objects, and quantity of social struggle, but it is pervasive. In the second place, that analysis has demonstrated the coherence and intelligibility of social protest and class struggle. Although there are many different protest groups, and although Tilly would not defend the thesis of the fundamental character of class struggle in the same way Marx would, he finds that the intelligible bases of collective action and struggle are the identifiable social groups in opposed economic positions, with divergent economic interests.

In the third place, historical analysis has recovered the importance of social protest and revolutions for structural change. If history is everything that happened, then class and class struggle are important to it, but you would not say history is the history of class struggle. If history is an account of radical, fundamental, "world-historical" shifts in social structure, such as the disappearance of feudalism and aristocracy, then class is much more important. When Marx says, "History is the history of class struggles," he is posing an empirical hypothesis that class is the main force behind such transformations. In the fourth place, Tilly's analysis reintroduced organization and politics into the analysis of social movements. Organization is the fundamental requirement of social action. There are times when class struggle is latent. Many theorists believe that this is not usually due to the absence of issues and sentiments of contention, but the absence of a suitable organizational vehicle of collective action. The interplay between organization and the social bases of politics will constitute the fundamental theme of chapter 3.

The great body of historical sociology like that of Tilly, even when it disagrees with Marx, has focused on the Marxist model of historical change. For Marx, the backbone of history is the transition between different modes of production. The history of the nineteenth century is the history of the expansion and concentration of capital. This expansion took the political form of the opposition between working class parties and liberal, largely middle class parties. More generally, the movement or transition between modes is accomplished by social revolutions.

Social revolutions are internally generated by the conflicts and contradictions within each mode of production. A social revolution means the rise of a political movement supporting structural change, in collision with existing laws and the state. Marx believed that all social revolutions are powered by class struggle because only thus can millions of people be mobilized in a persistent and enduring way. Depending on their relationships, some classes are easier to mobilize than others. For example, the peasantry is very difficult to organize into a movement, even when it constitutes the vast majority of the population. Moreover, not only are class interests important for the mobilization of millions of people, they are also important for their consequences. Marx argued that not all classes have the possibility of fundamentally transforming the social system. The peasantry, even if it is organized and conducts a successful revolution, does not have a set of interests and experiences which allow it to fundamentally transform the social system. There have been many successful peasant revolutions which have not created social revolutions. But the peasantry allied with and led by the working class may be an immense force for change.

Exercise 1.6: Marxism and Racism/Nationalism

Marx argues that the class struggle of capital against labor is the key to racism, and fighting racism is often the key to class struggle against capitalism. Can you find theoretical evidence relevant to these ideas? What is it? Do you have practical experience relevant to these ideas? What is it?

Anti-Marxists accuse Marx of neglecting the importance of forces like nationalism, racism, and sexism. In fact, Marx believed actual divisions of people by race, sex, nation, ethnicity, etc., and the corresponding divisive ideologies were the key to the class struggle. We shall see that racial and national divisions are part of a total system of alienation. Marx devoted hundreds of pages to the analysis of race and national divisions. Marxists examine racism, like other social processes, as an interdependent web of economic, political, social, and cultural processes. Globally, while racist exploitation and oppression based on "skin tone" has created a world where working class people of African ancestry are especially oppressed, we can find similar processes at work in various places against members of other supposed "races," ethnicities, and even religion. Most Marxists see the *origins* of modern racism as *economic*, based on the slave trade and reinforced by the extreme exploitation and subordination of minorities. The enslavement of Africans, the super-exploitation of black American workers, the extermination of Native American Indians, the importation of Chinese and other immigrants, along with economic expansion into Asia, Africa, and Latin America, all produced fantastic profits in the United States. Most Marxists also see the *ideological forms* of racism as important, because racist ideology makes it harder to change the social system.

Ignoring the economic aspects of racism, minimizing its connections to the roots of capitalism, underestimates how difficult it is to eliminate racism. If nobody, not even employers who pay less or slumlords who charge more, benefits from racism, then it would appear that it is easy to overcome by education and a positive attitude. Ignoring the ideological aspects of racism also underestimates how difficult it can be to overcome it. Without conscious, direct confrontation and refutation of racist myths, it is virtually impossible to organize the kind of action essential to challenge the profit system. Many non-rich "white" people may believe that racism benefits them, and indeed there are often measurable short-term advantages to them from racist structures in housing and jobs, but those structures and ideas maintain a capitalist system that hurts them in the long run.

For now, we shall focus on the ideological aspects of racism. One reason that Marx viewed racism as crucial is that he believed there is a pervasive struggle in society. In any fight or struggle, it is disastrous if a team is fighting among itself. In chapter 2 we shall see that Marx saw racial splits as very important for the economic division of the product into wages and profits. And in chapter 3 we shall see that racial splits are political dynamite.

Marxists have always treated the struggle against racism as fundamental to social change. Typically they have argued that it is impossible to do anything progressive in this society without coming into collision with racism. Racism does not just produce an occasional action by a small number of "racists" which only hurts a "minority" of the population. Every major setback, cutback, and rollback for working people as a whole—in health, education, organization, politics, consciousness, or security—is spearheaded by racism. It is one of the most powerful political forces in the United States, and history shows that it is always an immensely volatile, explosive political force. Not only is it not possible to make a revolution as long as the working class is divided against and fighting itself, it is not possible to make smaller reforms without coming into collision with racist ideology and often, overtly, with racist movements. Is this true? Do racial and nationalist divisions and ideologies constitute the fundamental obstacle to progressive change?

Marxists argue that racial and nationalist divisions are intimately connected to class divisions in a dual sense:

1. The class struggle of capitalist against worker produces racism. Theoretically, it is impossible to explain the increases and decreases in racism independent of a class analysis. Practically, it is only possible to address racism within the class struggle.
2. Fighting racism is the key to the class struggle. Theoretically, the Marxist model emphasizes the degree of unity or disunity of the working class. Racism is the key to that unity. Practically, any progressive ac-

tion brings one into collision with racist forces, and racism within progressive forces utterly destroys them.

We don't know what you thought of as theory and evidence about the impact of class struggles on racial division. We think that in different societies and communities, racial, religious, and other divisions are thrown up from the process of exploitation as surely as volcanoes are thrown up by the explosive forces beneath the Earth's surface. We don't know what you regarded as theory and evidence about the importance of racism to class divisions. We do think that Marx was correct when he wrote that nationalism and racism against Irish workers were Achilles' heels, both of the British and American labor movements. Such divisions fundamentally weaken the whole working class, no matter what the illusory or tiny benefits some workers might think they get from racism.

Obviously, any practical test of theories about race and class raises profound methodological and ethical problems, problems which are important in a less acute form in other areas of sociology and which are discussed in terms of participant observation and commitment. Both class struggle and race conflict can be dangerous. You should not do anything which is ethically wrong or practically dangerous; we don't recommend joining the Ku Klux Klan to see what it is like. But it may be that there are plenty of practical actions which are personally acceptable and which allow you to see the relations of race and class inequality. Community groups, social action groups dealing with issues of homelessness, fair housing, welfare rights, immigration rights, and education as well as workers' groups often deal with the interplay of race and class inequality. Otherwise, you can sometimes fall back on historical observation. The practical analysis of the role of racism often involves difficult judgments of what is going on, but those judgments are probably decisive in the long run, both for personal evaluations of the role of racism and for sound theoretical knowledge of its role.

The relation of class to other divisions such as race, religion, nationality, sex, and ethnicity is a huge topic of research. Making any real change in any one of them often seems so difficult that it is understandable that sometimes people wish to deal with them separately. But we think that you will find that they are always interconnected. They are part of package deals so that it is almost never possible to change them individually. In chapter 4 we shall relate such issues to very general ideas about the interconnection of the world and the "unity of theory and practice."

Suggestions for Further Reading

On contemporary theory of revolutions and social movements from an immense, rapidly moving field, three citations will have to suffice: a good example of the kind of analysis which has convinced many sociologists that no adequate theory of social movements and social change can fail to deal with social structure, especially class structure, is M. Schwartz, *Radical Protest and Social Structure* (Academic, 1976). From among Tilly's voluminous writings, a substantive summary of his findings, counterposing Marxist to Weberian and Durkheimian approaches, is *From Mobilization to Revolution* (Reading, 1978) and an argument that sociology should replace functionalist analyses of differentiation, legitimation, and strain with conflict analyses of the effects of capital accumulation is *Big Structures, Large Processes, Huge Comparisons* (Russell Sage, 1984). The concept of a "social revolution" consolidates the insight that there are other, nonsocial revolutions, like the perennial Latin American coup, which do not accomplish fundamental social change. See, for example, T. Skocpol, *States and Social Revolutions* (Cambridge, 1979). For examples of the pervasive effects of racism on whites, see B. Bowser and R. Hunt, *The Impact of Racism on White Americans* (Sage, 1981).

SECTION 1.7: ARE EVENTS INEVITABLE? WAS THE FRENCH REVOLUTION INEVITABLE?

Modern liberal society did not just happen. Epic historical battles were needed to get rid of feudalism. History not only describes different social forms and the trends within them, but also the events leading from one to another. It describes the path we followed and any forks on that path. The French Revolution destroyed the French monarchy and aristocracy; the Napoleonic armies carried republican institutions throughout Europe. How would our lives be different had this not happened? Could the French Revolution not have happened? Would it have made any difference? Questions such as these arise with respect to every major event of human history: the rise of ancient Greece, the fall of Rome, the American Revolution, the Civil War, World War I, the Russian Revolution, World War II, the defeat of Hitler, and so forth.

Suppose that Louis XVI had been a little bit smarter or more forceful. Could he have prevented the French Revolution? If not, why not? Would it have saved the monarchy? Would that have saved feudalism? Would other monarchies have been able to keep afloat? Would diplomacy still consist of the marriages and meetings of the crowned heads of Europe? If not, why not?

In chapter 4, we argue that the question whether history is determined *in general* is a mechanistic, bad question. So is the question whether a concrete historical event was determined *in general*. We shall suggest that some aspects of those events might have been changed easily; others would have been difficult to change; and still others were bound to occur. It is always a matter of approach. Not every aspect of the French Revolution was inevitable. Any event, and certainly any event as large and complex as this, has an indefinitely large number of idiosyncratic aspects. But such events also have an indefinitely large number of historically lawful, determined aspects. With regard to any event of world history, any nonmechanistic question of determinism must specify what aspects of the events were determined by what processes.

By the "French Revolution," Marxists and sociologists mainly have in mind the establishment of liberal, capitalist society, for that is the main role the revolution played in European and world history. It destroyed the monarchy and established the rights of man and the Napoleonic Code. With Napoleon's defeat, monarchies were reestablished, but they were moribund. Since many other institutions were built into the old regime, it was not possible to transform them without a political battle. The argument that the French Revolution was a determined, inevitable event then takes the form that the battle was so unlikely as to be impossible in the thirteenth century, for example, but it became more and more likely as time went on.

The main reason for this, according to Marx, was that there was a steady rise of numbers, power, influence, and organization of precisely the class with the most to gain from the new, liberal society. More generally, unless there is a class whose interests lie within the development of a new social form, then it is impossible that it will be built. The rise of these new economic arrangements and their beneficiaries was an international phenomenon. If the French Revolution had not taken place in France, France would no longer have been in the center of European history.

Within contemporary historical sociology, Barrington Moore's book, *The Social Origins of Dictatorship and Democracy* (Beacon Press, 1966) had a powerful impact on analysis of events such as the French Revolution. Moore aims to give a large scale map of the events which brought different countries into the modern age. It may seem that such a large scale map is impossible. At first glance, the differences between events in France, England, Germany, the United States, and other countries seem to be indefinitely complex. However, underneath those particularities there are fundamental similarities.

Moore's specific question starts from the gradual, peaceful transition of the British government, and especially the "glorious revolution" of 1688. Moore asks how it was possible for Britain to have relatively peaceful political change. His fundamental answer is that peaceful development followed the violent revolution of 1642. That accomplished the violent overthrow of the feudal system. In all developed countries, bourgeois groups arose who were hemmed in and limited by the aristocracy and its prerogatives. There is a fundamental contradiction or conflict between two different kinds of social system, represented by opposed social groups, beneficiaries of opposed social arrangements. The crucial arrangements of the rising middle classes and of the aristocracy were **contradictory.** They were **fundamentally opposed** or antagonistic. For feudalism to continue, particularly when feudal landholders were faced by sharp foreign competition, it was necessary for people to be tied to the land; for industrialism to continue it was essential that the workforce be free. To this condition and to the large group of interrelated social classes that stood to benefit or lose most from the change are connected all the divisions between the liberal and the feudal worldview and policy which we have discussed.

In every developed country? What about the United States? How was there a feudal aristocracy in the United States? Was the American Revolution analogous to the French Revolution? Most Marxists argue that the social revolution in the United States was not the American Revolution, but the Civil War. The American Revolution involved mainly national independence. The Civil War was far bloodier and involved the social form of the society. The Civil War involved the same groups and the same principles that motivated the revolutions against old regimes in Europe. The same landed groups opposed the same industrial groups, as in the bourgeois revolutions in Europe. The industrial groups were forced to mobilize the same masses, urban groups with similar slogans and principles, as in the French Revolution.

But what about those countries where no violent revolution marked the transition to modernity? According to Moore's analysis, in other countries such as Germany and Japan, the rising middle class was not powerful enough or bold enough to risk a collision with the landed aristocracy. Instead, they became a junior partner politically, in a deal in which the landed aristocracy was granted political influence in return for the rising bourgeoisie's right to make money. Peace was maintained, but in every single country characterized by this kind of arrangement in the eighteenth and nineteenth centuries, the twentieth century witnessed the peaceful victory of fascism. Why? The social merger of the industrial and landholding groups—the famous marriage of "iron and rye"—could be accomplished precisely on the basis of an agreement to maintain a system of repression and control over workers and peasants. In the absence of a violent social revolution destroying and expropriating the old groups, one had an alliance of elite groups on the basis of their joint interest in suppressing the masses of the population. The ideas characteristic of these groups (racialism, militarism, nationalism) were precisely the basis of fascism. Thus those societies came into the twentieth century with elaborate police and military systems. A middle class which comes into conflict with an aristocracy, and which is forced to appeal to a mass base, has to allow some ideas and arrangements which go against the repressive system. When it later comes into conflict with workers and socialism, the middle class may support fascism, but the ideas, the repressive apparatus, and the confusion of oppositional groups are greater if there has been no bourgeois revolution. Thus, those societies (and the human race) paid for a peaceful nineteenth century by their coming into the twentieth century ripe for fascism.

In a third set of countries—especially Russia and China—there was neither a strong bourgeois development nor an alliance of the bourgeoisie with the landed aristocracy. Instead, one finds agrarian bureaucracies. In the twentieth century those countries saw an alliance between working class parties and peasants leading to communist revolutions. Thus Moore's theory can be summarized in two sentences: no violent bourgeois revolution, no liberal democratic society. Then either the marriage of iron and rye prepares for fascism or the alliance of workers and peasants creates socialism. What these sentences summarize is a large scale map based upon a small number of key alliances between class groups—the aristocracy, capitalists, workers, and peasants. The analysis says that twentieth-century politics resulted from nineteenth-century revolutions, which in turn shaped and were shaped by the kinds of class alliances each country experienced.

The tendencies which dominated in some countries appeared as secondary tendencies in others. Countries are complex. Parts of France resembled Germany, and they experienced the dominance of similar groups, leading to fascist politics. Others were like Russia, and they experienced a worker-peasant alliance in the nineteenth century and supported socialist slogans in the twentieth. Similarly, in the American South, the continued power of antebellum landed groups, allied with capital on the basis of a labor-repressive system. In the twentieth century, those areas experienced large, powerful racist and profascist political influences. Just as France was nearly paralyzed politically by fascist groups prior to World War II, in the United States, some people estimate that as many as twenty state governments were dominated by the Ku Klux Klan.

Moore's analysis is a celebration of liberal, bourgeois revolutions. Some Marxists believe that he fails to see the ironic outcome that awaits liberal political structures at the end of the twentieth century, and that he treats liberal, fascist, and socialist outcomes as more fixed and predetermined than they are, ignoring the actions of political groups. Active political organizations played a role in fascist challenges in some countries in the 1930s; everything had not been predetermined in the nineteenth century. There are other respects in which Moore's analysis can be challenged. But Moore's positive contribution to American sociology was a reintroduction of large scale, historical macro-theory based upon the analysis of class alliances. There are a relatively small number of crucial class forces, and there are a relatively small number of bases on which alliances between them can be built. These two elements, class forces and class alliances, are the stuff of the fundamental dynamics of history.

Exercise 1.7: What Was the Effect of John Brown's Raid?

Suppose that you lived at the time of the Civil War, that you were committed to defeating slavery, and that you led a dedicated, multiracial group of about 100 people. What would you have done? Why?

In 1859, a militant opponent of slavery, John Brown, led a multiracial, armed raid on a U.S. government arsenal in the town of Harper's Ferry, West Virginia. The purpose was to seize arms and pass them on to slaves in the South, in order to start an armed uprising against slavery. Brown and his supporters took over the arsenal, but they were captured by the U.S. Army. Brown and most of his followers were executed. The slave uprising never occurred. What did occur, ending slavery, was the Civil War, the single bloodiest and most important event of U.S. history, a convulsion which shaped much of what one sees today.

Historians have argued about the origins of the Civil War. What effect did the raid and the furor about it have? Was the Civil War inevitable? What were the historical forces, the political, economic, and social processes, that led up to that war? Some historians explain the Civil War by moral outrage against slavery; they say that it was not inevitable but rather was the result of the good intentions of the anti-slavery groups. Other historians have argued that anti-slavery ideology was irrelevant; the war, they say, was the result of sectional conflict that would inevitably result in armed conflict. Both kinds of analysis would argue that Brown's raid was not particularly important: according to the first, because it was not in the mainstream of anti-slavery moral opposition; according to the second, because nothing would have made any difference. The **voluntaristic** analysis that you need not bring about institutional change if only you accomplish moral change is one common liberal counterargument to Marxism. The **deterministic** analysis that you cannot alter the course of institutional change is another common liberal counterargument to Marxism. When situations in places like Central Africa or Central America arise which cry out for action, both responses commonly come into play.

Many Marxists think that by the second half of the nineteenth century, slavery was doomed in that it could no longer coexist with capitalism. It had to change in some way. Moreover, it would never fade away peacefully, either. In *Political Economy of Slavery* (Vintage, 1967), E. Genovese argues that Southern slaveowners could have accommodated the demands of the North only by committing suicide as a class. Given the connection between slavery and their entire way of life, they would not do this. By the early 1800s, the invention of the cotton gin gave a new lease on life to slavery, increasing the profitability of slave agriculture but making it more unstable. It also brought slavery into sharper collision with forces opposed to it. Competition between the North and South intensified. On the one hand, many Northern banks had actually become partners or owners of plantations, benefiting from slavery. On the other hand, their primary concern was turning a profit. The international profitability of industry depended on a series of policies legitimized by principles directly opposed to slavery. There was increasing conflict over who would control the West and the federal government. Slavery needed room for future expansion. This need to expand brought it into collision with Northern interests.

Sometimes people attack Marxist analyses for supposedly saying that people have no ideals, or that it does not matter what ideals people have or what they do because history is determined. This is a shallow caricature of Marxism. Of course people have ideals, and one can even analyze which sets of ideals can be especially important historically. Of course it is important what people do, and one can even analyze when there are turning points in history in which it matters more what people do.

Suppose that you led a dedicated, multiracial group of about 100 people, committed to defeating slavery and you were able to field about a fifth that number for dangerous action. What would you have done? Of course, to answer that, you must first make a general analysis of slavery and its future. If it is doomed to fade away, then you need do nothing whatsoever—perhaps you will redirect your energies to moderating its effects, maybe by running stations of the Underground Railroad. If it can be eliminated legally and peacefully, then you will no doubt want to follow that course. If it requires violence to end it, then you will have to figure out whether there is a more effective way of using force than the way John Brown chose.

Most historians portray Brown as an irrational fanatic. Given that his speech and writing were not irrational, this is the historical equivalent of the sociological portrayal of all social movements as irrational. Of course Brown, like any other mortal, made a number of mistakes. Tactically, he allowed himself to be bottled up in the armory, when earlier he could have escaped. The reinforcements under the leadership of Harriet Tubman were delayed, and better planning may have made the whole action more successful. But, far from being a product of an irrational fanatic, most Marxists view the raid on Harper's Ferry as so well conceived that it succeeded even though it failed.

Slavery was a system of terror. Nothing was better calculated to demonstrate this character than the specter of slaves with guns. The slave system was, and had to be, backed by the military power of the federal government. Nothing was better calculated to underscore this than a raid on a federal arsenal. It took force, the Civil War, to destroy slavery. Nothing was better calculated to underscore this than the crushing of Brown's raid and his execution. Brown's raid swung the abolitionist movement onto the path of destroying slavery by force rather than moral persuasion. It enormously increased the fears of slave owners. This is one of the reasons that the marching song of Union troops became "John Brown's body lies a-mouldering in the ground, but his truth is marching on."

In an historical contradiction there is a *crisis*. Opposed historical forces exist, leading to opposed, possibly different historical trajectories. Under these circumstances, individual actions, while constrained by history, may have powerful consequences. Both the forces requiring the expansion of slavery and those behind its abolition were very powerful. The collision between these two sets of forces was unavoidable. *But that still left numerous possibilities for the outcome of that collision*. To say there was a contradiction is to say there was a fork in the road.

Could Northern bankers and politicians have worked out a peaceful co-existence with Southern slave owners? The analysis in the preceding section implies that an accommodation along the same lines as the German "marriage of iron and rye" might have happened, enormously accentuating elitist, repressive, and racist forces in the society—possibly leading to fascism in the United States in the early twentieth century. As Marx wrote,

> Secession, indeed, only took place because within the Union the transformation of the border states and Territories into slave states seemed no longer attainable. [But had the North ceded the contested territory,] there would in fact take place, not the dissolution of the Union, but a reorganization of it, a reorganization on the basis of slavery, under the recognized control of the slaveholding oligarchy. In the Northern states, where Negro slavery is in practice unworkable, the white working class would gradually be forced down to the level of helotry. This would accord with the loudly proclaimed principle that only certain races are capable of freedom, and as the actual labor is the lot of the Negro in the South, so in the North it is the lot of the Germans and the Irishman, or their direct descendants. (Marx, *On the Civil War* [a selection of his articles] International, 1974, pp. 67–68).

When massive forces are in motion, how can one prove that any action makes any difference? Even if Brown's cause became the rallying cry on the central issue, how can one prove that something else would not have done as well? Indeed, the same argument applies to the Civil War as a whole. It was the process that broke slavery and dominated the future development of the United States, but had it not happened, might not something else have had an equally powerful effect? It may seem that historical judgments concerning the long-term consequences are very iffy, unscientific, and academic. In a sense they are. But for participants, on such judgments rest the issue of what we should do. All our actions have consequences which **proliferate** indefinitely. It seems impossible to say with certainty what the effects of an action will be.

Practically, we act or fail to act all the time. That is the human condition. The effects of all our actions are uncertain. If you leave the house, it is impossible to say with certainty that you will not be struck by lightning. But staying home does not solve the problem. Staying home does not even help, since being struck by lightning is not, in fact, a common cause of death—but house fires can be.

Suggestions for Further Reading

On the French Revolution, a standard class analysis, the work of A. Soboul, *A Short History of the French Revolution* (University of California Press, 1965) was attacked by those (such as F. Furet) who saw the Revolution as successful and liberal until it was "blown off course" by more radical, socialist currents, for example, *Interpreting the French Revolution* (Cambridge, 1981). Of the immense literature on class alliances and political-economic developments, see, for example, D. Rueschemeyer, E. Huber, J. Stephens, *Capitalist Development and Democracy,* (University of Chicago, 1992) and E. Huber and J. Stephens, *Development and Crises of the Welfare State* (University of Chicago, 2001) as well as R. Brenner, "Agrarian Class Structure," *Past and Present* 78, 79, 80, and 85 (1978–1979). A powerful class analysis of slavery, its expansionist impetus, and the fundamental contradiction by the Civil War is E. Genovese, *The Political Economy of Slavery*. Still useful a century after it was written is W. E. B. DuBois's *John Brown* (International, 1962 [1909]). The idea of an historical contradiction as a time when action can lead two possible trajectories is pursued in chapter 4.

SECTION 1.8: WHAT ARE THE DYNAMICS OF THE MODERN WORLD?

Capitalism became the most productive system the world had ever seen. Life on Earth changed more in the last two centuries than it had in the previous twenty. The science and technology to control or wipe out diseases which had ravaged humankind for thousands of years allowed life expectancy and population to increase dramatically. The science of plant genetics along with machinery and fertilizers allowed a tiny fraction of the population to feed the rest. The steam engine, the internal combustion engine, and thousands of other ways to supply and use energy were invented and mass produced. The use of electricity was developed. People born before the automobile was invented lived to see men walking on the moon. All of these things happened in the latest instant of human history. Capitalism was the system which allowed them to develop.

Profit (money) is a very powerful motivator. Profits were the driving forces behind the diffusion of technology and the transformation of society. Investments in the development and production of inventions could yield profits, and therefore, though they might seem risky or destroy traditional ways of life or family arrangements, immense resources were devoted to their production. Money is not the most powerful motivating force in all human societies, not even in this society. But it is a very powerful force, and the drive for profits moves and transforms capitalism. If financing the development of research leading to more food production is a profitable venture, then capitalists will make those investments. If financing a cure for diseases that ravaged humankind for centuries could be profitable for those involved, then such medical research would be financed. If financing autos, TVs, or even computers for some working class people could be profitable, then capitalists would do it. If it was profitable for BP to mobilize the huge amounts of money, labor, and technological development to drill for oil on the ocean's floor, it would be done

But by the same token, if it was not profitable to build good housing in some neighborhoods—if one could make more profit by allowing apartments to fall apart and then burning them for the insurance—then good housing would not be built. If it cut too much from profits to clean up the environment or to make the workplace safe, then capitalism could not be bothered with it. If profits could be saved by dumping toxic wastes which would produce tens of thousands of cancers and grotesque birth defects in the following generation, then someone would do it. If it was profitable for BP to cut corners in deep-sea drilling and to convince regulators to look the other way, they would find a way to do it. For a while, government controls could deal with some of the ways capitalism spoils the environment and wastes its people. But government controls are limited. For example, the Johns Manville company poisoned thousands of workers with asbestos over a period of decades. Eventually they were forced to pay billions in reparations, and went bankrupt. Does this show that poisoning doesn't pay? Consider this: the stockholders and managers who made the profits years ago by cutting corners are *not* necessarily the ones who lost during the bankruptcy. For them, polluting did pay. If capitalists in other countries were doing something which was profitable, then it became increasingly difficult for any capitalists to resist. Capitalism is an addict for profits, not only because each and every capitalist is a junkie for profits but also because those who are expand at the expense of those who are not, and eventually govern the system. If profitability required poisoning the environment or invasion of other countries to install dictators using mass torture, then capitalists did it. For a time, capitalists could say that in the long run, growth will supply all needs, that stopping to satisfy short-term needs at the expense of investment is less wise than growing, to satisfy more needs in the long run. *But now we see that what is profitable can also be the most shortsighted and irrational.* We see future generations' health, water, and resources—indeed their very existence—squandered for profits.

For Marx, capitalism, like other modes of production, places its stamp on all other social institutions and relationships, from mathematics to marriage. He also believed that this stamp was not very attractive, that it involved buying and selling, greed and selfishness, inequality and coercion. But for him, the most important thing about a focus on production and inequality is that it allows us to see transformation and change. Production changes things, but it also changes people and relationships. Inequality and the structures needed to maintain inequality are the subject of conflicts which are dynamic. Capitalism, like every system before it, has internal contradictions and goes through changes. As we shall see in the following chapter, Marx believed that the key to these changes was labor—the productive process itself.

In the passage we analyzed in section 1.2, Marx speaks of a contradiction between **forces** and **relations of production.** How might relations of production fetter and strangle forces of production? A great deal of the theory of historical materialism represents the working out of these ideas of conflict and correspondence. As we shall see in chapter 4, contradictions refer to tensions between two sets of processes or sets of requirements. Contradictions also refer to tensions between groups of people. Using the term *contradictions* in this very general way highlights the connections between them. It risks the danger that some people will try to substitute conceptual analysis for the practical and empirical investigation of the real world. But so long as one avoids that error, Marx's usage is useful because there are, in fact, usually connections between the two kinds of tensions. For the moment it is enough to note that forces of production are usually considered to include things like machinery, science, technology, skills, and the skilled workers themselves. Now a machine, or a scientific discovery, or anything else does not have automatic effects. It is theoretically possible that property relations could cause scientific discoveries to hurt, choke, and threaten us, so that people try to suppress them and they stagnate. It might be that production relations mean that skills are undeveloped and that workers and machines lie idle. In such cases, there is a potent contradiction between what is possible and what happens. Marx believed that such contradictions do arise, and he saw them as the motor of history.

Exercise 1.8: The World Development of Capitalism

One of the striking things about the world today is the immense and often growing gap between the richer nations and the poorer ones. A dialectical analysis suggests that the riches and the poverty are not independent; they are the flip sides of a single coin, like the hydrogen generated at one electrode and oxygen generated at the other, when you pass electricity through water. There are many different aspects of these processes. Sketch out what you think are the main—the most important—processes linking developed capitalist countries such as the United States, and poorer countries, such as Afghanistan or Haiti.

The striking and obvious world-historical accomplishment of capitalism was its rapid expansion to cover the world. The European conquest and colonization of the rest of the world started before capitalism matured. But there can be no question that in fact the development of capitalism and its expansion occurred simultaneously. Recall Marx's summary of the process of capitalist development as expropriation, the entanglement of all peoples in the net of the world market, the diminishing number of magnates, and the growing mass of misery, oppression, slavery, degradation, and exploitation.

A dialectical approach emphasizes how everything is interconnected. Consider the world economic system and ask, "How is it interconnected?" For the sake of concreteness, imagine a square block of a shanty town in Rio de Janeiro, Brazil, or San Pedro Sula, Honduras, or any other part of the less developed world. Connect it mentally with the square block in which you are now living. Now, use Google Earth, go down and look around enough so that you can get some sense of how the people there are living. Your task is to visualize the *concrete relationships and interchanges* which connect those groups of people with yourself. In terms of actual labor—doing—and in terms of the transfer of material objects, what are the connections which you can visualize between yourself and them? Recall our previous exercises on this issue; the one answer which will almost certainly not work is "There are no real connections; we are the way we are, and they are the way they are without any relations or connections

Are there real connections? What about the shirt on your back? Whenever we have checked, we have found several people in the room (no need to look elsewhere on the block) wearing clothing manufactured in places like India or Central America. Or perhaps the machinery used to manufacture goods in the room used labor or materials from there. Or perhaps the accumulation of profits which made possible the construction of the machinery was fueled, in part, from that country or from others like it. What is the dynamic of those relationships and interchanges?

There are two main theories you will want to consider: **modernization theory** says that the two sides have been basically unchanged by any interchanges between them—that the shanty town is all too unaffected by its relation to advanced industrial capitalism; that they were poor before we got there and will only stop being poor when they have enough contact with advanced industrial capitalism so that they become like us in the more developed countries. **World-systems theory**, focused on the work of I. Wallerstein, has argued that in large part it is the relations between the two sides that has made them different. Rather than becoming similar, the two sides started out relatively similar, but there has been a single two-sided process which has resulted in the development of some economies and the underdevelopment of others.

The issue carries a lot of ideological weight. Modernization theory was the single thing making the liberal analysis of capitalism seem most plausible to many people. "Well, we are certainly better off than they are," many people have been tempted to say, "and so it must be that our liberal capitalist institutions make us better off. We are more modern." Given the crying misery in most of the world, few people want to think of themselves as benefiting from that. Most people would like to help reduce it.

Modernization theory contrasts modern, Western, European, bureaucratic, "universalistic" forms of organization to traditional, non-Western, particularistic forms. It was mainly inspired by Weber and secondarily by Durkheim, and it held almost absolute sway in American sociology during the 1950s and early 1970s. We think it gives two bad answers to the question, "What connects us to that South American slum?": (a) nothing does, and (b) handouts and gifts, especially the gift of knowledge, from us to them. According to those analyses, the only real connection between the two groups of people is mental: "We show them the way."

This picture is implausible. There are, in fact, massive interchanges of labor, goods, and guns between the masses of people. Europe, in its relation to Africa, Asia, and Latin America did not restrict itself to showing the way. Marx stressed the predatory, colonial character of capitalism. This history suggests that Europe and North America have often taken things from the Third World, and have set up organizations to do that. This is what Marxists call **imperialism.** The analysis of imperialism was a main foundation of Leninism. During the 1950s and 1960s, a small number of Marxist theorists argued that part of the reason Westerners were better off than people in Asia, Africa, and Latin America was the fact that the economies of the Third World were being robbed of millions of dollars per year. But the mainstream of sociology took it for granted that every country followed the same path of development, and that we were merely somewhat more advanced along that path. Any view of history which sees societies as following independent developments tends toward that view.

Against it, Wallerstein and his collaborators argue that there is a single irreversible process producing the development of some countries and the underdevelopment of others. Wallerstein argues that a host of tangled theoretical problems become tractable if one analyzes the process producing development at one pole, and underdevelopment at the other. Wallerstein points out that in the seventeenth century there was not a sharp difference between the technological, economic, and political development of Europe and the continents that Europe conquered. Only with the exploration and conquest of the underdeveloped world did sharp differences began to appear.

This might help explain a question many people ask of Marxists: "If the U.S. is so oppressive, how come so many people from other countries are trying to come to the U.S.?" That is a reasonable question, and to answer it, one has to look at imperialism. Simply put, economic and often political conditions in those countries are so bad that it may well be a matter of survival for all, or even one family member, to come to the United States get some sort of low-paying job, and either support the family here, or send the few dollars back that could be the difference between penicillin and death for a family member. Furthermore, conditions in that country are often so terrible because of imperialism—corporations from imperialist countries, aided by their governments, often including military aid, are what keep the people living in such dire circumstances.

Imagine that you are living in Pennsylvania in 1850 and you oppose slavery. You are having a debate with a plantation owner from Georgia who is arguing that slavery is fine. You argue that the slaves are unfree and miserable, and he responds: "My slaves are happy. I know they are. Why, I have two groups of slaves on my plantation. Some of them work in the house as servants, and the rest work in the fields, and you know, the ones who work in the fields would much rather work in the house. Some of them would do *anything* to work in the house. If I am such a bad guy, how come my slaves want to be *closer* to me?"

You would probably respond that conditions in the field are so terrible, chopping cotton in 100 degree heat, always in terror of the whip, while conditions in the house, while still abominable, are quite a bit better by comparison. It has nothing to do with the slaves loving the system of slavery, loving the master, or wanting to be near him.

Is the misery in a poorer country such as Brazil, Haiti, or Honduras unconnected to the relative comfort in some parts of the United States? What are the actual interchanges that connect them? It might be that even if relationships and interchanges shape and connect the whole world, any two particular pieces of the world are not well connected. But we think that even if you chose some particular block in the United States and some particular slum in Brazil, you will find interchanges which connect them. For example, Wallerstein has suggested that if any commodity is traced back through its constitutive commodities—in "commodity chains"—the great majority of those chains *now and over the last four hundred years*, cross national borders. From a given block in the United States, hundreds of thousands of these chains extend all over the world.

Since before the nineteenth century, the developed capitalist countries have been able to make the rules concerning their economic and social relations to Third World countries, either by using direct coercion or by using allies in those countries or by using their financial and organizational clout in international organizations. The common element of virtually all

Marxist analyses is that they believe that the developed capitalist countries have made those rules in such a way as to benefit themselves. For example, huge masses of profits are made in a country such as Honduras, and then repatriated to the home offices in New York or London.

The analysis of the interdependent dynamic of the world system is complex. The capitalist world system that encompasses the world today is the most powerfully interconnected, the largest and the most technologically advanced world system that has ever existed, but in another sense, it is merely the latest of a series of multistate economic and political systems which have risen and then fallen. The main world-systems analyses view the system as having been maintained by the constant incorporation of new populations. This process is now hitting its final limit, as the total population of the globe is incorporated, and so some transformation is inevitable.

Suggestions for Further Reading

On the dynamism of capitalism: a brief general introduction to the world-systems treatment of the history of capitalism is I. Wallerstein, *Historical Capitalism* (Verso, 1983). On the world system: fundamental works outlining the world-systems perspective are I. Wallerstein, *The Modern World System* (Academic, 1974) and *The Capitalist World Economy* (Cambridge, 1976). The argument that the analysis of commodity chains and the process by which people are pulled into the world market shows absolute as well as relative immiseration appears, among other places, in T. Hopkins and I. Wallerstein, *Processes of the World-System* (Sage, 1980), C. Chase-Dunn and T. Hall, *Rise and Demise: Comparing World-systems* (Westview Press, 1997) and T. Boswell and C. Chase-Dunn, *The Spiral of Capitalism and Socialism: Toward Global Democracy* (Lynne Rienner Publishers, 2000). Mike Davis, *Planet of Slums* (Verso, 2007) shows that in the world as a whole, capitalist development has been a process that deposits hundreds of millions of people in "mega-slums" that surround most of the giant cities, particularly in the periphery. He provides a useful guide to the task of observing such areas with tools such as Google Earth.

SECTION 1.9: WHAT ARE THE FUNDAMENTAL PROBLEMS OF THE MODERN WORLD?

As we have seen, Marx saw the sequence of modes of production as the backbone of history. We have also seen that in Hegel, the concept of **alienation** was the basis of a complex and abstruse philosophy of history. Marx wanted to separate useful ideas about alienation and human history from what he regarded as Hegel's quasi-theological mysticism. The natural way to do so was to analyze concrete forms of alienation in production and how they related to concrete historical, social, economic, and political phenomena. There is a difference between works that Marx wrote at different periods of his life. Some people argue that the early Marx was concerned with a fundamentally different set of issues—philosophical issues of alienation and freedom—than the later Marx. In his maturity, Marx wrote quantitative economic, political, historical, and social analyses, which he clearly regarded as the foundation of a social science. People who celebrate his early works often view them as a philosophy of freedom, fundamentally different from science. Other people argue that there is complete unity between the analyses that Marx made at different times in his life.

Marx always regarded people's alienation, their powerlessness over their situations, especially their work, as the fundamental problem of our time. The concept of alienation (powerlessness) is very abstract as a concept. But the *fact* of powerlessness is not abstract: it is when you have to ask a supervisor for permission to go to the bathroom, when you have to eat dog food because of poverty, when you have to sleep in the street. Being ripped off for a parking fee or being caught in traffic is not abstract, but the question of what is alienating about them may involve analyzing what other possible arrangements there are. In his later works, Marx did not often speak of alienation. If you consider Marx's early works an ethical/philosophical analysis as opposed to concrete, quantitative, scientific analyses of exploitation, poverty, brutalization, oppression, and intimidation, then there is a big difference between his early and later works. And certainly the philosophers who talk most about alienation do not often talk about how many poor people eat dog food or how many dollars it takes to run a campaign for the U.S. Senate. But having to eat dog food and having someone else control the government are forms of alienation. In his early work, Marx focused on concepts which, in his later works, were developed into quantitative and empirical analyses of exploitation, oppression, and class struggle. Marx distinguished different kinds of alienation, and we shall discuss them shortly. But for the moment, it will be useful to develop a concrete image to fix in our mind the idea of alienation as a whole—the image of an alienated society:

Imagine a dark tower, peopled by slaves. It is a tower of fear. The slaves in the tower live in constant fear. They are physically afraid. They are insecure. They are afraid of losing their jobs. They are afraid of being poisoned. They are afraid of each other. They are afraid of diseases they cannot control. They are afraid of war. But they can do nothing about their fears. They feel powerless. In large part, the fear results from the fact that the rulers of the tower have to use a considerable amount of intimidation to get the slaves to do their bidding. Millions of them have to be thrown into prisons to be raped, brutalized, and fed on food riddled with maggots, to keep a constant flow of the fear in them. The rulers need an elaborate apparatus of guards. People are divided against each other, and the most sordid, corrupt motives and attitudes—racism, selfishness, sexploitation, violence for the sake of violence—are force-fed to people so that they are split apart and willing to do almost anything for the sake of money and security. Thus people are not only unfree, but they are constantly subjected to *chains on their mind*. People are forced to build their own chains. Not even the rulers are free. They are so constrained by the system that any attempt to act in a more human way brings disaster down on them. That is a system of alienation.

Does it sound like Hitler's Germany? Does it sound like the worst dictatorships in the world today? Yes, it probably does. Those systems were and are deeply alienated. But *look closer to home*. Walk into most neighborhoods of any city in this country. How secure are most people? How secure are most people anywhere in this society? Recall the shape of the income distribution and the tendencies in ownership. Even those who have a house, farm, or business have reason to be worried about losing them. To what extent is this society based on powerlessness and lubricated by fear? Why are millions of people in prison in the United States? It is important to see to what degree a system of alienation characterizes American society.

According to Marxism, the central economic, political, and social arrangements in this society are alienated, and that is why people are split apart and powerless. From the standpoint of the future it may be as difficult for people to understand this system as for us now to understand why slaves put up with slavery or feudal serfs put up with the aristocracy.

Some people think this picture is exaggerated—hopelessly exaggerated—that the United States is just not like that. Some people are hungry, in prison, or insecure, but not a lot. They think that the United States is an affluent, middle class society. But where do the people who feel this way live? Are they simply wearing blinders? A picture of the society as not alienated is transmitted by TV, education, politicians, etc. But we think that that picture is ideological, that it is distorted, that it is not real and does not fit most people's real experience. The issues and data involved will come up many times. Certainly it is *possible* for someone to live in a very alienated society—in Nazi Germany for instance—but to have a way of life, information, and a "set of eyeglasses" that keep it all out of sight.

Some people grant that American society is characterized by persistent fear and powerlessness, but they think that is the human condition, that all possible societies are like that or worse. They think that the problems of the poor, prisons, and power will always be with us. Is this true? Or is it an ideology? Is the very sense that nothing can be done a kind of alienation? Marx believed that since the emergence of class divisions, millennia ago, all societies have been based on the exploitation of human by human. For millennia all societies have had antagonistic class contradictions, and therefore, they have had the whole complex of brutality and distortion just pictured. But not forever. He believed that it was possible to have a different ("communist") society based on equality, community, and cooperation.

For Marx, economic alienation is the foundation of other kinds of alienation. While the main outlines of economic alienation will appear in chapter 2, we can introduce the concept of alienation by beginning, as Marx did, with alienation at work. In his early works, Marx distinguished four aspects of the alienation of labor. Something is alienated when it is outside of one's control. If you sell me a tomato or a piece of land, you have alienated it. It no longer belongs to you—it *belongs to someone else*—it belongs to me. Under capitalism, buying and selling things extends to all aspects of social life. Everything has a price. And everyone supposedly has their price. The sale of labor is the key arrangement of capitalism, one which characterizes no other social system. Buying and selling labor becomes the center of social structure, and labor is alienated in several ways: (1) the *product* of labor does not belong to the worker and (2) the productive *process* is controlled by someone other than the workers. If what one makes belongs to someone else, then that work must be tightly controlled.

> What, then, constitutes the alienation of labor? First, the fact that labor is *external* to the worker, i.e., it does not . . . develop freely his physical and mental energy but mortifies his body and ruins his mind. . . . Labor is therefore not voluntary, but coerced; it is *forced labor*. It is therefore not the satisfaction of a need; it is merely a *means* to satisfy needs external to it. . . . Lastly, the external character of labor for the worker appears in the fact that it is not his own, but someone else's, that it does not belong to him, that in it he does not belong to himself, but to another. (Marx, CW III, p. 274)

Marx goes on to argue that the alienation of product and process is tied to two further elements of alienation:

> (3) *man's species-being* . . . It estranges from man his own body, as well as external nature and his spiritual aspect, his *human* aspect. (4) An immediate consequence of the fact that man is estranged from the product of his labor, from his life activity, from his species-being is the *estrangement of man from man*. . . . What applies to a man's relation to his work, to the product of his labor, and to himself, also holds of his relation to the other man and to the other man's labor and object of labor. (Ibid., p. 277)

The term "species-being" is a technical, philosophical term from the Hegelian tradition, which can also be translated "collective or social essence." Humans make humankind; while one is making pins, one is also making oneself into a pinmaker. Alienation is a particularly important concept if you view humans as social animals, who become who they are by making commitments. The alienation of species-being means that one is not able to control the kind of laborer that one is making oneself into. This means that the human whom one is making oneself into is distorted. Moreover, in the example of a parking permit in exercise 1.2, we saw that you can describe the subjective feeling of alienation without very much analysis of power, fairness, or alternatives. But if one considers alienation as an objective variable, as Marx does—if one views alienation as a loss of control over time, resources, relationships, and institutions—then one will have to analyze power, fairness, and alternatives. We think that an explicit analysis of social alienation connects all the works of Marx. The four aspects of alienation above do not exhaust the concept. It is possible to picture the core of Marx's theory of society and history in terms of other kinds of alienation. They are represented schematically in figure 1.7.

These nine forms of alienation have powerful logical, causal, and historical connections to each other. The analysis of those interconnections is one core of Marx's historical and sociological theories:

1. **Product.** Essential to capitalism is the following: at the end of the productive process, the product does not belong to the laborer. It belongs to the owner of capital who hired the laborer. The shoemaker or farmer who produces for himself or herself, on his or her own time, and sets his or her own pace, subject to the market, is inexorably replaced by the GM worker or migrant farmworker who produces for someone else.

2. **Means of Production.** The alienation of the means of production is also essential to capitalism. As capitalism develops there is an historical process of **expropriation** of producers. At the beginning of the process, producers have their own means of production. At the end of it, they

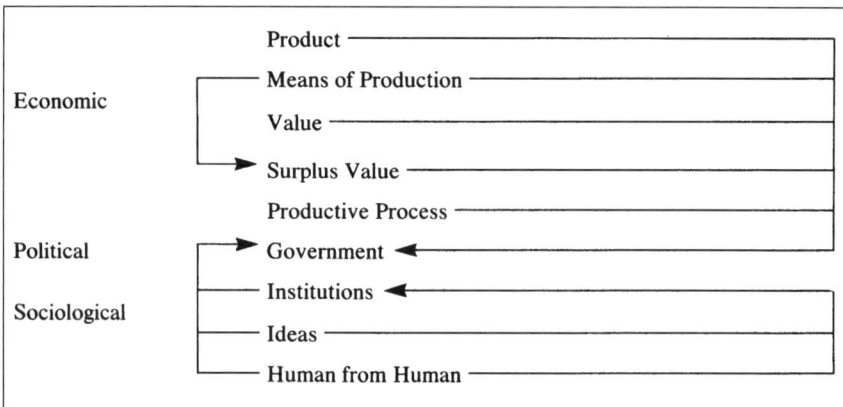

Figure 1.7   Types of Alienation

do not. "And this one historical condition comprises a world's history" (K. Mark, *Capital: A Critique of Political Economy* [CAP], p. 170). At the time Marx wrote that, the great body of producers were still self-employed. Marx could see the process by which the self-employed group would effectively disappear. And he could see that it was one of the master trends for the rest of social structure.

3. **Value.** Money represents a claim on the labor of others. You don't have to grow potatoes if you can pay someone else to do it. This is the social structure underlying market relations. Historically, buying and selling increasingly determines other relationships. Value is also alienated from most people because capitalism requires and generates enormous economic inequalities. The lion's share of the value of labor goes to a very small number of owners of capital. Some people have bank accounts that can command the labor of thousands of other people for hundreds of years. When you combine the fact that buying and selling become the master relation of modern society, with the enormous concentration of buying power, you get a society of immense social inequalities.

4. **Surplus Value.** The key portion of the alienated value is not that which goes to sustain life but the further portion which is used to create the cultural and social systems which Marx calls "superstructural." The surplus value is the cutting and growing edge of social development—science and whether we learn to cure people or kill them; art and whether it is poison or nourishment for the mind; the kinds of formal and informal organizations that are set up; and so forth. Ordinarily, this surplus goes *entirely* to the capitalist class. The fact that all of the superstructure is constructed from value that is channeled through the capitalist class means that they inevitably dominate each portion of the superstructure. At the beginning of the historical process, capitalists directly hire unproductive workers (guards, maids, police, scientists, clerical workers, footmen, teachers, preachers, hired bullies, politicians, etc.). These occupations may be indispensable to the social system, but they do not produce a profit. They have to be paid from the surplus. Originally, when they are directly hired, **unproductive workers** have to do what they are paid to do. Later on, more subtle mechanisms develop. Unproductive laborers are not directly hired by capitalists. But the indirect mechanisms of their hiring and control amount to the same thing.

5. **Productive Process.** Under capitalist production, since the workers do not receive the product, they have no interest in producing more. Therefore capitalists must set up an authoritarian structure, a command structure, to watch over everything workers do. They break down the productive process into its simplest (and most dehuman-

izing and boring) elements so that they can fire anyone and replace them easily. There have been a series of historical transformations of the organization of the productive process, both during Marx's lifetime and since. These transformations have always been of central concern to both economics and sociology.

6. **Political System.** In all societies those who control the production process have the most influence in government. Under capitalism, capitalists' dominance in the political system stems partly from their direct control of institutions individually more powerful than states. Secondly, capitalists' dominance stems from the fact that only they have the millions of dollars needed to fund the political parties, as well as their supremacy in the other parts of the social system.

7. **Social System: Institutions.** Ownership of means of production is a direct form of political power. But besides this raw power, the political domination of the capitalists follows from the fact that they monopolize the other sources of influence in capitalist society. Over the last three generations, schools, churches, newspapers, neighborhoods, art, science, TV, sports, etc., have come to be dominated by capitalists. There is a long historical process by which the boards of these institutions have inexorably passed into the hands of capitalists.

8. **Ideas.** From the above follows the ideological distortion of every idea system of the society. One always "inherits" one's ideas from society, at least in part. The concept of **ideology** refers to the social reasons that ideas are promoted or persist. The social dynamic of ideas is mainly determined by ideas' usefulness in legitimating policies and social arrangements. The prominence of capitalists under capitalism means that everyone's ideas, to a greater or lesser extent depending on working class organization, will not reflect their own interests and situations, but those of capitalists.

9. **Human from Human.** Directly, the foundation of capitalist culture is **individualism,** selfishness, looking out for number one. As money, buying, and selling things becomes more important, individualism becomes the dominant ethical standpoint. Moreover, the indirect consequence of the domination of the capitalist class is the need to divide-and-rule. This leads to the production of **divisive ideologies:** *nationalism, racism, sexism,* ethnic and religious *chauvinism,* etc. These ideologies are both the initially unintended product and the necessary precondition of the continuation of capitalism.

These nine historical processes are deeply intertwined. Each of these kinds of alienation reinforces the others so that the system as a whole is a self-reinforcing system. That is one of the reasons that dismantling it by gradualist reforms does not work.

Do we really live in a dark tower? Well, whether you think so depends on your standpoint and options. Some people are in a better position to see how the system works than others. But the actual degree of alienation of each of these kinds and their objective interrelation are all subject to empirical investigation. Marxists believe that this investigation is the core of sociology.

Exercise 1.9: The Empirical Analysis of Alienation

Each of these nine different forms of alienation might plausibly reinforce the others. Find out whether this is true. Using your own experience (or an existing data source, if it is available), devise your own measures or indices of two forms of alienation. Then test whether they seem to reinforce each other. Are the people who are more alienated in one respect also more alienated in the other?

Each of these nine different forms of alienation plausibly reinforces the others. If this is true, then alienation constitutes a massive and immensely important complex of processes. To analyze it one must took at a system involving 72 causal interconnections. If those 72 interrelations are not mind-boggling enough, many of these forms of alienation are not single things easily measured; they are complex variables with many different aspects. To measure each would require several different measures. For example, to analyze any one divisive, "me first" ideology such as racism, sexism, or nationalism is a big task. To analyze their interrelation with each other is an even bigger task. But if any one of them is to be treated as something other than a set of free-floating ideas, if it is to be analyzed in its historical connection to concrete relationships of production and power, it will have to be viewed in relation to alienation as a whole. American sociology has not devoted much of its ingenuity to the analysis of alienation in this sense. To the extent that it has considered alienation at all, it has considered **subjective** measures of the dissatisfaction, powerlessness, or unhappiness of individuals. One would expect objective alienation of the kinds we have just considered to have *some* relation to subjective measures, but they are obviously not the same. Some theorists have gone beyond such measures to look at the degree to which different groups of people feel that they can or cannot affect their lives, the government, etc. These turn out to be powerfully affected by occupational control, income, and social class. But such studies are merely the beginning of an empirical analysis of alienation.

If X produces or reinforces Y, then when you compare individuals and groups, where there is more X you will find more Y. The fact that there is a fairly complex system involving many interrelations does not change that, though it may make it harder to see. Are those individuals who are more alienated in one respect also the individuals who are more alienated in another? This is not a perfect indication of whether one form of alienation as a social structure reinforces the other. But often you will find that there is the same relation among individual traits that there is among aspects of society. If people who are alienated in one respect are more likely to be alienated in another respect, this gives an indication that we are faced with a complex of mutually reinforcing processes.

The narrow task of hypothesis testing is merely to devise an index of two of the kinds of alienation and see whether individuals, groups, and structures which have more of the one also, in fact, have more of the other. Make a statement of the hypothesis you intend to test and the way you plan to test it (the **"operationalization"** of the hypothesis) before proceeding. Then try to carry out the analysis.

Different people handle this task in different ways. Often the evidence on an hypothesis does not "prove" or "disprove" it so much as to suggest ways of changing it. This will often be the case when one uses data about individuals to test a theory which mainly concerns the relation of different aspects of social structure. It is also often the case when dealing with a set of relationships as large and powerful as Marxist concepts of alienation. Nevertheless, we think that you will usually find the connections between these forms of alienation both theoretically comprehensible and empirically compelling. Inequality, coercion, and lack of control go with each other. Structures of privilege, accumulation of resources and goods, and power or influence are threaded onto each other in intricate ways. This set of structures is immensely important for how the society works and how it changes. We shall return to it over and over again.

Suggestions for Further Reading

On alienation: as noted above, there is an elaborate literature on Marx's concept of alienation, but it often divorces the concept from others such as class, surplus value, exploitation, racism, immiseration, centralization, political oppression, greed, inequality, and ideology. Divorced from concrete issues and examples, the philosophical concept of alienation becomes a feeling, unconnected to anything. A full analysis of alienation probably includes the whole of Marx's work, but we cannot deal with everything at once. Economic alienation is the core of chapter 2, and political alienation is that of chapter 3. Studies of the alienation of ideas, or ideology, are mainly useful when they are connected to concrete, substantive theories. But in addition to the works cited in section 1.6, the many works of R. Williams, such as *Problems in Materialism and Culture* (NLB, 1980), illustrate some of the main works in the field. Recent work on alienation is well-introduced by R. Wilkinson and K. Pickett's *The Spirit Level* (Bloomsbury, 2010), cited earlier, showing the powerful relation between inequality and a wide range of physical, mental, and social pathology such as short life expectancy, ill health, mental illnesses, drug use, obesity, educational failure, teen births, violence, crime, imprisonment, lack of social mobility, and anxiety.

SECTION 1.10: ARE CLASSES IN THE UNITED STATES BASED ON EXPLOITATION?

Just as the aristocracy lived off the labor of peasants, or slave owners lived off the labor of slaves, so capitalists live off the labor of wage workers. Profits pay the bills. Workers produce everything, but the product does not belong to them. Owners do nothing, but at the end of the process they not only have what they started with, but more. (Particular owners may manage the company or hire someone else to do it; they may be smart or foolish; they may work eighteen hours a day or lie on a beach. It doesn't matter. What they get paid for, what produces their profit, is the fact that they have a piece of paper that says they own the business.)

The system is based on inequality, it requires inequality, and it produces still more inequality. If one person has a billion dollars (and there are more than a few billionaires in the United States), he or she can hire thousands of other people for a year. At the end of the year, the owner will usually have the money he or she started with and more. That is what profits are. Profits refer to the fact that the owners—on average—end up with more than they started with. A particular multimillionaire owner might lose it, especially gambling in the stock market. But the capitalist class, as a class, makes profits even when the standard of living of the working class drops. Even incompetent owners can hire someone to look after their money or run their businesses. Because profit involves an amplifying positive feedback from property to increased property, it is immensely dynamic and it drives many other processes of change. It also produces large and growing inequalities. In chapter 1, we contrasted the Marxian picture of class to that of Weber. Let's look at what is the distribution of means of production, income, and wealth. Is it bulged in the middle, and becoming more equal? Or is it an elongated pyramid which is becoming still more elongated?

With regard to ownership of means of production, it would appear that the process which Marx foresaw has taken place. The number of people with their own means of production has decreased, and that decrease has been relatively inexorable. In the United States, the self-employed portion of the population has diminished from the great majority to about 10 percent, and only about 1 percent of the population gains the bulk of its income from employing others. The disagreement is not whether proletarianization in this sense has occurred (it has) nor whether it is a powerful, inexorable process (it is). Partly the disagreement is how important the process is. Is it a master process of social development? One process among many? Or is it not worth talking about? And partly the disagreement has to do with categories of jobs within those who are employed, especially professional and supervisory jobs. Marx recognized that college professors, bank tellers, foremen, police officers, farmworkers, factory workers, and government workers are all workers in the sense of being without means of production. But they are not proletarianized in the same ways or the same sense. *However, all this represents distinctions within an overall process that has essentially eliminated self-employment.* In general, analysts who concentrate on status have not presented arguments that the change in relations to production are avoidable or inconsequential; in general what they have done is to ignore the process.

The distribution of ownership of means of production is certainly unequal and becoming more unequal. What about the distribution of status? Is that a gradation with a bulge in the middle? Well, it obviously depends how you measure status. Most of the measures of status show a "normal" distribution, which bulges in the middle. That is how the measures were defined and constructed. It is a matter of definition, and it doesn't tell you anything about the real world, only about the measures. What about wealth and income? These can be measured on a natural, quantitative, nonarbitrary scale—money.

Later we shall argue that in the United States there are hundreds of thousands of people who sleep in the streets, many of them *not* surviving a given winter. Millions of people go hungry. Others spend tens of millions to oppose food stamps for the poor. We shall see that there is no tendency for the number of poor to decrease. Most people live lives constrained by need and insecurity. However that may be, the income distribution is certainly unequal, and it has changed little over time. Is it bulged in the middle or is it a pyramid?

The distribution of income in the United States is so unequal that it is hard to picture. If you were to construct an income tower or pyramid out of one inch children's blocks, with each block representing an income of $1,000, then the top of the pyramid would be higher than the Eiffel Tower. It would be ten times higher than the tallest buildings in the world. But most people would be within one yard of the ground! Virtually everyone would be on the ground floor. Figure 1.8 pictures the data from table 1.6. It distorts the data only in that ink cannot portray how tall the income pyramid really is or how squashed the bottom of it is. At the top of the pyramid are multibillionaires who, like many people, average perhaps 5 percent on their investments, for a yearly property income of hundreds of millions of dollars. You can see from table 1.6 that the great bulk of the very large incomes comes from **property,** like dividends and profits, not wages. (In fact, a certain amount of their wage income is disguised property income. Owners can decide how to pay themselves.) At the base of the tower, in the bottom foot, are the quarter of the population making less than $20,000 per year. In the next two feet are about half the population

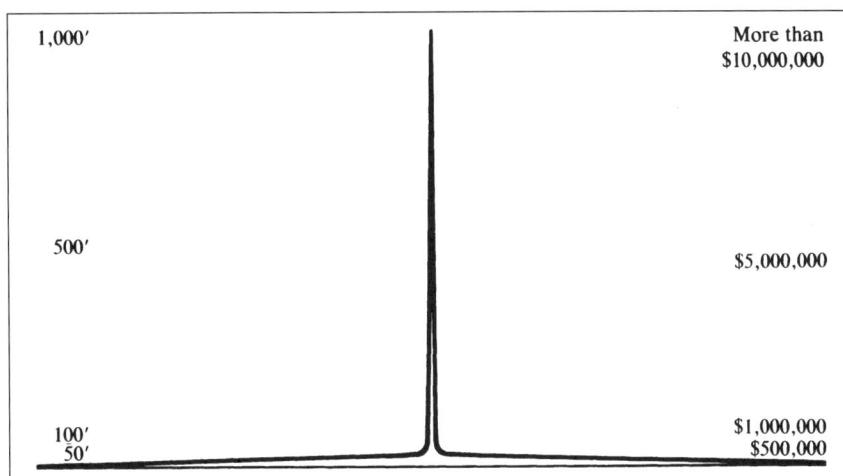

Figure 1.8   Tower of Income

Table 1.6   Income by Type and Size, 1982

1982 Income Size	Number of Recipients (1,000s)	Salary and Wages	Dividends	Capital Gains	Partnerships and Profits
0–$10,000	34,992	82.8%	2%	1%	4%
$10–$20,000	24,842	83.3%	2%	4%	3%
$20–$50,000	31,004	89.1%	2%	1%	3%
$50–$100,000	3,759	78.1%	5%	2%	9%
$100–$500,000	711	60.6%	10%	8%	18%
$500–$1,000,000	21	35.3%	18%	| 32% |*	| 14% |*
$1,000,000+	8	18.7%	19%	| 32% |	| 14% |

* combined.

Source: U.S. Internal Revenue Service, *1982 Statistics of Income Individual Tax Returns*, 1984

making $20,000 to $50,000. Nearly 90 percent of their income is wage income. From one yard to ten feet, we see about nine million income recipients making $36,000 to $120,000, while from 100 feet to 1,000 feet you have the 711,000 recipients making $100,000 to $1 million. And then there are the few who make one hundred times that! Under capital-ism, this degree of inequality has proved virtually impossible to change very much. This is not the only or the main way that capitalism produces inequalities of resources and opportunities and power for different people, but even by itself it is formidable.

The distribution of **wealth** is *much more unequal* than the distribution of **income.** And the enormously concentrated form of both direct and disguised income from property is a main source of income inequality. With respect to wealth, many of us are in net debt. Most of the rest of us have a mortgaged house; while at the other extreme, the wealthiest group is in a different world. They are over 100 miles high. The wealth distribution became sharply more unequal during the last decades, so that the top 1 percent of the society holds more wealth than the bottom 90 percent. Thus the distributions of wealth and income are not just pyramids, as in figure 1.2. They are grotesquely elongated pyramids, showing a tiny upper class whose property income places them in a different universe from everyone else. And this is within the United States. The differences would be much more extreme if we considered all the people of the world together and the wealth distribution. Where one inch equals $1,000 on the Earth as a whole, several billion people will be within an inch of the ground. The average black or Latino family in the USA will be within a foot or two; the average white family will be within a few feet, and Bill Gates, with $60 billion—60 million inches—five million feet, will be about 950 miles into outer space. Airplanes fly at about eight miles.

The process of the growth of inequality, particularly when it involves inherited traits such as race or ethnic group membership, poses a real threat to any rational and just society. Joe Feagin, in his 2001 presidential address to the American Sociological Association, illustrated this problem with respect to the hypothetical task of designing a viable, sustainable social system for a set of colonists in a spaceship for a trip that would take several generations. People were given the task of designing such an environment and therefore deciding how much inequality of wealth and power they would allow, as well as what to do about maintaining the biological environment—the ship's food crops, etc. Then they discussed the different plans and voted for a winning one. Even when conservative managers and engineers were given the design task, there was no great mystery about what such an environment would look like, and it does not look like the present capitalist system.

Biologically, the winning design was that there should not be pesticides and other toxic substances that could accumulate, and that the species— even of insects, let alone of food crops—should be genetically diverse. Single-crop ecostructures are fragile. Socially, the winning design proposed that the ship would have to avoid the accumulation of inequality and social separation, especially of inequalities that associated with race, gender, language, or other ascribed traits. The designing groups did not believe that there should be perfect equality, but they thought that it was obvious that the inequalities could not be allowed to get too large. The captain might have a higher income than a crewman, but not thousands of times as large; the captain might have larger and more luxurious quarters than a crewman, but obviously not quarters of hundreds of thousands of square feet, while many crewmembers had no quarters at all but had to sleep in the corridors. The designers suggested that the accumulation of inequality and privilege in a closed system could be as destructive as the accumulation of biological toxins. They thought that all inequalities of political influence, health, education, and the like should be restrained so as to prevent divided groups. Feagin suggests that no one would design a spaceship with the kind of inequalities visible in any American city today, both because it is inefficient, because it generates other social problems, and because it leads to divisions and conflicts that would almost certainly, sooner or later, explode. The Feagin thought experiment of "spaceship Earth" suggests that a structure of immense inequalities is unstable and unpleasant, even if there is a complete "safety net" of food, shelter, health, and education for those at the bottom. But a spaceship Earth where the elite lives in palatial suites, while substantial parts of the crew sleep in the corridors, is not viable in the long run. However, it is clear that capitalism not only generates such inequalities but it also tends to associate them with ascriptive groups, and to create the ideological rationales and mind-sets that justify arrangements of great inequality, inequality of opportunity, and coercion.

Exercise 1.10: The Growth of the Welfare State

In the United States, as in other Western countries, a welfare state was developed after World War II. What causes the expansion or contraction of welfare or other social supports? On a piece of paper, list what you think are the two or three main causes of the expansion of welfare in the 1960s and 1970s. What are two possible theories of that expansion/ contraction? What is the crucial evidence which would decide between those theories? What is their practical import, that is, what observable difference will it make whether the welfare and social supports structure expands or contracts according to the theories? Try to answer these questions before proceeding.

The topic of "welfare" is one which is important and politically charged. In the 1980s, a Republican administration came to power with the slogan of cutting back on government. In fact, the Reagan administration expanded many parts of government, but it cut back on social supports. One's attitude toward welfare was often the principal determinant of whether one was a Republican or Democrat. It was also the topic of an elaborate mythology. Many people in the United States believed that most welfare recipients are black or that they are able-bodied males. Many people believed that "welfare," especially aid for dependent children, was the main cost which was cut by Reagan, and that that was cut because it took up a huge chunk of the federal budget—as much or more than defense. Many people believed that welfare recipients live well—even affluently—on public aid. Paradoxically, they also believed that welfare has made little difference to the number of poor people in the United States.

A large literature has shown that these beliefs were wrong. Most welfare recipients were white; the overwhelming majority were ill, disabled, over 65 or under 14, women with children, or people already working who still fall below the poverty line. Even before the cutbacks, all welfare payments together made up a small fraction of public expenditures, especially compared to the military, Social Security, or education costs. Aid to Families with Dependent Children (AFDC), which is what many people meant by "welfare" and with which we shall mainly be concerned, was a small fraction of all public welfare expenses which included things like aid to the blind and Medicaid. Aid to Families with Dependent Children was dwarfed by expenditures on the military, highways, health, or police. Far from allowing recipients to live affluently, welfare payments kept many people living on the very edge of subsistence. Now many of them are living on the streets. But to say that many people were being personally hurt by welfare cuts does not get at the long-term social causes or consequences of welfare. That requires a general theory.

In terms of causes, let's consider three main kinds of theories: (1) that welfare expansion is a simple function of need; (2) that welfare expansion is a function of the number of liberal politicians; and (3) that welfare expansion is a function of how hard people fight for it.

1. Supporters of welfare characteristically viewed it as a function of social need. They argued that the development of modern industrial capitalist society leaves some people especially vulnerable. To prevent their being destroyed or trapped over a series of generations, they need social supports, social policy fulfilling social needs. Ergo welfare.
2. Opponents of welfare often saw it as resulting from the political influence of liberal politicians—their attempts to get votes or their ethical sensibilities.
3. In opposition to these views, a third view, associated most strongly with Frances Piven and R. Cloward, *Regulating the Poor* (Vintage, 1971), argued that welfare is not instituted either to fulfill needs or in response to liberal majorities. Rather, they argued that welfare is a response to disruption of the society: "A placid poor get nothing, but a turbulent poor sometimes get something" (Ibid., p. 338). Programs of social supports were instituted or expanded in large part because of the fear of rebellion. By 1969, virtually every major city in the country was in flames—there were tanks rumbling through the streets and blood running in the streets of Los Angeles, New York,

Newark, Detroit, and a host of other cities. One of the things that this implies is that much of the money "saved" in the cutbacks has to be earmarked for the use of force to put down the rebellions which will ensue. (This argument does not depend on the intentions or motives of any person who supports or opposes the cutbacks. In general, people who support social service cutbacks want more military and police. But even if that were not true, the cutbacks are arguably part of a structural dynamic which involves a shift from butter to guns, from the carrot to the stick.)

In 2010, two years after the election of Barack Obama as president of the United States and one year after the presidency of the American Sociological Association of Frances Piven, the conservative talk shows of Glenn Beck, Rush Limbaugh, and the "tea party movement" spent several months talking about the "Cloward and Piven conspiracy." Glenn Beck devoted more than a dozen programs to arguing that Cloward and Piven, along with other "left wing academic Marxists," operating through community organizing groups like ACORN, had organized a conspiracy to wreck the economy, elect Barack Obama, cause a crash of the housing market, nationalize the banks, and install communism. He based this fantasy on a popular article that Cloward and Piven had published in the *Nation* magazine in 1966 arguing that the welfare system did not and could not grant recipients the benefits that they were entitled to on paper, and so if everyone applied for the benefits for which they were eligible, this would force change in the system. In fact, the change that was brought about by increased welfare rolls was the abolition of welfare.

Piven and Cloward's thesis that welfare is a result of public disorder and mass agitation has led to a substantial amount of empirical research which has considerable implications for the welfare state and for political change in general. Some of that research takes the form of historical case studies. Other research involves the statistical analysis of when and where welfare payments increased. The synthesis of these very different kinds of investigation on common theoretical issues is one of the main tasks of historical sociology. A powerful, typical quantitative analyses was that of A. Hicks and D. Swank, "Civil Disorder, Relief Mobilization, and AFDC Caseloads," *American Journal Political Science* 27:695. Hicks and Swank examine a time series regression using data from 1948 to 1977. A time series multiple regression describes the relation of each possible cause (such as number of liberal politicians) to the effect (the AFDC caseloads) controlling all the other causes. Thus if one includes both the number of riots and the number of female-headed households, and the number of Democrats in Congress in an equation, the regression will calculate the importance of riots, controlling female-headed households, and Democrats.

Table 1.7   Influences on AFDC Caseloads at Time *t*

Variable	Lag	Beta	*t*	*p*
AFDC earlier	*t*–1	0.498	8.39	0.000
Riot (ln)	*t*–2	0.059	3.38	0.002
Robberies	*t*–1	0.200	3.15	0.002
Legal aid ($1,000s)	*t*–1	0.195	3.39	0.001
Unemployed	*t*	0.106	5.32	0.000
1966 (Effect of SSA)		0.013	1.15	0.131

Table 1.7 gives the results of the analysis. Table 1.7 includes only those variables which had a significant relation to AFDC caseloads after controlling the others. Variables absent from the table had essentially no relation to AFDC, and it is important for a correct theory to predict these cases of "no relation."

Among the variables that had some relation to welfare expansion, the statistic that measures the strength of the effect of each variable, is BETA. BETA is a standardized regression coefficient, roughly analogous to a partial correlation. Thus, the fact that the strongest relation is AFDC earlier shows that caseloads change relatively slowly and there is a certain amount of inertia in the system. The fact that the second strongest relation is ROBBERIES shows that when robberies have been high, there is a tendency for caseloads to increase. For each variable, LAG gives the number of years earlier that the cause was measured. It was chosen to maximize the relation. When one is looking at data over time, something may have an immediate effect, or it may take several years to have its effect. The symbol *t* gives an inferential statistic which is associated with *p*, the probability that a relation that strong or stronger could occur by chance, even if there were no causal relation between the variables. When *t* is high, *p* is low, and that indicates a stronger effect of the variable.

Hicks and Swank note that the Cloward and Piven analysis receives notable but mixed support from these data. There is a substantial inertia between current caseloads and those from the year before, but virtually any theory would predict that. The two variables to measure the disruption by the poor, riots, and robberies, both show a significant positive effect. However, in contradiction to the thesis that need has no effect whatsoever, there is also a positive relation between caseloads and contemporary unemployment as well as prior legal services spending. The variable designed to measure the effect of the 1965 amendment to the Social Security Act has a marginally positive relation, but it may be due to chance. In any case, it is not nearly enough to explain the effects of the other variables. What is striking about the analysis are the variables which turn out *not* to affect growth of the welfare state. Migration, female-headed households, and all of the measures of the strength of liberal politics turn out to have no measurable impact. This contradicts "commonsense" hunches about welfare.

Hicks and Swank's analysis of the effects of popular insurgency on welfare stipends suggests that mass disruption is often the basis of getting concessions from the state, as Cloward and Piven had argued. In other societies and at other times within the United States, these concessions obviously do not take the form of Aid For Dependent Children. Hicks and Swank are able to get a precise quantitative estimate of the effects of disruption (riots and robberies) by treating the institutional structure as given and narrowing their focus of what is to be explained. They do not examine other aspects of the process by which at some times more people are forced into the labor market, driving down wages, while at others, segments of the population may form a reserve army of the unemployed. Hicks and Swank's analysis must be compared with other studies of other processes. The period from World War II to the 1970s in the United States was a particular historical juncture and both the kinds of pressures and the kinds of concessions they produced were different at different times in different societies.

As an example of some of the other forces involved, section 2.9 will look at Hooks and McQueen's analysis of the emergence of the mixture of public and private provisions for pensions, health, education, and welfare that emerged toward the end of the New Deal. Hooks and McQueen (2010) consider the movement that emerged during the New Deal toward the kind of universalistic health, education, welfare, and labor policies analogous to those in most European countries. They argue that the congressional elections that produced gains for the Republican Party in the 80th Congress (1947–1948), making it possible, for example, to override Truman's veto of the Taft-Hartley Act, marked a watershed of the movement toward social democratic policies. Hooks and McQueen argue that it was the combination of militarism and military construction (especially the expansion of Air Force construction) and race conflict (consequent of massive migration of African Americans from the South to states with expanding war-time construction) that were the key basis of the political forces that established the institutional framework limiting that movement.

The kind of institutional structure that Hooks and McQueen are concerned with is treated as given by Hicks and Swank or by Cloward and Piven. The kind of insurgency that Cloward and Piven are concerned with is treated as given by the analysis of Hooks and McQueen. They are interdependent and both are being analyzed within a fairly narrow historical window of the local social and political forces, such as those that led to the party balance in the 80th Congress.

Class forces always operate within a unique, particular historical situation. This is true of the political struggles that established the post-World War II institutional structure, and it is true of the organizations and insurgencies that pushed for greater welfare benefits in the mid-twentieth century, within that institutional structure. Marx's analysis of class conflict is a way of addressing both the larger historical forces and options that are available at any time and also the unique, concrete, particular situations within which such forces operate.

Suggestions for Further Reading

On the relation of history and theory: for a long time the conflict between historical and systematic approaches was always the battle between an elephant and a whale. The participants had to keep to their own terrain. The section of historical sociology is one of the largest sections of the American Sociological Association. On welfare: the best introduction to the work of F. Piven and R. Cloward is still *Regulating the Poor* (Vintage, 1971). Piven has elaborated her view of "interdependency" as a source of social power in her presidential address to the American Sociological Association, "Can Power from Below Change the World?" *American Sociological Review* 73:1–14 (2008). Important analyses of the welfare state are: J. Quadagno, "Welfare Capitalism and the Social Security Act of 1935," *American Sociological Review* 49:632 (1984); L. Griffin, et al., "Capitalist Resistance to the Organization of Labor Before the New Deal," *American Sociological Review* 51:147 (1986); A. Hicks and J. Misra, "Political Resources and the Growth of Welfare in Affluent Capitalist Democracies," *American Journal of Sociology* 99:668–710 (1993); and Hooks and McQueen, "American Exceptionalism Revisited," *American Sociological Review* 75:185–204 (2010). Feagin's spaceship Earth analogy appears in "Social Justice and Sociology: Agendas for the Twenty-First Century," *American Sociological Review* 66:1–20 (2001).

SUMMARY AND CONCLUSIONS: HISTORY, HISTORICAL SOCIOLOGY, AND COMPARATIVE HISTORY

Can history be a science? Should history be a science? Must any science of society be historical? We have argued that an historical analysis which looks at the scientific lawfulness of the past is indispensable for sociology. There are some aspects of the past that one may be interested in as an historian, but that are uninteresting to many sociologists. And some parts of sociology may not be useful for some historians. But there are many other areas where an historical and a theoretical analysis have to go together. Marx constructed a bridge between the two studies which profoundly shaped each of them. It is a bridge which needs to be strengthened and expanded.

One of the reasons that bridge is so important for sociology is that without history, you don't even see social structure when you are part of it. It seems like background hills and mountains which have always been there. But when you investigate history, you often find that those mountains were not always there. Indeed, sometimes you find that they are volcanoes which were not there yesterday or will not be there tomorrow. And so, at the same time that history makes us sensitive to social structure, it also makes us sensitive to crisis and change. We think that most things can be understood well enough to understand their change only when they are examined historically.

Further, we have argued:

1. **Human Life Is Social and Historical**. In the last year, how many days have you spent without interacting with others? Probably very few, as humans are social. Even mountain climbing is usually a social act. In the last week, how much of your existence was independent of prior historical and social development, not using the collective products of human history? We venture to predict that none of it was ahistorical or asocial in this sense. Our parks and gardens are as much a social, historical product as our computers and cities. Does this make us unfree? Is this what makes us free? Both things are true. It is in our interactions that we become who we are. Every human society develops from a previous society. But every previous society had conflicting possibilities, developing in conflicting directions. Capitalist culture often emphasizes individualism and selfishness, but doesn't the widespread explosion of Internet networking and the hundreds of text messages we send each month show our craving to be connected with each other?

2. **We Live in an Era of Class Societies**. Prior to the development of classes, the development of states, armies, prisons, and law, in highly egalitarian and traditional communities, human existence was still social. In a sense, it was even historical. But it was social and historical in a very different sense from modern society. And if and when we move to an egalitarian, classless society based upon the principle "from each according to ability, to each according to need" our existence will be social and historical in yet another sense. Marxists believe that that kind of society would guarantee the highest material standard of living for mankind. It would unlock the greatest human potential for scientific, intellectual, and other achievements; problems which have proved insoluble would be solved. Decisions about education, production, and all collective action would not have to be put to the final test of whether they are profitable or useful for a few owners. And this would allow real, popular, democratic control of our historical destiny. The reverse of that vision is the realization that we have not had real, popular, truly democratic control of our historical destiny.

3. **In Class Societies, Some Control the Labor Power of Others**. A Greek politician, playwright, and philosopher had women and slaves

to make his clothing and grow his crops. Their labor made his leisure possible, while his leisure made their life slavery. Male, slave-owning citizens dominated the society; they were a ruling class. Not every citizen owned slaves, but those who did set the tone. An American politician, profiteer, or philosopher lives off the labor of others just as surely. The labor is extracted by markets and taxes rather than personal servitude and military capture. But in an era of class society, some control the labor of others. They use their position to create the institutions, ideas, and arrangements that maintain those relationships. This means that the labor which they extract from others is *alienated*. Not only does the dominant or ruling class extract a surplus, materially depriving others, but they decide what labor is to be done. Their decisions are ultimately guided by what enhances their wealth and position rather than meeting the needs of the society. Unfortunately, to keep that kind of a system going requires the distortion and degradation of many human impulses. Selfishness, greed, sexism, racism, nationalism, and other mean impulses have to be fostered as in a great hothouse. Thus, there is a fundamental contradiction between meeting the needs of some and meeting the needs of all. This contradiction takes the form of struggles over control of the state and other social institutions.

4. **Class Struggle Has Been the Motor of History**. One can look around and see production, classes, states, and culture. From an ahistorical and nondialectical perspective, it is possible to believe that social arrangements have always been and will always be pretty much as they are, and it is possible to focus only on the aspects that seem most general. But a familiarity with the actual change and diversity of social arrangements shows that little can be explained that way. The conclusion that things will always be pretty much as they are usually requires combining very vague concepts with colossal ignorance of human history. In fact, the short period of recorded human history has seen the rapid transformation of all human institutions. That short period has also been the period of class divisions—a period of rapid change, tension, and struggle. Even when it is impossible to mobilize classes, the process of exploitation or extraction of surplus has a profound effect on other social institutions. In the great social revolutions which have launched new modes of production, classes (defined in relation to production) have played the major roles. Some classes are more capable of being mobilized than others. Some classes have experience which makes them more capable of supporting the reconstruction of the social structure. In any case, the antagonistic relations of classes have been the essential motor behind historical change. Class struggle is not just a struggle between haves and have-nots over material assets.

It is much deeper than that—it is the struggle that determines what is produced and how, as well as how it is distributed.

5. **In Capitalism, Owners Buy the Labor Power of Workers**. The distinctive, novel, defining trait of capitalism is that most people (workers) are paid by others (capitalists) to work. The social fact that is necessary to this arrangement is that capitalists must find laborers *free*, as Marx put it, in a dual sense. They must be legally free, unencumbered by traditional bonds of personal and political dependence, and able to sell labor power. They must be without property, "free" of means of production of their own, looking for work; they must need to work. The fundamental concern of every capitalist class is its supply of labor. Ensuring this supply of labor requires an elaborate structure of social institutions, which are as they are in order to ensure that supply. If we study the history of United States immigration policies, for example, we see the need for labor of some sections of the capitalist class supporting "welcoming diversity" and alternately, others generating racist propaganda, most recently directed at immigrants from Latin America, from Africa, or Muslims. The freedom allowed by liberal institutions is a dual, mixed, ambivalent freedom. The fulfillment of these two conditions, extending back into the feudal period, is the guiding thread of the immense historical battles which gave rise to the modern world.

6. **This Process Creates Conflicts, Poverty, and Misery.** The immense dynamism of capitalism does not exhaust itself with the creation of liberal, bourgeois, capitalist society. It goes further, to spread all over the world, liberating and enslaving those in pre-capitalist societies. To promote freedom of commerce, we now see human trafficking, even of children. Capitalism devours and strangles itself, creating social, political, and economic crises. The liberal conception of society and history, which sees history as ended with the establishment of free labor, has grave difficulty explaining fascism, world wars, and racist, nationalist, irrationalist movements, brushfire wars, or increasing hunger and poverty. Those occurrences seem like some kind of mistake, an accident, which will never recur. By contrast, Marxist sociology sees them, and all of modern history, as resulting from tensions, conflicts, and contradictions built into capitalism.

2

Surplus Value

Marx's Economics

INTRODUCTION: MARXIST ECONOMICS
AND THE SCIENCE OF SOCIAL CHANGE

Marx worked for the last twenty-five years of his life on his economic model. Only fragments were completed by his death, but four of those fragments, the *Grundrisse*, the *Critique of Political Economy*, *Capital* (three volumes), and *Theories of Surplus Value* (three volumes), amounting to eight volumes (more than 5,000 pages), constitute the core of Marx's economic writing. It is a model of formidable complexity. What is so complex about the economy? Why did Marx spend so much time and effort analyzing it? Did he overestimate its importance? Many "Marxists" believe that they can understand the essence of Marx without any familiarity with those analyses. Many sociologists who haven't read them still regard themselves as perfectly conversant with Marx's social theory. But if you lay these works aside, you will never understand certain fundamental tenets of Marxism. We have already seen several reasons economic analyses were important for Marx.

Economic alienation is at the center of other kinds. Economic analysis is the key to classical liberalism, while arguments concerning liberalism are basic to the justification of other institutions. The mode of production is at the center of social structure; class is defined by the process of exploitation; our social class position conditions our social existence. Class is itself complex and intertwined with other social divisions. Above all, classes and class contradictions are the key to any practical change we can accomplish. Given the importance of economic conflicts to historical and political change, one virtue of a sociological approach which places class at the center is that it represents a way to connect philosophical, political, historical, and sociological analyses. Can we really understand a supposedly "moral" issue, such as human trafficking, without taking into account the economic hardships in some countries caused by globalized capitalism's intense drive for profits? Can the terrible human cost of some natural disasters, such as the 2010 earthquake in Haiti that killed perhaps 250,000, be understood without taking into account the economic poverty caused by political, military, and economic processes set in motion by capitalism's intense drive for profits? Can environmental problems that affect all of humanity really be understood without understanding how they are caused by capitalism's intense drive for profits?

Furthermore, it is important to recognize that in Marx political economy is a considerably broader subject than modern economics and much more sociological. It focuses on real relationships, not on market transactions and money. Marx realized that economic forces could not be understood in isolation from the political system, history, social relationships, and social institutions. It is only in the context of politics, history, and social organization that we can understand the great financial crash of 2008 and the resulting worldwide recession. Economic analyses of markets, which abstract from the actual relationships inside firms, have difficulty even analyzing economic relations. Moreover, those economic relations are, in fact, deeply bound up with and dependent upon noneconomic institutions.

Anti-Marxist theorists in sociology commonly accuse Marx of "economic determinism." They use phrases such as "avoiding reductionism," the "basic importance of culture," or the "relative autonomy of the state," to argue that Marx ignored key elements of social structure. In these debates there are real, practical disagreements involving what would be required for change. But it cannot be evident what those disagreements are until one clarifies what is "material" and "economic" in Marx. Above all, without some idea of dialectics and dialectical contradictions, one will always interpret Marx as an economic determinist.

Marx never wrote a treatise on method or dialectics. But he did make methodological comments within his main works. This is discussed in more depth in chapter 4, but we have to anticipate a few of those ideas here. The notion of *contradiction* links three methodological principles, all of which are very important for modern sociology: there are contradictions between *points of view*, between *processes*, and between *groups*. Even a simple statement like, "the beer is on the table," is *truly conditional* on a given frame and theory. At the very least, there must be assumptions about what one is talking about when one says "beer," "table," or "on." These assumptions involve points of view. Is the beer spilled on the table or is it in a can on the table? Moreover, even such a simple process as sitting on a table involves a host of pulls and pushes and counteracting tendencies, which appear contradictory. Its "on-ness" involves the beer's spinning around with the Earth, flying around the sun, interacting with a host of people, etc. And finally, "the beer's sitting on the table" may make someone better off or worse off. People may have feelings about it; they may act on them; they may even fight about it.

In social theories, the meanings of terms and the assumptions making up a theoretical framework are far more problematical than in the statement "the beer is on the table." The relationships which got the beer to the table are complex and contain enormous tensions; both the beer and the relationships are being transformed. The beer and the table are processes; these processes are parts of many other processes. The same is even truer of the human relationships involving the beer or the table. All are changing; understanding these changes involves looking at history and at production as well as at the present. Dialectical language, even if it sounds awkward at first, is very useful in connecting different considerations relevant to an issue.

Marx says that his goal in *Capital* is to show the laws of motion—the dynamics—of capitalism. He regards this as the main task of any science. In the afterword to the second edition of *Capital*, Marx gives an extended quotation from a reviewer who, he thinks, has correctly understood his dialectical method. It is the natural place to begin if we want to know what he is trying to do:

> "The one thing which is of moment to Marx, is to find the law of the phenomena with whose investigation he is concerned; and not only is that law of moment to him, which governs these phenomena, in so far as they have a definite form and mutual connection within a given historical period. Of still greater moment to him is the law of their variation, of their development, i.e., of their transition from one form into another, from one series of connections into a different one. This law once discovered, he investigates in detail the effects in which it manifests itself in social life. Consequently, Marx only troubles himself about one thing: to show by rigid scientific investigation, the necessity of successive determinant orders of social conditions, and to establish, as impartially as possible, the facts that serve him for fundamental starting-points. For this it is quite enough, if he proves, at the same time, both the necessity of the present order of things, and the necessity of different order into which the first must inevitably pass over; and this all the same, whether men believe or do not believe it, whether they are conscious or unconscious of it. Marx treats the social movement as a process of natural history, governed by laws . . . The old economists misunderstood the nature of economic laws when they likened them to the laws of physics and chemistry. A more thorough analysis of the phenomena shows that social organisms differ among themselves as fundamentally as plants or animals. Nay, one and the same phenomenon falls under quite different laws in consequence of the different structures of those organisms as a whole, of the variations of their individual organs, and of the different conditions in which those organs function, etc. . . ." Whilst the writer

pictures what he takes to be actually my method, in this striking and [so far as concerns my own application of it] generous way, what else is he picturing but the dialectical method? (CAP I, pp. 17–19)

We see here the fundamental importance of the linking of theory to history. Marx's central criticism of the "old economists" is that they failed to see history; they failed to see change; they failed to see the dependence of the regularities which their theories pictured on the rest of social structure. A scientific analysis must be simultaneously concerned both with the regularities which operate within a given structure and period and also with "laws of motion," the dynamic by which that structure changes. The analysis is one of natural history and of history.

Instead of transhistorical generalizations which are a function of human nature or psychology, one must construct theories to deal with complex, structural effects, "the different conditions in which those organs function." Any social phenomenon—classes, the state, money, wage labor, etc.—is not well understood if it is analyzed as though its present form always existed. For example, the concepts of inequality, leadership, exchange, or work are all much more general than the specific social forms just listed. (And much more empty.) Analyses focused on absolutely general aspects of social structure become very vague. To neglect or ignore the specific social and historical structures *which have not always existed* and *will not always exist* makes it hard to explain change, or anything else. Marx's analysis requires abstracting from some characteristics and focusing on others, but the aspects on which it focuses highlight dynamic change rather than obscuring it.

If Marx's political economy does not focus upon money transactions, what is its essence? In chapter 4, we shall see that the key concept is that of **contradictions.** In all Marxist analysis, the basis of dynamic change is the existence of contradictions in things. There are contradictory processes and possibilities and there are opposed groups with contradictory standpoints. Marx's use of the term *contradiction* forces one to pay attention to the linkages between these. The contradiction key to Marxist economics is the view of **labor as a contradictory process.**

A dialectical analysis of the contradictions in the labor process generates overlapping contradictions within capitalism as the basis of its change and development. We have looked at some of these contradictions. Sometimes the relations of production strangle and fetter productive forces; science and technology are perverted so that they threaten and enslave us rather than free us; labor and resources are devoted to waste and destruction; industrialization, under late capitalism, is often de-industrialization; "labor-saving" devices can create slavery, misery, poverty, and powerlessness; and so forth.

This contradiction generates and reinforces *class* contradictions. In capitalism, the entire product belongs to an owner who does not labor, but who owns the productive process and can abort it. This fact is the center of other contradictions in capitalist society. One of the classic, summary expositions of the essence of Marx's economic analysis is that of Engels in his book *Anti-Duhring*. Engels points to four contradictions: capitalism is characterized by the contradiction between the socialized (increasingly socialized) character of production and the private appropriation of the product. This generates a contradiction between those who labor (the proletariat or working class) and those who profit (the bourgeoisie or capitalist owners of production). Both contradictions are accentuated by the increasing organization of labor in the workplace and the anarchy of production in the society at large. And all of these come to a head in crises of overproduction in which the mode of production comes into contradiction with the mode of exchange. These contradictions are schematically listed in table 2.1.

Much of this chapter will deal with these, but do not wait for us or anyone else to give you examples of these types of contradictions or to tell you how they are related or how they are relevant to sociology as a discipline. Right now, try to think of two or three concrete examples of each. What does it mean to say that production is social but ownership private? What tensions, conflicts, and opposite pulls are implicit in this? What are some examples? How does it relate to the other contradictions? Is that something important about the society, or is it merely incidental?

Suggestions for Further Reading

There are a host of popular introductions to Marxist economics. Howard Sherman, in addition to his *Introduction to Sociology*, noted above, has written introductions to Marxist economics: *Radical Political Economy* (Basic, 1972) and *Stagflation* (Harper and Row, 1976). A standard introductory work which was used in the Soviet Union for many years is A. Leontief, *Political Economy, A Condensed Course* (International Publishers, 1974). Among his many works, E. Mandel's *Marxist Economic Theory*, two volumes (Monthly Review Press, 1962–1968), assimilates a massive amount of empirical data. M. Linder and J. Sensat, *Against Samuelson*, two volumes (Urizen Books, 1977), represents a detailed chapter-by-chapter critique of a major liberal introduction in that it highlights many important empirical and theoretical issues.

Table 2.1   Contradictions of Capitalism

I	Socialized production	v.	Private appropriation
II	Workers	v.	Capitalists
III	Organization of work in the firm	v.	Anarchy in the society
IV	Mode of production	v.	Mode of exchange

SECTION 2.1: WHAT IS A COMMODITY?
WHAT IS THE LABOR THEORY OF VALUE?

Marx's model is an analysis of the *sociological* aspects of the economy. It deals with the social relationships which undergird the market or money exchanges. What is really going on when you buy a tomato? It looks as though you are exchanging inedible green cabbage (money) for a perfectly edible red fruit. Why and how does it come about that a certain quantity of money is accepted as equivalent by a producer of tomatoes?

Classical political economy, exemplified by the writing of Adam Smith in 1776, answered this question based on the labor theory of value. Marx did not invent the labor theory of value, but he developed and consolidated it. Above all he showed that previous ways of accounting within it for **property income**—for profit, interest, and rent—contained contradictions stemming from their attempt to ignore classes and exploitation. Since the labor theory of value is the foundation of Marx's accounting of surplus value, and that is the foundation of Marx's economics, it is important to be clear on what it says and what it does not say. It is not a price theory.

The basis of the labor theory of value is the conception that **money is a claim on the labor of others**. One could also say that value is crystallized, objectified, or alienated labor. Money itself is useless, but it commands labor. The classical economists imagined deer hunters and corn growers on a desert island. They said that it was clear that if, on the average, killing a deer took about the same amount of labor as growing ten bushels of corn, then one deer would exchange for ten bushels of corn. If a deer was priced at more than ten bushels, then corn growers would hunt their own deer. If a deer was priced at less than ten bushels of corn, hunters would grow their own corn. What about the value of an object like a diamond? The classical economists said that its value was the labor which would take to replace it or find an equivalent. What if it takes a while to learn how to grow corn? Then the actual time spent growing it gradually uses up the time spent learning how. But in one way or another, the classical economists said, every product is a product of a portion of the total labor of the society, and that is what is most important about it. In other words, **the value of commodities is ultimately determined by the labor that goes into them.**

Very often students (or orthodox economists) attempt to "disprove" the labor theory of value by demonstrating that, in fact, prices are not a simple function of labor. But Marx acknowledges this over and over again. This misunderstanding involves confusing **paradigms** or **models** (questions one is asking) with **empirical results** (answers, facts, statements). The labor theory of value is a model that examines the *underlying trends and limits* of the economic process. Under special assumptions it predicts the same prices as the mainstream, liberal explanation, but it is a fundamentally different analysis, both in the questions it asks and the answers it gives.

Now, in the presence of monopolies of various kinds, price will not be determined solely by labor. If you have private property in land, and the corn growers can prevent the hunters from growing their own corn, they may successfully offer less than ten bushels of corn for a deer. If one person owns all the land, he or she might prevent anyone from growing or hunting anything without giving him or her a rake-off, which would affect prices. Or a group might invest in hired bullies and coercion to make everyone pay them a surtax as a protection racket. In the real world, price is not determined exclusively by labor. And in the real world, objects do not fall at thirty-two feet per second per second. But it is correct to base one's fundamental model of gravity on the situation without friction, accounting for deviations later. And it is correct and useful to base one's fundamental model of exchange on the labor theory of value.

One of the reasons that the labor theory of value establishes a sociologically useful model is that it focuses upon the social relationships which underlie market relations. Those social relationships are key if one is even to understand the dynamics of the economy; but they are absolutely crucial if one is to understand the articulation of the economy with politics, with history, and with other social institutions. Every society has some way of dividing up its total labor, the sum total of actions or doings of its members. Even in this society, and certainly in most societies, some of the most important of those relations do not take place in the market; they do not involve buying and selling things. But to start out, we should analyze money, buying, and selling because they provide the dynamics that alter other kinds of relations.

Any society has to have some mechanism for dividing up its total labor. The labor theory of value says that the mechanism is what is fundamental or foundational for the economy. What does it imply about the accumulation of wealth? What is the radical core of the labor theory of value, which pre-Marxist political economy evaded—a core so fundamental that once it was pointed out, academic economists had to abandon the whole framework? Ownership of wealth yields property income. Where does it come from? Go up to members of the Rockefeller family, whose collective wealth is estimated at over $100 billion, and ask where their wealth came from. Like the bankers who, after wrecking the financial system, awarded themselves $10 million bonuses, they will answer that they *earned* it, they worked for it, or they inherited it from someone who worked for it. What does the labor theory of value have to say about that? If one has $20,000, then one can hire someone of average skills at a subsistence wage for a year; if one has $2 million, then one can hire him or her for 100 years, or can hire 100 people for a year. If one has

$5 billion—and there are more than fifty people with that wealth in the United States, members of the Rockefeller family among them—then one can hire a quarter of a million workers for a year, or a 2,500 workers for 100 years, or one worker for 250,000 years, etc. The fundamental question raised by the labor theory of value is the question: did that original Rockefeller, who started that wealth machine, *really* work for 250,000 years? Or even 2,500 years? Of course not! Classical political economy made a series of efforts to try to account for property income: it was the income for "waiting," for "directing," or for "risking" the start-up capital. But all such arguments really fail to convince.

Now, the fact that some people have a claim on the labor of hundreds of thousands of others might not be so important if the money got used up. But what are the dynamics of a system where an owner who hires 100,000 other people for a year, then reaps a profit which allows him to hire *more* people the next year? The issue is not only or mainly one of ethics and fairness. *The point of* **surplus value** *is the expansion of capitalism.* This drive within capitalism to expand is crucial to understanding the dynamics of capitalism.

Capitalism is *not* the "logical extension" of the selfishness of individuals, because on the individual level there is a limit to how much one can consume, how much one can spend to make life as comfortable as possible on Earth. It is probably impossible for someone to truly consume $100 million (except through mass destruction), though they can "spend" it by converting it into other forms of capital. But capitalism as a system does have a drive to constantly expand; unlike individual people, corporations, no matter how wealthy, must expand economically or risk economic ruin.

If one profits from hiring people, then at the end of any period, one will have even more money to hire even more people. At the level of individuals, different individuals have different resources which get different rewards. But at the structural level, Marx says, we can see where the capitalist got capital—from employing workers. On the average, capitalists end up with more than they began so that that form of relation will gradually invade every other sphere of the society. Not only that, but it is not just more gold that the person who hires labor has at the end of the process. The surplus value is real. There is more value, more crystallized labor, goods, and services. All the rest of social structure—art museums and pornography, science and comic books, basketball and society balls—whatever else they are, are funded out of the surplus value. The production of surplus value is so dynamic that it will not only change all the relationships in the society, it will expand all over the face of the Earth.

Surplus value is based on value. Value is based on **commodity** production. Let's first distinguish between **commodities** and other things that are produced. Commodities are products that are *produced in order to be sold.*

Commodity production is at the heart of capitalist economic processes, and it imposes entirely new dynamics on the economy than when goods were usually produced for use. Not all commodity production is capitalist production—capitalist production, properly speaking, occurs only when there is the *buying and selling of labor*. Even if buying and selling of labor has the same rules as buying and selling of shoes and houses, it is fundamentally different. Sociologically, we think this is certainly true. There were pockets of commodity production within the slave and feudal systems of the past. But under capitalist production, labor power becomes a commodity, the sphere of commodity production expands, and virtually every sphere of life comes to be regulated ultimately by whether it is profitable to produce things.

Marx says that two contradictions are key to understanding a commodity. A commodity is a contradiction between use value and exchange value, and it is a contradiction between general labor time and particular labor time.

> We saw in a former chapter that the exchange of commodities implies contradictory and mutually exclusive conditions. The differentiation of commodities into commodities and money does not sweep away these inconsistencies, but develops a modus vivendi, a form in which they can exist side by side. This is generally the way in which real contradictions are reconciled. For instance, it is a contradiction to depict one body as constantly falling towards another, and as, at the same time, constantly flying away from it. The ellipse is a form of motion which, while allowing this contradiction to go on, at the same time reconciles it. (CAP I, pp. 103–4)

One of the mutually exclusive conditions to which Marx refers is that the commodity be a use value (or it would not be purchased) and *not be* a use value (or it would not be sold). It seems that producing something in order to sell it is very simple. But it means that the thing must be a use value for the buyer at the same time that it is an exchange value for the seller. And this contradiction is just the beginning of a process which is at least as complex as an orbit, in which a body both falls toward another and flies away from it. It is the beginning of the process by which the kinds of relationships in tribal or feudal society are replaced by impersonal money transactions. In the opening, very difficult portion of *Capital*, Marx analyzes a series of forms which contain a phenomenology—an implicit anthropology, history, and sociology—of different kinds of exchange, such as barter. Marx regretted the difficulty of these chapters, but he believed that it was very important to show the origin of the roles and the dynamics which come to be built into property law. For the moment, all we need to know is that when all production is geared not to use but to making money, this produces new social dynamics. And it produces social relationships which are alienated in especially powerful ways.

Exercise 2.1: Behind the Veil of Money

Consider: How is your life interconnected with the lives of workers all over the world? As your life is going right now, today, this minute, sketch out the network of relationships and sets of goods and services which make your life as it is. Next, look at the label on the shirt you are wearing, and then use Google Earth to look at the kind of factory in the country where it was made. (You can just look at a major manufacturing concentration in the country, or you can easily find on the web a major textile manufacturing area.) Usually you can get close enough to make an estimate of the way of life. Construct in your mind the chain of inter-actions that got the shirt from there (from a factory to you.

Look around you. What you see are **commodities.** Clothes and tables, walls and windows, objects of use and the land outside are all infused with labor and they are bought and sold. Now wasn't it nice of someone to raise the sheep and dig the iron and make the machines that knitted your sweater? What did you ever do for them? Wasn't it nice of someone to build the roads and mine the oil and fly the planes that brought you the sweater? What did you ever do for them?

Take any commodity, such as a shirt, that you see in front of you. To sketch out the complete, concrete network of relationships which connect you to the people (many of whom are not alive and not in this country) who propelled those commodities along their individual trajectories to you uncovers the world economy, globalization, the capitalist world system, and the enormous interdependence of people in the modern world. Many, perhaps all, of the people and relationships in your sketch may have to be hypothetical, but try to make it coherent and hypothetically complete, that is, try to include all of the relations or institutions which led to their doing what they had to do to get the commodities to you.

You will probably find that the relations are so complex that it is almost impossible even to *imagine* them as they really are (Fred did X for Joe be-cause Y; Mary did Z for Fred because . . .), rather than in highly stereotyped ways. After all, it took the combined labor of hundreds of people, many of them long dead, to get you a shirt. You will see why you need a model, rather than merely observing an immediate reality. You will see why a model has to be somewhat intricate. And you will see that production re-lationships involve a lot more than money. They involve politics, power, knowledge, and much more.

We think that if you really visualize the network of relations involving a few commodities, you will discover that we are one human race. If you find that your shirt was made in Cambodia or in Mexico, so that if you use Google Earth to look into Mexico City (one of the largest cities in the world) or Phnom Penh (a vast industrial complex) you will discover sets of relationship that you probably took for granted. We may be split apart by barriers of nation, religion, sex, race, and class. But if you look at what makes your life livable, it is the combined labor of the human race.

You cannot investigate very many of the relationships you have just sketched out. Right now they are speculation, and probably infused with a good deal of ideology. But they are real enough. If they weren't, you would have starved or frozen long ago. And it might even be possible to go into some one of the factories, plantations, neighborhoods, or corporations which got those commodities to you. This is one of the fundamental inspirations of sociology. Why don't you investigate one of those factories, plantations, neighborhoods, or corporations? It will be hard. In general, you will find that they are not a bit like a school, a public library, or a family. You will find that they are often surrounded by barbed wire; there is no question there about free speech or freedom of movement. Indeed, we think you will find that most productive establishments are rather like the dark tower of alienation sketched in chapter 1.

The main appeal of the book *Roots* was the idea of going back to find out how it *really was* for your biological forebears. But there is an important sense in which the people to whom your three commodities connect you are more important to you than your biological forebears. That mass of living human physical and mental labor makes your life possible, and it is the future.

Suggestions for Further Reading

One demonstration that labor theory of value, under special assumptions, gives the same price model as liberal economics, is in H. Sherman, *Radical Political Economy* (Basic Books, 1972, pp. 359–67). One of the best overviews of the structure of capital is still P. Sweezy, *The Theory of Capitalist Development* (Monthly Review, 1942, 1970). As Sweezy shows, Marx's analysis moves toward the concrete by relaxing assumptions posed at the beginning. Even the rich historical material, concerning the state, at the end of vol. I of *Capital* still operates within assumptions which are relaxed later. At a more advanced level, J. Roemer's *Analytical Foundations of Marxist Economics* (Cambridge, 1981) and *Free to Lose* (Harvard, 1988) show that the labor theory of value, which he ultimately rejects, gives a powerful analysis of many kinds of exploitation. He considers labor markets to be equivalent to others, but many Marxists think that he is mistaken on a number of crucial sociological issues. Some limitations of market analysis are explored in A. Sen, *Commodities and Capabilities* (North-Holland, 1984). On real commodities: I. Wallerstein, among others, has insisted on the importance of looking at the world economy in terms of the concrete movements of real commodities in commodity chains. As noted, if one does so, he argues that:

(1) most commodity chains, now and during the last five centuries, cross national boundaries; (2) most laborers on those chains, now as during the last five centuries, are not full-time wage workers for a lifetime; there are a series of other groups (women, peasants, underemployed workers with subsistence farms) who are being pulled into the net of the world market; (3) if one takes account of the real losses and gains of these groups, one finds that absolute immiseration (e.g., a net decline in calories or protein consumed) is and has been taking place; and (4) this is one of the reasons that the process of pulling them into the world market is one of violence and violent resistance. See T. Hopkins and I. Wallerstein, *Processes of the World System* (Sage, 1980).

SECTION 2.2: WHAT IS SURPLUS VALUE?

Marxist analysis starts from the production of commodities. In commodity production, producers sell goods for money which they use to live and to produce more. Thus, Marx represents the process of commodity production by the formula *CMC*, the movement from commodities to money to more commodities. The story that begins *Capital* is how that system gives way to a different system governed by different dynamics, which Marx represents by the formula *MCM'*, in which some people start with a stock of money (*M*) and use it to get commodities (*C*), which are worth a larger amount of money (*M'*). The difference between M and M' is the **surplus value.** Marx argues that the labor market, the buying and selling of labor power, is the key to producing surplus value. The fact that surplus value is produced makes the capitalist system incomparably more dynamic than all previous systems.

If every commodity has a value—no matter how that value is established—and if every commodity is exchanged at that value, then at the end of all the exchanges, you still have the same total value that existed at the beginning. Even if things are not exchanged at value, even if some people are able to cheat and steal or to buy cheap and sell dear, then at the end of the process you still have the same total as at the beginning. The labor theory of value shifts attention from the exchange process to the production process, and this shift is especially important if one is to see the dynamics of the system as a whole.

In his analysis of the production process, Marx assumes that there is no cheating, stealing, etc., going on; he assumed that property income does not arise from shifting around a given amount of value, but rather from production of real surplus value. Cheating, stealing, etc., were very important, especially for the production of the great accumulations of money that started the process, which Marx calls "primitive accumulation." Often those fortunes resulted from war and piracy, from shifting aristocratic fortunes into plantations or business, or the use of coercion to squeeze money from Indians or powerless groups at home. But these processes move value around; they do not create it. The dynamism of capitalism lies in its production of surplus value. (We shall see later that as the political-economic system reaches its limit, and extracting profits has become more difficult, a decaying, rather than dynamic, system comes to rely more and more on the same practices that characterized primitive accumulation, although now it is more out of desperation than strength. But for now, we want to explore the dynamism of the core processes of capitalism.)

As class societies developed, owning classes accumulated wealth by exploiting laboring classes. In a slave economy, you could buy slaves, and if you could make them produce more than their cost of subsistence (plus the original price), then at the end of the process you would have a surplus. In a feudal economy, the aristocracy could extract the same kind of surplus from enserfed peasants. But under capitalism, there is only one commodity which one can buy and use up, and at the end of the process, have more left than one started out with. That is labor itself. Or rather, it is not labor, but labor power. Capitalists do not buy services. They don't contract out the production process. They buy the right to tell the workers what to do for the day or for the month. They buy labor power which is *all* the services of their workers.

Expressed differently, capitalists do not buy labor; they buy a problem. Their problem is how to get labor out of their laborers. In *Capital*, Marx constructs a model in which everything is bought at just what it is worth. Anything is worth the labor it takes to produce it. Capitalists buy labor power, just like everything else, at what it is worth. What labor power is worth is what it takes to produce it. Capitalists pay the laborer the historically and socially determined subsistence wage required to support the laborer and his or her family. But laborers produce more than this during the period that they work. This is the fundamental dynamic of the system. The capitalist then pockets the difference, the surplus, including the profit.

But what ensures that there is any profit? Suppose that workers work just long enough or just hard enough to replace the value laid out in raw materials, equipment, and wages but with no profit left over? Capitalism runs on profit. Once capitalism is established, profit is not only indispensable for the growth of the system; it is the indispensable condition for there to be any production at all. *Unless workers produce more than they are paid, capitalists would refuse to have any production.* But what prevents that from happening? The answer to this question is not short. The supply, the compliance, and the pay of workers are not determined strictly within the firm. They are affected by organization; they are affected by laws, by families, and by a host of different political issues and choices—from immigration to schooling. Capitalists are intensely concerned with these issues, and the profitability of production involves virtually every institution in the society and, over time, it involves the transformation of these institutions. However, the bare outline of an answer is short enough: there are two ways of increasing surplus. Either workers must work longer and harder (which Marx called the production of **absolute** surplus value) or workers must be able to produce their own replacement costs in less time by increased productivity (which Marx called the production of **relative** surplus value). The analysis of battles over relative and absolute surplus value leads directly to analysis of the main sociological structures of the firm.

Marx's own analysis of it leads directly into several hundred pages of discussion of the historical process by which capitalism first adopts and then transforms the technical relations of production as it finds them. In handicrafts, the actual production process remains as it was; in cooperation, workers are brought together; in factory production, the production process itself is transformed. And this is only the beginning of the process. In vol. II of *Capital*, the genesis of industrial sectors, banks, and interest is discussed. In vol. III, the genesis of rents and interaction of industry with the old agricultural class system is treated. Nor does the process of development stop in the nineteenth century. Contemporary neo-Marxist analyses have taken the process of the extraction of surplus value as the key to a host of social developments in the twentieth century.

Exercise 2.2: Super-Exploitation

Consider: When one group of workers is exploited more intensely than others, what effect does it have on the exploitation of the other workers?

Capitalists generally buy labor power at its value. At that value, labor is exploited; the worker works, the capitalist consumes; and at the end of the process, the capitalist has more than he or she started with. When labor power is bought at less than its value, Marxists speak of **super-exploitation.** That value is determined by the labor required to produce it—that is, the historically and socially determined subsistence required to support the laborer and his or her family. Super-exploitation means that some group of laborers gets less than this historical subsistence.

> If the owner of labour-power works to-day, to-morrow he must again be able to repeat the same process in the same conditions as regards health and strength. His means of subsistence must therefore be sufficient to maintain him in his normal state as a labouring individual. . . . [T]he number and extent of his so-called necessary wants, as also the modes of satisfying them, are themselves the product of historical development. . . . In contradistinction therefore to the case of other commodities, there enters into the determination

of the value of labour-power a historical and moral element. Nevertheless, in a given country, at a given period, the average quantity of the means of subsistence necessary for the labourer is practically known. (CAP I, p. 171)

What is this "historical and moral element"? The value of labor power is determined outside of the production process by the unity, organization, and traditions of the working class as a whole. Earlier, we discussed how Marx and Marxists view divisions within the working class as an important part of this moral and historical element. How long the workers work and how hard they work is also determined outside of the productive process. The value of labor, the intensity of work, the length of the working day, and a host of related questions all become the object of intense political struggles. From the point of view of capital, if any group of workers can be forced to work for less than their value, it is a windfall. Accordingly, capitalists will always be on the lookout for ways to accomplish this. Certain groups—blacks, women, foreign workers, and other subordinate groups—are especially vulnerable and thus they can be forced to work at less than value.

What effect does this have on everyone else's wage? Would wages for some workers go up because there is more left for them when wages for others are lower? Would wages go down? What effects does this have on the battles within the workplace over intensity, length, and conditions of work? What effect does this have on the larger political struggles within the society? Briefly sketch out your best answers to these three questions before you proceed.

A major portion of Marxist theory is devoted to these three questions. Marx himself sketched out many lines of argument and analysis with respect to them, and later Marxists have extended those. These constitute possibly the largest single coherent body of theory in sociology concerning race, sex, and national differences. With respect to slavery, Marx argued,

> In the United States of North America, every independent movement of workers was paralyzed so long as slavery disfigured a part of the Republic. Labour cannot emancipate itself in a white skin where in the black it is branded. (CAP I, p. 301)

The essential Marxist argument is that when any group is forced to sell labor power at below its value, this ultimately undercuts the wages of the rest of the workers. It lowers the historically determined subsistence. The attempt to prevent undercutting each other's wages is one of the main forces driving workers to combine in unions.

While many answers are clear, others are the subject of dispute among Marxists or between them and liberal theorists. Processes of these kinds are complex and they have extremely powerful consequences which involve virtually every aspect of society.

Perhaps many white male workers *do not know* that their wages are undercut, their unity is undermined, or their overall political position is weakened by racism or sexism. But in fact, they are. Some would argue, "So what? If they *think* that they benefit from excluding minorities, then it might just as well be true." The opinions might be the same; but *how deeply rooted they are* might be different. It is one thing to convince people to oppose something that is hurting them, and something quite different to try to convince people to oppose something that benefits them.

Suggestions for Further Reading

The production of surplus value is briefly described in chapter VI of vol. I of *Capital* (pp. 167–176), but there is no major segment of his analysis which is unconnected to it. Brief accounts by popularizers, in which the extraction of surplus value is disconnected from other processes, distort Marx's political-economic theory. Marx himself wrote two useful, brief popularized accounts: "Wage Labor and Capital" in 1849 (SW, pp. 64–94) and "Wages, Price, and Profit" in 1867 (SW, pp. 186–229). We shall return to super-exploitation in section 2.6. Contemporary discussion of exploitation and its relation to other processes creating difference between racial, ethnic, gender, or other segments of the work force stems largely from C. Tilly, *Durable Inequality* (University of California Press, 1998) to which we shall return in section 2.6. A brief argument that Marxism contains the analytical tools essential to deepen a descriptive understanding of gender and race, as well as class, is M. Gimenez, "Marxism and Class, Gender and Race: Rethinking the Trilogy" Race, Gender and Class 8: 23–33 (2001).

SECTION 2.3: WHAT IS OVERPRODUCTION? HOW CAN THERE BE TOO MUCH FOOD, HOUSING, OR HEALTH CARE?

We said that a commodity is the focus of two contradictions: the contradiction between **use value and exchange value** and the contradiction between **general and particular labor.** With regard to the contradiction between use value and exchange value, a commodity is something which is exchanged. The exchange implies that something is and is not a use value. It is useful to someone, or nothing would be exchanged for it; it is not a use value for the exchanger, or it would not be exchanged. What is the more general significance of this? The most striking way that capitalism is characterized by a pervasive contradiction between use value and exchange value is the coexistence of crying needs and superfluity: waste. Consider the wealthy countries of Europe and North America: at the time when there is desperate need for clothing, medicine, and housing—at a time when hundreds of thousands of people are going hungry and sleeping in the streets—there can be inadequate *market demand* for food, clothing, medicine, or housing. To prevent resources going completely to waste, they have to be redirected to the production of weapons or luxury goods. What explains this contradiction, this paradox?

Under commodity production, things are produced only to be sold; it is a by-product if they happen to fulfill human needs. Thus there may be food, clothing, and housing unsold while there are people who also desperately need them. In a capitalist economy, production is guided by the production of exchange value; the demand for an item has nothing to do with the needs people have for it. Only those needs which are backed up by money, which are backed up by exchange, count. Only that is "effective demand." At a time when millions of people are starving in parts of Africa, some of those countries are *net exporters of food!* Why? Those who owned were producing profitable cash crops for those who could pay rather than producing food for the hungry.

Supporters of capitalism claim that the marketplace has the consumer as king, that it only produces what people want and need. They say free enterprise is like a system of voting what to produce, but much more efficient than actually voting on what to produce, without all that red tape and bureaucracy. Economist Milton Friedman says that only capitalism makes people free; only when every possible decision is made by markets is everyone free to decide what they want for themselves.

The classical liberal paradigm is founded on the notion that free competition leads to the most needed goods being efficiently produced. Pluralism, libertarianism, utilitarianism, and a host of other individualisms are based upon the paradigm of free competition in the economy. Is it true that competition assures that needed goods are efficiently produced for the good of society? Marxist research strongly challenges that assertion. Capitalism does not satisfy most people's needs, and it does not make most people free. In the first place, a major distinction must be made between commodity production and voting on what to produce. In markets, some people have more votes than others—a lot more. In economics, effective demand is demand that has money to back it up. Some people have no "votes" at all and some people have millions of "votes." When you have millions, capitalism is oriented to satisfying your needs. Capitalism's job is to make a profit, not to satisfy needs. There are plenty of things that are profitable which do not satisfy needs. There are plenty of needs which are unprofitable to satisfy.

Second, the whole liberal conception slides between two social relationships which are fundamentally different: *small scale commodity production* where self-employed producers own means of production and *capitalist production using wage labor*. These two systems have the same property laws, but they have fundamentally different relationships. The self-employed shoemaker owns the shoes that he or she makes. There, what private owner-ship of production means is the greatest possible dispersal of control. What it means is that no one can or has to tell him or her when or how to make shoes. He or she makes his or her own decisions within the market. But in a shoe factory, the people who make the shoes don't own the shoes they make. We saw that from this follows a host of other alienations. For exam-ple, since the benefits of making more shoes go to the owner, the produc-tive process has to be organized as a command economy. Every move that anyone makes must be controlled and watched. What private ownership of production means, then, is the greatest possible concentration. What it means is that even if every single worker in the plant stands to lose from the closing of the plant, but if the owner benefits from closing it, the plant will be closed. Even if every single person in the community, the country, or the world stands to lose from actions which benefit the owner, it is the owner who decides. Private ownership of the means of production once seemed to represent dispersed and popular control; eventually it became the fundamental barrier to popular control.

Competition devours itself. The game of Monopoly is a familiar example of the dynamic that results when access to further resources is, at least partly, a function of how many resources you already have. In Monopoly, your properties are your resources. The more properties, the higher your rents, and thus your income and wealth; but players with plenty of money can keep buying and improving properties, increasing their income. The result is that the rich get richer and the poor get poorer; inequality grows, and the game polarizes until ultimately one player wipes out all the others. Any game in which access is a function of resources, and thus most forms of accumulation, has this dynamic.

We saw that Marx's central model of the circuit of capital, analyzed as MCM', is an example of this dynamic. A capitalist starts out with a quantity of money (M) which he or she turns into a set of commodities, worth the same amount, which can be used to make something that he or she can sell (C). There is a difference between the money the capitalist has at the begin-ning (M) and the money at the end (M' called "M-prime"). This difference, called "surplus value," is the basis for profit and other property incomes; it is the basis of the dynamic by which capitalism grows and extends itself; and it means that the capitalists not only have an advantage in getting more money, but also in gaining access to other resources in the society. This dif-ference between M and M' is structurally built into capitalism. For capital-ism to work, the capitalist must make a profit; the commodities that he or she sells at the end must be worth more than the money at the beginning. In many respects, the distinctive and decisive elements of Marx's analysis are the kind of social, organizational, and political decisions and processes that result from this and ensure that the capitalist ends up with more than he or she started with. In Monopoly, a player with a lot of money can buy more properties, and that is just about all that the player can do. Perhaps he or she will buy a GET OUT OF JAIL FREE card from another player, just in case. But he or she cannot buy better lawyers or better health care or better education. Certainly he or she cannot buy senators or newspaper companies to try to get the rules of Monopoly changed in his or her favor. However, in the real world, it is possible to accumulate resources to acquire many other kinds of resources and privileges, and in a capitalist society, where the entire productive plant is privately owned, Monopoly becomes the master game of the whole society.

In real-world situations, in which the rules are not pre-set, the consequences of human actions on their capacities, resources, identities, and organization very often take the form of accumulation and polarization. Marxist dialectics provides a natural language and conceptual framework for analyzing these structures and processes. A positive feedback loop such as that between resources and access to further resources in Monopoly appears conceptually simple, but the dynamics that result from such feedbacks are complex, nonlinear, and discontinuous. Up to now, in social theory, dialectical analysis has made the main attempts to explore those dynamics. The main attempt to deal with these holistic properties of social structures during the twentieth century was systems theory, but systems theories have been almost entirely concerned with the stabilizing and self-maintaining processes of negative feedbacks, rather than the unstable, self-reinforcing, and self-destroying dynamics that result from positive feedback.

The supporters of "free competition" maintain that competition not only benefits the winners, but also the public. Is this basic claim true? Sometimes, in some limited forms of competition. But it is not true in a fundamental sense. Very often, the drive to get the reward is in contradiction with the way to achieve the best job, and conversely, attaining the reward is not the same as having done the best job. There are two points to consider here: (1) what if the best way to get the biggest *individual reward* in the short run actually goes against what is best for the group as a whole, including often even the individual striver; and (2) *advantages can accumulate* to give the competitor with the fastest start the victory, even if he or she does not have the best ability.

Consider the first point. It is true that runners will often run faster against other runners than when just running against the clock; it is true that the promise of a monetary reward can motivate some people to work harder, and that the promise of a high grade (or the threat of a low grade) can motivate some students to attend class more often or study harder. But imagine a basketball team (the "I" team) where each player is rewarded *only on the number of points he or she scores* and not on whether the team wins the game. Will that team rise to a higher level of overall achievement than another team of equal ability (the "W" team) where each player is *rewarded only if the team wins?* The "W" team will probably beat the "I" team most of the time. Furthermore, it might even be the case that the individual highest scorer might also be from the "W" team, because of the lack of teamwork and, in fact, the level of competition among the "I" team members themselves.

Similarly, if a student is sitting in a room because attendance is mandatory and absences will automatically lower the grade, and if the student really does not want to be there, the same contradiction arises. The immediate "reward" for the school is achieved; higher attendance in the room. But will the long-run goal, more learning, really take place? The drive for grades not only leads to more attendance and studying; it also leads to shortcuts, cramming, taking special courses for the medical school and law school exams to "beat the system" and, in fact, even to cheating itself. It may have been the profit motive that drove the Ford Motor Company to mass-produce automobiles, so that today the United States has the most automobiles in the world. But it was also the profit motive that encouraged Enron, Anderson, and AIG executives to lie to their employees and the public and to bankrupt their companies.

The second point about competition raised above is a little more complex, but it too shows the frequent inconsistency between achievement and final reward. Picture, again, a basketball game. Add just one more set of rules . . . *for every five points ahead* that one team is, *they get to have an extra player on the court* plus four free shots at the basket. Obviously, you can see what will happen. It would be like a game of Monopoly "gone wild." In nearly every case, whichever team gets five points ahead first will get an extra player, probably get ten points ahead, get another extra player, etc. Real competition, the alleged benefit of the system, will vanish. This is often how the corporate structure works. There are exceptions and we often hear them trumpeted in the media; but they are newsworthy exactly because they are so rare. As mergers form giant companies, small businesses have been squeezed out. It is possible for an underdog to win, just as it is possible for a minority child born into poverty to become head of the Chase Manhattan Bank. But how often does it happen? Billionaire Bill Gates dropped out of college—but the college he dropped out of was Harvard. Has the profit-competition system given us the best we can have? Are the economic winners really the winners because they made the greatest contribution to society? And does this drive for profit eventually cause the winners' own profits to drop as well?

How does this work itself out in economics? Once capitalist production is established, self-employed commodity production inexorably gives way to capitalist production. In fact, it is only under capitalist production— the situation where labor power becomes a commodity—that commodity production becomes dominant and invades all other spheres of human relationships so that self-employment is relentlessly reduced. Marx says, correctly, that he is not out to expropriate the producers; capitalism has already done that. Marxists aim to expropriate the expropriators.

Exercise 2.3: Commodity Production and Capitalist Production

Private ownership of means of production may connote a small, self-employed shoemaker who makes and sells shoes. But it may also connote a giant factory where one owner controls the work and livelihood of thousands of workers. How do each of these systems of production influence individual autonomy as well as cultural and political ideas and institutions?

The first 170 pages of *Capital* deal with commodities and exchange relationships. At that point, there is a sudden sea change, a sudden dive down into the productive process. There is a similar transition in the *Grundrisse* and the *Critique*. It is a basic element of Marx's economic analysis. The contradiction between production and exchange is fundamental to Marxist analysis. Below, we have reproduced the transitional passage from *Capital*. Analyze it and answer the questions which follow it. Remember that **commodity production and capitalist factory production** are governed by the same laws, the same rules. And remember to analyze capitalism as a process, understanding the centuries-long transition from dispersed commodity production to concentrated, capitalist factory production. Remember that we live in a social system which is characterized both by commodity production and by factory production. Many jobs operate according to both dynamics. For example, we can picture workers, managers, and capitalists within capitalist factory production, but the petite bourgeoisie are found in commodity production, and small employers and semi-autonomous workers are found in both. In *Capital*, in the sphere of exchange, the capitalist is Mr. Moneybags, someone who just happens to have a stock of money. In the sphere of production, he becomes the owner—the boss.

> The money-owner buys everything necessary for (production), such as raw material, in the market and pays for it at its full value. . . . The consumption of labour-power is completed, as in the case of every other commodity, outside the limits of the market or of the sphere of circulation. Accompanied by Mr. Moneybags and by the possessor of labour-power, we therefore take leave for a time of this noisy sphere, where everything takes place on the surface and in view of all men, and follow them both into the hidden abode of production, on whose threshold there stares us in the face "No admittance except on business." Here we shall see, not only how capital produces, but how capital is produced. We shall at last force the secret of profit making.
>
> This sphere that we are deserting, within whose boundaries the sale and purchase of labour-power goes on, is in fact a very Eden of the innate rights of man. There alone rule Freedom, Equality, Property and Bentham. Freedom, because

both buyer and seller of a commodity, say of labor power, are constrained only by their own free will. The contract as free agents . . . Equality, because each enters into relation with the other, as with a simple owner of commodities, and they exchange equivalent for equivalent. Property, because each disposes only of what is his own. And Bentham because each looks only to himself. The only force that brings them together and puts them in relation with each other, is the selfishness, the gain and the private interests of each. . . .

On leaving this sphere of simple circulation . . . we think we can perceive a change in the physiognomy of our dramatis personae. He who before was the money-owner, now strides in front as capitalist; the possessor of labour-power follows as his labourer. The one with an air of importance, smirking, intent on business; the other, timid and holding back, like one who is bringing his own hide to market and has nothing to expect but—a hiding. (CAP I, pp. 175–76)

Consider these questions:

1. When did groups first arise with slogans of freedom, equality, property, and the greatest good for the greatest number (i.e., Bentham, founder of utilitarianism)? Who were they?
2. Historically and politically, how important are these conceptions of freedom, equality, and property? Do they involve superficial or basic elements of the society?
3. What makes a money-owner a capitalist? List the other social arrangements necessary if capital is to yield a profit.
4. About 1 percent of the population has substantial property income, and most of them hire people to run their property. Some owners jet to the Bahamas; some manage factories; some use alcohol or cocaine; some run for president. They can do whatever they want with their incomes. How does/doesn't that promote freedom, equality, property, and the greatest good for the greatest number of the rest of us?

Suggestions for Further Reading

Overproduction is often used in a narrow sense to apply to the depression/recession stage of the business cycle. We will consider that below. *Forbes* magazine publishes a special issue every autumn that estimates the wealth of the richest people in the United States; while some of the information is not precise, it does offer some insight as to how and where the fortunes were made—much more from property income than from labor. The link between famine and commodity markets is explored in A. Sen, *Poverty and Famines* (Oxford, 1981).

For the view of Monopoly as an example of dialectical, positive feedback, see P. Knapp, *One World*, second edition (Thompson Publishing Group, 2002). The logic of Monopoly is identical to the logic of Risk. In Risk, the players are not individuals, but nations, and the object is not to acquire properties in order to increase your rents, but to acquire territories in order to increase your armies. Since armies, in Risk, are then used to acquire more territories, the logic of the Risk is the same kind of positive feedback as Monopoly: there is a dialectical process of acquisition, polarization, and the game ends when one player takes over the world. P. Knapp, "Evolution, Complex Systems and Dialectic," *Journal for World Systems Research* (5:74–103, 1999) argues that the analyses of such processes of positive feedback is one of the major uncompleted tasks of twenty-first century sociological theory. Because systems theory was the principal twentieth-century way of representing holistic systems, there are many ways of representing Marxian theory as a form of systems theory, e.g., A. Stinchcombe, *Constructing Social Theories* (University of Chicago Press, 1968); P. Sztompka, *System and Function* (Academic, 1974); G. A. Cohen, *Karl Marx's Theory of History: A Defence* (Princeton University Press, 2001); R. Levin, "Dialectics and Systems Theory" in *Science and Society* (special issue, 1998). However, we shall suggest that these all tend to privilege self-maintaining structures of negative feedback, ignoring crucial structures of positive feedback.

SECTION 2.4: WHAT ARE THE DYNAMICS OF PRODUCTION FOR PROFIT?

Capitalist production is immensely dynamic. It invades all other relationships in the society and transforms them, making buying and selling fundamental to every relation in the society. All kinds of relationships which used to be governed mainly by custom, consensus, law, or religion come to be governed by the sale of goods and services. Capitalism expands all over the face of the Earth, and its spread destroys local and parochial bonds. What is the nature of this expansion?

When an area of production develops where there is a higher rate of profit, the company in question makes a lot of money. But then other companies see that the first company is doing well, and they too enter the field. The more companies that enter the field, the more is produced; the more that is produced, the more pressure to lower the price. The more the price is lowered, the more pressure on the profits. The more pressure on profits, the more pressure to produce more and produce it more efficiently. In addition to competition, a company's own production can flood the market, to the detriment of that company's profit. If a company can only make $100 profit on something it used to make $1,000 profit from, then it will have to produce ten times as many to get the same profit. But of course, if more is successfully produced, this further lowers the rate of profit, as the market is flooded with more goods. Businesses are concerned with absolute profit, but they are especially concerned with *rate of profit*, especially in modern corporations where investors demand a return on their investment and are not especially impressed with overall corporate profits if their own rate of return on investment is not high. That is why companies with great wealth still must seek higher rates of profit. Owners of money are forced to look to other spheres of production to maintain profitability. They search all over the world, looking for cheaper labor and cheaper raw materials (which are cheaper because they require less labor and less expensive labor to extract). Owners are forced to revolutionize the production process, but doing so undercuts their profits. Profit is calculated on the total investment. There is an increase in the amount of capital invested for each laborer ("capital deepening," roughly, an increase in the "organic composition of capital"). Therefore, unless the profits extracted from each worker can be forced to rise even faster, the rate of profits falls. Marx formulates some of the developmental tendencies of capitalism in terms of the "failing rate of profit" and the series of countertendencies which capitalists must institute to halt this decline.

Why don't the companies make a deal to divide up the market so that none of them will flood the market? Often that is what they try to do. But there are difficulties in sustaining such agreements, since the companies are in competition with each other. The ups and downs of OPEC are an example of this. Furthermore, even if a single company has a complete monopoly on the production of an item, some of the same pressures exist, because of pressures from abroad, or because other items may be substituted for it. If the head of a company does not move to maximize profits, bankers and investors apply pressure for him or her to do so. And besides, any company which does not grow is gradually left in a backwater, and the economy comes to be dominated by companies which do grow. Profits—surplus value—are the stuff of growth.

As the rate of profit falls, the weaker and smaller companies fall away, either run out of business or bought out by the larger businesses. Even "craft businesses" such as barbershops and shoe repair shops are vulnerable—the barbershops by the large companies that can employ cheap labor in bigger shops and undercut the price, and the large companies that can use very cheap labor from all over the world to produce new shoes for less than what an individual shoe repair shop would have to charge to just stay in business. Sometimes, even larger businesses are overcome by intense pressure, especially from mergers by their opponents and from international competition. This leads to a process of increasing monopolization, with a larger and larger market share falling into fewer and fewer hands. The intensity of competition increases among the winners, as in a game of musical chairs or the end of a game of Monopoly. A given company may want only to be left alone to quietly go about its business. But they know that if someone else gets to a technological innovation, a market, a stock of raw materials, or a supply of labor first, then they may be frozen out. The companies try other means to maintain their rates of profit—mainly by lowering their labor costs or their raw materials costs. It is difficult to lower the costs of raw materials, since they either have to enter the raw materials industry (say, by buying mines) or they have to find ways of pressuring their suppliers, who may be overseas. Even then, the government or the military may be able to help get suppliers who are cooperative, but lowering raw materials costs is difficult. Lowering the costs of labor is the main way to produce rapid results.

What are the fundamental social consequences of this frantic search for profits? It has many consequences, but perhaps the fundamental one is the creation of the proletariat and the creation of a labor market. We said that commodity production was the focus of two contradictions: the contradiction between use value and exchange value and the contradiction between general labor and particular labor. As an object of use, every commodity is qualitatively different from every other. As an object of exchange, every commodity can be measured on the same scale; every commodity has its price. The qualitative difference between commodities corresponds to the fact that every commodity is the product of a particular kind of labor; linen is the product of weaving and coats are the product of tailoring. The quantitative comparability of different commodities corresponds to the fact that they are a product of simple, abstract, homogeneous labor; they are a product of some fraction of the total labor of the society.

One might object that all labor is qualitatively different and incomparable, that the very notion of general labor is an abstraction. Indeed it is. Marx notes that only at the end of a long social development can the concept of "labor in general" appear. The concept of simple, abstract, homogeneous labor is the intellectual reflection of the long historical process of the development of a labor market. Moreover, Marx comments,

> There are, however, states of society in which one and the same man does tailoring and weaving alternately, in which case, these two forms of labour are mere modifications of the labour of the same individual, and no special and fixed functions of different persons; just as the coat which our tailor makes one day, and the trousers which he makes another day, imply only a variation in the labour of one and the same individual. Moreover, we see at a glance that, in our capitalist society, a given portion of human labour is, in accordance with the varying demand, at one time supplied in the form of tailoring, at another in the form of weaving. This change may possibly not take place without friction, but take place it must. (CAP I, p. 44)

Imagine the death and replacement of a tailor in a little feudal village 500 years ago. What is the "friction" preventing most people from moving into the slot he vacated? A partial list might include the following: poor communication and probably law required that that replacement be a local person;

traditional bonds and obligations created other restrictions; custom and possibly law required that the replacement be of a given sex and religion; and kinship was a barrier, maybe the replacement had to be the tailor's son or nephew. Certainly property laws passed on the tools and shop through kinship, and it's hard to sew without a needle. The movement of people from job to job is not frictionless today, but virtually every barrier has lowered. The needle goes with the job. There are barriers of nation, sex, kinship, religion, and property. Often this means that there is more than one labor market—that the labor market is socially segmented. Capitalism is not a liberal utopia. But compared to feudalism, for some purposes, everyone in a country is in one labor market, and for other purposes everyone in the world is part of one labor market. What are the implications of this?

All sociologists, not only Marx, have believed that this process is connected to a phenomenon of immense sociological importance. For Durkheim as for Weber, the disappearance of local, traditional, **particularistic** bonds and relationships is the key development in modem social structure. A system based on passing one's position on to a relative is fundamentally different from a system based upon impersonal, social, universalistic rules. Durkheim, Marx, and Weber all analyze this shift and see it as the key to many other social changes. It is not just the development of means of communication and transportation—though these are products of labor which are a function of capitalism. The collision between the world market and local bonds is one of the keys to social change in the last three generations. Capitalism as a system comes into collision with kinship and particularism, but it is also based upon them.

Marxists believe that someday the main barriers of class, race, sex, nation, etc., will be destroyed; the international working class will be the human race. They do not believe that those barriers have already disappeared. Those barriers will not vanish all by themselves. Marx did not treat them as something one could merely watch disappear. Instead he constructed an organization to combat them as the principal enemies of humankind. The concept of working class internationalism is one of the keys, if not the key, to Marxist politics. Marx's view that it would be possible to destroy such barriers was based on the analysis of the many ways that the development of a world system of capitalism had already pulled most people out of particularistic communities based upon ties of personal dependence. It did not make us a single human race; but it created the basis for our doing so.

Exercise 2.4: Different Rules for Monopoly: Liberal Reforms to Slow Down Polarization or Change of the Game.

We have seen that many processes have a dynamic similar to a game of Monopoly, in which the rich get richer and the poor get poorer. We further saw that this dynamic results whenever access to further resources is, at least partly, a function of how many resources one already has. While the game of Monopoly only looks at rents and properties, in the real world, many other kinds of resources become concentrated in the hands of the owners of capital. We also saw that there are some respects in which the concentration of resources is even more prominent in the real world than in the game of Monopoly. While in the game of Monopoly the only players are individuals and each individual starts with exactly the same amount, in the real world families and other groups start with very different amounts of cash and can make all kinds of alliances to gain further advantages.

Think about various ways that one could change the rules of Monopoly to slow or reverse the process of polarization or to make it more fair (see discussion of these questions below). (1) What are some rules that would work in the actual game of Monopoly? (2) What other kinds of rules would be needed in the real world? (3) Think about coalitions of various kinds. **How will organization and group solidarity affect the play of the game?**

Question 1: The dynamic of Monopoly is that of positive feedback, similar to having a speaker behind a microphone, so that the amplified output of the speaker is fed back into the microphone. The system is unstable. It explodes. What one needs to do to prevent the high-pitched squeal that results is to move the microphone behind the speaker—to eliminate the feedback. Is it possible to do that in the case of Monopoly? How? Is it possible to do that in the case of capitalism?

In the game of Monopoly, the rules cause polarization to occur very rapidly. A game ends in a couple of hours, and players rarely get to circle the board as many as thirty times. The rules that cause this to happen include:

1. The amount of money you get for passing Go is tiny compared to rents on a hotel.
2. You need a monopoly of the same color properties to build.
3. Taxes and other elements uncorrelated with property are small.
4. There is no real income except property income (rents).

Obviously, any of these rules can be changed, and most of the political conflict during the twentieth century involved struggles about such issues: progressive taxation, health, education and welfare policies to insure that the children of the poor get some opportunities, even if they are not the same as those of children of the elite, borrowing credit unions and cooperatives.

A little change in the rules, such as increasing the money for passing Go by $100, will make a little difference. A big change (such as increasing the money for passing Go to $5,000) might prevent polarization from occurring.

Question 2: In the real world, the concentration of resources occurs in many different spheres: health, education, status, political power. These were central issues for twentieth century capitalism, and they will continue to be central issues as long as capitalism persists. The decisive thing is that the rules are not made by some neutral party, from outside the system. Different groups, with different resources for making their voices heard, and with different interests, have a push and pull about the rules. Someone with billions of dollars has billions of dollars to spare for making their voice heard, should they decide that it is very important. Someone with little savings, who is having trouble paying the rent or the mortgage, probably has nothing to spare. For example, election rules in the United States ensure that wealthy people are about twice as likely to vote as poor people, and so two-thirds of the electorate comes from the top half of incomes. The Supreme Court's *Citizen's United* decision of 2010 made it unconstitutional to prevent a huge corporation from buying expensive political ads whose costs are often beyond the reach of individual candidates and from flooding (or threatening to flood) the media during a campaign to destroy any candidate that fails to protect or extend that corporation's legal advantages.

Question 3: Ultimately, any game of accumulation, in which one's access to resources is a function of the resources that one already has will tend to polarize, more or less rapidly. And ultimately, those with a lot of resources will be interested in using those resources to make sure that the rules give them and their children superior life chances. In Monopoly, players are not allowed to make coalitions against other individuals or groups, but real world capitalism promotes group disadvantage in many different ways. An individual may be disadvantaged by the disadvantages of those around him or her; growing up in a poor family, neighborhood, or group can hurt one's life chances. Moreover, the existence of poor, disadvantaged, or vulnerable groups may be an active benefit to employers, landlords, and other property owners. We saw that the objective interest of capitalists may be to destroy any process that raises the floor of life chances in the society ("Shmoos") and the accumulation of advantages or disadvantages will often lead to qualitative differences in life chances. The relationship of class inequalities to qualitative characteristics such as race, gender, ethnicity, language, religion, or nationality is one of the foremost issues of Marxian dialectics.

Suggestions for Further Reading

Gunnar Myrdal's analysis of cumulative causation, *An American Dilemma* (Harper & Row, 1944) and *Asian Drama* (20th Century Fund, 1964), led to his Nobel Prize in Economics in 1978. More recently R. Blauner, *Still the Big News: Racial Oppression in America* (Temple University Press, 2001) and S.

Steinberg, *Turning Back* (Beacon, 1995) criticized the idea that the American creed was the principle source of the progressive movement.

SECTION 2.5: WHY IS THERE UNEMPLOYMENT?

Marxist social science emphasizes how capitalism is characterized by contradictions. On a number of different levels, there are two developments happening at once—there is a contradiction between the forces and the relations of production and there is development of science and technology and skills and machinery. All of these are good and useful, except that the capitalist relations mean that we're already gagging on what we've got. There is an increase in use values, but at the same time, things are not and cannot be produced simply because they are useful; they are produced only because they are wanted by those who have money to buy them. Because things are not produced to fulfill needs, crying needs coexist with waste, luxuries, and excess. While thousands of children suffer from malnutrition, more is spent on a single debutante ball than it would take to feed them. Oprah Winfrey reportedly spent several million dollars on a birthday party for herself. There is no money for food stamps, except when it serves the big corporations, but there is money for mink coats and for thousand-dollar-a-plate dinners to oppose food stamps. Farmers are paid by the government not to grow crops, or paid to grow crops and food is left to rot even as millions of people go hungry. The market is "free" of "bureaucratic" controls, except when it serves the big corporations, but at the same time that means that workers are organized into immense "command economies," subject to close supervision, in a structure of ownership which is often passed from one person to another by inheritance. The system is driven forward by the fact that competition is devouring itself.

Perhaps the most striking contradiction to capitalism's dynamism and the claims for capitalism's efficiency is unemployment, the coexistence of joblessness with idle productive forces. At the same time that millions of people are destroyed by lack of jobs, a large percentage of the productive capacity of the country is wasted. Unemployment is immensely important both dynamically and in human terms. Many studies have documented the massive human destruction and waste resulting from unemployment. We contrasted explanations of unemployment which depend on the attributes of individuals and which try to explain why Fred Jones is unemployed, considering social structure, and why the level of unemployment is as it is. It is time to pursue this topic.

From one point of view, everyone is against unemployment, depressions, and recessions. But is unemployment really equally against the interests of everyone in the society? Aren't there some people who think that a depression—or at least a recession—though unfortunate in some respects, is nevertheless necessary in others? Indeed there are. And they happen to be the most powerful and influential people in this society. At a time when millions of people are out of work, *Time, Newsweek,* and *Fortune* feature analyses that say we should "squeeze the fat out of the labor market." What is the issue?

The price of labor power is not determined in the firm. In a sense it is not determined in markets at all. What people are willing to do, for how long, and at what wage is largely a function of what alternatives exist. A host of different political, organizational, and social forces play an important role. From a Marxist perspective, battles over the cost of labor power are the central issues of capitalist society; in one form or another, they are pervasive. But in all this, the key to the social and historical subsistence package is the **industrial reserve army.** Whenever a worker or a group of workers is not willing to work hard enough, long enough, or cheap enough, the boss needs to be able to take them to the door of the plant and point to the other (unemployed) people who want that job. This is the fundamental control over the price and the conditions of labor. If there is full employment, if everyone has a job, then this fundamental control does not exist. As was suggested in exercise 2.2, when and only when you can get one group of workers to work for less, the wage structure of all the other workers is undercut. Unemployment is the main determinant of the price of labor. Profitability within the enterprise is determined by things which occur outside. Above all, capitalists in all times and places have to be concerned about their supplies of labor. If people don't want to work for what a capitalist wants to pay them, doing what they are told to do, then the capitalist can't make a dime. A more colorful age spoke of "the whip of hunger." The unemployment of some people is not something that only affects the 5, 10, or 33 percent of the population who are unemployed. It drives down the wages of those who are employed. It is the fundamental lever by which the wage level is set and profits maintained.

Every liberal (procapitalist) analyst would like to get rid of unemployment, but unemployment is the main way that workers are forced to work cheaper, longer, and more compliantly. In the 1950s and 1960s liberal theorists believed that the whip of hunger was out of date. They believed that it was possible under capitalism to maintain full employment by a variety of government programs. Very few liberals believe that anymore. They deplore and minimize the amount of unemployment and hunger. But it is hard for them to deny the facts in front of their eyes. At the time of this book's revision, the official rate of unemployment is over 10 percent, and the rate of actual unemployment (including those involuntarily out of the labor market or employed part time) is nearly twice that. So undeniable, actual unemployment tends to be explained away: "Someone made a mistake; it is temporary; it's the fault of the Chinese; it will soon go away."

One liberal analysis of unemployment sees it as a consequence of frictions and automation. "It is the by-product of progress," said Henry Ford. Does increased automation and technology mean that unemployment is inevitable? In one sense, the obvious answer is, "Of course not." Over time, unemployment does not go up and down with technological change. And one can obviously imagine a society with lots of science and technology and no unemployment. But ours is not an imaginary society. In this real, capitalist society, **technology** is one of the main ways that you can get workers to bid against each other. If all clerical workers demand a living wage, but electronics workers in Taiwan or Silicon Valley work cheaper, then a capitalist can set the "dead" labor of technology against living labor. Technology makes human labor more efficient so that it takes less labor to produce the same amount of goods. This means that some jobs will be lost if exactly the same amount is produced. In theory more could be produced, sharing the benefits of productivity with the society as a whole while those who lose their jobs can be educated into scientific fields with limitless potential for growth and human betterment. But the job of capitalism is not to increase jobs any more than it is to increase goods; it is to increase profits.

Another mainstream liberal analysis of unemployment is voiced by many neoconservatives. It sees unemployment as due to the obstinacy of workers. If only they would work cheap enough, then it would be so profitable to employ them that no capitalist could resist. They would generate so many profits that the capitalist would employ others with the money burning holes in their pockets. Then wages would rise. This analysis is the archetype of all liberal economic analyses. In one form or another, every liberal-capitalist economic analysis rests on the claim that the only practical solution to all economic problems must come out of the hide of the working class. Whenever the economic machine begins to stagnate or shudder, it can always be lubricated by squeezing the working class a little harder. If only workers could be forced to work cheaper, longer, more compliantly, then more would be produced, then U.S. goods would be competitive in world markets, and everyone would be better off.

In this liberal analysis, the capitalist stands for the general interest. The capitalist squeezes workers for our sake; the capitalist organizes production for our sake; the capitalist makes profits for our sake; no doubt the capitalist eats expensive caviar for our sake. The analysis says that if the resistance of workers can be broken, so that people are forced to work harder for less money, then everyone is better off because more is produced more cheaply. All workers would work at their marginal level of productivity, all profits would decline to a minimum, working conditions would be as safe as workers wanted them to be, everyone would have the goods they need, and there would be no unemployment. Has this ever happened?

Are "we all" better off when workers are squeezed more? If you are un-employed, then being used as a club against the rest of the working class does not make you better off. If you are a worker, being forced to work at a more frantic pace, for longer, for less money, to support someone's sum-mer house on the French Riviera, does not make you better off. The human cost is measured not only in hundreds of thousands of injuries and nervous breakdowns, but also in indirect costs. Large sections of major cities look as though they had been bombed. People put bars on their windows, so that they live in a cage. Many put pistols under their pillows. Human relations decay, and it still does not keep the economy from stagnating. No matter who you are, the disasters and breakdowns of the capitalist system have never been prevented or reduced by remedies of breaking the resistance of workers and lowering their standard of living. Later we shall examine the brutal, vicious kind of society that does result. Profits are not what makes us better off; Marxists would say that the main thing that will make us bet-ter off is getting rid of the profit system. Short of that, there are defensive, reform-oriented tactics that workers use. Some of these help unite the work-ing class, but others are actually harmful to the working class as a whole.

Exercise 2.5: Correlates and Noncorrelates of Occupation

Try to predict what different occupational groups will say about some com-mon social issues. Make a short list of common attitudes such as, "politi-cians are crooks," "women's place is in the home," "too much money is spent on welfare," or "sex before marriage is wrong." Which will be more common among blue-collar workers? Which among those in white-collar occupations? Which will show no difference between different groups?

How important is one's job? How important is one's social class? Does it affect the way that one votes? Does it affect one's taste in music? Does it affect the likelihood that one leaves the lights on when making love? Does it affect the way that one says "potato"? Is there anything it doesn't affect?

Within sociology, there is disagreement about the nature and effects of class. Some studies have found social class to be related to voting, music, lovemaking, speech, and virtually everything else. Others argue that it is related to almost nothing. Some people argue an Archie Bunker theory of class that says that most white workers are racist, sexist, and conservative. (This viewpoint has very powerful political implications. If the working class is conservative, change must come from elite groups.) Other soci-ologists have argued the opposite, the "you have nothing to lose but your chains" theory, according to which the working class is the main progres-sive force for change now and throughout history. As to the nature of class, some sociologists have argued that social status is the most important element of class. (Social status is honor or prestige. A man addressed as

"Sir" has more status than one called "Mr.," who has more than one called "Fred," who has more than a "boy.") Other sociologists have argued that relationship to means of production (whether one lives off profit, salaries, wages, sale of one's product, etc.) is most important.

Table 2.2 presents typical data relevant to such questions. Use it to test your own theories and to develop better theories. An adequate theory of class is an important task which has eluded the best minds in sociology. The data in the table are taken from the *1982 General Social Survey*. In this book, we shall almost always use data from this source because it is widely available in many schools for use in sociology and political science courses. The data are given over and over again, and so it is possible to look at trends using current data. You should check anything we assert using these data for yourself, and you can further investigate anything which seems relevant.

Table 2.2 shows the relation of occupation to various attitudes, behaviors, and beliefs in the survey. Occupation is only one part of class, but it is an important one. Each row of the table portrays the relationship between two variables: occupation and one attitude, behavior, or belief. The population is divided into four occupational categories: upper white-collar, lower white-collar, upper blue-collar, and lower blue-collar. Upper white-collar includes businessmen, small proprietors (the owner of a small shop), professionals (a lawyer or teacher), technical workers (a dental technician), and managerial workers (a supervisor). Lower white-collar includes clerical workers (the postman), or sales workers (a cashier at a supermarket). Upper blue-collar includes skilled workers (mechanics) and crafts workers (a carpenter). Lower blue-collar includes service workers, laborers, and operatives (an assembly line worker).

This is not all there is to class. It is not what Marx usually meant by class, and it does not include the occupational divisions which Marxists think are most important. In general, the difference between blue-collar and white-collar is a kind of *status* difference. By contrast, Marx and Marxists usually define class in terms of relationship to means of production, according to who owns and controls the means of production and the product. For Marx, the difference between employers and employees, between bosses and workers, is more important. Some carpenters are employees, others are self-employed, and some employ others. As we shall see, most of the uppermost group are workers rather than bosses and some of the lowest group are bosses rather than workers. Nevertheless, occupation is one important aspect of class. A good theory of the effects of class should predict the differences between these broad occupational groupings. That has been a main focus of American sociology.

The first thing you should do with the table is to cover up the actual percentages and predict roughly what you think the total responses will be. What percentages of the total population do you think will believe that, "The lot of the average man is getting worse," "The courts are not harsh enough on criminals,"

Table 2.2   Correlates of Occupation

GSS Variable	Total	Professional Technical	Clerical Sales	Craft	Unskilled
ANOMIA5: Lot of average man getting worse (% "agree")	65%	52%	68%	69%	68%
ANOMIA6: Not fair to bring child into world (% "agree")	34%	19%	32%	41%	39%
ANOMIA7: Officials not interested in average man (% "agree")	65%	55%	61%	73%	72%
ATTEND: Attend religious services (% more than once a month)	44%	45%	48%	33%	40%
COMMUN: Feeling about communism (% "OK" or "good")	13%	17%	12%	12%	14%
COURTS: Courts dealing with criminals (% not harsh enough)	43%	41%	38%	51%	43%
FEWORK: Should women work? (% approve)	74%	86%	78%	72%	68%
HAPPY: General happiness (% saying "very happy")	33%	40%	36%	29%	29%
JOBINC: High income (% listing as most important aspect of job)	25%	21%	19%	31%	31%
JOBMEANS: Work gives feeling of accomplishment (% most important)	41%	52%	39%	43%	36%
JOBSEC: No danger of being fired (% most important)	10%	4%	4%	15%	15%
MEMNUM: No. voluntary assn. memberships (% 2 or more)	42%	55%	43%	44%	30%
NATFARE: Fed. money on welfare (% "too little")	53%	45%	54%	50%	58%
NATRACE: Fed. money solving problems (% "too little")	59%	34%	63%	58%	59%
NEWS: How often respondent reads newspapers (% every day)	54%	63%	58%	55%	45%
PREMARSX: Sex before marriage (wrong sometimes or never)	60%	63%	63%	65%	60%

Table 2.2 (continued)   Correlates of Occupation

GSS Variable	Total	Professional Technical	Clerical Sales	Craft	Unskilled
RACMAR: Favor laws against racial intermarriage (% "yes")	29%	11%	28%	36%	37%
SOCCOMMUN: Spend evening with neighbor (sev. times/month or more)	37%	37%	34%	33%	41%
SOCFRND: Spend evening with friend (several times/month or more)	43%	43%	53%	36%	37%
TVHOURS: Hours per day spent watching TV (% more than 1)	75%	60%	75%	81%	81%
TOTAL	24%	26%	13%	37%	34%
	1506	331	362	181	512

or "Sex before marriage is only wrong some of the time"? These data allow you to check your impressions about how common these attitudes and behaviors are by looking in the column of total percentages. The General Social Survey contains a large and well-chosen sample of people. The total at the bottom of the table shows that there were 1,506 people in the survey. While the people in a survey are never exactly like those in the population at large, a large, well-chosen sample means that the survey adequately reflects the population. If 65 percent of the sample agreed with the statement, "The lot of the average man is getting worse," you can be pretty sure that about 65 percent of the overall population would do so (see appendix A). But it is not the total proportions which are important. Mainly, you should predict in each row whether there will be differences between people in different occupations and, if so, what the differences will be. That is, you should test theories about the differences between occupational groups. Since it is a good sample, the percentages within each occupational group in the sample are approximately the same as the differences in the population. Fifty-eight percent of the upper white-collar respondents in the sample agreed, "The lot of the average man is getting worse." You can be sure that very nearly 58 percent of the upper white-collar respondents in the whole population would have done so. The attitudes, behaviors, and beliefs in Table 2.2 are referred to by their General Social Survey acronym—a code of eight letters or less that refers to one of the questions. If you want to find out more about the questions or the sample, you should consult a General Social Survey codebook. For those students who have not taken a course in statistical methods (and for other students who would like a review), appendix A of the first edition online reviews topics in quantitative methods.

Getting a theory which accurately predicts the differences between various occupational groups seems easy. All of us have an intuitive sense of the difference between lawyers and mechanics on any given item. You need not predict exact percents, but you should try to predict the following: will there be a difference? If so, in what direction? Will blue-collar or white-collar respondents be more likely to give the answer in parentheses? Will the difference be large (more than 15 percent), or small (5–10 percent)? For each question, make a prediction or hypothesis of the effects of occupation, and try to devise a theory that predicts correctly. Note that it is just as important to predict correctly the cases where there is no difference as to predict the cases where there is a difference.

Our intuitive sense of the differences between lawyers and mechanics is often right, but it is not infallible. One of the reasons it is often wrong is that we often pick up our impressions from TV shows which give a distorted picture of the class structure. Getting a theory which always predicts correctly whether and what differences you will find turns out to be hard. What is needed is not memorizing these particular attitudes at this particular point in time. A powerful theory of class would predict correctly all the effects of different aspects of class. But it would also correctly predict how the patterns change over time, in response to changes in the economy, organization, and political forces. The construction of such a theory has eluded American sociology.

The theory that class is related to almost nothing does not do well. Occupation shows strong relationships with most of the variables (seventeen out of the twenty). The only variables with which occupation is unrelated are COMMUN (blue-collar workers are not more anti-communist than anyone else), SOCCOMMUN (they do not do more or less neighboring), and PREMARSX (they do not have a different attitude toward premarital sexual relations.) What we call the Archie Bunker theory also does poorly. The variables which are *not* related to occupation are some of the main ones which the Bunker theory says should be so related. Moreover, the Bunker theory often predicts incorrectly. While blue-collar workers are somewhat more likely to support harsher courts and laws against intermarriage, on other issues (such as welfare) they are considerably more liberal than white-collar workers.

Suggestions for Further Reading

On stratification: a bibliography of recent titles on stratification would be longer than this whole book! American sociology was long dominated by the Bunker theory, technically called the "thesis of working class authoritarianism" and developed by M. Lipset, *Political Man* (Doubleday, 1960). This view was demolished by R. Hamilton, *Class and Politics in the U.S.* (Wiley, 1972, pp. 399–506) as well as A. Levinson, *The Working Class Majority*

(Penguin, 1974), and others. Rhonda Levine, *Social Class and Stratification: Classic Statements and Theoretical Debates* (Rowman and Littlefield, 2006) gives the major works. The thesis that class affects little was recently put forward by J. Davis, "Achievement Variables and Class Culture," *American Sociological Review* 47:569. For a critique, see P. Knapp and B. Jones, "Class, Occupation, and Education," *Sociological Viewpoints* 4:17–45 (1988). One corrective to the neglect of class in stratification studies was R. Levine, S. McNall, and R. Fantasia, *Bringing Class Back In* (Westview, 1991). Approaches toward Marxism that are much more consistent with that taken here are covered in R. Levine and J. Lambcke, eds., *Recapturing Marxism* (Praeger, 1987). A useful recent introduction to class in the United States is M. Schwalbe, *Rigging the Game* (Oxford, 2008).

SECTION 2.6: WHO BENEFITS FROM RACISM AND SEXISM?

Who benefits from racism and sexism? Where do they come from? Marxists and many other sociologists think that the answers to these two questions are linked. If there is an intractable social problem—if something persists over a long period of time even though it hurts a very large number of people—then someone is probably getting something out of it. If it is really difficult to change, then probably the groups dominant in the society are benefiting from it. Rather than seeing racism and sexism as isolated, individual psychological problems, Marxism examines how they are connected to social processes and the class structure.

Some theorists say that Marx thought that the only important divisions in the society are class divisions. The way that class divisions combine and interact with other divisions has been discussed in chapter 1. Capitalism creates divisions because that makes it easier to control and to extract a profit from a labor force, and the same profit imperative generates divisive ideologies of racism, sexism, nationalism, among others. Marx argued that such divisions can be key to who wins class struggles at certain junctures. Over the course of time, what happens to those divisions?

On the one hand, the development of the capitalist world market homogenizes labor. The search for new fields of profitable investment, new markets, and new supplies of cheap labor, forces capital to batter down barriers of tradition, nation, language, race, religion, and custom. Yet there is one barrier, one division, which capitalism does not and cannot eradicate: **class** divisions. *And because of that, the leveling process is twisted, perverted, and often reversed.* It is not a simple homogenizing process. Some divisions are created for the first time. Others are elaborated into grotesque forms. It is as though a river rushing down to the sea is dammed by an insuperable, impenetrable obstacle, creating enormous pools, lakes, and swamps. This contradictory process has appeared and reappeared previously. Now is the time to examine it a little more carefully.

Before immersing ourselves in the economic and historical processes, let's step back and get an overview. From a Marxist perspective, class conflict is the fundamental social process in class society. Conflicts create unities and divisions, and in a conflict, unity is the key to victory. Super-exploitation—paying one group of workers less than the average—has a powerful effect on wages and profits. Marxists analyze the ideas of racism in terms of their material basis in super-exploitation. Beyond merely getting more profits, it is a matter of life or death for the capitalist class to get various segments of the working class divided. The capitalist class has enormous resources to foster such divisions in the production process; it has direct control over what people do, with whom, for what rewards; it sits astride the political system, as well as all the other institutions of communication and information. Most sizable organizations which might serve as a nucleus of working class unity or might transmit information promoting that unity are owned or controlled by the ruling class.

The newspapers and churches, the schools and the political parties, the unions and the neighborhood organizations, all to one degree or another are dominated by the capitalist class. Those which are not owned can usually be influenced. If the capitalist class has both a powerful interest in creating divisions and also the ability to create them, it seems plausible that it creates the divisions in order to insure its rule. But even if none of this were true, one has a situation in which the rules of the game promote competition, individualism, and selfishness. From "me first" to "my nation first," "my race first," "my sex first," "my ethnic group first," "my city first," and so forth, is merely a matter of applying selfishness in particular policy areas.

Liberal and pluralist theorists argue that racism is not the creation of capitalists. They say that this analysis would require a conscious, far-sighted, and omniscient ruling class. They argue that it is a *conspiracy* theory of racism, a witchcraft theory. "The capitalist class is not that smart," they say. How would they ever be able to figure out that they need workers to be divided? How would they be able to coordinate their efforts? How could they be so nasty? Instead, some liberals say that racism and other kinds of divisiveness are just built into human nature—humankind is inherently nasty. Other liberals say that all such divisions are just a hangover of past events, such as slavery, which is gradually disappearing. But over time, there have been both enormous increases and decreases in all social divisions. Marxists believe that neither that fact nor the timing of the swings over time can be explained from the standpoint of these liberal theories.

The capitalist class doesn't have to be very smart or coordinated to see the advantages of divisions or to foster them. In the ordinary course of events—within a factory, for example—the question whether people can get together or not is an obvious and immediate source of resistance or nonresistance. In creating divisions, what could be more natural than physically segregating groups of workers and paying vulnerable groups—*especially members of racial minority groups and women*—less? That spontaneous tendency for capitalists to divide workers in the workplace is reinforced by the fact that the basic ideology of capitalism is "being out for number one." Certainly, to maintain social peace or to win a section of the minority group to supervise the rest, various sections of the capitalist class will put a damper on overt racism in some settings, even passing laws against it or preaching tolerance. But the fundamental pressures remain. The capitalist class is already elitist, intent on building exclusive status walls around itself. Within the political system, they are already intent on class collaborationism—on the search for bases on which they can appeal to one or another group of workers to say, "You and I are in this together. Let's present a united front against those other groups." There are times when those supposedly "spontaneous" tendencies to produce divisions in factories, neighborhoods, and parties have to be reinforced by more conscious, long-term policies and movements in schools, literature, or other ideological institutions. There have been times in history when individual members of the ruling class have had to see what the keys to the political situation were, and have devoted their immense resources to racist, sexist, and nationalist organizations, or to promoting other divisions. But even without such explicit organizations, the capitalist class has only to follow its own instincts and the tendencies built into the rules of the game—its competitive selfishness and elitism—in order to find the one strategy most likely to assure its continued dominance.

But, in addition to all this, racism is intertwined with capitalism in other ways. Modern racism began with plantation slavery. Modern racism is tightly connected to nationalism and imperialist policies and ideas to be discussed shortly. Above all, capitalism creates enormous inequalities and separates people both physically and in terms of lifestyle. The splitting and segmentation of labor markets reinforces racism, which in turn provides a pool of extra low paid workers which is both directly profitable and which drives down wages and makes it extremely difficult for workers to organize.

This analysis implies that racism benefits bosses and hurts workers. As to the question of who benefits from racism, there is a very sharp empirical difference between Marxist and liberal economics. From a Marxist standpoint (from the standpoint of a class struggle over the product) workers lose and bosses benefit from divisions among workers. From a liberal capitalist standpoint (the standpoint of maximizing production, with labor being paid its marginal product) white workers supposedly benefit and bosses lose from discrimination against blacks. In response to the obvious fact that workers do not have the power to discriminate in hiring and wages while bosses do, liberal theories imply that if bosses discriminate it is because their workers force them to. Empirical data are directly relevant to the question. When there are big race differences, who is better off, workers or bosses? M. Reich has compared different areas to see whether those areas with greater racial differences have more or less inequality *among whites*. Does the race difference appear to have a positive or a negative effect on white incomes at the top and at the bottom?

Reich notes that the neoclassical, marginalist model says that white workers should gain from racial inequalities and bosses should lose. In the marginalist model, the absence of discrimination is the system which is most profitable, and every time a boss pays someone less, he loses. In complete contrast, the Marxist model says that white workers should lose, and white bosses gain. This is because the Marxist model is based on a conflict at the point of production, and so the unity and/or undercutting of wages is the key phenomenon. Since there is a sharp conflict in the predictions of the two models, it is possible to convert them to data.

For each of the fifty largest standard metropolitan areas, Reich collected data on the degree of inequality among white wage earners (G is the Gini index, which is an overall measure of inequality; S_I is the share of the top 1 percent of whites). Reich also collected data on the ratio of median black to median white income (B/W), as well as other measures of racial inequality (SEG is a measure of segregation). Reich also examines data on other variables known to influence the degree of income inequality (M_{FG} is the percentage of employment in manufacturing; W_C is the percentage in white-collar occupations; I_{NC} is the overall level of income.) If you just compare G, the level of inequality among whites, to B/W, the ratio of black to white income, they are negatively correlated at the level of -0.47. The more inequality between blacks and whites (the lower B/W) the *higher* the inequality among whites (the higher G). The more inequality between races, the more inequality among whites. This certainly suggests that discrimination and racism help whites at the top and hurt whites at the bottom. But this effect might be the spurious effect of other processes. To check whether it is, Reich controls other variables known to affect inequality. How does the picture change if one looks at all of the variables we have just listed? Table 2.3 gives the results of three regression analyses of the data.

The three rows give three different analyses with different variables. The first two rows show the effect of racism and various other things on overall inequality among whites. The third row shows the effect of racism and various other things on the income share going to the top income group. All three analyses show approximately the same thing.

Each column shows the effect of some variable, such as segregation, on some measure of income inequality among whites. Since the regression coefficients are unstandardized, the simplest indication of the relative size

Table 2.3   Effects of Race Inequality on Income Inequality

Dependent Variable	Constant	B/W*	SEG	MFG	WC	INC	R^2
G	0.492	−0.097		−0.134	0.066	−0.012	0.685
		(−3.29)		(−5.50)	(1.89)	(−3.49)	
G	0.370		0.069	−0.153	0.055	−0.010	0.642
			(2.09)	(−6.01)	(1.50)	(−2.58)	
S[1]	0.094	−0.059		−0.043	0.029	0.001	0.511
		(−4.32)		(−3.80)	(1.81)	(0.72)	

*t statistics in parentheses
Source: M. Reich, *Racial Inequality* (Princeton, 1981), p.134.

of different effects is the size of t. When it is not close to 0 but is less than −3 or more than +3, then one is dealing with a powerful effect. In the first row, one sees that with controls, the effect of racial inequality (a low B/W) is still to increase inequality among whites. (The effect of B/W on inequality among whites is -0.097; t is -3.29.) Inequality is also greater if there is a lower proportion of the work force in manufacturing or with a lower overall income. Together, these variables account for the better part of the variation in inequality, which suggests that no conceivable control of other variables is likely to affect this finding very much. In the second row, one sees that the results are fundamentally similar if one uses the degree of segregation rather than the relation of black income to white income. (The sign of the coefficients is opposite. When there is more segregation, the ratio of black to white income is lower. Segregation has a positive effect on inequality: 0.069; t is 2.09.) Finally, in the third row, one sees that racial inequality has the effect of increasing the income of the top stratum of whites, just as it has the effect of lowering the income of lower whites and increasing white inequality overall.

While only one study, these findings help provide support for a Marxist conflict model of income, rather than a neoclassical marginal productivity model.

They also have practical significance. Racism appears to be in the objective interests of white bosses and in the objective disinterest of white workers. Does that mean that white workers are never racist? No. Learning whether something objectively makes a given group better off or worse off does not tell you what that group will feel or do. People may not see or act on their objective interests. But, in contrast to views that objective interests don't really exist at all ("Who is to say what is in someone's objective interest?"), we believe that it makes sense to say that overall, white workers are objectively hurt by racism. We must temper this statement with the reality that it is not just erroneous ideas and capitalist propaganda that reinforce racist ideas among white people. There are short-term material advantages (biases in housing, employment, and education) that do make life significantly less oppressive for many white people than it is for members of certain minority groups. And these advantages can even mean life or death. Marxists should not minimize the intensity of racist oppression nor underestimate how racist ideas get reinforced with material bribes. But Marxists believe that no section of the working class fundamentally benefits from capitalism, and racist exploitation, oppression, and racist ideas sustain capitalism. That is why Marxists assert that in a fundamental sense, racist oppression and racist ideas are against the interests of the whole working class.

It is of obvious practical importance to learn who is objectively hurt and who objectively gains from any arrangement you wish to explain or change. If something they are doing is objectively hurting someone, then their behavior is objectively contradictory—it runs counter to what they want and are trying to accomplish. There is an objective basis for resolving the contradiction by having the person change their behavior. Finally, it provides powerful evidence that one of the main causes of the racial inequality is the dominance of a class of people who benefit from it.

When exploring how divisions are fostered in the working class, the ubiquitous reality of sexist oppression, which saturates every aspect of modern life, must be understood. A few radical theorists dismiss the issue of sexism, the oppression of women, as being relatively unimportant. "Class is the principal important factor," they say, "and when capitalism is abolished all people will be equal." At the opposite extreme are those who say that class analysis is irrelevant to the issue of sexism, that the fundamental conflict is between males and females. Marxists have attempted to understand the complex and reinforcing interplay between sex and class divisions. In this light, there has been renewed interest in research in how the segmentation of the labor market interacts with sexism. This is not to say that sexism is just like racism, for obviously it is not. On the other hand, sexism today, like all major institutions, including racism, is not merely an extension of historical and cultural sexism. We live in a capitalist world and major institutions have been cut, molded, shaped, and saturated by capitalist interests. While there are many important aspects of sexism, the sexist division of labor and the operation of a segmented labor market is one of the most important.

The sexist division of labor has many forms. One of the most obvious is on the job. Men and women are often segmented into different labor markets. When they work together, they are often segregated and treated differently. In a cafeteria, for example, male workers might be called "chefs" and female workers might be called "cooks." Even when they have the same responsibilities, male workers usually make much higher wages. The same is true within the university system, factories, farms, and hundreds of other occupations. Because of the organized struggles against sexism, it is a little more difficult today to pay women less than men on jobs where they do exactly the same work. A way to disguise the inequity is to give them different job titles or even somewhat different responsibilities. Often, the responsibilities that the female workers have may even exceed those of the male workers, but because they have different job descriptions, the employers can claim that they deserve different (less) pay. As in the case of race, extra profits can be taken from both sections of the segmented labor market. Much of the very inexpensive labor in the "global assembly line"—especially of clothing and electronics—is done by women, who increasingly are becoming a larger and larger percentage of the proletariat.

Another aspect of sexist oppression lies within the way the capitalists want families to function. The labor that many women do as they take primary responsibility for raising children and maintaining the household is, in fact, labor that is necessary for the capitalist system to survive. Raising children is helping to produce the next generation of laborers, and all the household tasks associated with that are similarly necessary for the maintenance of the social structure. However, the capitalists do not directly pay the (usually female) household workers. Instead, they are supposed to live off of part of the wages that the husbands receive from their jobs. It is especially insulting when women who receive some government assistance to help raise children are not considered part of the working class. Raising children not only is "work," it is work that is necessary for the maintenance of civilization.

As with other aspects of capitalism, the sexist division of labor is also riddled with contradictions. In some circumstances, the capitalists want to keep women in the home as unpaid family laborers; in other circumstances, they press women into the workforce when they need them to serve as lower wage workers in certain industries; in still other circumstances, they even allow some women access to higher paying jobs. But maximization of profits and social stability are critical needs for capitalism, and the fundamentally subordinate role of women remains an inherent aspect of the profit system.

Finally, the oppression of women also has an aspect that might appear to be totally separate from the economic structure of society. Capitalism often encourages men to treat women as objects, things, commodities to possess. Just as capitalism uses the possession and control over other commodities as a bait to get men to ignore the true sources of their alienation and escape into a fantasy land where they can pretend to be master and king over their possessions, so too the treatment of women as commodities diverts men away from understanding the roots of their powerlessness. In this sense, it shares an aspect with racist ideology. However, the immediate material reinforcement of this myth can sometimes be quite powerful. Men can sometimes receive immediate physical satisfaction, such as relaxing while a wife does housework, that can more intensely reinforce the myth that men benefit in a *fundamental* way from the exploitation and oppression of women.

Racism and sexism, then, play far more complex roles in society than simply being "wrong ideas." Nor are they explainable as minor aspects of general economic oppression. They are deeply intertwined with economic and political structures and can only be understood in those contexts. The explosion of research in critical Marxist and neo-Marxist sociology has led to a great deal of empirical and theoretical research in these fields, and current journals are always presenting recent studies of these issues.

Exercise 2.6: Monopoly with Coalitions: Group Interests

Consider which groups will tend to promote the processes and arrangements that lead to equality and inclusion and which groups will promote arrangements that lead to greater polarization, division, and inequality. Imagine that there is a closed system which, for simplicity, consists of white workers, black workers, white bosses, and black bosses. Imagine that there is a correlation between race and class, so that the great bulk of bosses is white and that there is some degree of racial and class solidarity. Also, we have seen that there are known processes that will tend to increase the amount of inequality and separation between bosses and workers and the amount of inequality and segregation between whites and blacks. What are some of the processes that will consolidate "durable inequality"—the existence of inequality that continues generation after generation, associated with categorical traits such as race (skin color), language, or gender? What are some of the processes that will cause these groups to support progressive policies? What are some of the mechanisms that will cumulatively disadvantage groups such as women, African Americans, Spanish speakers, or Muslims, under capitalism?

The mainstream economic models are based on the assumption that everyone is paid what they are worth. However, sociologists and Marxists have shown many different ways in which labor markets are segmented. People who get locked into the segments of the labor market with poor wages, poor security, poor benefits, and poor working conditions usually cannot work their way into the other segments. Racism, stereotyping, and urban segregation are among the processes segmenting the labor market. In different capitalist societies, the particular categorical groups that come to be cumulatively disadvantaged are different. Often, the only mechanism considered by mainstream sociology is stereotyping, leading to individual prejudice and discrimination, but such analyses ignore the ways that property holders may benefit from the exclusion, the vulnerability, or the divisions among disadvantaged groups.

We saw that the main Marxian models of economic and social processes involve positive feedback, like that in a game of Monopoly: players with resources are in an advantaged position to get more resources. The logic of the situation is one of polarization, increased inequality, alienation, and exploitation: those with advantages get to make the rules that consolidate their advantages; the rich get richer and the poor get poorer. We noted further that many theorists have argued that this process occurs between groups as well as between individuals. It is often families, communities, neighborhoods, or racial, ethnic and, national groups that accumulate the advantages or disadvantages, whether those are physical resources such as a home and bank account, or intangible resources such as health, political influence, contacts, or education.

We have seen that there are complex processes by which racial or ethnic disadvantages can reinforce each other and they can reinforce structures of segregation or stereotyping, as well as being reinforced by them. Joe Feagin has shown that racial inequality is a self-reinforcing process which he analyzes in terms of systemic racism. The inequality between, say, a Virginia slaveholding family (whom we can call William and Priscilla, for concreteness) and their slaves (whom we might call John and Mary) does not end with William and Priscilla's death. The advantaged descendants of William and Priscilla continue to accumulate advantages. Nor does it end with the abolition of slavery in 1865 or with the dismantling of Jim Crow a century later, because the structure of advantages/disadvantages has a self-reinforcing dynamic. Although both the nineteenth century abolition of slavery, and the twentieth century abolition of Jim Crow were progressive, neither attempted to dismantle and distribute the results of exploitation. Both put in place structures that continued the process in a moderated form.

Charles Tilly has analyzed four main mechanisms by which capitalism can lead to qualitative, categorical group disadvantage. Tilly stresses the need to analyze structure of inequality in terms of generative mechanisms. Tilly's analysis, *Durable Inequality* (University of California Press, 1998) sketches four main mechanisms that attach individual inequality to inherited traits such as race, ethnicity, and the like. He calls the two principal mechanisms "exploitation" and "opportunity hoarding" and he argues that they are then reinforced and consolidated by the supplementary mechanisms of emulation and adaptation in which inequalities and processes developed in one sphere become consolidated in others:

1. Exploitation: Exploitation is the process by which those in positions of power and control can manage to deprive workers of the value added by their work. In order to do so, they have to make sure that the workers remain fragmented and relatively vulnerable. Tilly illustrates this by the classic case of the creation of tribal identities in South

African Apartheid. Apartheid involved the oppressive segregation and subordination of the great bulk of the population, who were native African, who had to be segregated from the white minority, deprived of livelihood, and assigned to "tribal homelands" to which they felt no connection, and which were incapable of supporting them. In practice they were used as forced labor, as second class citizens in the diamond mines, the factories, and the plantations of white South Africans. Tilly argues that the oppression of women stems from the same process of exploitation.

2. Opportunity Hoarding: A group of workers (including self-employed artisans) may accumulate resources such as a network of contacts, customers, and information. For instance, Italian workers in Mamaroneck, New York, working largely as gardeners, accumulated equipment, skills, customers, etc. While it is useful to share these resources, the opportunities for gardening were not unlimited, and so they were not shared too widely—totally aside from the fact that the linguistic, religious, and national organizations which created the solidarity and sharing of opportunities tended to have a limited number of people in them. Exploitation by those with power and opportunity hoarding by groups of workers may be connected to each other, but they have a different logic and dynamic. A group that is hoarding a set of opportunities is largely indifferent to other groups; if anything they would prefer that others were not in the competition at all. But a group that is exploiting requires that other groups be there and be relatively powerless and vulnerable.

Tilly argues that the two main mechanisms generating durable inequality get reinforced and generalized by two others:

3. Emulation: What one institutional structure is doing is often then copied by others. For example, once one state in a system can accomplish a mass mobilization into a citizen army, all the other states adopt that institutional form or they are conquered; if African Americans are excluded from business, they will tend to be excluded from law schools.

4. Adaptation: The individuals within the system come to accept, adapt to, internalize, and work around the institutional arrangements.

Thus, we do not know what are the generative mechanisms you proposed to deal with group inequality. But we think that you may find it useful and interesting to compare your analysis to Tilly's analysis of exploitation, opportunity hoarding, emulation, and adaptation. These processes are certainly not the only ones going on. Tilly proposes them not as a full description of all the various individual and group actions and sentiments relevant to group inequality, but as the main generative mechanisms that produce those configurations. Since they are self-reinforcing and mutually reinforcing feedback processes, their operation is dialectical, dynamically complex, unstable, and difficult to analyze empirically. We believe that the analysis of such systems is one of the urgent agendas of the twenty-first century.

Many who are opposed to racist oppression and racist ideas put forward the idea that "white people in general" enjoy a "white skin privilege" because on average, they are less oppressed than people of color. It is certainly true that, on average, capitalism oppresses black, Latino, and other subordinated racial-ethnic minorities more than it oppresses white working class people. It is certainly true that there are tangible, palpable, measurable material "advantages" that many white people get, such as more job opportunities, less police brutality, higher pay, better housing, and more. And it is also true that many white people do not make a strong effort to oppose racist oppression and sometimes believe racist myths about racial-ethnic minorities. But we do not believe that the word "privilege" is accurate; perhaps a better term would be "less oppressed." The term "privilege" implies that white working class people benefit, in a fundamental sense, from the arrangements in capitalist society—arrangements that are strengthened by and that strengthen racist oppression as well. Marxists believe that the whole working class, including white workers, are exploited and oppressed by capitalism, and since racist oppression and racist ideas help strengthen capitalism, racism is therefore fundamentally against the interests of the white working class. Marx himself understood this interconnection when, writing about slavery in the United States, he wrote that labor in white skin can never be free as long as there is slavery against black people. However, while Marxists would assert that the white working class is oppressed by the processes of capitalism, including the oppression of subordinated racial-ethnic groups, Marxists certainly are aware of the intense extra oppression which such groups experience and, as emphasized above, Marxists see the struggle against racist oppression and racist ideology as the cutting edge of the struggle against capitalism.

Suggestions for Further Reading

Labor market segmentation is explored by many works including D. Gordon, R. Edwards, and M. Reich, *Segmented Work, Divided Workers* (Cambridge, 1982) and C. Tilly and C. Tilly, *Work Under Capitalism* (Westview 1998). An immense research literature pursues the effects of race and ethnic inequalities on the class structure and income inequality among white English-speaking workers, for example, C. Kim and C. Taborini, "The Continuing Significance of Race," *Sociological Inquiry* 76:23–51 (2006). Feagin's analysis builds on his earlier analysis of institutionalized discrimination,

which showed that institutionalized structures of racial inequality can produce discrimination as a result of structures of power and resources, with
or without attitudinal prejudice. His analysis of systemic racism is laid out
in works such as *Racist America* (Routledge, 2001) and (co-authored with
H. Vera) *White Racism, The Basics* (Routledge, 1995).

SECTION 2.7: HOW MUCH MISERY
IS THERE IN THE UNITED STATES?

According to historical materialism, the class structure of a society is the
single most fundamental fact about that society, partly because class divisions have a powerful, direct effect on almost everything else. Does this
mean that Marxism really is a form of economic determinism? Did Marx
believe that economic arrangements determine everything else in a society?
Part of the answer depends on how one defines "class," "economic," and
"determine." Economic analysis is very important to class analysis, but it
would not be correct to say that classes are only economic groups. Marxist
classes are economic, but they are not only or merely economic. Earlier, we
discussed how occupation affects virtually all attitudes, and that in important respects, blue-collar workers are more generally open to changing society than white-collar workers. Marxists critique the notion that the United
States is fundamentally controlled by the "middle class," and instead assert
that it is basically dominated by a capitalist minority while most people
are in the working class majority. Certainly, ownership of means of production, wealth, and income are very concentrated. In the Eiffel Tower of
wealth, most of us are within a yard of the ground. As relational groups
in production, Marxist classes can be contrasted to Weberian *occupational
prestige strata* based on lifestyle and consumption. Class is distinct from
occupational status, and it seems to determine the process by which other
variables affect income. Class is more important for understanding the relation between different components of stratification and for relating sociology to history, economics, and political science. And, in terms of political
movements, class is key to change.

  Class divisions are dynamically and historically important. They are
lines of fracture, determining further development and structural change.
At any particular point in time, you may not be able to see those lines of
fracture. Because they are *implicit* in the objective possibilities open to any
society, one must *infer* what the lines of possible division are on the basis
of other tensions and contradictions in the society. Among these, economic
alienations characteristic of private ownership are connected to other
forms of powerlessness. What are the main lines of division or fracture in
the society? Marx saw the conflict between workers and capitalists as the

fundamental division—the fundamental class contradiction—of modern society. He argued that the central issue of that division is the tendency of unemployment to depress the wage rate of the whole working class, in order to increase or maintain profits:

> The same causes which develop the expansive power of capital, develop also the labour power at its disposal. The relative mass of the industrial reserve army increases therefore with the potential energy of wealth. But the greater this reserve army, the greater is . . . official pauperism. *This is the absolute general law of capitalist accumulation.* Like all other laws it is modified in its working by many circumstances, the analysis of which does not concern us here . . . all means for the development of production transform themselves into means of domination over and exploitation of, the producers; they mutilate the laborer into a fragment of a man, degrade him to the level of an appendage of a machine, destroy every remnant of charm in his work and turn it into a hated toil; they estrange from him the intellectual potentialities of the labour-process in the same proportion as science is incorporated in it as an independent power . . . they transform his life time into working-time, and drag his wife and child beneath the wheels of the Juggernaut of capital. . . . It follows therefore that in proportion as capital accumulates, the lot of the laborer, be his payment high or low, must grow worse. The law, finally, that always equilibrates the relative surplus population, or industrial reserve army, to the extent and energy of accumulation, this law rivets the laborer to capital more firmly than the wedges of Vulcan did Prometheus to the rock. It establishes an accumulation of misery, corresponding with accumulation of capital. Accumulation of wealth at one pole is, therefore, at the same time accumulation of misery, agony of toil, slavery, ignorance, brutality, mental degradation, at the opposite pole. (CAP I, p. 645)

Is Marx right? Has there been an accumulation of misery, agony, slavery, ignorance, brutality, and mental degradation? Is Marx saying that average real wages decline? Would the analysis be proved right or wrong by the movement of real wages? If not, what are the data which would confirm or disconfirm this analysis?

Most non-Marxian theorists believe that raw misery for the working class may have characterized early industrialization, but is not true today. But as we write, one in four American children are on food stamps, and for some six million Americans, food stamps are their only income. A recent study found that from 2000 to 2008, the number of people below the poverty line grew by five million, reaching nearly forty million, and that does not include the data from 2009, when the recession really hit. And much of misery is longer term; some of it is visible from space: if you use Google Earth to view almost any part of Chicago, you see the signs of a labor market that is roughly equivalent to that of the Great Depression. But if you use Google Earth to view almost any area of Detroit, what you see is vast areas of grass or rubble. In the early twentieth century, Detroit looked like Chicago does now, but unemployment and job flight had an effect equivalent to a nuclear device or to the effects of Hurricane Katrina on our third largest port, when the levees were neglected.

Moreover, theorists critical of Marx misinterpret his analysis to say only that there would be an absolute decline in real income for the working class. Then they argue that real income has risen, so Marx is wrong. The movement of real income and poverty is important, but you can see that the argument is against a straw man. Even a very superficial reading shows that that interpretation distorts Marx's argument. Marx argues that there is a tendency toward pauperism, modified by various circumstances, but the lot of the laborer grows worse. *Be his payment high or low.* Why? Workers, not owners, produce everything in the society. All those glittering palaces of glass and steel in our cities, all the pleasure domes of country clubs and resorts, all the whole immense superstructure of institutions are a product of human labor and ought to be a means of human development. But Marx believed that so long as these are privately controlled by a privileged few, they do not enhance development and human freedom. We think that he is right. They become so many links in a chain of slavery and degradation. Workers see their spouses and children drawn into a brutal and degrading system which poisons all human relations. The apparent prosperity of one segment is always at the expense of misery at the opposite pole. In part, the opposite pole of a North American suburb is visible in any center city. Of course, if you follow commodity chains back to Mexico or Cambodia, polarization would be more visible. But suppose we just look at economic deprivation in the United States. It is very easy for middle class academics to believe that hunger, brutality, and personal degradation are a thing of the past, or limited to small, special, unusual groups. Against this, it is important to inventory the actual misery, toil, ignorance, hunger, and brutality which is produced within the United States by capitalism in the late 1980s and 1990s. If Marx had said that average real money wages always decline, he would have been wrong. That is not what he says. But does capitalism make everyone rich? Figure 2.1 gives the movement of average real wages in the United States during the long post-World War II boom.

Like any other tendency over the course of time, it fluctuates. It is subject to contradictory forces and it allows contradictory interpretations.

Another answer to the question "How much misery is produced by capitalism" lies in an examination of the number of people below the poverty line in the United States. This is not a perfect measure. People at the poverty line have steadily lost ground relative to everyone else. The poverty line was devised by M. Orshansky by taking the cost of an "economy food budget" of the Department of Agriculture and multiply-

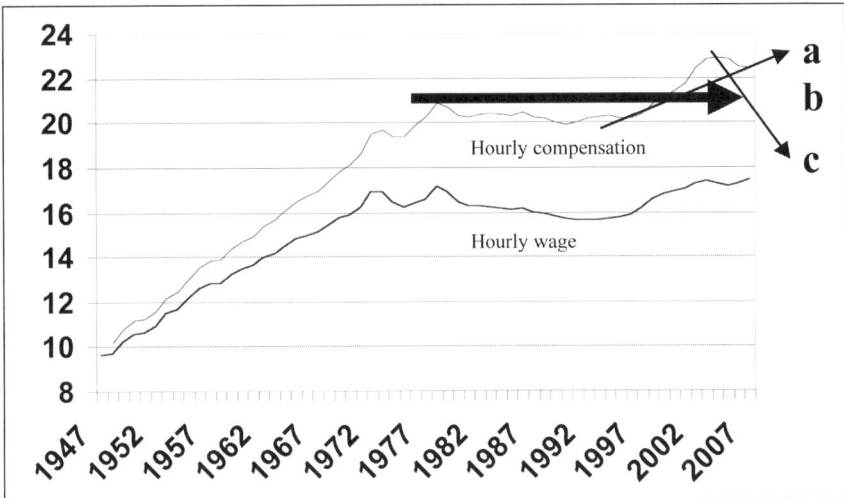

Figure 2.1　Spendable Average Weekly Earnings

ing by three to cover housing and other necessities, since most people spend about a third on food. The U.S. Department of Agriculture diet which was selected was meant for "temporary and emergency use only" and Orshansky has since estimated that among poor families, *one in ten* had a *nutritionally adequate diet*. In 1979, the poverty line for a nonfarm family of four was $6,662, which meant that they spent just about fifty cents per person per meal. By the late 1980s with inflation, it had risen to about $0.85 per person per meal, and by the twenty-first century that had risen to about a $1.14 a meal. A good exercise for those who think that poverty and hunger have been eliminated in the United States is to live for a few weeks on a $1.14 per meal. (Not surprisingly, most people below the poverty line are malnourished, partly because most of the people below the poverty line are just that—*below* the poverty line.) How many people are below the poverty line? Figure 2.2 shows that there were about forty million people living below the poverty line in 2008, the highest level since 1966. It has risen since, and in any case, it remains much higher than in the 1970s and is now near 15 percent again. Let us be clear what this means. It means that after transfers and supplements, more than thirty million people have less than a $1.14 per meal to spend. This in the nation where capitalism is supposedly the best.

Figure 2.2 is the number of people below the poverty line after government transfer payments like welfare or unemployment. It shows that the number of people below the poverty line decreased during the 1960s, but that decrease was wiped out in the 1980s. The number of people

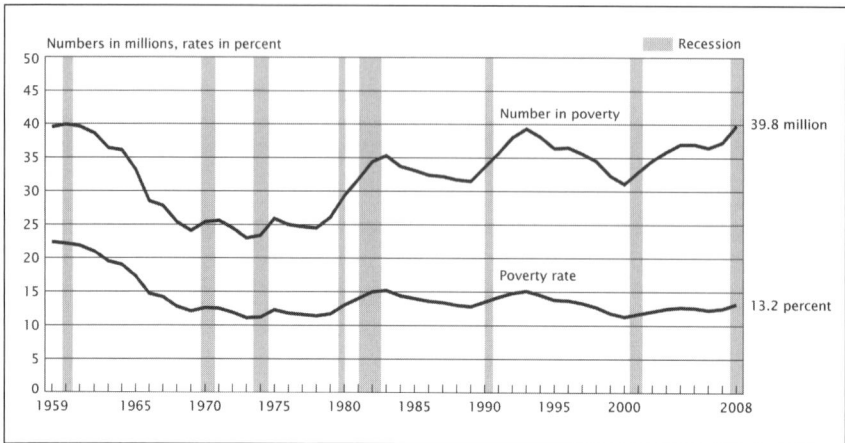

Figure 2.2   U.S. Number in Poverty and Poverty Rate, 1959 to 2008

who would be below the poverty line if there were not government transfers (i.e., prior to transfers) has also increased. For a time, this tendency
could be counteracted by a political climate which allowed us to reduce
the number of poor by means of welfare payments. But the same culture
which creates a need for welfare makes it politically impossible to sustain
support for welfare. Accordingly, political tendencies of the present society
have massively reduced government payments to counteract the economic
tendencies of the system.

Both in the case of real income and in the case of poverty, Marx seems
to be perfectly clear that the *tendency* of capitalism is modified by political
and organizational processes not completely analyzed in *Capital*. Certainly,
Marx is explicit that the be-all and end-all of his analysis is not the level of
pay of workers. That is important, but it is not all-important. Stagnant real
wages, enormous inequality, millions of people malnourished—this is unfortunately only the tip of the iceberg of the misery, toil, slavery, brutality,
ignorance, and degradation created by capitalism. There may well be more
people above the poverty line than below it who have their lives somehow
spoiled by crying need. But there are far more who will be needlessly mu-
tilated on their jobs, or who will have poisoned or deformed children. But
beyond that, the racism, violence, and brutality built into the system will
injure far more. Those closer to the bottom are merely the ones who see
the future the system has in store for everyone else most clearly. We think
that capitalism in developed countries is a system which has to collide with
needs of other parts of the world. The immense stockpile of weapons is ugly
enough when it appears as waste—as children unfed, and people's basic
needs unmet. It is far uglier when it is used.

Exercise 2.7: Does Economic Change Automatically Lead to Political Action?

Marx spoke of a class-in-itself becoming a class-for-itself. What do you think he meant? Think of some times when a group of people have done something, such that you would say, "They did such-and-such" or "They are able to do such-and-such." In the cases you are thinking of, how do the relations among the group members and between them and others affect their doing or being able to do things? How, if at all, were people changed by being in the group and in the action?

Apply these insights to the issue of long-term battles over political power and the shape of the society. What kinds of things might make a class become aware of its common interests and act upon them?

Does economic misery produce a political force for change? Does it produce political action, especially revolutionary political action? This question is important on two levels. In the specific sense, the question could be asked, "Is it merely deprivation that makes people rebel? Will the economic crisis lead to political and social change?" Marx certainly did not believe that raw deprivation leads to successful political action. Marx's economic analysis is caricatured to say that real wages always fall. His political analysis is caricatured (often by people who have read little Marx) to say that this automatically leads to revolution—that totally impoverished masses will mindlessly rise up and smash the system, like starving wolves. Marx's analysis is very different. Marx paid great attention to economic factors because those are what most powerfully affect how people live. But he recognized that human reactions through history are not a mindless response to the stimulus of hunger and that if hunger alone caused revolutions, India, Sudan, and Haiti would long ago have had communist revolutions.

At a more general level, what is involved is the whole question of crisis and change—the whole question, fundamental to chapter 3, of the relationship of ideology and politics to economics, of ideas to material reality, of organization to action. Just as ideology and politics for the ruling class flow from an economic base, but are qualitatively different from it, so, too for subordinate classes the economic basis and political ideology are connected. But saying that things are connected is different from saying that they are the same. Class is central to Marx's analysis, but classes are more than economic phenomena. In the first place, classes are defined in terms of production relations, which is a broader category than wealth or market relations. In the second place, classes are defined in terms of the overlapping contradictions in the whole mode of production. Liberal theorists object, "How can Marx define class in two different ways? That is inconsistent." But human action is not a mindless reflection of the economy, nor is it completely spontaneous, disembodied, and separate from material reality. It has contradictions and different aspects. Groups can both be classes and not be classes; for different analytical purposes a group may or may not be unified. Perhaps the classic example is the peasantry. Marx described the French peasantry as follows:

> A small holding, a peasant and his family; alongside them another small holding, another peasant and another family. A few score of these make up a village, and a few score of villages make up a Department. In this way, the great mass of the French nation is formed by simple addition of homologous magnitudes, much as potatoes in a sack form a sack of potatoes. In so far as millions of families live under economic conditions of existence that separate their mode of life, their interests and their culture from those of the other classes, and put them in hostile opposition to the latter, they form a class. In so far as there is merely a local interconnection among these small-holding peasants, and the identity of their interests begets no community, no national bond and no political organization among them, they do not form a class. They are consequently incapable of enforcing their class interests in their name, whether through a parliament or through a convention. They cannot represent themselves, they must be represented. Their representatives must at the same time appear as their master, as an authority over them, as an un-limited governmental power that protects them against the other classes and sends them rain and shine from above. The political influence of the small-holding peasants, therefore, finds its final expression in the executive power subordinating society to itself. ("The 18th Brumaire of Louis Bonaparte," 1852, SW: 172)

For the moment consider the two different elements of class to which Marx refers. He did not always integrate them by means of the particular Hegelian terminology of "for-itself " and "in-itself," but he always recognized the two aspects of class. The construction of an historically accurate, economically informed, politically predictive theory of class is the cornerstone of Marx's analysis. It is a difficult task.

When Marx says that the peasants are a class and they are not a class, he is not just equivocating. It is the reality that is equivocating. Marx is not being inconsistent. The reality is contradictory. Imagine this: a person, Maria, has all the knowledge, skills, ability, training, and strength to be a good engineer. But she doesn't know it. Or she sort of knows it but is afraid to try. The question is: is Maria an engineer? And the answer is: yes and no. *At junctures like this, the role of human consciousness can be a decisive factor.* And for that, organization is a decisive factor. The great temptation is to suppose that one or the other of these definitions of class is the real and the ultimate one: that a class should only and ultimately be defined in terms of a set of economic relations which put people into a common position, or that a class should ultimately and only be defined by the possibilities of imminent collective political action.

Various Marxist sociologists have taken each of these options. But under-estimating either aspect distorts not only the description of classes in society, but more importantly, analyses of the social processes that come from interactions within and among the different classes. Nor can one solve the problem by saying that it is half and half, by an arbitrary combination of the two aspects which interpenetrate and shape each other. Marx avoided the reduction of class to either of these ultimate bases. When Marx says that peasants both are and are not a class, he is pointing to the fact that the lines of the fracture within the society are objectively such that they are composed of several different processes, and they can go in several different directions.

One of the reasons that Marx stressed such factors as organization and racism is because it is only when a **class-in-itself** becomes a **class-for-itself**, realizing its actual and potential place in the world, that disorganized economic struggles can take the form of organized political struggles to change the society. The class-for-itself does not spring out of nowhere. While given individuals can abandon the class of their birth, for the most part it is as firmly rooted in the class-in-itself as your mind is in your body. But in itself, a class-in-itself cannot fight to change the whole society. The unique role of a revolutionary organization is to spread the ideology fundamental to collective action. The ideological task involves much more than exposing economic injustices. There are many powerful aspects of procapitalist ideology, including racism, nationalism, sexism, anti-scientific mysticism, anti-working class stereotypes, cynicism, and a thousand forms of "me first" individualism. Unless they are defeated, they will channel action back into procapitalist activity. Ideological work is not simply speech-making or writing pamphlets. It encompasses organizing short-term political and economic struggles, bringing about key changes themselves, building strong social ties, and being involved with others. But no amount of skillful organizing, brilliant speeches, or charismatic emotional appeals can succeed for long if large numbers of oppressed people do not consciously grasp their role in the process and give leadership to it.

Thus, there are no simple answers to the two questions posed above. "In-itself " and "for-itself " refer to two fundamental dimensions of class analysis. They are tied to each other by a series of different threads at different levels of analysis. There seems to be no simple, homogeneous way of constructing a theory encompassing both.

Suggestions for Further Reading

A useful analysis of poverty in the United States, some way into the recession that began with the financial crisis of 2008, is R. Haskins and I. Sawhill, *Creating an Opportunity Society: Economic Mobility, Children and Families, Federal Budget and Family Formation* (Brookings, 2009). On subjective and objective class: from an historical standpoint, one of the classic definitions of class from the standpoint of culture and possible action is E. P. Thompson, *The Making of the English Working Class* (London, 1963), which can be contrasted to Ste. Croix, cited above.

SECTION 2.8: IS THE UNITED STATES A LAND OF EXCEPTIONAL MOBILITY? DOES IT MATTER?

The United States is a society of profound *inequality*, and that inequality has increased in recent years. Those who defend free market capitalism would accept this picture, but they would argue that the United States is a society of **equality of opportunity.** People may be very unequal, they would say, but every child has a chance to be president, and every child has a chance to be the next Bill Gates. Indeed, they would argue that equality of opportunity requires and implies the inequality and that people end up unequal because they are given the chance to make themselves unequal. What is the relation of equality and equality of opportunity, and what is the relation of each of them to Marx's analysis? How much equality of opportunity is there in the United States? To what extent do children end up in the same or in different positions from those of their parents? What are the main mechanisms which determine the amount of mobility?

Equality of opportunity is usually understood as the opportunity to have unequal accomplishments and hence unequal rewards. Thus, it requires and implies inequality. Moreover, ideas about opportunity are the main ideology which justifies inequality in the United States. However, inequality also conflicts with equality of opportunity. Can you have equality of opportunity when there is actually massive inequality? When some children grow up malnourished, poisoned by lead paint, and miseducated in schools that are almost prisons, do they have equal opportunity with other children who grow up well nourished and educated at elite schools? It is obvious that they do not. When some children inherit controlling interest in a corporation, like Exxon-Mobil, that means that other children don't have the same opportunity. Within capitalism, every way that one group of people assures itself of power and privilege necessarily freezes out others. Economic, social, and political inequalities are inevitably turned into inequalities of opportunity. Equality of opportunity logically implies inequality, and inequality inevitably produces inequality of opportunity. Equality of opportunity is a *contradiction*.

There is a sense in which equality of opportunity and the dream of mobility have been particularly important concerns in the United States. The notion of equality of opportunity has functioned to legitimize inequality. This required forgetting that effective equality of opportunity is both logically and practically inconsistent with large inequalities. Equality of opportunity plays an important ideological role in the United States. Rather than people being promised pie in the sky when they die, they have been promised that their children will eat pie if they work hard. This ideological role does not require that there be any opportunity; only that people be promised it and believe it. It is important to separate the question of whether there is a greater ideological concern with mobility in the United States than in other advanced capitalist countries from the question of whether there has in fact been greater mobility in the United States than in other countries.

How much mobility is there in the United States? The traditional view of the United States, enshrined in Fourth of July speeches, has been that the United States is a land of opportunity, where anyone can be anything. That is, many people see the United States as a society of great opportunity, with more mobility than other countries. Is it true that there is a greater chance than in Europe that a poor boy or girl will end up as president or as the head of a large company? Many studies have found that the rate of mobility in the United States was no higher than in other industrial, capitalist countries. The ideological perception of and concern with mobility may have been greater, but the actual extent of mobility was neither very impressive nor very exceptional. A number of studies have shown that rags-to-riches mobility into the elite is quite restricted. The main story is rags-to-rags, and mobility is reduced whenever there is very high inequality.

What about more modest movement—movement not into the elite but between occupational categories? What is the extent of intergenerational occupational mobility in the United States? To what extent do children end up in the same kinds of occupations as their parents? The American Dream is the idea that a poor child can, by hard work, move into the "middle class." For what fraction of the population is the American Dream a reality? Table 2.4 presents data relevant to this question from the 1972 General Social Survey, a generation ago, and table 2.5 compares that with data from the 2006 General Social Survey. Both tables are mobility tables, cross-tabulations of the occupational status (not class) of fathers with the occupational status of children. (Housewives are classified by the occupation of their spouse; retired persons by their former occupation.) Thus, in table 2.4, the first row shows that of 357 respondents whose parents were white-collar workers, 280 were themselves white-collar workers, 57 were blue-collar workers, 19 were service workers, and 1 was a farm worker. Analyzing the distribution of cases within the table as a whole gives evidence about mobility. A very large amount of energy of American sociologists has been devoted to technically sophisticated analyses of tables like this one.

Does this table show a relatively large amount of mobility or a relatively small amount of mobility? For how many people was the American Dream, in fact, a reality? To answer this question, the total sample of 1347 cases in

Table 2.4   Occupational Mobility in the United States in 1972

	Respondents' Occupation				
R's Father's Occupation	White Collar	Blue Collar	Service	Farm	T
White collar	280	57	19	1 **11%**	357
Blue collar	282	212 **41% immobile**	74	**DOWN** 6	574
Service	**UP** 32 **25%**	23	11	0	66
Farm	138	109 **structural**	60	43	350
	23%				
Total	732	401	164	50	1347

Table 2.5   Occupational Mobility in the United States in 2006

	Respondents' Occupation				
R's Father's Occupation	White Collar	Blue Collar	Service	Farm	T
White collar	1668	578	454	44 **30%**	2744
Blue collar	543	275 **48% immobile**	162	**DOWN** 19	999
Service	**UP** 105 **16%**	36	22	1	284
Farm	138	109 **structural**	60	43	350
	6%				
Total	2417	983	701	88	4188

the table has been divided into four groups: respondents who were **down-wardly mobile**, labeled "**down**;" those who were in **jobs similar to their parents**, labeled "**immobile**;" those who were **upwardly mobile**, labeled "**up**;" and those who moved **out of farm occupations** into urban ones, labeled "**structural**." One part of the answer to the question how much mobility there was in 1974 is to look at the proportion of respondents who were in the four groups: 41 percent were in the **immobile**, diagonal cells running from the upper left-hand to the lower right-hand corner: children of farmers who are farmers, the children of white-collar workers who are white-collar workers, etc.; 23 percent were **structurally mobile**; 25 percent were **upwardly mobile**; and 11 percent were **downwardly mobile**.

While the largest fraction of the population was **immobile,** nearly half the respondents fall in these four cells. Does that mean that the other half of the population is mobile and has achieved the American Dream? Certainly people are distributed throughout the table. It appears that there is a substantial amount of mobility. However, four considerations sharply reduce the impression of a very large amount of mobility which some theorists get from tables such as this.

In the first place, much of the mobility in the table is not large jumps. It is minuscule movement between adjacent positions. People may occupy jobs with different titles and classifications from their parents, but that does not really constitute mobility if the jobs are at approximately the same level as those of their parents.

In the second place, even much of the movement between separated categories is not real mobility. Some of this mobility is certainly pseudo-mobility. There are many people who certainly have not achieved the American Dream, but who nevertheless appear to be mobile in the table. Consider the son of a doctor, a college student who plans to and will attend medical school and become a doctor, but who is now working during the summer as a night watchman. He is pictured as being sharply downwardly mobile from an upper professional to a lower service job. During his lifetime he will be pictured as sharply upwardly mobile into a professional job. But in fact, he is simply going into the same job as his father. The night watchman job is merely incidental to his career. The daughter of a teacher who works for a year on a farm, and who then becomes a teacher is not really mobile. Or consider the son of a steelworker who is a small store owner, making, perhaps, $50,000 per year. Since most small store owners go bust, suppose that in a few years, if he is lucky, he will go back into work in a plant and will end up approximately where his father was. This is not to say that no one in the society is mobile. Some people are mobile—either through education or because they become sports stars or because they hit the number. But the people we have just pictured are pseudo-mobile. They are not really mobile, even though they appear to be mobile on this table. It is hard to estimate the amount of this pseudo-mobility, and different people will estimate it differently, but a substantial proportion of the respondents in the "**up**" (upwardly mobile) region are almost certainly pseudo-mobile.

In the third place, much of the movement in the table is not a function of the openness of the occupational system. It does not consist of people moving back and forth between different occupations. It does not indicate that anyone can be anything they want. Rather it is a function of a single, one-time-only change in the structure of occupations. Sociologists call the kind of mobility which involves movement back and forth between different occupations **circulation mobility**. They call the mobility that is produced by changes in the occupational structure **structural mobility**. The clearest component of structural mobility is the elimination of farming. This is actually a direct consequence of the reduction of self-employment, the expropriation of means of production, and concentration of ownership. About 26 percent of the respondents had fathers who were farmers; only 4 percent of the respondents were in farming. Thus about one-quarter of the respondents *had* to go somewhere other than farming; they had to appear to be upwardly mobile. But once family farming has been eliminated (which is rapidly happening in the United States), the mobility is gone. While it is logically possible that other forms of structural change will substitute for the decrease in farming, most theorists suppose that the decline in farming and the increase in other occupations is a one-shot irreversible process. No one has a plausible suggestion of any other process which is likely to substitute for it as a massive source of structural mobility.

Finally, in the fourth place, the whole concern with occupational movement ignores class. Other theorists concerned with mobility look at class rather than occupational mobility. Variables like education have different effects for whites and blacks, for men and women, and thus it is important to specify their effects. And there is reason to believe that those things like education which affect one's chances to get ahead affect it differently depending on one's class. Thus one can ask to what extent is one's class position a function of one's father's class position and of the kind of society one lives in? For example, R. Robinson, *Reproducing Class Relations in Industrial Capitalism* (Sage, 1984), notes that one would expect the effect of education to be different for people in different class positions and that education has different implications for different kinds of mobility. There is no reason to expect that education would improve one's chance to become an owner. One becomes an owner by having capital. Capital is often inherited. But education is often important for becoming a manager. Robinson obtains data on fathers' ownership for the United States, Britain, Ireland, Argentina, and Chile. He looks at the effect of fathers' class on sons' education, finding that having a capitalist father increases one's chance of getting education. It is one's class position, not one's education, that has the main influence on class position. Whether one looks at mobility into the elite, at occupational mobility, or at class mobility, one does not get a picture of equality of opportunity. **Equality** of opportunity is an ideology which serves to justify large inequalities and unearned incomes.

Thus, much of the apparent mobility in table 2.4 dissolves under closer inspection. Forty percent the respondents are on or next to the diagonal of immobility. Twenty-three percent of the respondents are in the four cells showing structural mobility out of farming. That leaves only about a third of the respondents with possible circulation mobility. A substantial fraction of that is likely to be pseudo-mobility, and the occupational mobility that does occur is often not relevant to class position.

The data in table 2.4 were from 1972. Since then, for a generation, the government has been dominated by politicians who have cut taxes and reduced social safety nets largely in the name of promoting mobility—of allowing people to keep more of what they earn without having to worry about others. Has this changed the pattern or the amount of mobility? If so, has it increased it or decreased it? Table 2.5 provides information from the 2006 General Social Survey relevant to that question.

Table 2.5 has the same form as table 2.4. In 2006, the "**structural**" mobility that resulted from the movement out of the farm sector essentially ceased. Once the farm sector is down to about 5 percent of the workforce, it cannot generate a significant amount of structural mobility. With regard to the question of whether policies of lower taxes on the wealthy and fewer social programs increase mobility, table 2.5 suggests that they reduce it. The population that was **immobile** increased from about two fifths (41 percent) to nearly half (48 percent.)

Besides the drop in the overall amount of mobility, the other effect of a generation of Reagan, Bush, Clinton, and Bush policies was a striking change in the nature of the mobility. In 1972 **upward mobility** was about three times greater than **downward mobility**. In 2006, even after factoring out the decrease in **structural** mobility, there was twice as much **downward mobility** as **upward mobility**. In 2006, nearly a third of the population was working in jobs with less pay, benefits, or status than their parents, and this was before the vast wave of foreclosures, bankruptcies, and unemployment from the great financial crisis and recession of 2008. One of the principal arguments for free market policies was called "Free to Choose," and a major critique of it in 1988 was called "Free to Lose." These data suggest that policies of reduced government services, reduced regulation, and taxes were a recipe for Free to Lose rather than Free to Choose.

What are the political consequences of the increase in downward mobility that we see in table 2.5 and of the financial and economic crisis that followed? While we cannot foresee all the political consequences of these shifts, it is evident that enormous political force is generated when many tens of millions of people suddenly lose the future that they thought they had achieved. In the absence of a strong left leadership, there are often leaders who will try to mobilize them with the message that internal and external "enemies" (often seen in racial terms as Muslims, Hispanics, African Americans) have stolen their future. Economic and social changes do not lead automatically to political actions. But one of the sources of the wave of racist and fascist movements that swept over much of the world in the early twentieth century was that millions of people had lost, or feared losing, their social positions. Such changes make political under-

standing, leadership, and political movements exceptionally important in
the coming period.

Exercise 2.8: Does Mobility Matter?

**How much difference does it make how much mobility there is in the
U.S.? What kinds of class privilege are important? What are they important for? If you think that class position is mainly the result of inherited
wealth and rank, what *evidence* does this conception rest upon? Are the
new rich nicer than the old rich? Are societies with more mobility less
oppressive than those with less mobility? In terms of mobility and in
terms of any measure of class moderation you can think of, how do you
think the U.S., Italy, Brazil, or China compare?**

When the rising middle class came into collision with the aristocracy,
they put forth an analysis of society which suggested that aristocratic privileges and legal restrictions on occupation were the core of class society. For
them, a titled aristocracy was the main form of class privilege; if there were
no inherited classes, there were no classes. Tocqueville argued that the
United States was different from aristocratic societies because it was characterized by constant movement of people up or down and by social equality.
This picture was adopted by many sociologists about the United States.

How did Tocqueville know? He talked to many middle class businessmen and landowners, and that is what they said. But since then, it has been
possible for historical sociologists to reexamine the amount of social mobility and social equality in the United States during the nineteenth century
to find out the empirical basis of Tocqueville's picture. There is an obvious
difference between real mobility and beliefs about it. But even when there
is real movement, does it matter? Most Marxist theorists would argue that
even if (as is clearly impossible) the membership of classes did change from
generation to generation or even from year to year, that would not substan-
tially affect the distorting, oppressive features of the system.

Consider the exercise questions above. Since all present-day societies with a substantial amount of inequality have substantial barriers to
mobility, there is not as much variation as one would like. Since many
people who experienced advantages from their class, race, or gender position think of themselves and represent themselves as "self-made men or
women," there is often considerable blindness to inherited advantages.
And since the issue is politically charged, you may have trouble getting
agreement on how much variation in mobility rates there is. But we suspect that no matter how you measure mobility, you will not find it correlated with openness, moderation, contact between top and bottom, etc.
There is no evidence for the implicit conceptual baggage in most theoretical discussions.

To some extent you can run rough checks on the plausibility of your findings. There are societies that have greater and lesser amounts of mobility, and there are persons who have experienced more or less. Do those situations and those persons have less class rigidities? By most measures of mobility, there was more in Eastern Europe after World War II than there is in the United States. If you like mobility, then you must love those societies or China. We think that you often find rigid, oppressive class societies with lots of mobility.

Similarly, the effects of individual mobility are not always greater openness. You often find that individuals who have experienced some mobility, rather than being grateful for the advantages they have had or sensitive to the disadvantages of others, are blind to whatever advantages they experienced and to the disadvantages of others. What that demonstrates is that in thinking about a free and open society, mobility or equality of opportunity is often the wrong thing to concentrate on.

Suggestions for Further Reading

A recent comparative study of intergenerational mobility from the London School of Economics shows that among developed countries, the more inequality, the less mobility: J. Blanden, P. Gregg, and S. Machin, *Intergenerational Mobility in Europe and North America* (London, 2005). A well-known critique of M. Friedman's book, *Free to Choose* (Harcourt, 1980) is J. Roemer, *Free to Lose* (Harvard University Press, 1988). The classic reanalysis of Tocqueville is E. Pessen, *Three Centuries of Social Mobility in America* (Heath, 1974), showing that the claim of openness and social equality was just as inaccurate in Tocqueville's time as it is today. L. Damrosch *Tocqueville's Discovery of America* (2010) confirms that Tocqueville badly overestimated the amount of mobility in America. R. Robinson, "Reproducing Class Relations in Industrial Capitalism," *American Sociological Review* 49:182–196 (1984), analyzes some of the relations between class and occupational mobility. P. Gomberg, *How to Make Opportunity Equal*: *Race and Contributive Justice* (Wiley-Blackwell, 2007) analyzes some of the issues concerning race and mobility.

SECTION 2.9: WHY ARE THERE ECONOMIC DEPRESSIONS?

What causes capitalist crises? Why are there depressions? Can they be controlled by Keynesian policies? Marxists often analyze the developmental tendencies of capitalism in terms of contradictions—overlapping, interconnected contradictions. The forces of production, including machines, skilled labor, and existing technologies expand, but are strangled by property law. The dynamic of producing what is needed (use value) comes into collision with production of what is profitable (exchange value), and that contradiction is acted out by distinguishable interests of owners (capital) and workers (proletariat). The development of capitalism brings together and unites classes by creating simple homogeneous labor and by the deskilling, degradation, and alienation of work; at the same time it splits and divides them by segregation, segmentation, durable inequality, and divisive ideologies.

From 1950 to the mid-1970s, the United States economy (and the world economy) experienced the single most dramatic period of growth and prosperity it had ever had. It seemed as though the fears for the life of capitalism which people had felt during the Great Depression were premature. It seemed that there was a certain trade-off between unemployment and inflation. When inflation got too high, one could arrange to slow down the economy, throw some (a few million!) people out of work, and cut down on inflation. When unemployment got too high, one could push credit into the system and get more people buying and selling so that jobs would be created.

The period of the 1970s represented a first strike against this conception. "Stagflation" developed, the coexistence of very high levels of unemployment with very high levels of inflation. It turns out that the sharp change in the relationship between unemployment and inflation occurred in virtually every country in the capitalist world economy. From 1970 to 1972, the unemployment rate increased without substantial decrease in inflation. From 1972 to 1974, the rate of inflation increased without a substantial decrease in unemployment. Then, the period from 1980 to 2007 represented a second strike against the view of a regulated, depression-less, capitalist economy. A kind of growth produced by expansion of the financial sector produced relatively jobless growth, fueled by debt. Finally, the great financial crisis of 2008 represented a third and final strike against the view of crisis management by credit management.

Could different domestic policy have deflated the housing bubble safely? Could different foreign policies have avoided the Iraq, Iran, Afghanistan, and Pakistan wars, with their resulting impacts on the world economy? Possibly. But beside the difficulty demonstrating the counterfactual outcome if only such-and-such a policy were different—the different policy would have directed the train onto a different track—there is the issue of how possible such changes would be. If you have a capitalist society, you will usually have a government driven by those with immense resources and an immense need to secure profits, and this need will often lead to grabbing oil from (to regime change of) societies that have vast oil resources. No serious Marxist advocates sitting back and doing nothing, because the future is "determined," but any effective intervention depends on understanding the contradictory processes and dynamics in play.

A dynamic system of this kind in terms of contradictions does not substitute for developing other kinds of quantitative theories. Marx and other Marxists have done those kinds of analyses. But it makes us aware of what other theories ignore: overlapping structures and structural change. The capitalist system does maintain itself, but only by being modified. An analysis which *assumes* its stable existence ignores the obvious fact that it came into existence in the past and it will pass out of existence at some time in the future. Nothing makes this more visible than crises.

In the normal development of capitalism, some sectors of the economy expand, while other sectors slow down, shut down, and are gobbled up. The drive for profits causes major industries and banks to ignore low-profit areas and concentrate on high-profit areas. The **neglect of the less profitable sectors** has a negative effect on the society, because there are many aspects of society that are necessary for the long-term well-being of society but do not offer an immediate high return on the investment. And capitalists need a high return on the investment. As the less profitable industries wither away and shut down, the intense competition taking place in the more profitable areas of the economy eventually results in that market being flooded as well. And as that market gets flooded, the rate of profit begins to drop, more production is needed to keep the dollars rolling in, and the increased production further depresses the rate of profit in a continuing self-sustaining cycle. Eventually, the rate of profit in once-profitable enterprises has also fallen so low that many of those enterprises have to be run with fewer and fewer workers or shut down altogether. This is a long-term trend and is not necessarily easily observable in every business all the time. There are many attempts to resist this—price fixing, monopoly practices, government intervention, and credit management. Some companies thrive for a while as the many deteriorate. But ultimately, the capitalist class simply will not—*cannot*—plan the economy and especially production, because the capitalist class is at war within itself. They must ultimately go for the immediate profit while other considerations remain very secondary.

A major crisis or depression erupts when larger, powerful businesses are forced to shut down and topple others, in a self-reinforcing process. Contradictory processes do not simply unfold gradually forever. There may be long periods of slow, quantitative change, but there are also periods of very rapid change, especially as the process reaches a limit. When large numbers of businesses are producing more than they can sell, when they are all in debt, when there are not enough customers and every layoff reduces that number, even many of the powerful companies have to shut down. What else can they do? Continue to produce goods that people won't pay for? The decline of the auto industry in the United States is one of the more profound examples of this process.

Dialectical terminology is especially useful to show the interconnection of interdependent and overlapping processes. In a crisis, other contradictions focus on the contradiction between the mode of production and the mode of exchange. Ignoring other interrelations at different levels, we can formulate the process in familiar terminology using a medical analogy. A person who loses six pints of blood very quickly would die even if the remaining blood could carry enough oxygen and enough nutrients to keep the person alive. The person would die because there is not enough pressure to force the blood around and keep the blood circulating. Similarly, if there is an economic shut down, there still are raw materials. There still are workers to do the labor. There still is food to feed those workers and housing to protect them. Those material things do not just evaporate into the air. But they will not be utilized. The money is not circulating, and the system will shut down. Production of goods would be greatly curtailed, and there would even be conscious destruction of many goods in order to try to drive prices up again. There are examples of this today. If this sounds far-fetched, consider the "Cash for Clunkers" program of 2009. The federal government used money "borrowed from the future" to pay people to turn in their old cars if they used that money to buy new cars. The old cars, which were still functional, were destroyed. Military spending during peacetime, and especially during war, is another way to artificially increase production for destruction—again with "fake" money borrowed from the future. The problem of balancing the economy between extreme inflation and a complete drop in circulation (economic slowdowns) is always a problem for capitalism. During a full-scale depression the situation is far more extreme.

The essence both of the contradiction between forces and relations of production and between the mode of production and the mode of exchange is the same. *The spontaneous tendency of the capitalist system is to produce more than can be marketed profitably.* This is a direct effect of the profit system, and it is what is self-contradictory about it. The drive for profits creates a long-term tendency for the rate of profit to fall, creating deep tendencies toward stagnation and leaving plants, skills, laborers, and technologies idle.

These tendencies bring into being institutional arrangements to try to keep the machine in motion. Three techniques for maintaining capitalism have dominated in the United States: borrowing against the future, exporting capital, and war. **Keynesian** adjustments have emphasized massive borrowing against the future by the government, to keep the economy circulating. The export of capital or runaway shop often feeds both other tendencies. And, in practice, key supporters of the Keynesian strategy have been groups also interested in maintaining a world empire. The objective situation which has supported the apparent victories of Keynesian solutions was the fact that the United States had free run of most of the world from 1945 until the early 1970s.

What is most distinctive about Keynesian solutions is borrowing, and borrowing is not something restricted to the government. Keynes argued that government spending can be used to make up the difference between the effective demand which exists and that which is needed to maintain full employment or nearly full employment. This was one of the principal characteristics of the New Deal. The analogy which Roosevelt used was that there had to be pump priming. What can one do if there is no blood available for a transfusion? One can use a substitute: plasma or even salt water. They will not bring nutrients to the body, but they will maintain blood pressure and allow the real blood to circulate. Keynesian policies do the same thing with the economy; private credit and government spending create adequate effective demand—for a while. Thus, the trillions of dollars that were channeled to banks and corporations to restart the economy in 2009 is another stopgap that somewhat revived the economy, at a huge cost, that will have to be paid back. By 2010, cutbacks of teachers, of social services, of environmental protection, and of other needed work illustrated the attack on the standard of living of the working class to squeeze out money to repay the debt.

During the last decades of the twentieth century, there was increasing reliance on military spending and the encouragement of financial speculation to overcome the stagnation tendencies of late capitalism. Reagan had argued, "Government is not the solution; government is the problem." However, this did not mean lowering government expenditure, so much as channeling it into military procurement, while deregulating financial institutions and instituting tax cuts, generating demand based on private debt. These policies were extended by Clinton, G. H. W. Bush, and especially G. W. Bush. While the expansion of the U.S. economy in the mid-twentieth century was based on growth of mass markets, increased productivity, and employment, the growth during the last decades of the twentieth century and the first decade of the twenty-first century, based on a series of speculative bubbles, was relatively anemic, jobless, and accompanied by an enormous increase in inequality. Figure 2.3 shows the inflation of stock prices in the dot-com bubble and the inflation of housing prices in the housing bubble that drove the system.

Both produced a kind of Bernie Madoff world in which investors' and owners' listed assets kept rising, and those paper assets even led them to purchase goods and services, producing some jobs and the appearance that the stagnation tendency was under control. But the Bernie Madoff worlds of bubbles in the stock market and the housing market were not real. The paper value of the assets in figure 2.3 was absurdly inflated above the values to which they had to return. A Ponzi scheme (a pyramid scheme like those chain letters that promise big money if you can recruit more people to just send money), like the one that Madoff carried out, is illegal, and he went

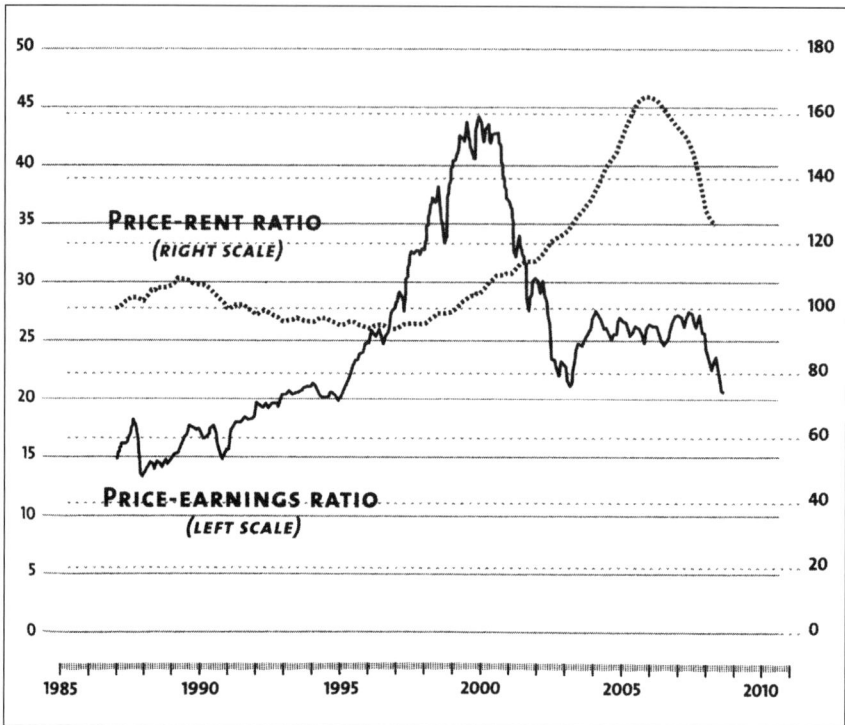

Figure 2.3 The Dot-com and Housing Bubbles

to prison, partly because fraud is necessary to run a Ponzi scheme, and because he defrauded some very powerful people. No one would invest in something doomed to crash. The supposed prosperity of the Reagan, Clinton, and Bush bubbles was not illegal, but they rested on fraudulent claims, such as the claim that financial markets are self-regulating, that were merely a more sophisticated Ponzi scheme, with an equally certain collapse.

Fiscal and financial changes can alleviate a short-term crisis, but they cannot supply a permanent solution. *Over-reliance on borrowing creates the basis for other types of instability later,* sometimes more sudden and more devastating, especially if many of the debts have to be paid back all at once. Massive expansion of private credit and Keynesian economic policies only temporarily alleviate capitalism's crises.

Exercise 2.9: Military Keynesianism

What determines the level of military spending? Is it simply a response to foreign threats? Is it mainly the result of which political party controls

the presidency? List the factors that you think have the most important impact on the level of military spending.

The Keynesian model addressed the situation in which the capitalist system produced inadequate demand—a situation in which the money available in the society does not buy all of the goods and services, leaving plants and labor idle. It addressed that problem from an apparently neutral standpoint, not from the standpoint of this or that group, but from the standpoint of the good of the system as a whole. Is it not the case that the partisanship of a social theory is often built into it? *Someone* is going to implement the theory; *someone* is going to benefit from its implementation. In a situation in which, in fact, there are conflicting interests and political battles, the failure to explicitly consider what groups are being appealed to often leads to certain groups' interests being smuggled in. What were the class interests that would or could be infused into Keynesian spending to maintain full employment? To the extent that the analysis sees the capitalist situation as eternal and tries to undergird and strengthen it, those interests are capitalist. Beyond that, from a Marxist standpoint, the government has limited possibilities for expanding civilian spending without coming into conflict with profits. Expansion of the civilian state sector competes with private enterprise. Provision of services or redistribution of income weakens the power of capital over labor. To the extent that capitalists have dominant political influence, they can block spending which threatens them. However, one virtually inexhaustible kind of expenditure can achieve a substantial ruling class coalition: military expenditure.

Fundamentally, a military exists to protect the foreign and domestic political and economic control of the ruling class. The *nature* and *amount* of military spending have a powerful impact on the domestic economy. Its "virtue," from the point of view of capitalist economics, is that it is absolutely useless. It does not compete with business. It does not shackle the "whip of hunger"; no one is going to eat guns. It is easily manipulated by the state and has built-in obsolescence. It undergirds highly profitable American foreign investments, and it is easily rationalized on the basis of "national needs" or "foreign threats": the Cold War, the need for energy, patriotism, the war against terrorism, or the war against drugs; which is to say, it boosts profits by increasing effective demand (spending a lot of money) without undermining the position of capital (without giving the working class anything).

But the interpretation of national needs and foreign threats is never class neutral. Marxists have traditionally seen external government policies and military Keynesianism as the usual outcome, with further policy implications. Investigating the variation in military expenditure, during the long boom after World War II, L. Griffin, J. Devine, and M. Wallace undertook a time-series analysis of the relation of military spending to the other variables listed in table 2.6. Structural variables (such as revenue and civilian government expenditure) give some indication of the amount of money available for the military. Political variables (such as whether Republicans or Democrats have the presidency, or whether it was an election year) show the possible dependence of military spending on the democratic process. Economic variables (such as a decrease in monopoly profits, the occurrence of a recession or an increase in unionized unemployment) measure ways in which military spending may be a way of solving economic problems. Griffin, Devine, and Wallace undertook a time-series regression to see whether, in fact, during the period from 1949 to 1977, military expenditure went up or down in response to each variable. Table 2.6 gives a partial list of the variables they considered and a brief rationale why some theorists suppose that each of those variables might be related to the increase or decrease of military spending.

Table 2.6   Partial List of Possible Causes of Variation in Military Spending, 1949 to 1976

Civilian expenditure/GNP	Virtually any theory will say that if more is spent for civilian expenditure, there will be less for military.
Democratic president	Throughout the period, the Republicans tended to be pro-military. If there is a political dynamic at work, this variable will have a negative relation.
Election	Many political economists hypothesize an election cycle such that spending increases just prior to an election to maximize the reelection chances of the incumbent.
Inflation	If inflation is promoted by all government spending, periods of high inflation will produce a pressure to lower government spending, including military spending.
Percent change monopoly profits	Military spending may be needed to beef up profitability of monopoly capital.
Percent change in USSR military	An arms race would make this a main determinant of US military spending.
Recession	If military spending is countercyclical, a general recession ought to cause an increase.
Revenue/GNP	Most theories predict that more revenue makes more military spending possible.
Unemployment	If military spending is an outlet for spending to bolster demand, this will show a positive relation.
Unionized unemployment	If the only sagging demand which counts is in unionized sectors, this will correlate to military spending.
War years	Theories which give any autonomy to political events predict that wars should have positive effect.

Adapted from source: L. Griffin, J. Devine, and M. Wallace, "Monopoly, Capital, Organized Labor, and Military Expenditures in the United States, 1949–76" *American Journal of Sociology* 88:130–3 (1982).

Before you proceed, examine the table and decide what you think you will find with respect to each variable. What does Marxist theory predict? What do liberal theories predict? For each variable, decide whether you think it will have a relation to military spending. Which variables will show the strongest relations? What will happen when a foreign threat disappears?

Table 2.7 gives the results of Griffin, Devine, and Wallace's investigation. As in previous analyses, only the variables which showed a significant relation to military spending are included in the table. That does not mean that the variables which do not appear in table 2.7 are without interest. Indeed, some of the most interesting of their findings concern things which turn out *not* to be related to military spending. All of the geopolitical items (the ostensible reasons for the military expenditure), such as spending by the Soviet Union or whether the United States was at war, turned out to have *no* significant relation to military spending! Similarly, most of the political items have no relation to it; only the short-term election cycle (essentially an increase in spending as a kind of pork barrel) shows any relation, and that is not a powerful one.

As in previous regressions, each coefficient shows whether military expenditures went up and down at the same time that the variable listed at the left went up or down. As previously, the specific numbers depend on how the variables are measured; therefore, the thing to pay attention to is whether the coefficient is positive or negative and the *t*-statistic and * (indicating significance which shows how strong the relation is). Table 2.7 gives two equations; one gives the effects of the structural variables (revenue and civilian expenditure) and three economic variables (monopoly profits, inflation, and union unemployment). A second equation gives those variables and also whether it was an election year. In both, revenue has a positive relation to military spending, with a very large *t*, which is statistically significant.

Table 2.7   Sector-specific Determinants of U.S. Military Spending

Independent Variables	Lag	Equation 1	t	Equation 2	t
Revenue/GDP	(*t*)	1.16	(8.60)*	1.23	(9.24)*
Civilian expenditure/GDP	(*t*)	−0.525	(7.03)*	−0.523	(7.07)*
% Change of monopoly profits	(*t*–1)	−0.036	(3.29)*	−0.025	(2.30)*
Inflation	(*t*)	−0.138	(2.23)*	−0.097	(1.43)
Union unemployment	(*t*–1)	0.138	(1.45)	0.165	(1.84)*
Election	(*t*–1)			0.563	(1.95)*
Adjusted R^2		0.877		0.890	

*$p < 0.05$.

Source: L. Griffin, J. Devine, and M. Wallace, "Monopoly Capital, Organized Labor, and Military Expenditures in the United States, 1949–76," *American Journal of Sociology* 88:130–3 (1982).

The reason that revenue is positively associated with military spending is mainly that to spend more money on military, the government has to collect more money. Similarly, civilian expenditure has a large, significant, negative relation because the more money is spent on the military, the less there is for civilian government expenditure and vice versa. In both equations, change in monopoly profits, lagging one year, has a strong negative relation to military spending. This means that if monopoly profits dive in 1965, say, military spending will tend to rise in 1966, controlling the other variables. If military spending rises in 1965, domestic spending will tend to fall. Inflation has a negative relation to military spending; when there is a lot of inflation, military spending tends to be a little less, relative to what it would be, given the other four variables. The same relation shows up in the second equation when you take account of the election cycle, but then it is not statistically significant. Similarly, unemployment in unionized industries, lagging one year, has a small relation to military spending, which is barely significant when one takes account of the election cycle. If unionized unemployment rises in a given year, military spending will tend to rise the next year; and conversely. Finally, prior to an election, military spending tends to rise.

These data suggest a picture of an economy choking on its own productive forces, politically unable to spend its money on needed goods. But the corporate elite, dominating the monopoly sector, is able to use military expenditure to prop up its own profits, and secondarily, to keep inflation and the unemployment of limited groups of workers within bounds. A secondary and weaker tendency is for political leaders to time military expenditure so that more government contracts are handed out just before they try to get reelected. These data are *not* consistent with any of the main rationales which are given for military expenditure (like, "We have to do it because they are doing it") or the main explanations usually put forward (such as, "It is the warlike Republicans, and would be stopped by electing more Democrats").

This analysis is especially interesting in light of the political-economic events of the Reagan, G. H. W. Bush, Clinton, and G. W. Bush terms. The great puzzle of those years was that the disappearance of the alleged Soviet threat was instantly and seamlessly replaced by a supposed Islamic terrorist threat. This becomes less puzzling when the institutional (corporate and government) power and the economic demand for a permanent war economy is taken into account. Whatever differences including those years might make in the coefficients of the analysis by Griffin, et al., and whatever differences in rhetoric and in social, health, and educational programs, some of the main elements of Reagan's program merely continued that of prior administrations, and they were continued by G. H. W. Bush, Clinton, G. W. Bush, and now by Obama. This was especially true of using massive military spending to spend our way out of a recession.

However, imperialism, world domination, and the military apparatus to maintain it is not merely a politically convenient way for the government to spend money in order to prevent inadequate demand. We saw in section 10 of chapter 1 that Hooks and McQueen ("American Exceptionalism Revisited," 2010) argue that the combination of militarism (military construction) and racism (tension between the large recently migrated African American workforce in military procurement industries) were powerful forces in the states that switched to the Republican Party in the early years of the Truman administration after World War II, bringing the New Deal to a halt.

Hooks and McQueen analyze the thesis of "American exceptionalism"—the view that deeply rooted peculiarities of American society made it impossible to develop the kinds of social democratic policies about health, education, welfare, and labor that came to characterize many European societies. Hooks and McQueen argue that the United States had many of the same developments up to and through World War II, but the first decades after the war put in place distinctive practices about health, education, and labor that set the country onto a path of development with a smaller fraction of the labor force unionized and more limited social policies. The fact that the Congress passed the Taft-Harley Act in 1947, overriding Truman's veto, was a key moment and a good illustration of the political process that let to that distinctive historical trajectory. Hooks and McQueen argue that the two main characteristics of the states which went to the Republican Party in 1947, making it possible to halt or roll back parts of the New Deal, was the combination of high military expenditure with high African American migration from the South.

The concept of military Keynesianism, like other theories that stress the power of the Pentagon, often focuses on the political and bureaucratic forms within which policy unfolds with less attention to the larger political forces driving national and international change. What the kind of work illustrated by Griffin et al. (1982) and by Hooks and McQueen (2010) suggests is that such policies are often driven by some simple, basic economic and international contradictions (the main ways to generate demand domestically erode domestic profitability); this can be partly alleviated by use of racism and undocumented workers, with further consequences that we shall consider later; and it can be partly alleviated by international expansion and preparation for war, with other problematical consequences.

Suggestions for Further Reading

Like many topics reviewed here, a bibliography on depressions, Keynesian policies, and inflation would be much longer than this whole book. Introductory accounts appear in the introductions to Marxist economics cited above. A liberal account of the Reagan, Clinton, and Bush bubbles is P.

Krugman, *The Return of Depression Economics and the Crisis of 2008* (Norton, 2009.) A basic Marxian account, written as a series of articles as the crises unfolded from 2006 to 2008, is J. B. Foster and F. Magdoff, *The Great Financial Crisis* (Monthly Review, 2009). Military Keynesianism: the analysis by L. Griffin, J. Devine, and M. Wallace, "Monopoly Capital, Organized Labor, and Military Expenditure," *American Journal of* Sociology (Supplement) 88:113–153, is further discussed by C. Jencks, *American Journal of Sociology* 91:373–390 and G. Hooks and G. McLauchlan, "Reevaluating Theories of U.S. War Making," *Social Science Quarterly* 73:437–455 (1992). The fundamental theories of the election cycle, as well as capitalism's need for unemployment to discipline the workforce, were elaborated by M. Kalecki, "Political Aspects of Full Employment" (1943), in *Selected Essays* (Cambridge University Press, 1971). The literature looking at the economic, military, and geopolitical sources of the Gulf wars is overviewed in J. Carroll, *House of War* (Houghton Mifflin, 2006) and Frances F. Piven, *The War at Home* (New Press, 2006). A class analysis of relations between capitalism, imperialism, and development is B. Berberoglu, *Globalization of Capital and the Nation-State* (Rowman & Littlefield, 2003). A recent view of the concept of military Keynesianism is J. Cypher, "From Military Keynesianism to Global-neoliberal Militarism," *Monthly Review* 59:37–55 (2006).

SECTION 2.10: WHY HAS
THE UNITED STATES BEEN "NUMBER 1"?

Some people believe that the current economic problems of the United States were caused by other countries, or at least that current economic problems may be solved by our relations with other countries. Certainly, U.S. corporations' relations with the rest of the world have deeply affected us in the past, and so it is understandable that some people hope to solve problems by policies such as overseas investment. They support the search for foreign markets for goods and services from the United States and policies that reduce our economic and social problems, often at the expense of people in other, weaker countries.

How else can one raise the rate of profit when there is downward pressure? Marx stressed the importance of England's colonies, and Lenin made the analysis of imperialism (the scramble for colonies) central to his analysis of the changes in capitalism and trends to world war. It is possible to get raw materials cheaper overseas; it is possible to hire workers for lower pay overseas; it is possible to sell goods overseas which cannot be sold at home. This creates formidable pressure for overseas involvement. Moreover, the giants who stand to gain most from overseas investment also have immense political influence on the government. This is one of the reasons for the enormous dynamics of capitalism. Once capitalism exists everywhere, it transforms the entire world. Foreign investment starts as a lovely windfall from the standpoint of capital. Later, it becomes a matter of *survival* for capitalism. The threat of the runaway shop can be used to increase profitability at home and help circulation. And the high rate of profit there represents a transfusion—the extraction of real labor, hence profits—from abroad.

The very important role of foreign investment and foreign involvement has meant that the analysis of the dynamics of capitalism now certainly has to be done on a world scale. From that standpoint, it is clear that people in the United States have one of the highest standards of living in the world. This fact is crucial to understanding why the United States has had a relatively high standard of living, and a looser, less repressive political atmosphere than many other countries. Simply put, the U.S. economic standard of living and the absence of major political repression are directly tied to the high profits that U.S. corporations were able to make overseas, which helped forestall economic crises at home. In fact, most of the countries which are considered to be more "democratic" are also the countries which benefit from imperialism. We use the term "imperialism" rather than the bland term "globalization," because "imperialism" makes the unequal, exploitative relationship central to the analysis, while "globalization" is a vaguer, more general concept.

Does that mean that working class people should support these kinds of overseas investments? There is a debate among Marxists as to the effect of foreign investment on U.S. workers. Some theorists believe that U.S. workers benefit from it, and this is sometimes used to explain why there have not been revolutions in advanced industrial societies. According to this "trickle down" theory, American workers would rationally support American investments abroad, at least if they pursue their narrow, short-term, economic self-interest. The money that the companies make overseas would supposedly trickle down to workers at home. Most Marxists disagree with this line of reasoning. They argue that there are a number of problems with overseas investment as a way of sustaining growth and capitalism and that U.S. workers are mainly hurt by U.S. foreign investment, in a number of ways:

1. The most obvious and immediate effect of foreign investment is the **runaway shop**. Plants close here and open up where labor is cheaper. This loss of jobs actually lowers wages at home. There are people who benefit from Ford's foreign profits: the Ford stockholders and bosses. But the direct effect on Ford workers is negative. The only sense in which Ford workers should support this is if they support corporate control of the system and wish to see it sustained. As the system becomes more and more malignant, it is less and less in their interest to sustain it.

2. Workers in those other countries do not like to work for a few dollars a day. (Social scientists debate the most accurate term to describe these places formerly called "Third World"—sometimes they are called "less developed countries," sometimes "poorer countries," sometimes the Global South, and we use the term "neocolony" to describe some of those countries as well.) Given the starvation and misery which is present there, workers in those countries, the neocolonies, begin to fight for their rights. (We use the term "neocolony" to describe countries which have formal political independence, but which have their economies dominated by corporations from imperialist countries.) As those workers organize for higher pay, better working conditions, land reform, or anything else that cuts into profits, neocolonial governments are faced with the choice of supporting their workers or supporting the multinational companies and the banking groups. Usually they support the multinationals—who are often more powerful than they are, and have them over a barrel in any case. In that case they are caught in a cycle of increasing the amount of brutal, military, and dictatorial policies which are necessary to keep their local populations subdued, but in turn causes them to rebel more. Increasingly, the United States has to send more and more military aid and even troops to prop up fascist military regimes in the developing countries. Do working class youth benefit from policies which can put millions of them into military combat?

3. Not only the workers and peasants, but also the capitalists in the neocolonies increasingly decide that they want a bigger piece of the profits that are taken out of their countries. There is increasingly an opposition between the multinationals, backed by the power of the U.S. government, and a broad coalition dominated by imperialists within the neocolonial countries. The rise of OPEC is a good example of this. The defection and rebellion of former U.S. allies, such as Iraq's Saddam Hussein, of the Taliban, and of Manuel Noriega of Panama, further destabilizes the political-economic power of the imperialist country, sometimes in powerful ways. The development of Latin American drug cartels which are controlled by capitalists sometimes in alliance and sometimes in conflict with the U.S. ruling elite is another example. The United States has completed two major wars in Iraq, protecting the profits of oil companies. As we go to press, it has ongoing wars in Afghanistan and Pakistan, with other wars, in the Middle East and elsewhere, waiting in the wings.

4. Perhaps most urgent in the next decade is that attempts to maintain profits by overseas investment bring capitalists into collision with the interests of the capitalists of the other countries, including Russia, Germany, Japan, France, and the state capitalist managers and own-

ers in China. The dynamics of expansion are such that soon there is no more world to divide up into spheres of influence. Then the only way to get more is to take it away from the sphere of influence of some other world power. Twice before, in World War I and World War II, this has led to global conflagration. Proxy wars and brushfire wars are more common. Some people argue that the situation is different now because of fear of nuclear war. The leaders of recent administrations argued that the United States military was so dominant because the Soviet Union was no more, that we could almost effortlessly enforce our interests abroad. Unfortunately, these don't change the underlying dynamics. For example, the development of a more united Europe under the European Economic Community, or the rise of China, of Russia, or even of India, will only further intensify global economic competition with the United States. There is increasing desperation as the economic crisis emerges at the level of the world system.

Exercise 2.10: Dependent Development and Poverty Traps

The location of a capitalist firm in a poorer country such as Peru is social dynamite, bringing about massive transformation of virtually the whole of the social structure. Is the transformation benign or malignant? To get an overview of the kinds of effects one must consider, imagine a hypothetical country like Peru. To consider political and social effects as well as economic ones, distinguish different groups such as peasants, workers, landholders, capitalists, politicians, and others who might be important. Now imagine the entrance of a multinational, a conglomerate which may be richer and more powerful than the entire country. This conglomerate might either be in the business of extracting raw materials, such as Exxon-Mobil, or it might be in the business of manufacturing. In either case, try to make a list of the effects the multinational will have on each group. Note that it will not ignore those groups, but in order to assure its continued operation, it will form alliances with some of them. How? Which groups will do what? How will this affect their relations with each other? How will this affect the overall pattern of growth and development of the country?

Think about the similarities and the differences between the relationship of a conglomerate from the United States or Europe to a country in the Global South and the relation of the white, Anglo majority to the largely African American and Hispanic dwellers of a ghetto community in the United States or the poor immigrant communities in Europe.

Just as there is debate among Marxists as to the effects of overseas investment on the workers in the home country, so too there is debate about its long-term effect on the country where the investment takes place. The dominant picture for a long time was modernization. Sociologists thought investment would lead to the eventual capitalist development of those countries as well. They thought those countries were being hurried along the same path that the developed country had already taken. This corresponded to the common-sense perception that capitalism spreads—that setting up a Ford plant or an IBM plant in a country like the Philippines has to provide a certain number of jobs, currency, and training that would not otherwise be there.

However, those countries either did not seem to develop, or seemed to develop far more slowly or qualitatively differently. As we noted above, dependency theory and world-systems theory emphasize ways in which the development of the advanced countries and the underdevelopment of the peripheral countries were the two sides of a single coin, two halves of a single process. As all peoples are entangled in the world market, there is a growth of riches at one pole, and the growth of misery, starvation, oppression, and degradation at the other. Those countries have been falling further and further behind the advanced countries. Often their real standard of living (e.g., grams of protein consumed per person) has declined, especially if one takes into account the disappearance of nonmoney income. This corresponded to the perception that capitalism does not spread equally—that Ford or IBM are out for their own interests, and that the shipping of tens of billions of dollars of repatriated profits to the United States does not help the workers from whom that profit is extracted.

Does foreign investment promote or retard development? It might seem that this is a simple, empirical question. One looks at the countries that have lots of foreign investment and sees whether they have developed. In fact, the question is complex. Foreign investment powerfully affects many things about the country where the investment happens. There has been a burst of research on the economic development, the political relations, and the social structure of countries with lots of foreign investment. This research considers investment by multinational corporations as one of many causes which together have various effects. In general, what that analysis has found is that close ties to U.S. multinationals does not so much lead either to development or to nondevelopment; it produces a *different kind* of development.

The scenario you laid out was a hypothetical one, like a science fiction story. The aliens arrive and society changes. The crucial next step is to move from scenarios to actual evidence. To do so, you must figure out what are the crucial kinds of theory and evidence which you would need to find out whether the processes you have sketched out are the real, main processes there.

Dependency theory suggests that on the one hand, investment by a multinational, like any other investment, makes a short-run contribution to growth. But, on the other hand, it distorts the political system, the economy, technology, and the social system in a way that prevents growth. The heads of the multinational make their decisions so as to help themselves. They create a political, economic, and social dependency deadly for most people in a less developed country. For example, P. Evans and M. Timberlake, in "Dependence, Inequality, and Growth in Less Developed Countries," *American Sociological Review* 45:531 (1980), look at the effect of foreign investment and level of development on inequality and the growth of service employment. (Economically, producing services rather than raw materials or manufactured goods is classified as the **tertiary sector.** Maids, waiters, barbers, soldiers, teachers, clerks, transport workers, government workers, and salespeople are examples of tertiary sector workers. The tertiary sector is roughly, but not exactly, equivalent to nonproductive labor in Marxist theory. Some dependency theorists had suggested that the presence of multinationals causes a bloated tertiary sector.) Like analysis of military Keynesianism in the previous section or analyses of the world system and mega-slums in section 1.8, the analysis of dependency illustrates the interaction of Marxian theory with empirical research.

Thus you should make your general scenario more specific by predicting: (1) What will be the effect of foreign investment on income inequality? Why do you think so? (2) What will be the effect of foreign investment on growth of the tertiary sector? Why do you think so? (3) What part of the effect of foreign investment is due to the growth of the tertiary sector? (4) What are the theoretical implications of this for a general theory of development? (5) What are its practical implications for groups in less developed societies?

Evans and Timberlake note that there is a substantial body of empirical research indicating that foreign investments increase the amount of inequality—increasing the mass of very poor people at the bottom and of rich people at the top. Often the foreign investment is conditional on government policies, such as union busting and lower social services, which lower wages. At the same time, some upper and middle class groups make a lot of money from it. Evans and Timberlake first show a tendency for inequality to be greater and for the tertiary sector to be larger in countries with more foreign investment, measuring foreign investment in several different ways and controlling the size of the per capita gross domestic product.

Table 2.8 is one of their data tables, showing effects of one measure of investment dependence, and of change in the tertiary, controlling gross domestic product, on seven aspects of inequality. The Gini index is an overall measure of inequality. Column 1 shows that it has a positive relation to growth of the tertiary sector and a somewhat weaker negative relation to the gross domestic product (GDP). The other six columns of table 2.8 allow one to see how investment dependence, the tertiary sector, and the gross domestic product affect different income groups. Growth of the tertiary sec-

Table 2. 8   Regression of Income Inequality of Investment Dependence, Size of Tertiary Sector, and Per Capita GDP

Dependent Variables		Gini Index of Income	% Income to Poorest 20%	% Income to 21–40%	% Income to 41–60%	% Income to 61–80%	% Income to 81–95%	% Income to Richest 5%
Independent Variables		Inequality	Grouping	Grouping	Grouping	Grouping	Grouping	Grouping
Investment dependence II	a	45.064	5.554	8.37	12.926	21.962*	29.260	21.928
	b	2.858	-0.451	-0.414	-0.759	-1.858	0.135	3.332*
	Beta	0.544	-0.380	-0.310	-0.446	-0.910	0.040	0.728
	s.e.	1.898	0.406	0.494	0.781	0.916	1.701	1.878
	F	2.27	1.27	0.70	0.94	4.12	0.00	3.15
Change in tertiary 1950–1960	b	113.684**	-31.580**	-34.174**	-15.491	20.302	17.338	44.327
	Beta	0.511	-0.629	-0.605	-0.215	0.235	0.118	0.229
	s.e.	49.362	10.417	12.844	20.313	23.813	44.222	48.826
	F	5.30	9.19	7.08	0.58	0.73	0.15	0.82
Per capita GDP	b	-0.029*	0.004	0.006	0.008	0.013*	-0.008	-0.024
	Beta	-0.597	0.394	0.480	0.473	0.700	-0.232	-0.552
	s.e.	0.016	0.003	0.004	0006	0.008	0.014	0.015
	F	3.59	1.79	2.21	1.39	3.20	0.29	2.36
R^2		0.48	0.55	0.45	0.16	0.20	0.04	0.33
n		21	21	21	21	21	21	21

Notes: a = Constant, b = metric coefficient, se = standard error, * = $p < 0.05$.

tor seems to have a negative effect on the income of the lowest half of the population; overall development (GDP) appears to have little relation to the income of groups at the top and bottom.

Evans and Timberlake's analysis had previously indicated that investment dependence was associated with growth of the tertiary sector and with inequality. There are a number of ways that foreign investment might serve to increase the tertiary sector. The multinationals will use labor-saving technologies from their home countries; they may increase the tendency of people to move off the land; they create a big reserve of unemployed and underemployed people; they may generate more demand for maids, waiters, barbers, soldiers, salespeople, government workers, etc., than demand for manufacturing. Evans and Timberlake hypothesize that foreign investment bloats the tertiary sector, and the growth of this sector promotes inequality. Table 2.8 suggests that growth of the tertiary sector increases inequality, and that this effect explains much of the effect of foreign investment. It is part of an ongoing stream of research which suggests three important theoretical conclusions: (1) development is not a uniform process of modernization which independently happens in different countries. Rather, the relation of less developed countries to more developed countries and their position in the world system powerfully affects their options; and (2) the process of development is not a simple economic process. Powerful social, economic, and political changes proliferate. Moreover, practically, the fact that foreign investment seems to help the groups at the top and hurt the groups at the bottom suggests that a very common situation will be that where landowners and businessmen, backed by the force of the government, want very much to be part of the "free world" of Ford, IBM, and Exxon-Mobil. But workers and peasants at the bottom who appear to be hurt by that form of development may be far less enchanted by the prospect.

Thus, (3) capitalist development does not happen uniformly but by a Monopoly-like process. There is an accumulation of wealth by some countries at the same time that there is increased poverty in others, and even within developing countries, there is an accumulation of wealth by some and an accumulation of poverty and disadvantage for others. Such dependency effects are often analyzed today in terms of "spatial effects" and "poverty traps." They produce mega-slums. They occur both between neighborhoods, groups, or states within a society and between societies, and they constitute a vigorous area of sociological research.

These dynamics of accumulation, with their resulting inequality and polarization, are not only processes that happen far away in less developed countries. Robert Blauner based his theory of "internal colonialism" on the analogy between the relation of ghetto communities to the rest of the society and the relation of less developed countries to European or American colonialism. A different form of this analogy was also central to Gunnar

Myrdal's mid-twentieth-century analyses of American race relations (*An American Dilemma*) and of institutional economics (*The Asian Drama*). Myrdal argued that whether we consider the poverty of a less developed country or the poverty of a racial group within a society, the crucial thing to analyze is a vicious cycle. A country or a group has little capital because it has low income; it has low income because it has low skills, little capital, and poor health; it has a lack of skills, income, and healthcare partly because it lacks capital, social services, and political mobilization. In turn, these conditions are caused by and reinforce such other conditions as family disorganization or high crime rates. And so it goes; wherever one starts, one is led to a tangle of self-reinforcing and mutually reinforcing disadvantages and pathologies. Myrdal called this self-reinforcing structure "cumulative causation." It is also the dynamic of positive feedback and self-reinforcing alienation or accumulation, which we have analyzed in terms of games of Monopoly.

With regard to race relations and race inequality, Myrdal argued that the vicious cycle of minority deprivation is exacerbated by racism, which it further reinforces. The racism of the dominant group reinforces the disadvantages of the minority group; the disadvantages of the minority group reinforce the racism (such as stereotyping or segregation) of the majority group. These cycles of disadvantage or of racism and disadvantage are both polarizing and self-reinforcing so that a historical difference in initial conditions don't vanish over time; rather, in the absence of countervailing policies, it tends to snowball.

If one is affected not only by one's own resources and actions, but also by those of the people around one (and there are very many ways that this is true), then self-reinforcing cumulative causation (with polarization and crises which result from this fact) is a very common dynamic. It is not an occasional oddity of social science. Rather, it is a common result of processes of accumulation, and it produces polarization and a crisis-ridden pattern of development. A great deal of contemporary research and theory explores these effects.

Suggestions for Further Reading

The contemporary literature on globalization from within the Marxist tradition is overviewed in B. Berberoglu *Globalization in the 21st Century: Labor, Capital, and the State on a World Scale* (Palgrave Macmillan, 2010). Another recent contribution to the immense literature on dependent development, world systems, and globalization is D. Harvey, *A Brief History of Neoliberalism* (Oxford University Press, 2007). There is a complex debate between those who argue that foreign investment eventually develops societies in which it occurs and those who believe it does not; the reason that it is not a simple, empirical matter of fact is that self-reinforcing dynamics produce complex discontinuous effects. See also, P. Krugman, *The Self-Organizing Economy* (Blackwell, 1996). J. Stiglitz, *Making Globalization Work* (Norton, 2006) and James Petras, *The New Development Politics: The Age of Empire and New Social Movement* (Ashgate Publishing, 2003). S. Bowles has edited a useful collection on *Poverty Traps* (Russell Sage, 2006).

SUMMARY AND CONCLUSIONS: ECONOMICS AND POLITICAL ECONOMY

In the introduction we previewed our argument in twenty-four propositions, and we summarized chapter 1 by discussing the first six. Now we can discuss the next six ideas.

7. **The Value of Commodities is Determined by Labor.** Many people see economics as the core of Marxist theory. Marx devoted a major effort to understanding and explaining economic processes and development. But his view of economics, based on the labor theory of value, was different from U.S. college-level economics courses today. The common view that Marxism reduces everything down to economics, and therefore reduces humankind down to a group of greedy, hedonistic creatures, is simply not Marx's view. If we "are" what we "do," then the struggle for the working class and humankind as a whole to control our labor is, in fact, the struggle for human freedom. For Marx, economics was really political economy. His central aim was to understand the type of society which would unlock human physical and intellectual potential. Marx believed that collective production would not only improve the material level of people's lives, but much more, it would lay the basis for freer and more creative as well as more productive lives. His analysis contrasts with selfish individualism, either in its optimistic, neoconservative form, or in its pessimistic ones, which include fascist theory and liberal identity politics. Marxian labor theory of value is neither some abstract mathematical formula nor an abstract ethical postulate. By focusing on the social relations of work, it helps us to understand how capitalism generates other social arrangements and how contradictions arise within it. These contradictions, too, are not some mechanical interaction. They include human consciousness, human needs, politics, and most notably, class struggle.

8. **The Owning Classes Exploit Laborers to Accumulate Wealth.** The world has experienced several different modes of production. Capitalism is the current dominant stage. Productive laborers support a

leisure class through profit on wage labor. Capitalism develops racism, among other divisions, as an effective way of helping maximize profits. Workers are separated and split both physically and in consciousness. Sexist and other divisions segment the labor market as well. Capitalism allows for much more rapid accumulation of wealth than any previous system. It is also more unstable. Specifically, capitalism creates a working class. Globalization hides our dependence on the labor of others from some people, but the growth of a world market connects us all in an intricate net of relationships. Our shoes, our clothes, our cars, and the other things that make our daily lives possible were produced by someone, somewhere, often in relationships of exploitation. In pre-capitalist societies, widely separated people were relatively unconnected. In capitalism, they are *related* and *divided*. Under the slave or feudal system, a united, internationalist working class was blocked by divisions in language, transportation, religion, politics, kinship, and custom. Uner capitalism, people are still divided, but analysis of the production process allows us to see the root of these divisions and abolish them.

9. **Overproduction and a Falling Rate of Profit Are Endemic Capitalism and Cause Crises.** The immense dynamics of capitalism, like a game of Monopoly, cannot go on forever. It hits limits; it creates crises; it undermines its own conditions; bubbles burst. For Marx the evils of capitalism went beyond the simple, immediate suffering of deprived groups. For Marx, all class-divided societies, including capitalist, also distort, suppress, even destroy the productive capabilities of society and the creative potential of its members. The owning classes not only deprive the laboring classes of material wealth; *they distort the productive processes* in such a way as to deprive the laboring classes, and even themselves, of the ability to work, and to control production in a way that meets people's needs or develops their capacities. *Distribution and consumption cannot be permanently changed without changing production.* Marx analyzes how the accumulation of wealth by owners of the means of production affects what can and what cannot be produced. Economic production contracts and, with that contraction, there is the rise of a culture that deflates human aspirations, as well. In broader terms, it becomes a question of how human potential is being stifled in order to protect the property rights of the owning class. Marx examines the forms this issue takes both in pre-capitalist societies and, especially, within capitalist society.

10. **Private Credit and Keynesianism are Only a Temporarily Solution to Crises.** Keeping capital circulating can sometimes prevent acute crises. One way of keeping capital circulating is to borrow money

from the future. Private individuals borrow. So do large corporations and governments. But Presidents Reagan and Bush borrowed to stimulate the economy. When that wore off, and the United States economy really was on the edge of collapse, President Obama borrowed more, to stimulate the economy a little longer. This cannot stop the falling rate of profit, and it doesn't stop the disorder in the productive sector that causes overproduction, stagnation, and general chaos. Apparently vigorous but jobless growth temporarily floats on immense bubbles of debt. Individual corporate selfishness gives rise to continued economic problems. Furthermore, when economic crises again appear in the midst of a now-serious debt crisis, the problems are especially severe. Specifically, overproduction and the decline of profits emerge as inherent, fundamental problems for capitalism.

11. **Imperialist Foreign Investment is also a Temporary Solution.** What Marx was beginning to foresee did not come to full fruition until after he died. In some of the more powerful countries, the capitalists were able to stave off economic collapse by exporting capital, investing their money overseas to get higher rates of profit. Overseas expansionism is driven by the national and international competition of capitalism. Within this recent period, capitalism has meant not simply outright theft of land, gold, spices, slaves, oil, or uranium. Capitalism, which is choking at home, needs cheap labor and raw materials to sustain higher rates of profit, and it needs to prevent others from cutting it off from them. Inevitably, imperialism gives rise to new problems. In large countries and small, from Pakistan and China to Ukraine to Colombia, new problems arise. Economically, overseas expansion collides with the expansion of other capitalists, because the world is finite in size. China is now a major investor in Africa and Latin America, and U.S. corporate interests clash with Russian interests in Central Asia and Eastern Europe. Imperialist profits fall because of resistance from workers and from local capitalists in the neocolonies, as well as the competition of other imperialist powers who want to move into those highly profitable areas. In places like Darfur or in Latin America, that was once the playground of United States capital interests, there are now sharp conflicts between United States capital, local interests, and those of China and the European Union. Eventually, war becomes the main option to protect national interests, as it has in the past, even as all parties wanted to avoid it.

12. **As Temporary Remedies Falter, Economic Crisis Intensifies.** Neither private credit, nor Keynesian economic policies, nor imperialism can permanently solve capitalism's problems. As a result, the

capitalists must intensify their drive to squeeze extra profits from the working class. Mergers increase. Social services are cut back. Cities, bridges, and infrastructures decay. There is de-industrialization. Unemployment grows; tuition is hiked; jobs become temporary; repair of bridges or of the levees around New Orleans is not a priority. Maintaining a viable temperature or a viable ocean environment are not priorities. Superexploitation and segmentation intensifies and takes new and brutal forms. While some sections of workers could previously alleviate some of their problems by reform struggles, this becomes less true. While capitalists could previously give in to some demands, now they have little choice, and conditions worsen for most members of the working class and for many supervisors, managers, and professionals as well.

3

Class Struggle

Class, Party, and Political Theory

INTRODUCTION: ECONOMIC DETERMINISM VERSUS POLITICAL PROCESSES AND IDEAS—A FALSE DEBATE

Marx was a philosopher, an historian, and an economist; but he was also a political theorist and a political activist. For much of his life, Marx made a living writing about contemporary political events. He built massive organizations. Sometimes that work had to be begun over and over again. He thought deeply and continuously about the causes of advances or setbacks and learned crucial lessons from active involvement.

Marx was not an abstract theoretician, buried in the British Museum; he was an active fighter in the class struggle. Mechanical interpretations of Marx say that if he was a political activist, then he did not follow his own theory. After all, such interpretations go, doesn't Marx say that history is governed by scientific laws? And if it follows scientific laws, then it can't be changed. And if it can't be changed, shouldn't one merely understand it theoretically? Or, didn't he say that it is not the political system but the economic system which is the fundamental source of change? And if the economic system is the source of change, then doesn't that mean that political action and ideas make no difference? But obviously Marx did believe that political action makes a difference.

In opposition to such mechanical, **economic-determinist** interpretations of Marx, others propose idealistic, **voluntaristic** interpretations which say that one can do anything if only one has the will and the political organization. Was Marx an economic determinist who believed that politics made no difference? Was he a voluntarist who believed in the autonomy of political forces and the state?

193

Many Marxists believe that both of these interpretations are one-sided and lead to superficial analyses of complex institutions. Many of the issues are methodological and philosophical and will be discussed in more depth in chapter 4. But for the moment it could be argued that they represent false dichotomies; they represent confusions about idealism and materialism, necessity and freedom, the economic and the political. All of them are **mechanical**. They ask questions in the abstract, as if a "yes" or "no" answer in one time and place will always be the correct answer in all times and places—questions such as whether political ideas, ideals, and beliefs have *any* effect on social change, or whether it is *ever* possible to affect the course of history, or whether the economy is the *only* important basis of political movements and change. Posed this way, these questions lead to confusion. The first thing that a fertile and productive theory has to do is to "unask" these questions and ask better ones. That is one of the functions of the dialectical method.

Do ideas make a difference? When people act, it is because they think and feel a certain way. All forces, even hunger or fear or sex operate through the brain. Similarly, when classes and societies act, it is usually through political bodies. But to conclude from this either that political forces and bodies can do *anything whatsoever* or, conversely, that they are not real and affect nothing are both errors of one-sidedness. The real question is: what ideas are important and have leverage on what other forces? When there are opposing, conflicting forces in motion, particular actions or ideas can reinforce either of the contradictory tendencies. But to analyze such a situation, one needs a concrete, empirical, historical theory. No methodological catchphrase about the autonomy of ideas or politics *in general* will do the trick.

Is history so totally determined that it can't be changed? Is there a contradiction between determinist science and activism? Marx believed that science is what allows us to understand and to undertake change. Whenever people understand more of the laws governing something, they are in a better position to affect it. If we know about a cause and effect relationship, we can change the effect by changing the cause. And we can avoid wasting our time battering our heads against a stone wall by trying ineffective strategies that do not affect the underlying causes. It is not by ignoring the laws of gravity and mechanics that we fly—even to the moon. Flapping one's hands, talking to the birds, or eating mushrooms do not help us fly. Knowing mechanics and understanding gravity, the very force that holds us down, does. A powerful theory is a theory with practical import. Practical import is the information the theory gives about how doing something causes something else to occur. History, politics, and society do have certain patterns, or "laws," and understanding them is what allows us to change society.

Are political events determined by economic ones? Mainstream individualist explanations of social problems, accepted by conservatives and liberals alike, often end up concluding that "bad things" happen because people have "bad ideas" . . . leading to the conclusion that all we have to do is educate people or if that doesn't work, vote out or lock up the ones who just won't learn. Sometimes this interacts with ideas about a supposedly unchangeable, selfish "human nature" that should either be embraced (conservatives) or somewhat tamed (modern liberals), but accepted as unchangeable fact. Against that, Marxists first want to "follow the money" . . . to examine which interests are served by which policies. But of course ideas are important.

Marx discovered that class and organization of production have powerful political effects. But class and production involve more than money. Capitalist production contains many contradictory tendencies. Class struggle generates apparatuses of coercion, including the state, and it generates the forces and movements that transform those apparatuses, including forces that operate within the political sphere. Neither the state nor the economy is "autonomous" or "relatively autonomous" *in general*. To understand their impact, one needs a far more specific, detailed, and concrete theory.

Suggestions for Further Reading

As A. Gilbert shows in *Marx's Politics* (Rutgers University Press, 1981), Marx's extensive political activity repeatedly fails to jibe with the mechanical interpretations of some Marxist scholars. For example, it was not in advanced capitalist England, nearing a proletarian majority, that Marx saw the best prospects for socialism, but in backward Germany. Marx did not ignore the peasants as "reactionary"; he organized his first communist rally among Worringen peasants. Marx did not explain the rise and fall of Chartism in England by economic causes but by racism. Marx urged the International Workingmen's Association (IWA) to spearhead a campaign for Irish freedom to help overcome this racism.

SECTION 3.1: WHAT IS THE BASIS OF A TRULY FREE SOCIETY?

Political theorists have argued for centuries about the question, "What is the basis of a rational, just, and free society?" Modern political science seeks empirical, quantitative evidence to help find the answers.

Many political scientists and political sociologists say that there is a gulf between fact and value, between modern quantitative, empirical political science and old, value-laden political theory. They say that modern political sociology does not deal with questions concerning intangibles like rationality, justice, or freedom, but with things that can be observed and measured. Now a fundamental thrust of Marx's criticism of **idealism** was that he wished to move from abstract arguments to analyses which were rooted in what people were actually doing in the real world. But one cannot sidestep theoretical disagreements by sticking to raw facts. *People who think that they are avoiding all political theory are usually operating within the framework of a political theory which they do not wish to examine.* Rationality, justice, and freedom are just as measurable as the strength of party allegiances, but there are more disagreements about them because more people care and argue about them.

Theories of Freedom

In political theory, there are fundamental disagreements about "freedom." Marx's conception of freedom was **dialectical** and **materialist**. The dialectical approach examines the ways in which everything changes. Dialectical conceptions of freedom do not abstractly define a timeless condition. Dialectical approaches relate political freedom to other social conditions. A material conception of freedom focuses on **practice.** It hinges on what, in fact, people are *able to do*. People are not really free unless they have the resources, the time, and the organization to do the thing that they are "free" to do. Marxism seeks "freedom to"; it seeks substantive freedoms rather than "formal," abstract freedoms that might only exist on paper.

Most of the main answers to the question of how people can be really free were on the debating floor when Marx wrote. He supplied an important new answer. The history of modern political theory has been the debate or dialogue between Marx's answer and various other ones. (Some answers, like the pre-capitalist aristocratic and the theocratic ones, have essentially disappeared in the period since Marx wrote.) Marx's answer was that the basis of a rational, just, and free society was the power and organization of the working class.

Other conceptions of freedom stress not what people are able to do, but rather what they are legally allowed to do. According to those views, if everyone is allowed by law to set up Ford Foundations and political action committees, and radio stations protected by the government from competition, then there is complete equality under the law and a maximum of freedom. It does not matter if only 1 percent of the population really can do it. It doesn't matter that their ability to do so gives them predominant control over others. Everyone is allowed to do it, and therefore everyone is supposedly treated equally. Marxists argue that this formal conception of freedom is a metaphysical view—a kind of hypocrisy which celebrates the majestic equality of the law which forbids beggars and millionaires alike from begging or from sleeping in the street. Marxism's emphasis on what people can really do leads to saying that freedom depends on the power and organization of the working class. This follows from Marx's analysis of the obstacles to freedom in capitalism.

How does this conception of freedom relate to the question of democracy? For Marx, democracy is important; people should decide what will happen to them. Marx did not believe that you have real democracy when the most powerful and influential institutions in the society were private property to be handed on to one's heirs. Marx consistently argued that real democracy exists when working people run the state in their own interest. Marx called this workers' state "socialism" or the "dictatorship of the proletariat," and he regarded it as only a temporary condition leading to a time when classes, economic inequality, and the state would be eliminated altogether, a condition which he called "communism." From the very beginning to the very end of his life, Marx regarded socialism and communism as the realization of democracy and freedom. This is the most distinctive part of his analysis.

Marxism stands in opposition to two other kinds of analysis. Classical liberalism, or pluralism, an underlying philosophy of early capitalism, views freedom as the limitation of government. It believes that government is the main threat and so it pursues freedom by trying to minimize government. It believes that government is best which governs least. (At least that is what all classical liberals say that they wish to do; in fact, it is not what they actually *do*.) This type of liberalism regards socialism as an extension of big government and thus as the main threat to freedom. Even today's liberals in the United States, for example, who claim to want to use government to regulate business, are still fundamentally committed to the model of capitalist processes as the fundamental basis of society, with government secondary, mainly as a force to prevent extremes of inequality that might lead to instability. The third basic political position in the modern world is **elitism.** Elitism is the belief that elites always rule. There are a number of different varieties of elitism. What they all have in common is the belief that any conception of real democracy, according to which the majority governs, is utopian. Thus elitism is very congruent with varieties of empiricism which treat all questions of freedom as meaningless sentiment. Most varieties of elitism end up arguing that one particular elite (usually the elite which is in power in the society they write in) is best and that attempts to tear down that elite will end in substituting another one which will not be as good. (Not surprisingly, many who advocate for classical liberalism embrace elitism when they are on top and feel threatened.)

While liberals say that you don't need an egalitarian society because we already have democracy (the majority will prevails today), elitists say that you can never really get an egalitarian society because democracy is not possible and attempts at it may not even be desirable (an elite will always rule). Liberals believe that competing parties ensure that everyone has their say, and that public policies reflect what people want. Elitists don't believe this. They think that only a tiny fraction of the population exerts political influence or has co-

Class Is Key   MARXISM _____ ELITISM   Organization
to Freedom   \   /   Is Key to
                      \   /   Power and
                        \   /   Freedom
                    Social   Democratic
                    Democracy   Elitism
                    (Durkheim)   (Weber)
                          \   /
                           LIBERALISM
                           (M. Friedman)
                    Competition Is Key to Freedom

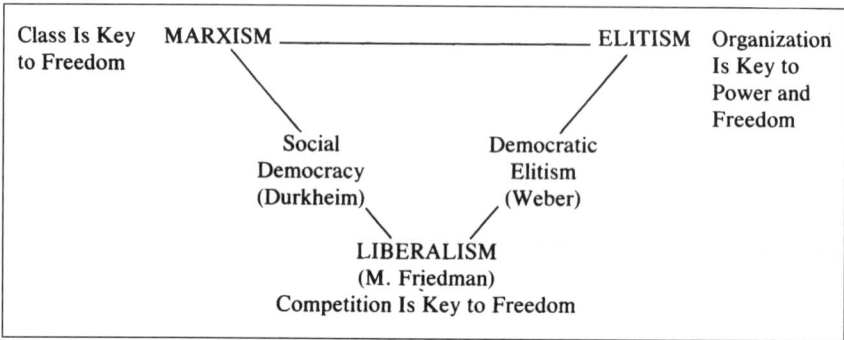

Figure 3.1   Fundamental Positions in Political Theory

herent political views. But elitists don't believe that can be changed. They argue that people need to wield influence through organizations, which come to be controlled by an informed, engaged, powerful few. Attempts to break up the great concentrations of private power, they say, will just lead to great concentrations of public and/or party power. For example, Weber argued that instituting public ownership and control over factories and production would merely lead to the proliferation of bureaucracy. One of his students, R. Michels, argued that without a mass party organization, the working class can exert no influence but, he argued, any such organization inevitably comes to be run by a small elite. Against elitists, Marxists argue that the actual tendencies toward elite control today are largely a *product of capitalism,* and the human race can (and must) develop forms of society without concentrations of economic and political power in the hands of an exploitative minority. However, among those who consider themselves Marxists or influenced by Marxism, there is considerable debate as to the degree of elitism and the mix of factors that cause elitism, as there is debate over the relative weight to attach to economic, cultural, and political factors in given situations. The elitism debates become especially intense when discussing practical political issues including, for example, whether support of liberal Democratic Party politicians is good; whether the Bolshevik Revolution was basically Marxist or basically elitist; and what is the nature of China or Cuba today.

American political theory, and hence American political sociology and political science, have been mainly dominated by classical liberalism, either in a conservative or a welfare-liberal form. One version of liberalism says that socialism (in the sense of public ownership of the means of production and public control of industries and factories) is fundamentally incompatible with freedom. This kind of liberalism merges with the elitist argument that public ownership and the planning process will necessarily create an expansion of government and government influence. For example, Milton

Friedman argued that there is freedom only if there is the maximum possible extension of "free enterprise," to all human relations. He believes that public education, roads, or regulation of toxic wastes are opposed to freedom. Certainly all of those things involve telling some people that they cannot do what they want to do.

A second version of liberalism, which we sometimes refer to as "welfare liberalism," says that public ownership of means of production and economic institutions is not inconsistent with democracy, but it is irrelevant. This second version says that freedom has to do only with political processes, and it is equally compatible or incompatible with capitalist and socialist economic arrangements. For example, today **socialists** or social democrats, or democratic socialists pursue a parliamentary strategy toward socialism and regard the gradual extension of public ownership as inevitable and a progressive extension of freedom. They assert that society can counteract the private concentrations of power with nationalization and government regulation, preventing excess government power through constitutional protections of political rights. They also believe that they are pursuing a moderate middle way between capitalism and Marxism, and that we should moderate the excesses of private concentration, making gradual changes. They often assert that the combination of a multiparty system with a mixed economy leads to a gradual drift toward socialism. Durkheim is pictured as a conservative, but actually he was such an evolutionary socialist who believed that private inheritance of wealth would eventually be abolished. But Durkheim detested class struggle, and he opposed groups who fought to abolish inheritance.

Against all forms of liberalism, Marxism asserts that real democracy is impossible under private ownership of means of production. We have already analyzed some of the reasons that capitalism does not give people control of their lives, either at home or on the job. *While procapitalists talk about "free markets," capitalism actually directly produces command economies, so that a few private individuals have command over the livelihoods of millions.* It produces an income and wealth distribution in which some people have hundreds of thousands of times the yearly incomes of others. In the shadow of this "dark tower," real democracy does not flourish. When all the sources of power and influence are in the hands of a small class, allowing the free play of those influences merely reinforces the control of that class. Under these circumstances, regardless of the formal political arrangements, the substantive effect is the concentration of power and influence in their hands.

The issues dividing evolutionary socialists from revolutionary Marxists are more complex. Against modern social democracy, revolutionary Marxists argue that capitalism cannot be gradually abolished. The gradual extension of government ownership within a capitalist framework just leads to a corporate state, with government merging with business and serving capitalists more directly. Many people are confused by this because systems such as Mussolini's fascism and Hitler's Nazi system merged business and government to serve the capitalists, but are mistakenly called "socialist." (There is also debate among Marxists as to the degree to which Franklin Delano Roosevelt and Barack Obama increased government control in ways that actually served sections of the capitalist class.) The effect of public ownership depends upon who controls the state. In a sense, many social democrats view public ownership as a sufficient condition while revolutionary Marxists see it as a necessary condition of real democracy. While Lenin himself remains a controversial figure among academic Marxists, Leninism, which stresses the importance of a working class party, continues to be the main form of revolutionary Marxism today.

Leninists think that elitists are accurate in so far as they say that no group can exercise power without organization. We saw that the importance of organization is the main theme of contemporary historical sociology of social movements. An unorganized mass does not have any interests; certainly it does not have any way of formulating or acting upon interests. But Leninists think that elitism is *mistaken* to view real democracy (in the sense of the rule of the many) as impossible. Rather, it is only impossible under capitalism. Under capitalism, an apparently unorganized mass is actually organized around capitalist ideas, interests, and institutions. In countering that influence, organizations are always the key. In the absence of working class organization, the vacuum will be filled by capitalist organization. It is over this question that one of the major schisms within the Marxist tradition exists, with both those who support the idea of a revolutionary political party and those who oppose it each claiming to be the true inheritors of Marx's legacy. The answers, however, will be settled in practice, in the real world of class struggle. While it is critically important to study the evidence and arguments of Marx and others, Marxism is not an anti-scientific dogma where truth is supposedly revealed to those who find the missing scripture.

Exercise 3.1: How Does Capitalist Politics Change *Monopoly* with Crises?

We have seen that for Marx, capitalism has the dynamic of a game of Monopoly. The accumulation of surplus value, *MCM*, is an immensely dynamic process. In the first place, it leads to "deepening" of capital: there is constant creation of capital goods, which can lead to increased productivity and a constant transformation of the productive process. This, in turn, leads to a constant transformation of the whole of the social structure built upon it. Moreover, the increased intensity of the exploitation of nature can lead to catastrophic ecological problems because the unfettered market is blind to the consequences that one actor's profitable activities will have for others. In the second place, it leads to the spatial extension, the worldwide expansion of capital, as owners seek to exploit new markets, new raw materials, and new sources of labor for their accumulated stock of capital. In the third place, it leads to polarization and concentration of capital as accumulation of capital leads to increased inequality. As we have seen in chapter 2, not only is wealth and ownership of property a direct source of inequality, but it also requires a labor market that involves immense inequality and oppression. In the fourth place, we have seen that it leads to "durable inequality," as access to jobs, to skills, and to other resources becomes connected to categorical variables such as race, gender, religion, or ethnicity by processes of exploitation, opportunity hoarding, emulation, and adaptation. Finally, in the fifth place, it leads to processes of the accumulation of power, as owners of production accumulate political, ideological, social, and institutional resources to influence the rules of the game.

In the game of Monopoly, these many different crisis tendencies of accumulation in markets are flattened down to the process of assuring rents: the only thing that is accumulated is properties, and the only advantages this accumulation brings is increased rents. However, in that simple system, the process of accumulation *hits a limit* and provokes a crisis. The immiseration of the population undermines the conditions of accumulation. As players are expropriated, they are forced out of the game so that there is soon no one left to pay rents. A crisis ensues that ends the game; later a new game starts with a new deal.

What are the limits of the more complex processes of accumulation in the real world? Think about the interrelated economic, social, ecological, and political processes of accumulation in the real world over the last generation and over the last century. What are the games of Monopoly that play themselves out in these processes of accumulation, and what limits do they hit? What crises and changes do they lead to and how are the various crises related to each other?

We do not know how you conceptualized the various "games" of Monopoly in the domestic economy, the world economy, and the domestic and global social and political structures. Because the board game of Monopoly is simplified to a single kind of accumulation, in which everyone starts from the same point, and the rules do not vary, the resulting crisis is relatively simple. In the real world, many different processes of accumulation hit limits in different ways. The result is a turbulent process producing discontinuities, whose dynamics are indefinitely complex. We do not know what kind of a model of the crises and turning points in these economic, social, political, and ecological process you created. They are a challenging area of current research and theory. Nevertheless, it is hard to miss powerful polarizing processes leading to worldwide crises. The task of producing a general theory of crises has taken up some of the main energy of Marxist theory and is the core of Marxist dialectics. Probably the simplest model is that of a logjam. Each of these processes creates its own vested interests that create blockage, until the whole system appears to be incapable of any real change. However, that produces increased tension and pressure for change, which, once it begins, cascades through the system, producing a dynamic of change that comes in fits and starts. This dynamic is often called a "punctuated equilibrium."

Some Marxists stress the economic polarization that has led to the greatest inequality of wealth and income since the Great Depression—a second "Gilded Age," which like the first Gilded Age of the robber barons has led to a second worldwide recession, the deepest since the Great Depression. Others stress the ecological catastrophe that appears to be staring us in the face. After decades of denying that global warming and other threatening environmental changes were happening at all or were leading to any limit that was unsustainable, it became apparent that the Arctic ice pack was "suddenly" gone, and that more frequent and violent hurricanes had utterly destroyed the third largest port of the United States. Therefore the tune shifted to claims that the environmental changes were inevitable, that they were not the product of human action, or that they were the product of someone else's actions, and so nothing could be done. Still other Marxists stress the replacement of the Cold War by the oil wars. Within a year of the disappearance of the Soviet threat, there was suddenly a new terrorist threat, ostensibly requiring much the same institutions and the same trillion dollar outlays of military materials and blood.

One simple example of a contemporary approach is the essay on "Sociological Marxism," by Michael Burawoy and Erik Wright (2001). They develop a set of ideas about the ways that social structure is shaped by class relations in production, specifically relations of exploitation, which lead to periodic crises and transformation. As **analytical Marxists**, they develop these ideas as a set of analytical categories that often appear to be constructed out of concrete. To flesh out the categorization they refer to a dozen recent studies of different kinds, operating with different models. Chapter 4 on dialectics will consider some of the limits of that approach. Nevertheless, underscoring the dynamics of crisis, by stating some of the things that have to be explained and some of the elements of that explanation, is useful. Burawoy and Wright state the basic elements of crisis that have to be explained in terms of three main principles. (1) The **inverse interdependent welfare** principle states that the material welfare of exploiters depends on the material deprivation of the exploited. Mansionization and homelessness are the flip side of a single coin. (2) The **exclusion** principle states that exclusion of the exploited from access to productive resources is the necessary condition of their profitable exploitation. (3) The **appropriation** principle states that this exclusion generates advantage because it enables the exploiters to appropriate the labor effort of the exploited. These principles then generate distinctively Marxian analyses of the contradictory reproduction of class relations.

A set of political and ideological institutions is necessary to assure the reproduction of class relations and production. This crucially concerns the division of the surplus—the rate of exploitation and the historically determined surplus. At the same time, this institutional structure leads to change in technology, labor markets, and international relations, that erode the ability of the institutions to contain class struggle. The result, Burawoy and Wright argue, has been a set of class compromises that have led to periodic crises which, so far, have led to renovation of capitalism and capitalist profitability on a new basis.

We believe that the world political crisis with its economic, financial, ecological, and political aspects, at the end of the first decade of the twenty-first century, is now a new political crisis or turning point.

Suggestions for Further Reading

The most useful general account of the opposition between pluralist, elitist, and Marxist theory is R. Alford and R. Friedland, *Powers of Theory* (Cambridge, 1985). A good exposition of elitist theory is K. Prewitt and A. Stone, *The Ruling Elites* (Harper & Row, 1973). An important investigation of the Marxian analysis of relationship between capitalism and ecological devastation is John Bellamy Foster, *Marx's Ecology: Materialism and Nature* (Monthly Review Press, 2000). The essay, "Sociological Marxism," by Michael Burawoy and Erik Olin Wright appears in J. Turner, *Handbook of Sociological Theory* (Kluwer/Plenum, 2001).

SECTION 3.2: WHAT ARE CAPITALISTS' POLITICAL RESOURCES UNDER CAPITALISM?

From a liberal standpoint, we are all politically equal because we are all legally equal and there are competing political parties. All of us can vote, buy politicians, or move our establishments to Delaware if tax laws or unions become troublesome, and none of us, poor or rich, can sleep under bridges. From a liberal standpoint, since the parties need every vote, and since the capitalist class is tiny, its influence must be tiny. From a Marxist standpoint, we live in a "dictatorship of the bourgeoisie." We live in a state that capitalists constructed to protect their property. Laws are written so we lose every decisive encounter with capitalist interests. Both political parties are funded and dominated by capitalists, who own the politicians. Millions of people rot in jail, tens of millions of people are threatened, and hundreds of millions of people are gradually squeezed dry in testimony to capitalists' power. In section 1.9, we called this a system of **alienation** and discussed it in general terms. Figure 3.2 adapts that analysis to the issue of political power.

From the standpoint of political theory, one can ask three questions. To what extent does capitalists' economic dominance assure them social dominance? To what extent does their economic dominance assure them direct political influence? To what extent does their social dominance assure them political influence? That is, we can consider what the implications of each of the other eight kinds of alienation are for freedom and the distribution of power.

Large capitalists, the very wealthy, are a tiny fraction of the population. Small capitalists and the petty bourgeoisie are another small minority. Nevertheless, it can be argued that their direct economic position gives them massive political resources. At the end of the productive process, the product belongs to capitalists. Virtually every single product in the society passes through their hands. They can bring the entire economy to a halt (the so-called "capital strike") if they lack confidence in or wish to pressure the government.

Means of production: an immense apparatus of buildings, machines, materials, and land—an apparatus which was socially produced—is private property. It is privately owned. However you measure size, in terms of budget, employees, resources, or whatever, many of these corporations are larger than some states.

Value: we have noted that parties, campaigns, fact-finding, and all other political functions have to be financed. They constitute labor and they have to be paid for. The liberal viewpoint is that everyone pays for such things, out of nickels and dimes. In fact, a politician or political party would rather

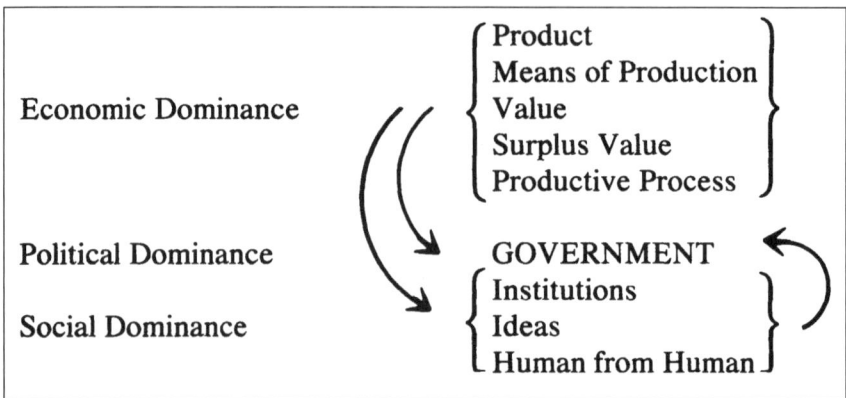

Figure 3.2   Kinds of Alienation

have one nice $10,000 contribution than a thousand nickels and dimes. All political parties have to appeal to capitalist support, at the same time that they have to obscure the fact that they are doing so.

Surplus value: society is constantly growing and developing. New possibilities, new technologies are produced and have to be paid for. Capital pays, and capital calls the shots.

Productive process: even if none of the above considerations were true, the ability to tell people what to do for most of their working day is a potent source of political power by itself. Only a very stupid boss would ask workers to vote a certain way, trusting in their gratitude to make them do so. But a smart boss can use the control over people's actions within the work process to affect actions, behaviors, and beliefs outside the work process.

But capitalist production also produces a capitalist *society*.

Institutions: there was a time when most schools were owned and run by teachers or ministers, when sports were mainly controlled by the teams, when newspapers or citywide associations were local affairs. Inexorably they have come to be owned by boards of trustees who are predominantly big businessmen. This ownership and control is not a secret—pluralists have to work hard to ignore it.

Ideas: in capitalist society, the circulating ideas are capitalist ideas: the movie director may believe that he or she has ignored the producer, the writer may believe that he or she has fooled the publisher, the college teacher may resist the board of trustees, and the newspaper reporter may resist his or her editor or advertisers, etc. But the main reason that there is not constant conflict in all those spheres is that in each, *most people operate inside limits* that are set up beforehand. In every social sphere, long historical battles defined some ideas as reasonable, and others as radical, un-American, or crazy. Marxists believe that when you reexamine these historical battles, they usually involve capital against labor or one group of capitalists against another group of capitalists. When you think about it, how could the capitalist distribution of resources and the different worlds in which bosses and workers live not be involved in such battles?

Human from human: under capitalism, the fundamental message and ideology—the thing which is built into the rules of the game—is "being out for number one." Racism, sexism, ethnicity, religious bigotry, regionalism, and a host of other ideologies translate selfishness into the systematic atomization of the society. In addition, groups are separated physically and occupationally and given different privileges. The result is that the whole society is pulverized and people are split apart. This increases the control of those on the top. Capitalists are not omnipotent, but their political resources are formidable. Wherever one looks for a force which might serve as a counter to capitalist interests—in unions, in political parties, in religion, in voluntary associations, etc.—one usually finds direct capitalist influence. One certainly finds various kinds of indirect influence in which groups are shaped by prevailing ideas and institutions. This is why Marx argued that "the executive of the modern State is but a committee for managing the common affairs of the whole Bourgeoisie" (SW, p. 37). However, there is an important debate between Marxists as to the nature and the limits of capitalist control. **Instrumentalists** and **structuralists** disagree about what is really going on. **Instrumentalists** believe that the capitalists directly control and run the government. **Structuralists** believe that capitalists neither can nor have to do so. Rather, they believe that the capitalist system sets up structures such that whoever runs the government has to run it in the interests of capitalists.

To oversimplify a little, instrumentalists believe that people like Bill Gates can (and sometimes do) call up people like the president, the Speaker of the House, or a Supreme Court justice and tell them what to do. Instrumentalists believe that capitalists are the people who put the politicians where they are. The politicians know this, and if they ever forget it, capitalists can break them. Of course Bill Gates may not want to or may not be able to call the president directly, but instrumentalists believe that they can call the people to whom the president listens and has to listen. By contrast, structuralists believe that capitalists don't and can't control the individual actions of individual politicians. If they could, then the politicians would not be as effective in doing the main thing that the capitalists want them to do, which is to act on the "common affairs of the whole" capitalist class. This means to maintain order, to maintain legitimacy, and to keep the system operating. But the system operates on profits, and so the one thing that whoever governs has to do is to make sure that the profits keep flowing. What are the facts and arguments that each group presents?

The instrumentalist perspective can be illustrated by the work of the elite theorist, W. Domhoff. Domhoff starts from an examination of the social elite of the United States: the hundred thousand or so families that are in the social registers, who constantly appear on society pages, who went to elite prep schools, or belong to elite clubs like the Rittenhouse. Domhoff calls this the **upper class.** He conducted a series of empirical investigations which ask: where did the status of these families come from? What is their relation to the **capitalist class?** To what extent do these groups know each other and get together? Is it a class-conscious group? What is the degree of their representation in the government? Is it a **ruling class?**

Note that although these people are a tiny fraction of the population, that means they still number in the hundreds of millions. There are too many to be studied individually, or listed in one book. To investigate the relationships and the various forms of relationships between them is complex. Domhoff finds that money is the main prerequisite of entry into this group, and the way that they got money is not by winning the lottery or playing baseball, but by owning capital. The upper class is a capitalist class.

How do they get together? Many institutions tie this group together. They form a coherent social group because a large mass of social resorts, associations, educational institutions, political organizations, and other arrangements allows the upper class to communicate with itself, to come to agreement on what has to be done, and to socialize a modest number of newcomers into the group. Some of these organizations are the elite clubs, resorts, and ranches such as the Bohemian Grove. They form a coherent political group and work out common political attitudes in elite organizations, such as the Council on Foreign Relations (CFR) and the Committee on Economic Development (CED). The various organizations may represent different sectors of the capitalist class—heavy industry, or international oil, or domestic oil, or agriculture, and might therefore lean toward one or another group of politicians and policies; they also might differ among themselves in how to best balance out the tension between increasing exploitation and using force to subdue resistance or sacrificing some of today's profits for some political stability. But these differences do not mean we have a pluralist democracy; they only mean that there are conflicting interests and conflicting ideas within the capitalist class about how to extract profits from the working class and how to protect those profits.

Not every member of such organizations is a member of the upper class or corporate elite. But those groups predominate and they control entry into such organizations. Because they include hundreds of members of the elite, they command immense resources. The enormous influence of such groups is not a secret around Washington. They have filled a majority of the important cabinet posts of the last eight presidential administrations, and their deliberations and policy recommendations are very powerful in determining the agenda of other groups, such as the Congress. Domhoff argues that the upper class has disproportionate political influence. The upper class is a ruling class. It is able to place many of its own members in positions of power, and it is able to determine the assumptions and presumptions in which others operate. He presents a mass of data, some case histories, some membership studies, some analyses of policy, to argue that the main structures of policy formation in the United States are as pictured in figure 3.3.

The main inputs into the policy-making process are from bodies which are predominantly composed of ruling class members. Those inputs then are acted upon by governing groups which are themselves enormously biased toward ruling class membership.

In opposition to the instrumentalist analysis, the structuralists argue that capitalists don't and need not rule. Structuralists think instrumentalists are asking the wrong questions about capitalist influence. Instrumentalists at-

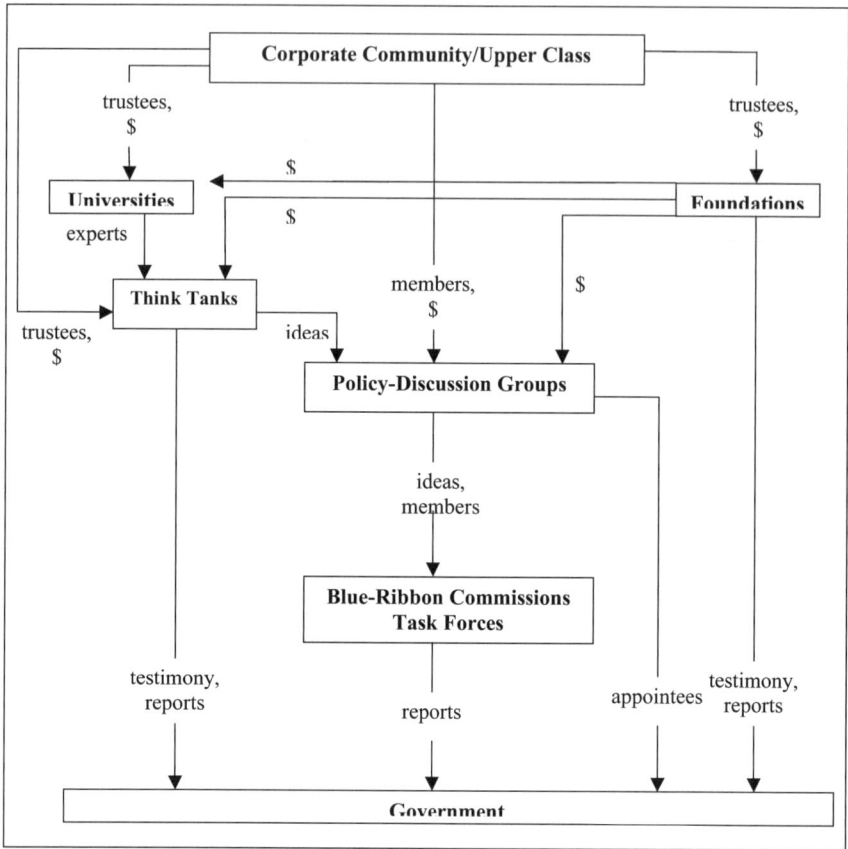

Figure 3.3   The Policy Formation Network

tempt to decide whether the capitalist class is a ruling class by examining the extent to which individual capitalists can or do influence individual decisions by government. But that might not be very important. Bill Gates does not tell any of the hundreds of janitors in Microsoft how to empty the trash, and he does not hire any of them either. He doesn't want to. And if he did tell one what to do or how to do it, the janitor might say, "Who the stew are you?" And if Bill Gates told the janitor how to do the trash, he or she might be polite and impressed, but he might do whatever he wants if no one is looking and might even make a rude noise. That doesn't mean that Bill Gates doesn't have the trash emptied to his satisfaction. Rather, he has set up a system which works well enough to suit him. Having set it up, he has no reason or inclination to mess with it. Structuralists argue that the same is true of capitalist control of the political system.

The fundamental arrangements of capitalism ensure that the system runs on profits. If there is a sustained decline in profits, the system creaks and groans to a halt. It is also an interdependent system so that the various portions of it all have to run smoothly. To the extent that this is true, *anyone* who runs the government will have to maintain an adequate level of profits, maintain business confidence, maintain profitable areas of foreign investment, etc. Or to be more precise, anyone who does not fundamentally contest the system as a whole will have to do these things. The logic of the system is such that it is pretty much a package deal. You either have to contest it fundamentally, or you have to go along with the things necessary to make it work. And what is necessary to make it work is exploitation.

Thus, if the capitalist class can eliminate groups that fundamentally contest the legitimacy of the system—and they have been able to do so—then, the structuralists argue, the details of government policy would just take up their time and make the government less effective at doing what the capitalists want it to do. What is more, capitalists have many different interests about all the details, but they also have joint interests as a class. To have these joint interests enacted, government has to be insulated from acting on particular, divisive interests.

Do the capitalists rule? The instrumentalists say, yes. The structuralists say, no, they actually don't have to. We think they are both right to some degree. The question is posed ignoring differences between different issues and differences between periods of time. We think there is no power in general—there are only powers. It depends on the time and place, and a dialectical understanding, one shared by most sociologists, actually, seeks to understand the interaction among institutions as well as the ways that institutions shape people and people shape institutions. Capitalists do not have distinct unified interests about every single issue that comes up. The process of coming to a common interest against opposed alternatives is a protracted one. But by the same token, no structure of rules—not "Hands off private enterprise," not "Maintain government balance of powers," not "America first; hate the Russians"—maintains itself indefinitely. In a series of historical battles capitalists have had to forge a general consensus as to their common interests. Sometimes individual capitalists have gone in for individual plums, often at the expense of others—that is one of the engines of accumulation. It is easy to underestimate the degree of direct capitalist influence. Both parties have an interest in hiding it. But more significantly, during the periods when there have been real threats to capital as a whole, capitalists have come together to defend their interests as a whole, even as they continue to battle with each other, as Watergate, Irangate, Wedtech, Madoff, and many other political scandals have shown.

Exercise 3.2: What Are the Resources of the Working Class?

Struggle implies two forces. We have seen that capitalists have resources, but what resources does the working class have? Write down a list of some of the main resources the working class has in conflict with the capitalist class. For example, money and influence in extra-political organizations are resources, unity and organization are resources, contact with each other, and desire to help each other are resources. One way to think of resources is to ask yourself what people could do, if they could get together on it; for example, setting up roadblocks everywhere or cutting off people's phones, or staging "newsworthy" events are all things capitalists do now. Could they be done by workers? Do your best to make a list of short- and long-term resources and how they combine and change before you continue.

Struggle implies two forces, two parties, two sets of wishes and possibilities and interests. If one ignores the ruling class, one gets a static, liberal view of the political process. If one ignores the working class, one gets a static, elitist view of the political process. Marxist theory always faces both of these. And, with respect to major changes, either of these views implies there is not much that can be done.

The dominant picture of the political process is one which is liberal, which regards the government as essentially acting in the general interest, as a servant of general values, rather than mainly serving the wealthy. But we have stressed the immense resources of the capitalist class. Those resources are so massive that *formal* democracy (political equality and competition, which leaves them intact) invariably makes a mockery of *substantive* democracy (popular control). Is the capitalist class invincible, then? Marx argues not only that politics is bound up with classes, but also that the existence of these classes is bound up with a particular historical phase. He believes that it is doomed and will lead to a classless, stateless society. He obviously believes the working class has massive hidden resources in this struggle.

If Marx thinks that they will not only struggle but win, what makes workers so strong? What resources did you think the working class has? Certainly workers do not have the money, the organization, or the access to the political elite, and so the main suggestions people often make leave them at a disadvantage. Different resources are relevant to different kinds of fight. Divide your paper into two and list short-term resources, which are the visible resources which we see in day-to-day conflicts over government policy and law. Then, also list long-term resources which are those relevant to or mobilized during a crisis involving the structural transformation of the society. At the bottom of each list, make a sketch of how the resources combine with each other. To what extent are they dependent on being conscious, aware, or organized?

This thought-experiment concerns measuring power. In some ways, the whole discipline of political sociology needs to measure power the way economics needs to measure money. It is hard to do, and there are a lot of disputes about it. Power is much harder to measure than wealth. There is disagreement on the main elements to be considered. The reason that there is fundamental disagreement and power is a difficult concept is that over the course of historical struggles, as issues change and groups come together or fall apart, not only does the power of groups change, but what *power itself is* seems to change. Sometimes a group continues to have the "powers" it always did, but those powers are no longer relevant to changed situations. Sometimes the powers of a group depend on everyone else respecting them, like the credit of a bank. In a crisis that credit can collapse. Sometimes a group has all the powers in the world, but contradictions within the group and contradictions among the various things the group is trying to do paralyze it.

Marx believes that capitalist society is constructed so that capitalists pretty much have things their own way. But even with all this, the power of the capitalist class is doomed. All of the possibilities we have just mentioned work against them: its powers are relevant within a dying world, they depend on laborers, so capitalists are forced to square a circle. All these arguments are developed in terms of contradictions faced by the capitalist class. Mao Zedong, leader of the Chinese Revolution, used to say that the capitalists are a paper tiger—their power ultimately depends on a piece of paper which gives them these rights—because they do nothing. Marx often used the image of workers as an unconscious giant: "the lowest stratum of our present society, cannot stir, cannot raise itself up, without the whole superincumbent strata of official society being sprung into the air" (*Manifesto*, SW, p. 45). It is when and only so long as capitalists can keep everyone else fighting among themselves that they can remain dominant—whites against blacks, men against women, Protestants against Catholics, North against South, Poles against Germans, and so forth.

Workers do everything. They perform all the functions indispensable for the continuation of life. The super-rich owners do nothing that is essential to human production, life, and well-being. They do things we would be better off without. But to exercise their power, workers have to be aware and organized. Most wealthy capitalists can maintain their power without having to become active participants in political organizations of capitalists. As long as they have a state which will enforce their ownership rights, they can act independently. Nevertheless, Marx thinks, there are some circumstances where the workers' short-term disadvantages turn into long-term advantages.

What this implies is that the prime resource above all is conscious unity and organization. Unity is not just one power resource in addition to others. It is the resource that changes the value of all your other resources. It is only the relative disunity of everyone else and the relative unity of capitalists which assures elite dominance. Unity not as a thing but a process that changes and can be changed; it is complex and constantly changing. That is one of the reasons for the complexity of Marx's dialectical, historical analyses. We don't know what short-term or long-term resources you listed above, and we don't know how you see them as fitting together. We do think that if you go back through Marx's economic and historical analyses you will find the most powerful single analysis of structural power processes that exists anywhere in political theory. There is much that is unfinished and incomplete in Marx's analysis, but it is still the most powerful analysis around.

Suggestions for Further Reading

The debate between structuralist and instrumentalist approaches was popularized by the interchange between Milliband (instrumentalist) and Poulantzas (structuralist) in the pages of *New Left Review*. It has been ably reviewed by D. Gold, C. Lo, and E. O. Wright, "Recent Developments in Marxist Theory of the State," *Monthly Review* (1975), and by F. Block, "The Ruling Class Does Not Rule," *Socialist Revolution* 33 (1977) and "Beyond Relative Autonomy," *New Political Science* 2 (1980). Domhoff's five principal books are: *Who Rules America?* (Prentice Hall, 1967), *The Higher Circles* (Random House, 1970), *Fat Cats and Democrats* (Prentice Hall, 1972), *The Bohemian Grove* (Harper & Row, 1974), and *The Powers That Be* (Random House, 1979). M. Useem argues that one can measure the emergence of a single, central capitalist, the "inner circle," whose emergence underlays the political victories of Ronald Reagan and Margaret Thatcher. See *The Inner Circle* (Oxford, 1984). A Hollywood film that somewhat touched on the power of working people is *A Day without a Mexican* (2004). For an alternate view of the contemporary state and political power, see R. Norman, *Free and Equal* (Oxford, 1987), and D. Schweickart, *Capitalism or Worker Control?* (Praeger, 1980). See also D. Clawson and M. Schwartz in M. Schwartz, *The Structure of Power in America* (Holmes & Meier, 1987).

SECTION 3.3: WHAT ARE THE CRUCIAL POLITICAL CHANGES IN THE WORLD TODAY?

The decades around the turn of the twenty-first century were a turbulent time. To many, it appeared to be a time of massive change, in which most of the political structures that had governed the dynamic of the twentieth century were swept away forever. Yet, the great changes that were expected did not materialize.

In Europe, the nations and national rivalries that had dominated world history for centuries were absorbed into a European Union. Across Eurasia, there was the end of the Cold War, as the Soviet Union disintegrated into its component republics and overthrew the Communist Party, and China instituted capitalist market-driven industrialization. Both China and India roared into world economic and political importance. In the world as a whole, after decades of denying global warming, most of the world woke up to rising temperatures, a vanishing ice cap, and rising sea levels. In the United States, after a generation of Democratic Party dominance, there was a generation of Republican free-market policies, leading to a massive financial collapse and the most serious economic recession since the Great Depression.

Yet, early in the twenty-first century, if you blink your eyes and squint, you may be forgiven for thinking that nothing has changed and that you are still back in the last century. Africa continues to be ravaged by wars that appear to be "tribal" but in fact are proxy wars funded and armed by European, North American, and Chinese interests seeking minerals and cheap labor. The end of the Cold War led not to an era of peace and a peace dividend, but to increased military budgets to fund wars in Kosovo, two wars in Iraq, and the ongoing war in Afghanistan. As we saw in the last chapter, the great bursts of free-market speculation of the savings and loan disaster, the dot-com bubble, and the housing collapse led to anemic growth during their height, and major recessions upon their inevitable collapse. Though a Democratic African American, Barack Obama, was elected president on a platform of "change" and "hope," the amount of change was considerably less than many people had hoped for.

A dialectical approach analyzes change in terms of the opposition of contradictory forces. When contradictory forces—particularly forces of quite different kinds—oppose each other, the resulting pattern of change is often turbulent, erratic, and discontinuous. Change, when it is fast, is very fast, and when it is slow, is very slow. The only way to understand the changes of the twenty-first century is in the context of what went before. The dominant political dynamics of the United States in the second half of the twentieth century has been called "the treaty of Detroit." It can be summarized in terms of the five laws that tried to restrain class struggle in the Cold War era of United States world dominance and competition with the Soviet Union.

The **Wagner Act** of 1935 provided the legal framework for collective bargaining and instituted the National Labor Relations Board. The **Social Security Act** was the linchpin of the New Deal, and it marked a general commitment to guaranteeing a minimum standard of living to some segments of the population. The **Employment Act** of 1946 denied the legitimacy of *laissez-faire* determination of wages, and affirmed the responsibility of the state for maintaining full employment. The **Taft-Hartley Act** of 1947 established the form and limits of union activity, prohibiting secondary boycotts and other trade union practices essential to building class solidarity around political as well as economic demands. Finally, the **McCarren Act** of 1950 provided the legal basis for eliminating communists and other militants from the trade union movement.

Such policies led to what Paul Krugman calls the "great expansion." Krugman believes that to be a liberal is to be a true conservative in the sense of someone who wants to return to the "middle class society" in which "a rising tide lifts all boats" that characterized the fifty years after World War II. He believes that the reinstitution of such policies, suitably augmented by universal health coverage and ecologically sound policies, will return us to that "great expansion."

Thus, Krugman's argument rests on his analysis of the four historical periods pictured in figure 3.4. In that figure, they are pictured as four line segments superimposed on a graph of the movement of income inequality in the United States that he cites: the unfettered free-market capitalism of the late nineteenth and early twentieth century produced (1) the **Gilded Age**. That ended with the stock market crash of 1929, the worldwide Great Depression, World War II, and the Holocaust. These brought about (2) the **Great Compression**, New Deal policies that reduced inequality by a factor of two. The combination of policies such as progressive taxation, unionization, Social Security, and wartime regulation led to a sharp decrease in inequality. (3) This in turn, Krugman argues, brought about the **Great Expansion**. In the postwar period, policies such as the GI Bill opening up higher education to veterans led to a rising tide that lifted all boats, the longest sustained economic expansion in U.S. history. The thrust of Krugman's analysis is that while unregulated capitalism leads to polarization and crisis, it is possible to put in place a regulatory regime that will harness the market for the public good. *Conscience of a Liberal* is a manifesto for a new New Deal.

Krugman argues that around 1980, the liberal New Deal policies that drove the Great Expansion were replaced by free-market policies of the Reagan-Bush era, producing a steady increase in inequality, (4) the **Great Divergence**, leading to a Second Gilded Age. As we noted in chapter 2, and contrary to the views of those who believe that capitalist inequality cannot or should not be reduced, Krugman argues that social policies have a powerful, cumulative effect on income inequality and that income inequality does not produce growth. Rather, we have seen, the economy during the Great Divergence was anemic. Median take-home wages were essentially flat, and what economic growth occurred was predicated on speculation. Savings and loan speculation, the dot-com bubble, and the housing bubble produced relatively jobless growth built on debt which, ultimately, were il-

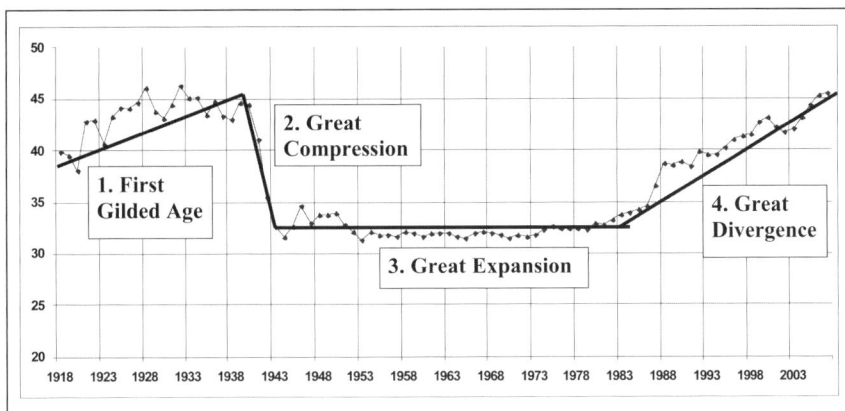

Figure 3.4   Krugman's Four Periods of Twentieth-Century Politics

lusory "Bernie Madoff worlds." Owners of stock or of real estate saw their wealth on paper increase many-fold, and this even caused them to buy various goods and services that were real. But the whole structure was built on a bubble, and it vanished in the crash.

Bernie Madoff was the former chairman of the NASDAQ stock exchange, who in the twenty years up to 2009, bilked billions of dollars from investors in a massive Ponzi scheme. Ponzi schemes are like chain letters, and early investors who cash in from their paper earnings are paid from later investors. They are illegal because, mathematically, you can only work a Ponzi scheme by robbing later investors, and so you can only do it by fraud. Krugman showed that, in the absence of adequate money to create sufficient aggregate demand in the hands of the mass of the population, a kind of Bernie Madoff influx of money was infused into the system from the top by trillion dollar speculative bubbles in stock and real estate. These bubbles are not illegal, but they have the same effect. It is the job of institutions like the Federal Reserve to deflate them, but it is always in the interest of political leaders to allow them, producing a boom in their term, and a mess for the next guy.

Thus, over the last generation, the "prosperity" of the Great Divergence was not based on increases in productivity. It was based on speculation, in the California housing market, and then in high-tech stocks, and then in the whole housing market and financial derivatives. It led to unhealthy accelerated expansion of the financial sector. A small number of people became fabulously rich, and a somewhat larger number of people saw a huge inflation of the listed assets, which encouraged them to spend money, often money that they did not really possess. Then, in the great financial crisis of 2008, all of the bills began coming due.

In Krugman's analysis, the policies that led to the inequality were not only against the interest of those in the lower half; they were against the interest of almost everyone. Why did so many people go along? He provides four main answers: firstly, those who stood to make a killing had enormous resources and were able to build a network of organizations, such as the American Enterprise Institute, the Heritage Foundation, and the Cato Institute, to develop "movement conservatism." Secondly, they were able to control media from *The National Review* and the *Public Interest* to Fox to telegraph that position. Thirdly, racism played a crucial role. Reagan instituted his first presidential campaign with a speech in favor of states' rights in Philadelphia, Mississippi, where civil rights workers had been killed. Fourthly, the actions of the movements of the 1960s had generated a substantial backlash, which movement conservatism could mobilize.

The kind of domestic political factors that Krugman stresses played a role in generating the Reagan-Bush rollback of New Deal policies, *but we believe that his analysis neglects more structural features of the political tendencies generated by late capitalism.* Many policies that are logically possible are not politically feasible except under exceptional circumstances. At the close of World War II, the United States was economically and militarily dominant. Under those circumstances it was able to make concessions that are not usually possible. Moreover it was subject to the political competition of the Sino-Soviet block, which meant that it was also motivated to do so. It was not only the rise of Reagan and the conservatives that caused the decline of the U.S. economy; it was also the rise of OPEC, the increased competition from Japan, Germany, and China as well as the structural crisis of capitalism—overproduction and falling rates of profit—discussed in chapter 2, now taking place not just on a national basis but globally.

A class analysis does not deny the political forces and the domestic political choices resulting from the forces in motion at some particular time. It does not recommend that we sit by and do nothing because at some times we cannot change the underlying conditions of those choices and forces. So long as one is operating within a capitalist system run by a capitalist class, or by politicians beholden to it, its attempt to solve its problems by exporting them to others—workers, migrants, or other countries—will lead to the grim outcomes we have seen: economic collapse, ecological collapse, political oppression, war, and fascism.

Marxists believe that these pressures are built into the capitalist system and will continue to intensify, leading to cycles of economic crisis, ecological devastation, political fascism, and war. As the wars become so much more devastating, the ability of the system to easily recover for the next cycle becomes more problematic. In any case, the human toll of death, destruction, and misery becomes almost impossible to imagine. Neither Marx nor serious Marxists hope for these terrible things to happen in order to supposedly fulfill some "master plan of history." On the contrary, serious Marxists strive to be scientific and accurate in order to help prepare people, so as to minimize the catastrophic effects of capitalism's crises. But many Marxists realize that there has never been a peaceful shift in the world balance of forces.

Exercise 3.3: Long Cycles and Short Cycles

The game of Monopoly has a cyclical dynamic that leads from the beginning of a game to a resulting polarization, to a collapse and new deal. Many people have suggested that such dynamics characterize a capitalist economy and that other linked cycles characterize the development of the economy, politics, war, and world history. They suggest that most social structures can only be well understood if they are seen in relation to such cycles.

 Take some social structure. It could be family relations, the divorce rate, a social problem like alcoholism or child abuse, an institution like education or religion. It could be anything in which you happen to be interested. It is particularly important to see the institutions that produce catastrophes for everyone, the Pentagon, big oil companies, and the state in these ways. Think of two or three of the ways that the social structure is connected to the overall economy—that is, ways in which it would be influenced by recessions, depressions, world economic collapse, and/or world war. How strongly, in fact, do you think such events will affect your structure?

 Possibly the most visible single characteristic of capitalism is the business cycle, the periodic alternation of economic expansion and contraction. This normal business cycle occurs within a very short time frame of less than a decade. While it is tied to other social processes, and while it can wreak untold misery by itself, it is not itself the basis of structural change. In the 1920s, an economist named Kondratieff claimed to have distinguished a much longer cycle of about fifty years. In recent years, this has become the focus of research, investigating the existence of such a cycle and its relation to many other phenomena such as the birth rate, changes in values, or domination or nondomination of the world economy by a single power. Different theorists have suggested different mechanisms which might drive such cycles, mechanisms which connect to economic expansion and contraction in different ways. One of the reasons that it is useful to think about the possible existence of such cycles is that they sensitize one to forces operating not within a given country, but in the world system. The striking economic booms and bursts have been worldwide, while liberal analysis of them tends to be entirely national. Another reason is that the periods of contraction have been periods of war and revolution.

Moreover, thinking in terms of such cycles recalls the problems of history, periodization, and context. Finally, it leads us to question the spell of the last forty-five years. The period from World War II to the 1970s has been the longest period of such massive, sustained expansion in United States (and world) economic history. It might be nice to believe that this situation will continue forever. Reason and history suggest that it will not. Neither past performance nor economic events in other countries give much reason for that optimism.

Table 3.1 gives one estimate of the main periods of the long cycle, the main structural changes associated with each upswing, and the main constraint appearing at the top. The data will be different depending on which indices, countries, and controls are used. Note however that the period around 1814 for the United States was close to the War of 1812, the period around 1866 was that close to the Civil War, and the period around 1920 was the conclusion of World War I and the preparatory period of World War II.

Sociology has consistently tended to propose theories which ignored problems of historical periods and different contexts. This has been connected to ignoring problems of structural change. Sociology has tended to predict by assuming that whatever trends have been occurring in the past will continue in much the same ways. In spheres like education, race relations, international relations, or attitude change, we have taken whatever trend appears in the last twenty years and viewed it as a master trend. But if one looks at large-scale cycles, there are obvious respects in which these smaller trends are often part of a larger pattern, such that the smaller trend undergoes sudden, discontinuous shifts.

World financial collapse, world inflation, world war—such phenomena are immensely powerful. The stock market crashes of 1987 and 2009 were much less powerful than that of 1929, but it is symptomatic of instabilities, and tens of thousands of people were financially wiped out. World war or economic collapse is far more powerful, and it is unlikely on the face of it

Table 3.1   Kondratieff Cycles and Restructuring

Minimum	Maximum	Restructuring of the Political Economy	Limit of Capital Accumulation
1790	1814	Handmade machinery	Low productivity
1849	1866	Machine-made machinery	Rising organic composition of capital
1896	1920	Monopoly capital	Underconsumption
1932	1970	Government management of the economy	Unproductive expenditures

Source: Weber, "Cyclical Theories of Crisis," in A. Bergesen, *Crisis in the World-System* (Sage, 1983).

that any of the particular trends and relationships which we observe would be unaffected by them. This section's thought-experiment can help you think about such dependencies. For example, if you are interested in the prison system, you might expect that the resources that could be devoted to it, the numbers of people that would be incarcerated, and the dominant beliefs about punishment might be powerfully affected by any process this powerful.

List two or three possible effects of this kind. Use what you know of the history of that social structure to estimate whether it underwent a periodic change in the last two centuries. We think that you will see effects of the four cycles listed in table 3.1. Finally, attempt to find some actual evidence as to whether your impressions are correct. Try to construct an historical series of data on the aspects of the structure that you think are related to long cycles of economic expansion and contraction. At the very least, it will help you to think about the interconnections of society. Indeed, many sociologists would say, "Well, of course society is interconnected in that sense. If you allow for world war and great depressions, then all bets are off, and no one can predict anything." This is going rather too far. Some processes are so powerful that they continue right through very powerful social upheavals. But to predict most things, you have to be able to think about such upheavals.

Suggestions for Further Reading

On long cycles: A. Bergeson, *Crises in the World-System* (Sage, 1983) and J. Goldstein, *Long Cycles* (Yale, 1988). The periodization given above is similar to that of D. Gordon, R. Edwards, and M. Reich, *Segmented Work, Divided Workers* (Cambridge, 1982, p. 45). Krugman's analysis in popular works such as *The Return of Depression Economics and the Crisis of 2008* (2009) was based on the Nobel Prize-winning work founding spatial economics and analyzing how international investor confidence creates crises like that of Greece in 2010 in which the breakup of the European Euro zone was threatened by the double-bind faced by countries in an inflation of prices and deflation of lender confidence.

SECTION 3.4: HOW DOES CAPITALIST POLITICS CHANGE?

We have seen that for Marxist sociology, the main motor of change is class struggle, which produces crises. The capitalist world economy periodically generates economic crises and wars. Moreover, the political rules of the game are not fixed, but rather they are one of the stakes in the struggle. These two facts lead to a complex pattern of discontinuous change. There are both major shifts, such as fascism, in which classes change their relationship to the state, and there are smaller changes in the nature of political parties or of the groups composing them, such as political realignments.

The analysis of shifts within the party system, or electoral realignments, has been an important field of study of American electoral politics. There is no theory of realignments that is accepted by all, or even a majority, of theorists, but even the sharpest critics of the theory of political party realignments grant that the conception of realignments remains the dominant perspective for organizing the interpretation of American political history, and it has interpretive authority approaching that of the periodic table of elements for chemists (Mayhew, 2002, p. 4)

Two historians, Arthur Schlesinger Sr. and Jr., suggested that over the course of the last 200 years of American history, the push for change and the resistance of privileged groups led to an oscillation in every generation (about every thirty-odd years) as the initiative of public attitudes swung to the left (for expansion of the franchise, of human rights, and of safety nets) and to the right (toward consolidation of social, legal, and economic arrangements supporting existing privileges.) Within political science and political sociology, the work of Key, Sundquist, and Burnham developed the idea that about once a generation, critical or realignment elections have produced major changes in the American party system.

Different theorists have different conceptions of what constitutes and what causes critical or realignment elections. Some stress the groups that are affiliated with political parties; others stress which party is dominant in presidential or in congressional elections; others stress the development of third parties and how strongly people are committed to parties; others emphasize shifts in what the parties stand for or what parties there are. These different conceptions of realignments produce very different lists of what have been realignment elections in the past. But almost all analysts treat the elections of Jefferson, Jackson, and Lincoln as critical elections in the nineteenth century, often leading to the disappearance of some parties, such as the Federalists or Whigs, and the appearance of others, such as the Republicans and the Democrats.

The elections of Teddy Roosevelt and Franklin Delano Roosevelt are usually taken as the prime examples of twentieth century critical elections, with greater disagreement about the elections of Richard Nixon, Ronald Reagan, and Barack Obama. The election of McKinley (assassinated) and T. Roosevelt in 1896 led to Republican dominance that lasted to the Great Depression, because even when the Democrat, Woodrow Wilson, was elected, he was operating with the framework laid by the Republican Party. Similarly, the election of Franklin Roosevelt led to Democratic dominance until 1968, because the Eisenhower Republican presidential terms were op-

Table 3.2   Party Realignments

Critical or Realignment Elections	
Year	President
1800	T. Jefferson
1828	A. Jackson
1860	A. Lincoln
1896	W. McKinley-T. Roosevelt
1932	Franklin D. Roosevelt
1968	R. Nixon
? 1980	R. Reagan
? 2008	B. Obama

erating within a New Deal framework. And the interruption of the Nixon-Reagan-Bush runs by the Democratic presidencies of Jimmy Carter and Bill Clinton did not change the significant movement of the political system to the right.

The main sectional pattern of voting has undergone an enormous flip. The free states and territories voted for Lincoln, and the election of 1896 consolidated the northeastern and west coast states for the Republican Party. Yet, by the G. W. Bush elections of 2000 and 2004, every one of those Republican states had become predominantly Democratic, and every one of the previous Southern Democratic states had become Republican, reflecting the movement of the conservative Southern Democrats ("Dixiecrats") out of the Democratic Party. There is currently sharp debate about the long-term meaning to the Barack Obama election. The question whether it was a realignment election has implications for whether, over the next elections, the left will be facing a centrist Democrat or a Republican administration.

In any case, it is evident that race has played a profound role in American politics for more than a century. In *The Emerging Republican Majority* (1969), the Republican theorist, Kevin Phillips, had argued that the "solid South" component of the New Deal coalition would become solidly Republican, and if one party holds all the states of the old Confederacy, the other party needs to win more than 70 percent of the remaining electoral votes, which has never happened. However, after the Reagan-Bush consolidation of the "solid South" for the Republican Party, northeastern moderate Republicans like Phillips were marginalized. He left the Republican Party and wrote half a dozen books critical of the politics of oil, conservative Christianity, the Bush dynasty, and unfettered free-market capitalism.

The period from Nixon's election in 1968 to Reagan's in 1980 was only twelve years, and the Reagan-Bush period represented a new kind of Republican Party dominance. Critics of realignment theory such as Mayhew describe it as a Rip Van Winkle theory, that the electorate wakes up and has an effect only once a generation. They argue that whenever you try to specify timing or state exactly what kinds of changes come about, the theory becomes fuzzy and unravels. Nevertheless, arguments about the periodic crises and transformations of American politics are unlikely to die out, and they will be accelerated by debates about whether the election of Obama and the increasingly Hispanic and African American electorate, marks a fundamental shift, or, like Clinton's presidency, merely a slight slowdown in the crisis-driven move to the right.

Even the most fundamental realignments of the American party structure have not been as basic as the changes that have occurred in many other countries, and must be seen in the context of theories about those changes, such as theories of fascism. We think that the reality is that change often comes about in jerky, discontinuous patterns, and the understanding of those patterns is one of the main challenges of social science today.

Exercise 3.4: Race and Political Crises and Transformations in Modern Society

Not only does race cast a long historical shadow in the United States, but in many other countries as well. But racial ideologies, divisions, segregation and inequalities, and their resulting political consequences are not a constant. There are times when they change slowly, and there are other times when they become one of the most volatile and turbulent social and political forces that we know of. This is highlighted by the history of fascism in the last century which blind-sided so many thinkers on the left. Suddenly in the period of the 1930s in virtually every country of the world, there arose primitive, racist, predatory movements. They specialized in raw terror, not only beating up and jailing opponents but also in **genocide**, taking groups of people such as Jews and attempting to wipe them off the face of the Earth—adults and children alike—by shipping them to concentration camps, practicing mass murder. Fascist movements came to dominate about twenty countries in the 1930s and led to World War II. Millions of people were shoveled into ovens; perhaps more than 100 million people eventually died as a result of war.

Often racism has been the crucial dynamic element of the fascist program. On the basis of racism, fascists were able to get mass support. Why should racism be such a key part of fascism?

There is a curious ambivalence about many people's sense of change in race relations, both in the United States and elsewhere. Many people have the sense that nothing ever changes—that it is a system that is immensely resistant to change. Many people have the sense that everything

changed qualitatively, in an all-or-nothing way. In the case of African Americans, the point where everything changed was once thought of as the Abolition movement and the Civil War; then it was the Civil Rights movement; and for some people it is now the election of Obama. Is it possible for the intuition of resistance to change and also the intuition of a volatile, unstable system that is subject to sudden changes both to be correct? If so, in what sense?

Perhaps the dynamic of jerky, discontinuous change is more evident when we look at the identities and mobilizations of national, religious, racial, and ethnic identities and movements in other countries. In the last century, the racial and ethnic identities and movements of good (Aryan) Germans or loyal Japanese (subjects of the Emperor) generated world devastation, only halted by world war. At the end of the century, bridging identities and organizations merged many of the European former combatants into the European Union, while divisive identities and movements splintered the former Soviet Union. These processes are analogous to the earlier ones that formed nation states, around the time of capitalist industrialization. List some of the groups, resources, and organizations that pursued these policies of fission and of fusion. Consider: are they active today? Where do the policies and organizations they lead take us?

Racism is not a constant; it is volatile. It changes rapidly. "Jim Crow" discrimination really did have a strange career over a century, with advances and retreats between 1865 and 1965. The Ku Klux Klan has gone through collapses and revivals. It is a central sociological aim to pose hypotheses which would explain the dynamics of those changes. Contrary to the view that discrimination, prejudice, and racism change gradually, racism goes through enormous sudden swings in periods of just a few years. This is evident from the history of fascism throughout the world and from the history of racist organizations. For much of the early part of the 1900s, Jews in Germany actually faced less hostility than they did in many other parts of Europe, but that changed within a few years. In the United States, the Klan has gone through at least three distinct periods of rise and fall. From memberships of hundreds of thousands and a potent, terroristic political force at some times, it has been virtually eliminated at others, only to be revived again. Similarly, race riots and rebellions have come and gone in distinct waves, as has racial conflict in schools, neighborhoods, and other institutions. Legal incarceration into concentration camps or expulsion, of groups such as the Japanese, Native Americans, and of immigrants, during the Palmer Raids, have occurred suddenly. The idea that race war and genocide are mainly cultural products of broad attitudes fails to see that there are enormous, rapid swings of actual conflict and treatment.

Racial conflict can escalate up to the point of genocide: the mass murder of a group. There are other important sources of division and conflict of which this is not true. We speak of the "war between the sexes," and sexism is an important component of fascism, but sex conflict cannot generate situations where there are tanks rumbling through the streets, blood running in the streets, and masses of people are rounded up, put in camps, executed or even exterminated. Such methods have been used in the United States with respect to Native Americans, African Americans, Japanese, "illegal aliens," and other immigrant groups. And in other countries, Jews, Palestinians, non-Arabs in Darfur, Salvadorans, Hmong Vietnamese, Pandits in Kashmir, Muslims in Gujarat, and other groups have been rounded up or even murdered *en masse*, at one time or another. The ability of racist conflict to escalate in this way is not linked only to visible differences such as skin color; it is characteristic of divisions like those between Jews and non-Jewish Germans, Protestants and Catholics in Ireland, and other invisible groups. Conversely, there are many biracial societies that lack intense racism.

Part of the explanation for these swings is the fact that racism is politically important. In earlier sections, we saw that where there is more racial division, those at the top benefit. Where there is more racial inequality, there is more class inequality. When racism increases, all working class organizations (unions, neighborhoods, parties, clubs) are split and weakened. Wherever there is more racism, schools and hospitals, unions and welfare, unemployment compensation and social solidarity—all sources of working class support—are set back and cut back.

Moreover, a crucial aspect of racism in the United States—one which is typical of the dynamics of racism more generally—is that black and Hispanic people are not just any segment of the population. They are not just segregated and socially separated, and they are not merely a lower income group which can be exploited more. Black and Hispanic people are concentrated in the working class, and they are often the most militant people fighting for change, whether in the unions, in the political system, in neighborhoods, or in schools. Whenever laws, ideologies, and arrangements are set up for the control of one group, they are used against other groups. But when that group is the most oppressed and militant, then those machineries of suppression are doubly effective against the working class as a whole.

In the United States, the future of racism is inextricably tied to the balance of class forces. That means that the increase of racism is powered by some of the most potent social and political forces that exist, and so, racism will increase powerfully.

For example, in the last decades of the twentieth century, the federal government began to cut back on all the gains of the War on Poverty and the New Deal. Both as a cause and effect, that led to sharp increases in racist policies and in racist ideas. This is a movement in the direction of a program and policy of external war and internal repression, using military force legitimated by racism. To the extent this analysis is right, the crucial opposition to racism has to be connected to opposition to the social and political system which feeds it and feeds off it.

As we pointed out earlier, major social developments do not unravel in a linear way, as if carefully planned; there are contradictions, twists, and turns; and a river going downstream might twist and turn and even go upstream momentarily when it swirls around as an eddy as part of its basic downstream movement. So too, in the United States, black and Latino people will likely be a majority in less than four decades; the capitalist class needs black and Latino youth to serve as soldiers, and some black and Latino people to serve as supervisors, managers, and even political leaders as high as president to dissipate or divert anger. Thus, we see some elements of a kind of "neoracism" where it appears that the old hardline racism is being softened in politics and culture. Similarly, an unintended consequence of working class life puts youth from all kinds of backgrounds in contact with each other, which also has the effect of weakening some aspects of racist ideology. But capitalism must maximize profits, and segmenting the labor force is necessary to accomplish that, and segmenting it by supposed "race" or ethnic identities remains a fundamental economic core process of capitalist society, as is "divide and conquer" politically. So alongside the seeming lessening of racism in some areas, underneath the smiles we see the material reality of the core . . . we see the increased gap in black-white incomes, "durable inequality," the mass incarceration of black youth, and the drumbeat in the media that acknowledges some "good" black folks but laments the many, many members of the black community who are still deemed unworthy of having the "American Dream." And when capitalism's crisis sharply intensifies, we can expect to see more of that "old time" racism surface as well.

The conflict in 2010 over an Arizona law giving police the right to search people who might "look like" an immigrant without legal papers (in other words, any person with a darker skin tone) shows this contradiction. On the one hand, the increasingly authoritarian forces in the United States, combined with high unemployment, wish to restrict and expel the same immigrants who were permitted a few years ago. On the other hand, the government does not want to alienate "legal" immigrants and citizens. Therefore, conservatives pass the authoritarian law, and liberals oppose the more extreme parts of it, while fundamentally agreeing with conservatives that more restrictions are needed.

The traditional Marxist analysis of *fascism* sees it as the result of the need of major sections of the capitalist class to impose order on an economy and political system that cannot be controlled, due to battles within the capitalist class, and due to a rebellious working class. Fascism results from an extension and logical development of late capitalism toward state capitalism, and it leads to the closer merger of certain sectors of the capitalist class with the state by means of a mass party.

Suggestions for Further Reading

The immense literature on realignments is critically summarized in D. Mayhew, *Electoral Realignments: A Critique of An American Genre* (Yale, 1982). Despite such critiques, in addition to the work that will be inspired by the attempt to understand the aftermath of Barack Obama, some of the reasons that electoral realignment continues to interest political scientists and political sociologists are evident in Merrill, Grofman, and Brunnell, "Cycles in American National Electoral Politics," *American Political Science Review* 102:1 (2008) and Brooks and Manza, "Sociological and Ideological Bases of Middle-class Political Realignment in the United States 1972–92," *American Sociological Review* 62:191–208 (1998); C. Tilly, *Durable Inequality* (University of California Press, 1999); D. McAdam, S. Tarrow, and C. Tilly, *Dynamics of Contention* (Cambridge University Press, 2001); J. Loewen, *Sundown Towns* (New Press, 2005); and Myerson and Roberto, "It Could Happen Here," *Monthly Review* (October 2006). Charles Tilly has overviewed the organizational and class dynamic of the fission and fusion of nation states in *Coercion, Capital and European States* (Blackwell, 1992).

SECTION 3.5: WHAT IS FASCISM?

Fascism is a word that has been used and misused in both academic and popular contexts. Some people think that it means just any kind of dictatorship. Others consider only the governments of Germany, Italy, Japan, and perhaps Spain prior to World War II to be fascist. Others use it only to refer to the party of Mussolini which came to Italy in 1920s, or the Nazi Party of Hitler which came to power in Germany. The most varied analyses have been put forward as to what caused fascism. Sometimes fascism is described as the rule of one evil dictator, often portrayed as "insane" and as having almost supernatural charismatic powers. Sometimes it is stated that fascism, communism, and socialism are all basically the same—a system where big government runs everything. During the Cold War, liberal political theorists developed the concept of **totalitarianism** to refer to any nonliberal political system which they opposed and to link fascism and communism. None of these definitions is very accurate.

Given these theoretical disagreements, it is best to start with an analysis of what fascism is not:

1. *Fascism is not the product of one particular kind of national culture.* One of the ways we know this is that even in the countries where fascists did not take power electorally, such as France, Norway, or the United States, similar movements grew and became powerful. For example, in the United States the Klan went through one of its main periods of expansion, becoming a formidable or dominant political force in many states. Certain conservative radio preachers, such as Father Coughlin, who supported fascism, developed followings of millions of people. And there was a burst of racism against such groups as the Japanese, which led to having their property confiscated and their being locked up in concentration camps. While fascism takes different forms in different countries, and while it always celebrates national culture and the peculiarities of one group over others, it is a general phenomenon which, unfortunately, can happen again in Europe and North America as it now characterizes many countries in Latin America, Africa, and Asia.

2. *Fascism is not the same as communism, socialism, or Marxism—it is the opposite.* Fascists usually represented themselves as a kind of "socialism"—a national socialism—but there was a huge difference in their ideas and platforms. Fascists supported racism and militarism; they did not expropriate the big capitalists; they did not have the same social base as Marxists; and they jailed and repressed workers' movements. During the 1920s and 1930s, there was a rapid growth of socialist and communist movements, because the failures of capitalism were especially visible. In the USSR, they expropriated capitalists and abolished private ownership of means of production. Ruling groups in all the other countries were terrified that they, too, would lose control. Fascism explicitly arose to stop the "red menace," and very large numbers of others joined with fascists because they believed that only the fascists would be able to stop the spread of socialism and communism. Fascists and Marxists were in constant conflict with each other, while liberal politicians often sat by and were willing to accommodate the fascists. This leads many liberal analysts to say Marxists caused fascism. How did they cause it? By fighting it so hard! They say the constant fighting eroded the legitimacy of the government and opened the door to fascism. But, in fact, fascism evolved out of liberal politics, unable to cope with crisis and disorder within the capitalist class and working class, and forced to resort to brutality whether or not there was organized Marxist opposition.

3. *Fascism does not result from a certain philosophy or ideology by itself.* It is significant that many of the ideas and philosophies which preceded the rise of fascism are becoming popular today in the United States and Western Europe. There is a revival of the same themes and often of the same thinkers. But it would be a mistake to view fascism as an intellectual phenomenon. Powerful as racist, elitist, and nationalist ideas are, fascism occurs only under certain conditions which are not essentially cultural, but rather economic and political.

4. *Fascism does not have any unique or distinctive set of ideas.* It is a mistake to evaluate or to try to understand fascism mainly based on the ideas and phrases that it uses. In every country, fascists put forward different, unique mixtures of ideas (e.g., against the Jews, against the banks, for the "little guy," for racial purity, for getting back into touch with traditions, against sexual freedom, against the rights of women, for toughness and macho, against liberalism, etc.). But the main people that fascists actually fought were Marxists. Very many church people, philosophers, academics, and others supported the fascists, allied with them, or at least refused to combat them because they saw fascism as the best chance to defeat the communists. This was particularly easy since there were large doses of racism and nationalism built into all those established institutions (as is also true today). Contradictory ideas were put forward side-by-side to win over different segments of the population: anti-modernism mixed in with phrases about a New Order, and anti-science spiritualism was combined with pseudo-scientific rhetoric about superior genes.

All of the fascist governments of the period between World War I and World War II carried out programs of external expansion and internal repression. Their ideologies had had a family resemblance to each other, combining nationalism, militarism, racism, sexism, and anti-communism. **Nationalism** (patriotism) merely heightened elements that had been present since the rise of nation states. Intense nationalism and support for expansion always involved **militarism**, support for arms, glorification of military men as patriots, and willingness to use force to solve international disagreements. The nationalism was also usually bolstered by ideological forms of **racism** (the view that the racial group dominant in a society was genetically superior), extreme cultural racism (the view that certain ethnic groups or religions were irrationally violent), **sexism** (the view that women are intrinsically inferior beings, who belong in the kitchen, bedroom, or nursery, serving men), and **anti-communism** (the view that foreign Marxists were worming their way into power and had to be exterminated). We have already analyzed many of these ideologies as forms of alienation and divisiveness which are built into the operation of capitalism as a social system. For the moment what is important to recall is that *there have been times when they have suddenly undergone a massive and cancerous growth.* This happened in many nations in the 1930s, such as Germany, Italy, Hungary, Spain, Japan, Austria, and Romania. It is important to recognize that fascism is a general phenomenon that happened in many different countries.

5. *Fascism does not result from one-man rule or from a weakness in democratic traditions.* There have been many open, brutal dictatorships that were not fascist. The pharaohs of Egypt, Alexander the Great, Julius Caesar, Nero, Attila the Hun, Louis XIV, Napoleon I, Napoleon II, and any number of other one-man rules were not fascist. They were not maintaining monopoly capitalism, and they did not have the capability of such enormous control and terror which develops with late capitalism. All unstable regimes are similar in that they increase brutality and suppression of opposed groups. But the ideological and organizational mixture we have called fascist, and the actual movements with their family resemblances, are essentially different from these other authoritarian systems.

Fascism is the specific form of open terrorist rule by the state in the period of monopoly capitalism. It therefore has fundamental purposes: sustain profits for major sections of the business class (which means squeezing more profits out of the workers and cutting services—even food—to some parts of the working class), intensifying racist/ethnic discrimination or other ways to intensify the segmentation of the working class (again to squeeze more profits from, as well as to politically divide, the working class), militarize the society to suppress dissent and often prepare for war, as well as taking other political-military steps to impose "order" on the "chaos" of "capitalism gone wild" as various businesses desperately battle it out for profits and the working class becomes more rebellious. There are some commonalities among its ideological forms, but these are somewhat more flexibly manipulated to meet the needs of the moment of the capitalists . . . sometimes individualism, sometimes conformity, and so on.

Liberalism and Fascism

One of the reasons that it is important to understand that fascism is not a mere absence of liberalism is that some people see liberal politicians as the main way to stop fascism. This sometimes seems reasonable because while liberal procapitalist leaders appeal to nationalism and anti-communism (and increasingly to racism and militarism) they always do so in the name of freedom, in opposition to fascism. But the strategy of such liberal leaders (particularly welfare-liberal politicians) is often to oppose fascists through such weak means that they are swept aside when the conflict sharpens. Often they take the leadership of a large number of people who were willing to use more militant means to stop the rise of fascism, and they divert them from effective actions to others which do not really halt the rise of fascism. Worse even than providing ineffectual leadership, then, some of the liberal leaders are actually *in league with the fascists*. And others will, with seeming reluctance, endorse fascism later if the threat to capitalist power by the workers becomes strong.

Given the pervasiveness of the image of fascists as an external force, conquering the government from the outside, it is important to underline the fact that fascist governments usually came to power as a result of the peaceful operation of the democratic political system under situations of economic and international crisis. It can be stopped only to the degree that people are willing to disobey the law and fight the main forces of the government. For more than 100 years, the many groups standing to the left of the liberal center have faced a choice when those parties were threatened from the right: to support the center as a "lesser evil" or to break ranks.

Suggestions for Further Reading

On fascism and explanations of fascism: while there is an enormous literature on fascism, analyzing its social and political base, its organization, and its historical origins, the literature is necessarily polemical and highly balkanized into the historical examination of particular countries. For example, the classic analysis of the class basis of German fascism is F. Neumann, *Behemoth* (Oxford, 1942). A classic general analysis which avoids this error is R. P. Dutt, *Fascism and Social Revolution* (1934, reprinted Proletarian Publishers, 1974). A contemporary brief overview is A. Szymanski, *The Capitalist State and the Politics of Class* (Winthrop, 1978, pp. 275–291).

Exercise 3.5: Politics of the Lesser Evil—Social Fascism, the Orangutans, and the Tigers

Periods of crisis, increased conflict, war, and change often produce increased polarization, and that often produces two contradictory responses. One response is conciliatory compromise; the other response is to sharpen one's actions and positions to avoid being swept away by the other side.

Consider some of the organizations in the United States that claim to represent common people: unions, community groups, welfare-liberal politicians, and the mainstream of the Democratic Party. In what ways

are they bulwarks against fascism? In what ways might they cave in to fascism or actively aid fascism? When violent conflicts arise between such groups, is there any way to decide whom to support? Can one avoid such conflicts and taking sides?

Imagine the following: we were at the zoo the other day, and to our horror we found that some cruel zookeeper had locked the orangutans into the tigers' cage. Seeing the orangutans, big and small, with their babies clinging to them, we looked all over for the keeper, to no avail. As long as the tigers slept, the orangutans huddled in one corner, with some pushing and shoving to see who would get up on a little platform. Then the tigers woke up, and they became very interested in the orangutans. Of course the orangutans became frantic. Some managed to find some tidbits left over from the tigers' last meal, which they tossed over to them. But that appetizer was soon finished, and the tigers began to approach the group. The pushing and shoving turned to biting. The bigger orangutans began to beat smaller ones, and tried to climb over them, up the wall. They chittered at passersby and threw refuse. Eventually, they hurled the smaller ones into the waiting jaws of the tigers. Only the bigger orangutans and their babies were left. Then, even their babies were thrown to the tigers. We couldn't watch any more.

In a "dog-eat-dog" situation, how do you get unity? When some of your own are collaborating with the enemy, how can you get together? We were reminded of the painful struggles before World War II concerning "social fascism," collaborators of fascism who claimed to be liberal or socialist representatives of the working class. We were reminded of the violent struggles that occur today in unions, radical groups, and other organizations between and among liberals, socialists, and revolutionaries. The big orangutans were behaving in a very pragmatic way; they were realists of a sort. "If you can't change the fact that you are all being devoured, maybe it is best to be the last one," they argued. Certainly they were keeping themselves alive. But when there are many orangutans and few tigers, then they *can* change the fact that they are all being devoured. But only if they band together. One by one, they will certainly all be eaten. Clawing to be the last one destroys everyone. The pragmatic orangutans were objectively feeding the tigers, and they were keeping others fighting among themselves so that no resistance was possible.

When fascism arose, many people in unions, churches, leftist parties, universities, even some Jews collaborated with them. Some collaborated because they believed in racial purity and the "national destiny." After all, the ovens, genocide, and death of millions only became visible later—what was visible to some were only upbeat themes of getting the country moving again, youth groups, patriotism, and summer camps. Some didn't like the fascists much, but hoped the fascists could stop the communists, whom they liked even less. *But also, many who collaborated hated the fascists.* They were being pragmatic and they didn't want to break the law. They thought that if one tried to fight back, one would be massacred. They were trying to get the best deal they could. They didn't want armed resistance because they were making deals, and fights spoiled their deals. Would trade-unionists, church groups, Jews, or other groups have been massacred if they had fought back? In retrospect it is obvious that they were massacred anyway—that being taken off one by one was the surest way to lose. Sometimes the leaders managed to get away, but they did so at the cost of their supporters' lives.

Were the liberal social democrats objectively collaborating? What should have been done? The question is immensely important because the present system has, in every single area of possible struggle, a series of "loyal oppositions"—oppositions which not only do not bring about change but which oppose sharp struggles and, in fact, do not seek any structural change. Often these "loyal oppositions" are more antagonistic to radicals than the authorities. Is there any general rule as to how one should relate to these groups? What produces unity? What produces the most action? Try to answer these questions.

With regard to the large number of socialists, trade-unionists, Christians, and others unwilling to break with the system, the Third Communist International, led by the then-revolutionary USSR, in the 1920s and 1930s adopted an analysis that said they were essentially no better than fascists— that they were "social fascists." This analysis said that those groups were the silent partners of fascism, objectively supporting its rise. There was a lot of bitterness. And in the United States today, there are often very bitter struggles between groups on the Left. Everything that one group is trying to do may be jeopardized by another.

For example, California migrant farm workers are subject to a lot of terror by farm owners, police, and the Immigration and Customs Enforcement (ICE), formerly called the Immigration and Naturalization Service (INS). There is a lot of racism. In a situation of very sharp struggle and a lot of intimidation, in the 1980s, Caesar Chavez's United Farm Workers of America, was pacifist, law abiding, and did not want to jeopardize its church support, its liberal support, and its radio station. Accordingly, it did little to organize the unorganized and did not resist the Immigration and Naturalization Service. In fact, in addition to actively discouraging strikes, its organizers actually did actively cooperate with the INS in patrolling the border.

Since the 1980s, in union after union—autoworkers, steelworkers, teachers, and more, the union leaders not only accepted concessions, they actively suppressed those rank-and-file groups of workers who wanted to take action to protect the workers' interests. When one group of workers wants to strike, union leaders discourage other workers from supporting them. Autoworkers, who do one of the most difficult jobs and were among the higher paid workers at $28 per hour recently accepted a contract where new workers are brought in a near poverty wage of $14 per hour. Nonunion plants in the South are replacing union plants, and deindustrialization has left Detroit and Gary, Indiana, as hollow shells of their former cities— depopulated to less than half their previous population. A view through Google Earth at those cities today will show many "green" rectangles, where empty lots now occupy former home sites. This is part of the irreversible, fundamental structural economic shift of the U.S. economy, and major concessions in this climate are permanent concessions to the crisis that continues to devastate that industry even after the concessions are granted. So it is not simply a matter of union leaders failing to organize the workers to win more; it is rather that they are smoothing the way for the continued slide of the working class into collapse. And then they rally their rank and file to support Obama's plan to have government committees "take over" the failing auto companies (after the capitalists have sucked billions in profits out over the years). So besides using taxpayers' (the working class's) money to save the company, the government committees that are overseeing these "takeovers" are mainly run by the biggest bankers of all! So a coalition of these union leaders and liberal politicians works to ensure the profits of a big company under the direction of big banks—the merger of business and government under more direct control of the banks. So, are those liberal leaders really opposing the slide toward a fascist corporate state, or are they facilitating it? Marxists are divided on this question, but many Marxists believe that these liberals are complicit if not actively engaged in this process.

The liberals who seem to support aspects of socialist reform reject the analysis that sees them as allies of "social fascism." They say that this analysis is what really helped the victory of fascism, that precisely what had to be done was submerge differences on the Left to build a broad coalition against fascism. This analysis within the Third International eventually led to the building of "popular fronts" against fascism with liberal and socialist oriented reformist groups. But the popular fronts never prevented fascism either. And submerging differences does not lead to unity in the sense of common action; often it leads to paralysis and getting picked off one by one.

This set of conflicts points out a very important and very painful set of problems on the Left. It is not an issue which just comes up now and then or which has only academic implications. It is a perennial contradiction with very powerful practical implications. Do you cooperate with someone who seems to be actively holding back or sabotaging struggle? Does maintaining unity require that one should never criticize other groups? Posed so bluntly, probably nobody would answer "Yes." On the other hand, if

one refuses to ally with someone unless the other person agrees 100 percent, there are many problems. Only the most arrogant pseudo-Marxists
would think that they have all the answers and have nothing to learn from
anyone else. Working together with people who disagree is the only way
to test, in practice, what the best course of action is. But concretely, there
are always very difficult questions for a radical group in terms of how it
should relate to other groups.

As we noted, in every area of struggle there are loyal oppositions which are
both theoretically and practically opposed to sharp action. Solving the contradictions in one's relation to them is politically crucial. The "Suggestions
for Further Reading" gives a number of the relevant arguments. But we think
that at least two principles clearly follow from any dialectical analysis:

1. One's stance toward such groups cannot be determined in the abstract. It depends on one's own total action program and the ways
   that such groups are opposing and resisting this program. This is not
   a matter of the subjective intentions of leaders of the organizations,
   but of what the organization is doing.
2. The main thing is not what is happening at any particular point in
   time. One has to make some kind of general analysis about how the
   situation is going to change, and what the organizations are going to
   be doing in a month, a year, or five years. This analysis is crucial because if it is wrong, the tactics will be wrong. Major labor unions are
   good examples of this contradiction. Without them, workers' wages
   and working conditions would probably get much worse in the short
   run. But the major unions really are so totally tied to the government
   and the capitalist class that they will invariably devote most of their
   efforts to opposing not only anti-capitalist organizing, but any rank-
   and-file organizing that seriously challenges the power of the capitalists. They are also a main force supporting fascism in other countries
   and work hard to win U.S. workers to support imperialist practices
   and fascist governments in many of those countries. Is it worth it to
   support a particular union leader today in the interests of unity and
   stability, if such support legitimizes that leader and encourages support for that leader, making it easier for that leader to betray the workers tomorrow on even more important issues?

Suggestions for Further Reading

On causes of fascism: as noted, one of the classical Marxist analyses of
fascism is R. P. Dutt, *Fascism and Social Revolution* (reprinted Proletarian,
1974). This is in sharp opposition to the line which came to dominate by
1935, articulated in G. Dimitroff, *United Front against Fascism* (reprinted

New Century, 1950). On social fascism: one of the sharpest critiques of the concept of social fascism is N. Poulantzas, *Fascism and Social Dictatorship* (NLB, 1976).

SECTION 3.6: WHAT DETERMINES DIFFERENT DEGREES OF DESTRUCTIVENESS OF FASCISM?

The severity of fascism can vary. Its severity is not mainly the result of how nice rulers are. The imposition of certain kinds of regimes have their own dynamics, and specifically race-ethnic war and international war can escalate up to the point of genocide relatively rapidly. The severity of fascism is not worsened by people combating them—one cannot moderate fascism by being nice to fascists. The instability of fascism is the nature of the regime itself. When a large percentage of the domestic population supports the regime, that makes fascism more brutal rather than less. However, while fascism does not result from a preexisting set of concepts, and while the opponents of it cannot change it by struggling against it mentally, the issue of how severe fascism is and how long a fascist regime lasts *is profoundly affected by the ideas* the population has.

Fascism in Germany from 1933 to 1945 is considered to be among the most brutal forms which ever appeared. The fascist regime and its puppets in other parts of Europe executed somewhere between 15 million and 20 million civilians. Moreover, they instigated a world war which, by combat casualties, by civilians who "got in the way" during the conflict, and by disease, starvation, and other side effects, produced somewhere between 50 and 150 million further casualties. The main reason that regime was especially destructive was that it was strong. At the other extreme, South Vietnam from 1956 to the early 1970s had a regime properly described as fascist. It was a brutal attempt to prop up capitalism by squeezing the working class using the ideas of nationalism and anti-communism combined with imprisonment, torture, and murder. But the regime had very little support among the people of South Vietnam. The only reason the government was able to stay in power was the introduction of one-half million U.S. troops, in a country with a total adult population of only about eight million, and even then the fascist regime was eventually destroyed. A similar example is the Afghanistan government of Hamid Karzai. That government, like the South Vietnamese government, can barely sustain itself and certainly is not in a position to invade any other country. In these instances with U.S. help, fascism was very deadly and destructive, but far less so than in countries such as Nazi Germany, where the fascists had more support from the local population.

What determines the difference between the two kinds of cases? The difference is not in the aims of the governments or sentiments about democracy. The difference is mainly one of the consciousness of the people living under fascism. How hard could they fight it? How much of the population actively supported fascism? When this number is relatively large, many civilians function as a kind of extra police force to keep the rest of the population down, and the super-rich can extend the false impression that they have a popular government with support of the working class and middle class. When, as in South Vietnam, there are few people prepared to die for the government (the desertion rate from the South Vietnamese army was 20 percent per year despite the fact that the penalty was death), the government was able to execute a great deal of repression, but its intensity would have been far stronger had the regime had more support. Clearly, then, even if ideology is not the genesis of fascist policies, it is a crucial force that sustains and strengthens fascism.

An important question becomes: what is it in profascist ideology that appeals to people, including many of those who are mistreated by capitalism. Profascist ideology is capitalist ideology (selfishness, racism, sexism, nationalism, commodification, and dehumanization of people) taken to a brutal extreme. The traditional forms of extreme conservative ideology that are bridges to fascist ideology are generally not that difficult to identify: religion politicized to justify conservative or even genocidal policies, celebration of irrationalism and anti-science, celebrations of brutality, seemingly contradictory coalitions of ultra-moralistic "family values" conservatives alongside hedonists who celebrate individualistic greed and militarists who justify torture and the aerial bombing of innocent civilians. But to understand the complex appeal of fascist ideology it is important to locate it within the context of "late capitalism"—capitalism in decline, where the crisis of overproduction has distorted the economy, where profits from consumption and speculation become more important and being productive becomes less important, and the winds of economic and political crisis can be sensed not just by the social scientists, but also by grassroots people. This is the setting where full-blown fascism—not just a vicious hiccup as the anti-communist witch hunts in the 1950s USA were, but full blown fascism—where the jailing and killings of many are routine ways of stabilizing a capitalism in crisis. Understanding the economic-political underpinnings is crucial to understanding the ability of some ideologies to grow and spread rapidly. In Germany in the mid-1930s, the capitalist economy had collapsed. Simply put, there wasn't enough for everyone to survive if corporate capitalism was maintained. Getting rid of capitalism wasn't on the capitalists' agenda—so getting rid of some of the people became the policy—starting not with the Jews, but with those the Nazis first called "useless eaters"—the mentally and physically disabled. Executing Jews, so-called "gypsies" (Roma), and millions of Slavs came later, as the increasingly desperate regime "threw some people overboard" in order to maintain the loyalty of others. But interestingly, just a decade or two before, Germany was one of the European countries where discrimination against Jews, while serious, was not as bad as many other places. It was not just the "embedded culture of anti-Semitism in Germany" (a very real and powerful force, of course); it was also the needs of some sections of the capitalist class to hire others to find a way to stabilize the system any way they could.

We purposely slide among such terms as "late capitalism," "capitalism in decay," "pre-fascist capitalism," "capitalism approaching crisis," "imperialism," and "monopoly capitalism," because Marxists variously use all these terms to describe a similar stage in capitalist development—the point at which the relations of production are holding back the forces of production to such a degree that important parts of the economy slow down or begin to contract. And in the later stages of this later stage, politics and culture become even more twisted and distorted as a consequence of the distortions in the economy. In earlier capitalism, when it had room to grow, it was accompanied by a culture, an ideology of optimism. Certainly it was racist and exploitative, but there was an optimism that somehow modern technology and science, including social science, could make the world a better place for nearly everybody. As will be discussed in chapter 4, every process has contradictory stresses within it that create change, and when a process also approaches certain limits, those stresses become more intense. In the USA, capitalism had a crisis in the 1930s, but by the 1950s, it was able to experience a period of growth similar to its growth from 1860 to the 1920s, but based on the creation of a temporary, somewhat artificial "market" for products, caused by the massive destruction of World War II.

Cultural/ideological trends do not simply reflect the moment. They include vestiges from the past, often modified to fit the moment, and they intertwine with other seemingly contradictory trends in complex ways. As modernist capitalism did bring improved material life and technological wonders to the United States and some other parts of the world, the dehumanizing aspects of that efficiency came under criticism from progressive sections. Big, modern institutions might provide good care, but could we go beyond them to a more humane way of treating those in need? Big schools might provide efficient education, but wouldn't alternative schools be more humane? Assimilating ethnic minorities into the mainstream could lessen inequality, but does it rob, even demean the heritage of these groups? Big medicine, big cities—big government itself—could provide many material things; didn't they also create impersonal bureaucracies and didn't this all just further make obvious the alienation of life where the main purpose was to accumulate possessions? These critiques, by progressive forces who wanted to go beyond capitalism to something more humane, have contributed important insights to the critique of capitalism. But in an era of declining production, it becomes important for ruling capitalist classes to promote a culture of declining expectations, especially when the modest gains of the 1960s were encouraging rising expectations just as U.S. capitalism was facing renewed competition from Germany, Japan, and OPEC, and as the Vietnam War was exacerbating the developing economic problems.

Ironically, then, many of the progressive critiques of capitalism were hijacked by sections of the capitalist class themselves. Major elements of the "safety net" were gradually dismantled, especially since the early 1980s, as government services to most people declined. The main types of alternative schools have been generally religiously conservative and even more conformist than the big public schools. Bashing "big government" as the enemy became a way to slash government services and cut taxes for the rich. Ethnic separation and segregation was embraced in the name of "identity politics," simultaneously applauding the heritage of ethnic minorities while often mystifying and essentializing supposed differences. And irrationalism, itself, was embraced as an alternative to "cold scientific logic," as politicized fundamentalist religions replaced the Woodstock Nation as the main countercultural force. It was liberal politicians like Democrat Jimmy Carter who promoted the mix of religion and politics before the "Religious Right" had become a potent force and who enshrined the concept of "austerity" and it was liberal Democrat Governor Lamm of Colorado who famously said that with resources getting scarce, the old should just die and get out of the way. The fashionable cultural trend that went under the broad umbrella of "postmodernism" similarly mixed some useful critiques of hegemonic modernist capitalist society with an embrace of subjective selfishness that would make a Wall Street stock manipulator believe he was as morally valid as Jesus of Nazareth.

Some commentators repeat the old cliché that the far left and the far right are the same because they both oppose liberalism. This is a very superficial argument, however, because the essential feature of communism is egalitarianism while the essential feature of the "far right," or fascists, is extreme inequality. But there are ways that some of the ideas of the "cultural left" have been hijacked by the conservatives, and ways that those on the "cultural left" actually foster some ideas consistent with the right-wing ideas that thrive under late capitalism. This is a different point from criticizing some left-liberals for being too weak in the face of fascism, and it is a different point from asserting that some left-liberals actually side with fascists in times of crisis.

The core of the problem, as we see it, is the abandonment of understanding that class relations, the particular kind of class society that we live in and the economic, political, social, cultural, and psychological processes that it engenders, lie at the root of today's social problems. Without that understanding, the emphasis is on the many complex forms that are manifested in society, but separated from the essential dynamic that generates and shapes those forms. So, for example, we learn of "globalization," a quantitative expansion of trade, migration, and communication, rather than "imperialism," which can incorporate the concepts of "globalization," but can do it in a way that ties it to the fundamental dynamic of the drive for profits. Progressive sociologists have developed many important insights about race and ethnic discrimination and about discrimination against females, critiquing the earlier liberal capitalist optimism that assumed that the post World War II prosperity would bring equality. Understanding the multiple oppressions of class, race, and gender is similarly important. But referring to these as "intersecting" implies that they have separate origins . . . and while every form of micro-oppression is not an immediate mirror reflection of the profit motive, what does it mean to imply that there are separate origins? Do they come from essential differences between people, or do they come from inherent ideas in different people that cause them to support the oppression of others? Can aspects of this perspective lead back to the idea that humankind does not have a core fundamental unity of interests (at least potentially) and instead revert back to the idea that we are ultimately so separate that competition, wherever it might lead, is the essential, eternal part of human existence?

While it is important to critique the modernist, rationalist optimism of early capitalism that reinforced the hegemonic power of the capitalist class, we should be aware that a generalized assault on the ideas of science and even rationality itself opens the door to a kind of ultra-relativism that appears to be super-democratic ("Everyone can believe what they want—there is no Authority") but actually can open the door to the most extreme kinds of authoritarianism ("If there are no common understandings, then I can do whatever I want to whomever I want"). Libertarianism is one of the outcomes of some of these ideas taken to the extreme, and while Marxists do aspire to a world without "states," as discussed in chapter 1, Marxists understand that as long as classes exist, the attempts to eliminate the state will just be a way of allowing the rich and powerful to exert their power more directly, while diverting the populace into believing that it is exercising individual choice.

Of course, many of the thinkers who promote some of the ideas discussed above consider themselves liberal or left or even socialist, and many have made valuable contributions to our understanding of the forms oppression takes when it is tied to globalization, to race, ethnicity, and gender. Our purpose here is not to critique them directly but rather to point out that individualist objections to modernist capitalism might sometimes appear to be moving the critique beyond modernist egalitarianism but in fact might be moving it backward, to the kind of individualism that encourages selfishness, ethnic exclusivity, and in the worst case, can build ideological support for more intense forms of oppression.

As capitalism becomes more unstable, then, the ideologies used to justify it embrace more extreme forms of individualism. Mussolini once said that fascism does not really have a consistent philosophy, but rather just reaches out to whatever will work at the moment to various constituencies. So sometimes we get extreme individualism, sometimes surrender to the capitalist-fascist state, sometimes regionalism, sometimes ethnic or religious chauvinism, sometimes patriotic nationalism, blacks are turned against Latino immigrants (and lower income blacks), Latinos are turned against blacks, white folks are turned against both, all are turned against targeted immigrants or countries. Sometimes modernism is promoted, sometimes traditional values, sometimes women are physically brutalized, sometimes they are treated as helpless and needing the protection of strong men, sometimes aggressive arrogance is promoted ("will power can do anything"), sometimes the passivity of feeling helpless and just giving in to the higher force—race, nation, religion, or "fate." These are all contradictory on one level, but in a fundamental sense, they all promote support for the stratification system, for capitalist inequality, even, sometimes, to the extreme of fascism.

The degree to which major sections of the population get won to these ideologies, most especially racism and its variants, can greatly strengthen or weaken the ability for fascism as a system to wreak its damage. A mistaken assumption about Marxism is that it is only concerned about economics and not about culture and ideas, but in fact, politics, social institutions, culture, and ideas are the ways that the class struggle takes place in the battleground of human consciousness, and Marxism has always been very focused on these.

Exercise 3.6: What Is the Effect of Violence on Social Change?

What is the effect of violence? What is the effect of nonviolence? Does violence alienate supporters so that violent movements usually fail? Does nonviolence create sympathy so that nonviolent movements usually win? What evidence would you present, and how do you know whether the movements you have heard about are typical?

What is the effect of violence? What is the effect of nonviolence? Often, people put forth analyses of racist or fascist movements which treat them as forms of "extremism." These analyses suggest that if everyone is moderate and follows the rules, you would not get those kinds of movements and backlashes. Is it true that political struggles beget more struggle, and political violence begets more violence?

Political struggles which concern deep political disagreements are often violent struggles. Often, in dealing with issues concerning racism, fascism, socialism, and communism, there not only are disagreements on the issues, but further disagreements on the means of struggling on the issues. There are some respects in which the theory of social movements is a relatively under-developed field of sociology. Every one of the founding theorists of the discipline constructed a theory of social movements. Nevertheless, some of the simplest and most basic questions have often been addressed more on the basis of intuitive judgments than systematic empirical analysis. One of these is the question of what causes the success and failure of social movements and especially what the effects of the use or the nonuse of violence are.

In any society, many different social movements come into being, grow or fail to grow, accomplish their objectives or fail to accomplish their objectives. Usually any given person is only familiar with the histories of a handful of these, and a handful is a pretty small number on which to estimate a pattern or base a judgment about causes of success or failure. Lacking data, we often come to conclusions which mainly reflect wishes, our prejudices, the selection of examples in high school history books, or conclusions which do not make us uncomfortable. Is it possible to do any better than this? Of course it is.

In order to investigate the determinants of the success and effectiveness of social movements, the first thing to do is to try to specify what one is talking about and to find a population of social movements. For example, W. Gamson, *The Strategy of Social Protest* (Dorsey, 1975), collected a list of several hundred movements in the United States which had been mentioned in ten or fifteen specialized histories. Then he selected a sample of those, obtaining about fifty movements which were a true sample of the population from which he started.

Some social movements used neither violent means nor had violence used upon them by either authorities or other movements. Changing Gamson's terminology, these are **neutral.** Other movements, whether they had violence used on them or not, used violence on others or on authorities. These are classified as the **violent** groups. Finally, there were a number of groups which had violence used upon them, but which did not themselves use violence, these are the **nonviolent** groups. What would you imagine was the success rate of the **violent,** the **neutral,** and the **nonviolent** movements?

Some people have suggested that violence turns people off, that it creates sympathy for the group that the violence is used upon, that it creates martyrs. If this is true, you would expect that violence is mainly counterproductive, and that the success rate will be highest for the nonviolent groups, lower for the neutral ones, and lowest for the violent ones. Others have suggested that violence, though difficult and sometimes disadvantageous, often works. If this is true, then the success rate should be highest among violent groups, lower among neutral groups, and lowest among nonviolent groups. Still other people have suggested that violence is a kind of mud that always smears both the group that uses it and the group that it is used against. This theory suggests that the success rate should be highest among the nonviolent groups, lower among the other two.

And other people have suggested that violence, in and of itself, is not a principled question, that violence or nonviolence does not have any particular effect, that it is other things that mainly affect the success or failure of a movement. To the extent that this is true, you would expect that the success rate of the three kinds of movements are not significantly different. One can even make one's theory more sophisticated by distinguishing different kinds of success. For example, Gamson distinguished between two different kinds of success. Some movements had major portions of their platform made into fact. The people or groups that enacted the platform might or might not grant any credit or recognition to the movement for calling for that change. But if a major portion of the platform of the movement was enacted, then Gamson classed the movement as having **advantages.** On the other hand, other movements were granted recognition by groups that they were dealing with. Regardless of whether their platform was enacted, they might be granted recognition and made part of the decision process. Gamson classed those groups as having achieved **acceptance**.

One can ask not only what the effect of violence is on success in general, but what the effect of the use of violence is by or upon social movements gaining advantages or acceptance? Instead of only four main possibilities, there are many more. Briefly write down what the ranking of the groups will be with regard to both kinds of success and why you think so, before you read further.

Table 3.3 gives the main Gamson findings with respect to violence. Gamson notes that estimating the effectiveness of a movement by the judgments of historians and the movements contemporaries is always problematic. But doing it formally with a sample is better than biased impressions of a handful of cases. There is a strong tendency for people to want to believe that those things which they find morally and normatively objectionable are also objectionable strategically—to believe that the things they do not like will not work. This tendency is accentuated in the selection of "instructive" examples of social movements in high school history textbooks. At any rate, these data suggest that the answers most typically volunteered by students of social movements are a product of wishful thinking and ideology.

With respect to **accomplishments**, you see that the poor nonviolent groups were utterly unsuccessful. The neutral groups were considerably more successful, but the violent groups were even more successful. Perhaps more surprising, even with respect to gaining official recognition, one sees the same pattern, although not as powerfully. These percentages are based on a small number of cases, but those cases are a true sample of a much larger population. It is thus a far better basis for evidence than taking many more than fifty movements but selecting them by intuition.

Table 3.3   Violence and the Outcomes of Social Movements

	Type of Social Movement		
	Nonviolent	Neutral	Violence-user
Percent gaining advantages	0%	53%	75%
Percent gaining acceptance	14%	50%	62%
Total	8	38	7

Source: W. Gamson, *The Strategy of Social Protest* (Dorso, 1975).

Does this mean that a movement should use violence all the time? Of course not. There is no simple guarantee to successful strategy and there is no simple answer to be found in this type of data analysis as to what one should do, either ethically or to ensure success. But, at the very least, it indicates why subjective feelings are not likely to be a good guide to effective action. It suggests that there are very important reasons why the question of violence comes up with regard to serious political conflict. To a considerable degree, the stories based on Gandhi, Martin Luther King, and others who supported nonviolence and saw violence as counterproductive, are consoling but superficial, misleading myths. And in those situations, and others with nonviolent movements, there was also often the threat of violence from other groups also active at the time, which provided an incentive for the powers to negotiate with the nonviolent groups.

Suggestions for Further Reading

The present sources of political fascism in the world are discussed in N. Chomsky and E. Herman, *The Political Economy of Human Rights*, two volumes (South End Press, 1979). An examination of organization and violence in black insurgency is D. McAdam, *Political Process and Black Insurgency* (University of Chicago, 1982). Among the works refuting the myth that the United States has had an open, nonrepressive political system is R. Goldstein, *Political Repression in Modern America* (Schenkman, 1978), which documents massive, consistent political repression, William Blum, *Rogue State* (Common Courage, 2000).

SECTION 3.7: WHAT IS A "DICTATORSHIP OF THE PROLETARIAT"?

For Marx, the first priority in achieving a free society is the end of exploitation, the end of arrangements whereby some people profit from the labor of others. Marx, like many of his contemporaries, called such a system "socialism." But the term *socialism* is used in different and confusing ways:

1. Some people use the term "socialist" to refer to big government, such as the Scandinavian welfare states, or to nationalizing industries. But government ownership does not necessarily mean popular control. If government ownership were socialism, Marx and Engels joked, then Metternich (the extremely conservative prime minister of Austria) was a great socialist, because he just loved state monopolies! In so-called welfare states there is still an exploiting class which lives off the labor of the working class. This is not "socialism" in the Marxist sense.

2. Other people call a society "socialist" if it eliminates private ownership of means of production (factories, mines, or land). The Soviet Union, Eastern Europe, Cuba, and China in the twentieth century were examples. Some Marxists believe this eliminates property incomes, which they see as the main class problem. However, a manager or a government official who does not have property income may live off others' labor. Marx was always very clear that the effect of government ownership depends on who controls the government. We do not think that the working class has controlled the government or the economy in those countries for at least four or five decades or more. For want of a more precise term, we use the term **state capitalism** to describe these societies.

3. A third position defines "socialism" as a society which is controlled and run by the working class. Marx did not expect that regime to be entirely egalitarian. Over the course of time, with the elimination of property income, the working class would come to include everyone, but in the beginning, there are other classes in a socialist society. How can you tell what class controls the government? Certainly a piece of paper saying there is popular or workers' control is not decisive evidence.

Dictatorship of the Proletariat

Marx argued that in the presence of enormous inequalities of resources, influence, and power, formal political equality does not achieve freedom or democracy. In the presence of enormous inequalities, equality of political influence is a contradiction in terms just as equality of opportunity is a contradiction in terms. When the rewards and control of the system go to inherited and other unearned property incomes, the entire system is perverted. Marx called socialism a "*dictatorship* of the proletariat." Why? He was perfectly aware that lots of people don't like "dictatorships" and see them as the main threat to freedom. Why didn't he call socialism a "democracy of the proletariat"? Certainly he believed that socialism is the only way truly democratic policies could be formulated and enacted. And "democracy of the proletariat" sounds nicer. So why didn't he call it that? There are two main reasons.

1. Marx wanted to underscore the fact that *capitalists would never give up their privileges without a fight*. He used the term "dictatorship of the proletariat" particularly after the Paris Commune of 1871, in which workers set up a democratic and egalitarian state. But at the same time, they had to fight against a capitalist French army cooperating with the Prussian army. Eventually the Commune was smothered in blood. Tens of thousands of French workers were executed or sent to prison colonies. Socialists are often strongly tempted to pretend that if they merely achieve a majority, or win control of the government through a legal election, there won't be a fight, that the former ruling class will quietly abide by the legal outcome. In Chile and many other places, this has led to the deaths of millions of people. The term "dictatorship of the proletariat" was meant as a warning that if you really plan to take away capitalists' billions, then you are going to have a fight. Marx viewed the state as an apparatus of power to protect the interests and members of a class, an apparatus for taking people who break the law and locking them up or shooting them. Marx was in conflict with anarchists who maintained that one could do away with government tomorrow. He wanted to honestly acknowledge that there would still be courts, laws, and jails for some time after a revolution.

2. At the same time, Marx wanted to emphasize that a state is a cold, cruel apparatus of coercion. Marx did not want to pretty up the state; but he *did* want to see it eventually disappear. He was also in conflict with liberals who maintained that as soon as there was formal, official political equality—the vote—then there would be freedom for the majority. Marx wanted to emphasize the fact that reducing government coercion, while leaving nongovernmental kinds of coercion—from the whip of hunger to private armies—in private hands was not the solution. *Marx wanted to underline—in a way that could not be missed—the fact that every government, socialist, capitalist, or feudal, represents an apparatus of force and uses force.* Initially a government of workers would have to do so as well. But it is either misunderstanding or a deliberate distortion of Marxism to say that Marxism favors "dictatorship" of the proletariat over "democracy." In Marxist terminology *the definition of "dictatorship" specifically applies to any government that ultimately depends on force to some degree, and that means all governments, capitalist as well as Marxist.* In other words, Marx counterposed "dictatorship of the proletariat" not to "democracy" but to "dictatorship of the bourgeoisie" (the capitalist system), the only other alternative in modern class society.

There is nothing pretty about the use of force. There was nothing "pretty" about the way that force had to be used in the South after the Civil War to prevent the ex-slaveowners from massacring free black people. There is nothing pretty about the way that present capitalist governments use force, and there would be nothing pretty about the force used by workers. People say that Marx should not have called it "dictatorship" because that ugly name might turn people off. But calling the state by pretty names is not a way of getting rid of it. Calling it pretty names only pretends that the violence of the state does not exist. Actually, it is a way of *not* getting rid of it.

Socialism and Communism

The fundamental difference between Marx and other social theorists is that Marx believes that we can eventually get rid of states—the instruments of domination—including prisons, courts, police, armies, bureaucracies, ministries, etc. From the very beginning, this was his disagreement with Hegel. Hegel thought that governments were eternal, that there would always be governments and wars. This is Marx's main disagreement with Durkheim and Weber. Marx believed that the fundamental reason for states is to hold down opposed classes, domestically and internationally. All of the other things that states do can be done in other ways. Marxists believe that before there were opposed classes, states did not exist, and after opposed classes are abolished, states will not exist.

Marx called this egalitarian society with no state **communism**. **Communism** for Marx was also a society where goods and services are distributed according to rule: "from each according to ability—to each according to need." More than just equality, what was meant by this was that human relations would progress to the point where people, working together to make a better world, would understand that the best kind of world was one where things are shared rather than where things are made for selfish reasons. In Marx's view, this could follow after socialism after the people no longer could make a profit from other people's labor, and people would not believe that they had to be greedy for themselves and their children— after the fundamental class contradiction in society had been eliminated.

Obviously, in this sense, what exists in China, today, and what existed in the Soviet Union for much of the twentieth century, were not communism—not even socialism, in the political-economic sense which we use in this book. We shall argue that such societies have a relatively small group of people who live much better than the average working class person, and the economy is controlled to meet mainly the needs of that small group, rather than the working class as a whole. A better name for that type of system is "state capitalist" rather than socialist or communist. The repressive measures in those countries exist not to protect the majority from a small group, but to protect a small group from the majority. It is certainly impossible to have socialism when private individuals control all the means of production. But when the means of production are officially owned by the public, the *essential nature* of the system still depends on who *controls* the state, including the economy. If the working class controls the state, it is socialist, but if a ruling class that lives off the labor of the working class controls the state, it is state capitalist.

In the corporate capitalist countries, there is also a move toward state capitalism, a move that actually may tie in with the development of fascism. This was especially apparent as Obama, with the strong support of Bush, restructured much of the U.S. economy in 2008, merging business with government under the guidance of the biggest bankers. Because capitalism often produces great disorders in the economy and political system, the most powerful capitalists try to bring order using the government against their foes. Everywhere in the world, as the international competition gets tighter, there is a tendency for the biggest corporations, who are already linked to their governments, to merge with them and institute more planning. *But the planning is not being done by the working class as a whole, and it is not being done in the interests of workers.* Marx and Engels made very explicit the fact that the merger of business and government is not socialist. In fact, it can be fascist. The issue is: who *controls* the government, the schools, the economy, and the state apparatus?

Exercise 3.7: Abiding by Majority Rule: Value Issues Concerning Democracy

Write down your preliminary position on the question of majority rule. When ought one to abide by the majority? When is it possible? Think of a number of cases where there are real disagreements about law, social arrangements, war, etc., and try to specify what you think ought to be the position of a group toward majority rule.

In Marx's day, democracy was very limited, even in the most democratic countries. In Britain, property requirements excluded most people from voting. In the United States, women and slaves could not vote. Everywhere governments greeted democratic movements with guns, armies, and prisons. The *Communist Manifesto* called for measures such as a progressive income tax, socialization of industry, and free public education. Movements to redistribute income, to give people the vote, to assure people access to a decent life or to socialize production all seemed to amount to the same thing.

By the twentieth century, the socialist parties had grown large enough to command near majorities in parliaments. Some socialists decided that they would be able to win without a fight. A fundamental dilemma for the Left centered on what policies they pursued and how they structured themselves to pursue those policies. Often they increasingly watered down their goals and platforms, trying to appeal to middle class people and small businessmen. In World War I, the socialist parties of Europe each patriotically supported their own governments, going to war against each other, wrecking internationalism, even shooting against their socialist comrades from other countries with whom they had been meeting at conferences just a few years before! The main places where there seemed to be real working class control, for a while, was not from such watered down politics, but from revolutions, especially the Soviet Union and China. These required a different form of political party. The development of the Bolshevik Party in Russia provoked a great deal of debate over the organizing principles of such a party.

Some of the issues seem to be causal questions about the effects of different party structures and political strategies. Others seem to be value issues. The causal questions about the objective consequences of a reformist strategy using a parliamentary strategy are probably the most important ones, and we shall consider those in exercise 3.10. But at the moment we want to consider some of the value issues concerned. Regardless of what the dominant groups do, and regardless whether a disciplined revolutionary party is essential to defeat capitalism, many people argue that if one once adopts nonelectoral, extra-legal methods, one has lost the whole show. "The failure to use legal democratic methods in a parliamentary party means that even if one wins, one will lose because the undemocratic methods one uses will corrupt the user," they say. This was how many European socialists criticized Lenin, and it is the view of most American socialists today.

Proponents of the idea that binding elections, such as we supposedly have in the United States, should be a sacred, noncompromisable feature of every society do bring up important points. They say that it is difficult enough to protect the majority from an elite even when there is voting; to publicly declare that voting will not necessarily be binding would seem to make it harder. Besides, they assert, the population should be allowed to vote, even to make their own mistakes, because that is how people will learn to govern themselves without elite "experts" giving them orders. These are all compelling points. However, even the staunchest proponents of voting do not actually believe in some *absolute* right of votes to be binding in all cases. These proponents of the absolute inviolability of binding elections are not simply "wrong"; they are being inconsistent.

During the Vietnam War, many opponents of that war opposed the presence on campus of military recruiters and Reserve Officer Training Corps (ROTC) programs. They argued that such programs were materially aiding the U.S. war effort and were helping to kill hundreds of thousands of Vietnamese, depriving them not only of free speech, but of other crucial freedoms (such as life) as well. One solution advocated by liberals was to let the faculty or students vote on that question. Many anti-war activists opposed such schemes. They said that if the government really wanted to carry on the war effort, it could and would simply ignore the votes, so why should the anti-war activists bind themselves to the outcome? More importantly, what right do a few hundred faculty, or a few thousand students have "voting" on whether to let hundreds of thousands of Vietnamese live or die? Who gets to vote? How about the Vietnamese? Can they vote in the campus election? How about the Canadians, the Russians, the Chinese, the Indians, the Swedes? Would the college president allow *them* to vote in the referendum?

Thus the point of the exercise is to bring the principle of majority rule (which majority rules on what?) into balance with the other principles that one must consider in politics.

Politics concerns power. It concerns times and ways that people are permitted or prevented from interfering with other people. Suppose the majority of students at a college in Scotland voted support for a British government's plan to bomb New York City. Would such a vote be binding on the people of New York? What if youth at a German university voted to expel Jewish students in 1936, or invade Czechoslovakia a few years later? We saw that before World War II, fascism was the outcome of the democratic process in many countries. In Germany, would you have abided by apparent majority rule in 1930? In 1935? In 1940? To the bitter end?

More relevant to the issue of postrevolutionary society are some other very real questions. Suppose a neighborhood, or a town, votes to keep black people out; would you, as a leader in government, feel bound to abide by that vote, or would you feel that the government had a right to not abide by that vote? What if you were a government leader after a revolution, and people in another part of the world desperately needed some food, or machinery, or minerals, or other resources that your revolutionary government had control over. What if the majority of people in your country voted against such aid because it would lower their standard of living somewhat—would you feel bound to abide by their decision? Letting people "make their own mistakes" not only has an effect on them, it can have profound effects on the freedom and lives of others. For example, in Bulgaria in 1990, thousands of Slavic Bulgarians marched, calling for the expulsion of all Muslims from Bulgaria. Like similar racial, religious, or national movements in Russia, China, Croatia, Hungary, and eastern Germany, this shows how little the previous regime had done to combat racism. But it also raises fundamental questions of whom democracy is for.

At this point, critics might say that the above is overly cynical. Why assume that the majority will vote the wrong way? Certainly one should not arrogantly dismiss the opinions of a large group; they may well be correct! This is a very good point, but it avoids the issue of what happens if they are wrong? Who will take responsibility? In sections 1.7, 1.9, and 2.5, we presented the Marxist argument that capitalists are a small but powerful group, and they maintain their dominance only by cashing in on the divisions and splits between people. Racial, religious, sexual, national, and other prejudices are strong. Sometimes they are immensely strong. Then, doing "what everyone wants" is a contradictory advice. To rely on binding votes as a main mechanism for preventing elitism only begs the question. Who will control the media in describing the candidates, who will be allowed to vote on which issues, who will count the votes, who will watch the counters, who will appoint the watchers, and so on? Is it "more democratic" to go through the motions of a binding vote, while all the time controlling the institutions that affect the outcome of the vote, and all the time reserving the right to overrule the vote? Or is it more honest to acknowledge that the procedure of voting will not always be binding and to strive at all points to involve people in the actual decision-making while struggling over the substantive issues?

Of course, the concerns of the anti-elitists need to be addressed. The rise of elitism within the Soviet Union and the elitist nature of some revolutionary organizations elsewhere reinforce the fears of concentrated power. One might say that these *political* questions are the most profound questions within Marxism today. The biggest disagreements between Marxists involve questions of how to take power and how to ensure that power will reside in the hands of the working class majority and not some privileged elite. Community organizations, block clubs, workers' committees on the job, anti-elitism, anti-competitiveness in the schools and workplace, and struggles to involve more people in making decisions, including even poll-taking, are all valid ways of training the majority to exercise power in the interests of the people and to resist elitism. But many Marxists argue that with all due respect to the important effects of program, technique, and forms, in the final analysis it is the *content*—the commitment to egalitarianism—that is the only way to truly overcome elitism. To the extent that "democratic" techniques help train people for egalitarianism, that will help develop anti-elitism. *But to the extent that these techniques are seen as the way to defeat elitism, the opposite will occur. If people are preoccupied with the techniques, devoid of egalitarian content, then elitism will be strengthened because people will be disarmed by illusions of real power when it is not really theirs.*

Obviously, much of the above is a major source of controversy with activist Marxist circles as well as within Marxist social science. Readers are encouraged to explore the range of literature dealing with Marxist politics, revolution, "dictatorship of the proletariat," the role of leadership, and other related questions.

Suggestions for Further Reading

On socialism and communism: studying the "classics" is not a certain guide to politics in the modern world. But ignorance of what Marx, Lenin, and others said is not a very certain guide either. A useful all-around source concerning Marx's own views of dictatorship of the proletariat and revolution is H. Draper, *Karl Marx's Theory of Revolution*, two volumes (Monthly Review, 1977–1980) which critiques most previous scholarship and which stresses the extraordinary character of "dictatorship," that is, it is government outside of, rather than within, the laws. Two of Marx's most explicit statements are his analysis of the Paris Commune in "The Civil War in France" and his "Critique of the Gotha Program" (SW, 288–313, 319–335). Lenin summarized and interpreted these and other writings in *The State and Revolution* (in many editions). One of the clearest theoretical arguments as to why abolition of private ownership of means of production does not necessarily produce socialism is C. Bettelheim, *Economic Calculation and Forms of Property* (Monthly Review, 1975). Most European communist parties recently eliminated the concept of the "dictatorship of the proletariat." One of the sharpest and clearest statements of the ensuing debate was that of E. Balibar, *On Dictatorship of the Proletariat* (NLB, 1978). On Leninist parties: the classical Leninist argument that there has to be a vanguard party is in *What Is To Be Done?* (in many editions). Among the many arguments whether Marx was or should have been a Social Democrat rather than a revolutionary, see R. Hunt, *German Social Democracy 1918–1933* (Quadrangle, 1970) and L. Colletti, *From Rousseau to Lenin* (Monthly Review, 1972). A well-known argument that social democracy can never produce socialism from within contemporary American sociology is A. Przeworski, *Capitalism and Social Democracy* (Cambridge, 1985).

SECTION 3.8: WHAT ARE THE MAIN VARIETIES OF MARXISM?

Issues of evolution versus revolution, socialism versus communism, and the like are necessarily controversial. People have very strong feelings about them. Most people's academic beliefs about them are related to what they actually do or don't do. American political sociology has tended to shy away from such issues, so that much of the analysis is by political scientists, historians, journalists, and activists. Does this mean that these are not objective empirical questions but rather a matter of value judgments? Does it mean that the disagreements aren't theoretical, but "merely" practical?

We think that the issues are objective and the disagreements on them merely indicate their importance. *Any* powerful, general theory has implications about what it takes to change what. "Theories" which purport to be above all that are not theories at all. If a theory really says something, then this has *practical* implications. In the case of Marxism, those political and practical implications are very visible. The main practical/theoretical disputes are spread out across history, existing political movements, and developed theoretical positions. As soon as people speak, the concepts they use, the works they cite, and the judgments they make allows one to place them. During the history of Marxism, the relationship between theory and practice has been displayed in a series of political splits between different political tendencies. The most important split, implicated in all the others, is the one which we have just examined, involving Lenin, concerning a disciplined revolutionary party. This occurred in the first generation after Marx's death between "socialists" and "communists," between parliamentary and revolutionary Marxists.

There still are major debates raging in the world today about such issues. In particular, the central division is between **parliamentarianism** versus **revolution**. **Parliamentarianism** is the strategy of trying to achieve change by participating in the election process as it exists under capitalism. Usually it is also tied to a strategy of reformism—attempting to achieve socialism gradually—within the law, in small bits. Parliamentarianism implies parliamentary parties. The Socialist Party of France is like the Democratic Party of the United States in most respects. In contrast to such strategies, the main revolutionary strategy was advocated most forcefully by Lenin. Lenin argued that one should not restrict oneself to operating within the law, which will always eventually be used to try to crush opposition to capitalism. In order to be able to battle against the law rather than operate within it, Lenin argued that anti-capitalists have to build a "democratic centralist" or **vanguard party**. Lenin argued that a party of that type is indispensable if capitalism is to be defeated because existing governments always try to crush opposition if it becomes a real threat to them. When fascist regimes arose in Europe, they threw tens of thousands of unionists and socialists into concentration camps. Only communists could mount sustained resistance movements. They had a kind of party and strategy which allowed them to oppose fascism.

The idea of "democratic centralism" that Lenin advocated is that after there had been a full discussion within the revolutionary party of some issue, everyone is expected to abide by the decision until the matter comes up for discussion again. This conflicts with the idea that one should keep on doing what one wants, regardless what other people in the group have decided. It also means that all decisions would not necessarily be resolved by the technique of voting. Within the revolutionary party, it means that the immediate majority opinion can be overturned in times of urgency. And outside the revolutionary party it usually means that members are ready to disobey the law if that party thinks that it is necessary. Such issues produced splits between revolutionaries and parliamentary gradualists, and many further splits have occurred since. Pluralist theorists, and many academics who consider themselves Marxist, are very hostile to this idea, which they believe will necessarily produce enormous abuses of power. They think the experience of the Soviet Union bears this out. But, on the other hand, without such a strategy, the tsar might still be running Russia. That situation would not have been "more democratic" than the revolutionary socialist governments were. This is not an easy question to resolve in a sociology textbook.

Lenin argued that since nearly all the organized political and intellectual forces in capitalist society are capitalist, there is a constant tendency for Marxism to be distorted in the direction of an accommodation with capitalism. Sometimes this takes the form of taking Marx's writings and revising them so as to systematically eliminate anything that gives them revolutionary perspective. Lenin called this tendency **revisionism**. The most prominent example in his day was the German social democrat E. Bernstein, who rejected Marx's dialectical method, working class leadership, working class revolution, and the labor theory of value. Politically and practically, Marx's politics are always focused on the future—on forces which are only in the process of coming into being. But there is always a powerful political tendency to be pragmatic, to limit oneself to what is possible now, and ultimately to accommodate with capitalist forces. Lenin called this tendency **opportunism**. An important example of opportunism occurred during World War I. French socialists supported French bosses in killing German workers and German socialists supported German bosses in killing French workers. (Most of the main political changes in the world have come about during wartime because the situation is very sharp then. If a group opposes its "own" country's war, usually they are vigorously attacked as traitors and put in jail. But Lenin felt that if Marxism was to reject nations and nationalism, wartime is precisely the time to do it.) To be patriotic kept the French and German socialists from being attacked as a traitors, but it destroyed the Second International as a progressive organization. In opposition to it, the newly victorious revolutionary Soviet leadership helped organize the Third International.

In practical politics, there are any number of philosophical questions of value which arise. But the main questions here are not questions of philosophical value but questions of fact, and the answers must be sought in empirical evidence. What are the inevitable consequences of nationalism? What are the necessary conditions of the working class gaining state power? Is it, in fact, true that in the absence of a centralized party, the working class will always be forced to make concessions of principle while ruling class concessions will be tactical? Are socialists always immersed in a liberal sea, so that they always tend to get wet? The fact that such questions have practical implications and historical supporters does not make them less objective or less theoretical.

The split between Lenin and Bernstein on revolution is only one of many splits among Marxist movements. During Marx's lifetime, there had been a split between the Marxists and the anarchists on whether any state was needed. After Lenin's death there was a split between Stalin and Trotsky, focusing on the question of whether socialism could be built in the Soviet Union. Trotsky set up the Fourth International which has since split into many Trotskyist parties. In the 1960s all communist parties split on the "question of the general line" between the Soviet Union and China. China argued that the Soviet Union had abandoned socialism and restored capitalism in actual practice. There have been further schisms and splits in all of these groups, producing a political spectrum which many people find confusing. Mainly the disagreements come down to the question of whether there needs to be a state, whether there needs to be a revolutionary vanguard party, whether there needs to be a violent revolution versus evolution through reformism, and whether the position of Marxists should be internationalist versus making concessions to nationalism. Not only are these divisions constantly reproduced because they involve perennial questions, but also past history produces some divisions and alliances. It is never possible to give an entirely nonpartisan, neutral account of the issues, because when there is sharp disagreement between two sides, there is usually disagreement not only on issues, but on what the issues are.

Exercise 3.8: Can Classes Be Abolished?

Often, people argue about equality as though no one could disagree with them. But there are opposing positions. Try to think through issues where there are such opposing positions. Divide a paper into three columns. Label the left column "egalitarians," the middle column "centerists," and the right column "inegalitarians." Now, write down the main thing that you think each of those groups could do today to strengthen and advance their position. Then write down what each group would do to react to the other two. Then at the next stage, write down the next step/reaction of the three groups, including alliances and breakaways.

Arguments about the possibility or impossibility of abolishing classes are partly a function of the different conceptions of class. One of the main reasons that there is an issue is that the concrete, material relations in the Soviet Union were similar in many ways to the concrete, material relations in the United States. We shall deal with that in a moment. But for now, it is important mainly to think about the different aspects of class that might be changed by different policies. In doing so, it is important to avoid two opposite errors concerning change, involving ways that class might be connected to other things.

The first error is to suppose that since everything is interconnected, nothing can ever be changed. All the different aspects of social stratification and class are connected with each other and with every other aspect of social structure. This is the functionalist illusion: everything is interconnected and therefore, nothing can change, and in particular, that the relationship between the classes will always stay fundamentally the same. But it is wrong to conclude that nothing can be changed. One could just as well conclude that everything about class can be changed, and can be changed in indefinitely many ways, by changing other things. In fact, history shows that the forms of social inequality are variable.

The second error is to suppose that anything can be conceived of as different, anything whatsoever about class can be changed *independently of other things*. Does one want equal incomes? Then one passes a law giving people equal incomes. Does one want equal political power? Then one passes a law giving people equal political power. Does one want an end of poverty, unemployment, war, sexism, racism, and other ills? One preaches charity, diligence, pacifism, anti-sexism, anti-racism, etc. In fact, the two opposite errors of supposing that nothing can be changed and supposing that anything can be changed independently of anything else feed each other and lead to each other. By not understanding the relationships between processes, many people one-sidedly bounce back and forth from one side to the extreme opposite, and back again, as each fails to explain the complexities of social change.

One can always legislate this or that, but if in fact the system is set up in such a way that inequalities emerge, then it does not matter what the law says. The key thing is that one is not really making a law from the outside, as a philosopher king, designing a society of puppets. The people who will carry out or change laws are the real members of the society. A law or constitution is just a piece of paper. It is only if you can find the forces which have actively strangled egalitarianism in the past, and stop them, that a piece of paper advocating it will have an effect. It is only if we can find a way of liberating forces, actively working toward an egalitarian and stateless society in the future, that we will achieve it. Issues about equality are issues where people disagree. If one is to avoid abstract and meaningless legislation in which "one" passes a law promoting that, you must consider opposed groups who have various governmental and nongovernmental resources for reacting to what opposed groups do.

When there is a battle between two groups, then the moves that each group makes are partly a response to the moves of the opposed group, as well as to what it has done before. If you took at such histories—particularly those in Europe at the beginning of the twentieth century—you will find that the "inegalitarians" become frantic when they appear to be losing. The political Left has often put itself into the position of supporting some strategy which appeared reasonable at the time, but which made it very difficult for them later on. For example, one often assumes that the main thing that egalitarians or inegalitarians must do now to strengthen their position is to grow larger, and the main way to do that is to move toward the center in the positions they take. And sometimes this may even be true. But there are also times when either group transforms the terms of the political debate, and it is often the case that moving toward the center makes it harder to do that. We shall return to these issues later.

The central issue in the historical and political analyses of what happened is whether there are some kinds of concessions which radically weaken the ability of the Left to act further. But since the issues, the composition, and the strategies of the Left (and of opposed groups) are all changing, and since all of those things depend on each other, there are serious difficulties in clarifying the questions and developing proof.

Suggestions for Further Reading

On main varieties of Marxism: you will find that this constitutes a whole section of the Library of Congress filing system, but not all of the relevant books are in that section. Moreover, all libraries are highly selective about what works they include. Two general works are: H. Laidler, *History of Socialism* (Cromwell, 1968) and N. MacKenzie, *Socialism, A Short History* (Harper & Row, 1966). On classlessness: an interesting contemporary analysis by an activist group is that of the Progressive Labor Party, "A Communist Manifesto, 1982," *PL Magazine* (Winter 1982). A standard Soviet account is A. Leontiev, *Political Economy* (International, 1974). A standard Maoist critique is S. Amin, *The Future of Maoism* (Monthly Review, 1981). The classic statement by Lenin is *The State and Revolution* (many editions).

SECTION 3.9: WHY DID SOCIALISM COLLAPSE IN THE USSR AND CHINA?

In most twentieth century revolutionary Marxist analysis, the picture of the future that was accepted ran roughly as follows: the tiny capitalist class in a capitalist society uses its economic and political power—in alliance with petty capitalists, managers, and other groups—to control the state. It holds down and exploits the working class. It has naturally the advantages that the working class can only acquire when masses of workers and their allies are organized by a party. But gradually in a series of conflicts with the capitalist class, the working class does unite behind a revolutionary party. The working class party then expropriates the tiny capitalist class and smashes its state apparatus, instituting socialism to abolish profits and property income, but retain unequal wages for some jobs. Money would remain the medium of exchange; products would still be produced, at least in part, in order to be sold. It is a society based on the principle, "(S)he who does not work, shall not eat," without the distorting effect of a leisure class living on profit, and without the domination of the capitalist ideology. There is rapid growth of productive forces.

The increased efficiency leads to a rise in the standard of living of those who are earning lower wages.

Living in this more equal, more efficient society, more and more people will come to understand that egalitarianism works to the best interests of all and that selfishness hurts everyone. People are more educated so that they can take more part in politics and they rotate between jobs. Collectively planned economies for people and not profits eliminate massive amounts of waste creating an ever higher standard of living for people. There is more to go around and it becomes increasingly possible to eliminate inequalities and material incentives, moving to a society based on "from each according to ability, to each according to their need." There will be less and less cheating, and less and less need for a government to protect the majority from the minority of would-be thieves and exploiters. The role of the state in maintaining social order becomes less and less, and the state "withers away" as what we call "government" becomes collectives of people cooperatively trying to figure out what plans will be best for everyone. In most twentieth century revolutionary Marxist theory, this completes the movement from socialism to pure communism.

Today, most Marxists see that process as being very rough and uneven, at best. The fundamental questions were raised by the Soviet Union and China. When the first edition of this book was published, the authors asserted that the USSR was state capitalist—with fundamentally capitalist class relationships but with much of the economy socialized, giving the appearance of socialism while the party and its allies functioned like capitalists. The authors suggested that this would collapse, and within a few short years, exactly that happened. Why?

Even according to the Soviet Union's own portrait of history, the classical scenario of abundance leading to increased equality and more movement toward pure communism did not happen. Other histories and analyses see a movement in the reverse direction, from socialism to state capitalism—increasing inequalities, increasing political monopolies, increasing selfishness—rather than from socialism to communism. Thus, the analysis of the Soviet Union and of what happened there has been a central question of theoretical, practical, and historical analyses during the last generation. Virtually no one argues that the Soviet Union achieved communism in the Marxist sense of abolition of the state and distribution according to need. Not even the Soviet theoreticians claimed to have made much progress in that regard, although they did claim to have abolished classes and class struggle. But their major claim was to have abolished exploitation, and with it the bureaucratic, vicious, predatory politics of imperialism, nationalism, racism, sexism, and other forms of domination. Of course, this begs the question of how traditional private property capitalism was able to retake power so quickly in the early 1990s.

We have noted that Marx and Engels did not equate public ownership of means of production with socialism. Public ownership is not necessarily the same as popular control. Private ownership is certainly not popular control either. In fact, private ownership is essentially inconsistent with popular, democratic control. The fact that Fred owns a factory means that he makes the decisions, and as long as Fred owns it, the workers in the factory or the community around it will never be able to control it. But the nature of government ownership depends on who controls the government, the working class or some other class.

Many Marxists around the world believe that there was a time when the working class controlled or had substantial control over the government of the Soviet Union, and the political and economic policies of that government mainly did serve the majority working class population. But they lost that control, and the Soviet Union moved from socialism back to state capitalism, eventually culminating in the abandonment of even the pretense of socialism, as some Communist Party leaders and allies in the military decided to move toward more traditional capitalism in 1991, the same year the first edition of this book was published.

Different analyses suggest different mechanisms as to how they lost socialism, each with different, practical implications as to how one would avoid that outcome in the future.

- Some people say that Stalin suppressed opposing political tendencies, so that an overly narrow political spectrum emerged.
- Some people say that the Soviet Union suffered a bureaucratic distortion mainly due to a failure to alter relations in production.
- Some people say that the rise to power of Khrushchev's faction increased privileges and failed to make communist political struggle primary.
- Some people say that the Soviet Union was locked into a capitalist world, and therefore nothing they could ever have done would have made much difference.

Which of these analyses is correct? Are any of them correct? Is there some other explanation, perhaps drawing on parts of them, which explains the setbacks of socialism where that has occurred and the degree of progress when some progress has occurred?

We think that none of the explanations just listed are adequate. Many of them contain important insights, insights that should be examined by anyone interested in Marxist theory. But we don't think any of them point to political-social-historical dynamics strong enough to *explain* the outcome. Thus, none of them point to political-social-historical dynamics powerful enough to allow us to *practically affect* that outcome. The exercise pursues the question and outlines one position on it. But, for the moment, let us sum up five things about the historical process of the Soviet experience which most Marxists consider relevant to the explanation of the setback there:

1. At the time of the revolution, the Bolsheviks, later the Communist Party of the Soviet Union (CPSU), were a small segment of a pre-dominantly peasant population. For many reasons, the CPSU did not have much of a base among the peasants (a main difference between Russia and China). This led to increasingly sharp conflicts with peasants, especially in the context of the rise of fascism and the movement of forces toward World War II. There was a dialectical, self-reinforcing historical process involving lack of a base or ties, lack of confidence, hierarchical and market controls, and conflict between city and country.

2. At the end of the revolution and civil war, the CPSU was suddenly in charge of the immense old establishments of the military, the minis-tries, the educational institutions, the firms, the scientific institutes, the police, the cultural institutions, etc. They wanted to run these effi-ciently to develop the nation rapidly, especially in the face of external threats. They believed that they could use the "progressive members" of the old tsarist military to run many of these institutions, so long as they were subjected to political supervision. But the old managers were not even won to socialist principles of work and politics—let alone to communist ones—and could only organize and run these institutions in the old way, as top-down hierarchies, infused with the elitism, the anti-worker, anti-peasant, and anti-ethnic minority atti-tudes which had been present before. With further layers of top-down controls and supervision, who was going to supervise the supervisors? Who was going to educate the teachers? The dynamics pushing toward an egalitarian society under popular control was often frustrated by these institutional arrangements and to self-reinforcing cycles of de-pendence either on competitive markets or on hierarchical controls, as ways of getting things done.

3. The CPSU believed that the most important thing to do was to increase economic production. Lenin once said, half seriously, that socialism plus electricity equaled communism. The main theoretical view which stood behind this attitude was that the development of the forces of production was the fundamental source of social change—that abun-dance would eliminate inequality. Instead of a dialectical theory, the CPSU tended toward a kind of technological determinism. Instead of solving a contradiction between two tendencies, they came to be-lieve that all they had to do was to increase production. Their theory enormously accentuated the tendencies toward nonmobilization of

peasants and increased reliance on hierarchies and markets. There was forced-draft extraction of surplus from villages, forced-draft urbanization, and proliferation of hierarchical controls and competitive markets. Thus, the theoretical analysis which stressed forces of production led to social structures whose principles were alienated and to increased wage inequality (**material incentives**).

4. The CPSU saw the rise of fascism staring at them over the German border. Hitler made no secret of his plans in the East. War was obviously coming. As the CPSU frantically pulled its industries behind the Urals (the equivalent of moving all U.S. eastern industries west of the Rockies), arguments about the need for forced-draft industrialization and use of the old elites became distorted. There was increased nationalism and with it a tendency to glorify individual leaders, but when socialists ally with nationalists and promote nationalist thinking, it is the nationalism that wins rather than the egalitarianism, and that "me first—my group first" attitude leads back to capitalism. This further strengthened tendencies to rely on old elites and structures.

5. The Soviets increasingly adopted principles of organization from capitalist countries, thinking that they were only borrowing technology and adapting it to socialism. They believed that the main way to get people to do things was to offer them money or to set up chains of command. These mechanisms do not convince workers that something is worth doing—the government can get a short-term productive behavior without changing motivation. This reliance on material incentives and hierarchical controls meant that people were increasingly faced with situations and structures which were essentially similar to General Motors or the U.S. government, in an intellectual environment increasingly rife with nationalism, sexism, and other divisive, selfish ideologies. One had the immense contradiction of a communist party, sitting on top of a society which was not organized in a socialist way. Something had to give. An immensely sharp, complex series of historical battles then occurred, analyzed by historical sociologists such as C. Bettelheim. It was not that some one group or individual was suddenly corrupted or crazy and went charging off in the wrong direction. Increasingly, *all* the various groups were operating with assumptions, within organizational structures, which made all of the choices bad choices. What is superficial about the dominant analyses of Stalinism, bureaucracy, Russian culture, world position, etc., is that they trivialize the problem. They suggest either that the only thing that had to be changed was individuals, or organizational principles, or that nothing could have been changed. This leaves out social structures and the dynamics of social structures.

In the Soviet Union, there was a contradiction between communist and capitalist principles of organization. Of course the CPSU never officially renounced "Marx," "socialism," or the "movement to communism" because those were, and are, very popular. But you can burn heretics in the name of love. Intellectual principles can always be reinterpreted. Increasingly, both domestically and internationally, we think that the Soviet leadership did abandon them. Meanwhile, some factions within the ruling elites had their eyes on privatizing major socially owned industries to greatly increase their own wealth. So when a major split emerged within the leadership of the CPSU (and various other Eastern European elites) between those who favored a move toward more overt capitalism and those who wanted to maintain the status quo, some large sections of the population, and especially the military, were so hostile to the leadership that they were willing to support any kind of change and take their chances that maybe they could be winners under capitalism. But when people were marching in the streets against the various communist parties in Eastern Europe, were they demanding an end to government-sponsored health care, child care? Did they wish that foreign companies would take over their industries and then shut them down? Were they really demanding that big companies, often from the United States, Western Europe, and even India, would now dominate their economies? Or were they just angry at the monopoly of wealth and power that the various corrupt communist parties had?

The combination of loss of support for the corrupt communist parties, the dream that capitalism could provide affluent lives for all as portrayed on television and in movies, and the split within the leadership of the communist parties and military created a situation where there were sudden upheavals and a removal of the communist parties from power in most of those countries. Ironically, many of the "new" capitalists and politicians were ex-communists who simply used their power to personally buy up what had been government property and then resell it to foreigners, making themselves even richer. Meanwhile, the life of the average person in most of Eastern Europe has actually gotten worse economically, although there is a minority, often well publicized in U.S. and European media, which has become more affluent.

China, with one fourth of the world's population, looks different. It is still run by its Communist Party, but the policies of that Communist Party are far from being based on economic equality. The number of millionaires in China has been increasing among the fastest in the world. Foreign corporations are exploiting inexpensive Chinese labor to make huge profits, with some of that going to local Chinese capitalists. China is investing heavily in U.S. banks and therefore relies on the successful profitability of U.S. business to protect its wealth, and Chinese corporations are exploiting labor all over the world, particularly intensely in some parts of Africa.

Within China, poverty in the countryside has greatly intensified, the gap between the rich and the poor has widened, and there are tens of millions of migrant workers who travel from one place to another taking temporary work. As in Eastern Europe, there is a visible middle income group more affluent than in the past, but even for them, their situation is not stable, while for many millions more, the situation is very unstable. Over fifty thousand factories closed in China in the past few years and China's overall economy is increasingly tied to the unstable capitalist economies in the rest of the world. What happened?

Within China, a complex set of conflicts and splits in the leadership goes back to the 1950s or earlier. As in the USSR, there was reliance on material incentives, wages, and commodity production. Agriculture was socialized in China more quickly; and through much of the 1950s and 1960s, those in the party who favored more equality also encouraged this type of culture within the working class. Throughout the 1960s there was a power struggle, and the Great Proletarian Cultural Revolution (GPCR) attempted to push the more procapitalist forces out of power and prevent China from going down the "capitalist road" that the USSR had gone down. Factories and schools were organized according to egalitarian principles and those officials, administrators, and teachers who were considered elitist or arrogant were subject to intense criticism. A main slogan was: "Better Red than Expert," meaning that having the correct, egalitarian policy was more important than relying on elitist experts who might improve production in the short term.

Immediate production was sometimes disrupted and there were instances where some of the rebels treated their opponents harshly. Mao, for whatever reason, compromised with his opponents. In the name of "spreading egalitarianism," he sent students to the countryside to work with peasants, which had the effect of splitting the students away from their worker allies in the cities. Mao then declared that the GPCR was a success and that the right wing was defeated. A problem that many observers saw, however, was that a main slogan of the GPCR was that 90 percent of the leaders of the party should be replaced, but at the conference that celebrated the supposed victory of the GPCR, 90 percent of the delegates were the same people who had been in power before. Not much change.

After Mao died in 1976, the elite consolidated its power and began to move China quickly in the direction of corporate capitalism. China today still has major parts of the economy controlled by the government, but in many cases, the government is using what appears to be the forms of socialism to protect the content of capitalism (exploitation of labor for the accumulation of wealth by private individuals). Today, there are still splits in the Communist Party of China over how fast to deregulate the economy versus concerns that moving too fast will destabilize the country and encourage more corruption. Neither faction, however, is seriously pushing toward the kind of egalitarian pure communism that is the goal of Marxist social revolution. Economically, Chinese production did increase dramatically, but so did inequality and instability, and as capitalism has shown, it can dramatically increase production in a short time, but in the long term the instabilities predominate.

Does the collapse of socialism in the USSR and China mean that Marxism is unworkable? Does this mean that socialism is inherently contradictory and that attempts to achieve popular control, abolishing private privileges (and the state that maintains them) always fail? Will it, as Weber suggested, merely expand the state apparatus? Well, obviously many people think so, but it certainly hasn't been demonstrated by the Soviet or Chinese experiences. What the Soviet experience does show is that if the party is a small group, isolated from the peasantry in a peasant society, using old elitist managers and generals to mobilize people on the old principles of material incentives and nationalism, then you might just end up with another version of the old system which eventually transforms into the more chaotic form of corporate capitalism. While the specific history of China is somewhat different, the essence is the same. In China, nationalism was and remains a particularly powerful force that undermines egalitarian consciousness, which combined with many of the same forces as in Russia.

After the fact, it is hard to see why anyone would think those cases would have turned out differently. It is always easy to be a Monday-morning quarterback. That is one of the ways that humankind slowly goes forward. The Soviets were trying something for the first time in history, and it is hardly surprising that they made mistakes. There were some fantastic accomplishments during that experiment, including greatly improved education and health care, some important attempts to spread egalitarian, communist philosophy, the destruction of the Nazi regime, and most important, the experiences of that period from which the world can learn. We think that socialism was reversed in the Soviet Union and China, and we think this was a world-historical disaster for the working class. But in some ways, it took the whole world-historical disaster of this reversal to demonstrate what, after the fact, is obvious: capitalist managers, using capitalist principles, set up state-capitalist ministries and factories, and promote nationalism and a culture that prizes above all acquiring consumer goods, and over time, that became the primary aspect of political-economic organization in the USSR, Eastern Europe, and China.

The answers to these questions ultimately can be found only by empirical investigation, not by substituting catch-phrases to fit a preconceived theory. The American media and Western academics discuss these changes often in highly oversimplified terms. Instead of analysis of underlying social and economic conflicts, they use simplistic versions of personality theory ("Gorbachev had a nice personality; Putin has a nasty one.") to explain events.

Dramatic recent events resulted from a longer, developing process. We believe that this process centrally involved economic and class conflicts. Over a long period, the Soviet bloc countries and China have been dominated by elites who used the state, rather than private corporations, to extract some of the labor from the working class and take it for their own use in the form of better housing, food, medical care, transportation, and salaries. Alongside slogans of Marxist equality, social policies and ideologies justifying the higher standard of living for these elites were disseminated throughout the society. A sizeable group of professionals, semi-professionals, technicians, intellectuals, and managers developed as a kind of middle stratum between the elite and the working class. Many members of this stratum, raised in a society that justified and reinforced special privilege, put forward their own demands to be given more rights and privileges but without challenging the essential inequality of those societies. In time, the size of this middle stratum grew considerably. The communist party membership in many of these countries consisted more of these middle stratum people than of workers. Some members of the elites saw the growth of this stratum as allies in their plans to privatize major assets for their own personal gain. Inequality increased. The "halfway" socialism of those countries stagnated. Workers were not motivated to produce for the good of the society; they could see the special privilege around them. These underlying processes laid the basis for what appeared to be sudden reversals. However, as the first edition of this book noted, the Soviet Union had already abandoned socialism, and the qualitative, discontinuous collapse had had a quantitative, gradual preparation.

Exercise 3.9: What Are the Lessons of the Soviet Union and China?

Suppose that Marxist revolutionaries had control of a factory, city, state, or country. (There are real enough differences between these, but don't make too much of them.) What would happen if instead of setting up a socialist wage/state system, they argued for and set up communist egalitarian/direct action institutions? No doubt there would be all kinds of problems of articulation between different structures—there always are. No doubt people would design ongoing solutions to those. What might they be? What further developments would occur? Thus assuming an egalitarian, communist solution within some structure,

1. List some problems that would arise.
2. List the solutions you think people would institute.
3. Describe the overall dynamic that you think would result.
4. Do you imagine the development would be a steady, gradual path in one direction or that there would be twists, turns, and unexpected contingencies?

5. But within that process, list three or four things that seem to you most crucial to maintaining and extending an egalitarian project. Is it some policy? Some organizational form? Some theoretical insight? Some situational factors?

What kind of evidence would corroborate or contradict your analysis of the dynamics?

As we have noted, the analysis of the past failures of socialism is a very basic question of Marxist sociology. It is an area where political theory, economics, and historical analysis come together with questions of method. The idea of "learning a lesson" seems like a very mental, a very ideal thing. On the other hand, what you learn the lesson from and what you do about it can be a very real thing. When it is a question of learning a lesson in world history, what is involved is the tension among the present, unique historical actions, and the general processes always active; between human consciousness and the real material policies and organizations; between voluntaristic factors (what one can do differently) and determined factors (what essentially follows from other things). These issues will be central to chapter 4 and we have argued that Marx's dialectic is opposed to two illusions: the illusion that nothing changes, that nothing can be different, that everything is determined; and the illusion that nothing is determined, that everything changes independently, and that anything can be different just by wanting it to be.

The debate over whether some major event in history "had to happen," whether it was determined by all the previous causes or not can sometimes be a useful debate. Other times, however, when the debate is framed in very abstract ways—extreme determinism versus extreme voluntarism—the debate can seem impossible to resolve.

As will be clearer in the following chapter, we think that some of the ideas of **dialectics** can be useful in resolving these very abstract and irresolvable issues, between voluntarism and determinism and ideas versus policies, concretely. The elimination of capitalism is a process. We have to look at the ideas and policies and memberships of organizations as interrelated and changing. We have to look at all the groups, ideas, and policies as being in tension or struggle with opposed groups, ideas, and policies. As we noted, some people believe that the experience of the Soviet Union shows how to do it, that there were not structural problems, perhaps just problems of leadership personality or psychology, but that the basic policies were on the right track and that it could have moved toward an egalitarian society. Some people think that it shows that capitalism is the only system consistent with "human nature," that it shows that you need good leaders or a less backward country, or that it shows that you need more of the kind of political arrangements we have in the United States.

We think a fundamental, radical rethinking of Marx from within a Marxist perspective is needed if we are to learn from the past. Some people argue that all the failures to sustain socialism—the Soviet Union, China, Vietnam, Indonesia, Cuba, Venezuela, Poland, Chile, and many other places—have the same form: one divides the process of change into several stages, a bourgeois-democratic stage, a nationalist stage, a "new democracy" stage, or whatever. This means that in the early stage, the concern need not be with real communism—with the policies and structures which one needs in a truly noncapitalist society. And the reason for postponing all that is in order to make an alliance with various (capitalist) groups which would be hostile to a truly noncapitalist society. Thus, concessions of various kinds are made to them: nationalism, inequality, restricted private employment, etc. But these concessions always become the tail that wags the dog.

The grandfather of all these stages is Marx's distinction between "socialism" and "communism," and we think that the attempt to maintain that distinction always fails. Recall that "socialism" was supposed to be a system which maintained the wage system and inequality while abolishing profits and maintaining a political state similar to the capitalist state, while establishing formal working class control of it. There are not many places where Marx uses this distinction, but there are some. Marx believed that you could see an overall movement, but he did not believe that you could lay out a blueprint. This kind of design was something millions of people needed to do, not some "genius." But why do you need a "socialist" stage?

No doubt a revolutionary party can only abolish a wage system of unequal pay in the areas and institutions where it gains control and has highly committed mass support. Popular alternatives to state apparatuses have to be set up one at a time. However, it might be that setting up a whole system of unequal wages and state bureaucracies merely slows down and then stalls the process of convincing people to do without them. And what if the entire system involves *convincing people that inequality is a positive good*? That does not seem like a way to move to an egalitarian system. Some people say that more people can be convinced to get rid of profits than to get rid of inequality. It is an empirical question. In a sudden, structural shift—depression, fascism, war, or revolution—it might well be easier or no more difficult to convince people to get rid of inequality altogether.

Suggestions for Further Reading

On the Soviet Union: within American sociology, the main argument that the Soviet Union remained a workers' state was A. Szymanski, *Is the Red Flag Flying?* (Zed, 1979). The main argument that the Soviet Union was bureaucratically deformed by Stalin was originally formulated by L. Trotsky, for example, *The Revolution Betrayed* (New Par, 1957). An analysis that stresses

Khrushchevism and privileges is S. Amin, *The Future of Maoism* (Monthly Review, 1981). The arguments that the Soviet Union's world position made socialism impossible are reviewed in C. Chase-Dunn, *Socialist States in the World-System* (Sage, 1982). A history of the Soviet Union is C. Bettelheim, *Class Struggles in the Soviet Union*, two volumes to date (Monthly Review, 1976, 1978).

SECTION 3.10: WHAT DOES THE COLLAPSE OF SOCIALIST WORLD POWERS MEAN FOR CHANGE?

Thus, we have suggested, the collapse of socialism in the world powers of the Soviet Union and China does not mean that socialism is inherently utopian. History often takes twisted paths. Nor does it mean that capitalism has solved its contradictions or that people have stopped struggling against it. The exploitation of nature and the exploitation of fellow human beings continue to bring devastation, misery, polarization, war, waste, and greed; they feed upon divisions of race, gender, ethnicity, language, religion, and politics, and they feed those divisions. Those forms of exploitation perceptibly move toward limits, crises, and catastrophe.

The fact that the Soviet Union and China cannot serve as models does not mean that everyone now sits on their hands. Everywhere in the world millions of people are engaged in struggles, movements, and tendencies directed against the capitalist dynamic of class and capitalist accumulation. With the exception of North America, every habitable continent on the planet has societies—usually the largest ones—that are explicitly inspired in various ways by Marxian anti-capitalism. Because there is no model in the form of a world power, that probably means that the movements directed against capitalism are more fragmented, with different opponents being set against each other. Even in Marx's day and in the twentieth century, there were times when, in Marx's words, communism was a "specter haunting Europe," rather than a power marching across it. Now, although the absence of a world focus of opposition lifts the burden of apologetics from the Left, it increases the problems of division and diffusion.

The analysis of the mistakes of the past is essential and, as we have noted, different analysts and different groups have stressed different factors of policy, program, organization, or situation. Some within the tradition of Marxism say that "the time has not been ripe." Those who emphasize economic determinism assert either that the economy has not matured to the point where scarcity is no longer a problem, or where collapse is unavoidable, or where the entire world system changes. We would place the main obstacle not in economic forces but within the ranks of the communist movement itself. At this point, the primary obstacles are subjective, not objective. In some ways, the very distinction is alien to Marx, who insisted that "ideas" become a "material force" when they grip the masses.

The main reason that communism has not been realized is that sufficient numbers of people do not *understand* why it is required and what it requires. Of course, like any analysis, this only states the problem and gives a guideline of the direction of a solution. It is often necessary for objective changes to occur in order for subjective changes to occur. But consider: (1) if objective misery were sufficient, then India, Bangladesh, and Haiti would have had egalitarian communist revolutions long ago. (2) If economic development were key, then the United States or Germany would have had egalitarian communist revolutions long ago. (3) If military destruction were the necessary objective condition, then parts of Europe should have embraced true egalitarian communism during the 1940s. Again, certain objective changes can create or greatly enhance the possibilities for a massive transformation of human consciousness. But what is most important is that people have to understand the need for total equality and the destruction of states. For this, some people have to present those truths uncompromisingly to those people who don't yet agree. Then, *even if objective conditions did preclude sufficient numbers of people understanding this for a time*, the fact remains that if the ideas are put forward, *more people* would understand it; we would be *closer* to achieving those goals. Marxists call the failure to put forward those ideas and positions **opportunism**.

Opportunism is the abandonment of principles in order to take advantage of immediate circumstances. *Opportunism has severely weakened most Marxist movements.* Within the Marxist movement, opportunism has taken many different forms. **Economism** involves hiding Marxist ideology in order to win immediate material gains, ignoring the issue of political power in order to build labor unions oriented to wages. **Nationalism** involves siding with the capitalists of one's own country in order not to be attacked as a traitor or to support one group of capitalists against another. **Pacifism** involves rejecting the principle of violent revolution or the use of force in order to avoid political repression. **Parliamentarianism** involves trying to build an electoral party, working for gradual reforms, hoping that the capitalists will give up control peacefully. Various forms of **anarchism** and **utopianism** reject the need for a strong leadership organization or for political changes in favor of building counterinstitutions. Each of these positions abandons important parts of Marx's own analysis. Traditionally, Marxists have seen them as the operation of liberal, capitalist ideas within the working class movement. Capitalist society is a sea. Marxists are bound to get wet. Marxists try to move to a new principle of social organization, but they have to do so with the people and the pieces of social structure trained and designed for the capitalist system. Thus there is a persistent pressure to abandon one or another element of the interconnected system of Marxism.

This does not mean that any variation from what Marx said, at one time or another, is opportunist. We do not think that Marx's own analysis should be accepted, or enshrined, just because it is Marx's. One of the reasons that it is difficult to overcome opportunism is because Marxism is a living science. Marxism says that concrete circumstances, not dogma, are what define reality. Therefore opportunists often claim that they are adapting Marxism to new circumstances and avoiding the error of dogmatism when they reject the essential principles of Marxism.

The question of opportunism is relevant in two different contexts—before and after the capitalist class loses state power. In the period of capitalist domination, Marxism is, at best, an oppositional force. In a thousand different ways, theorist and activist movements are tempted to find a middle way between capitalism and Marxism, combining elements of each. In every battle, groups will spring up to take a middle position, compromising whatever the main protagonists are standing for. If it was possible gradually and continuously to move from capitalism to egalitarian society, then this would be fine. But has this happened? What the working class has gotten from the gradualist strategy was either a weakened movement that was crushed by the capitalists or some temporary material reforms that did not actually break with hierarchical capitalist class relations and still had to confront the power of the capitalist state—and then economic and political crises developed. Often what was "won" was a corporate state which combines the *worst* aspects of corporate capitalism defended by big government, justified as updating and "enhancing" Marxist strategy. Often this opportunism involves appealing to special interests. Economism appeals to unionized employed workers, pacifism to many students and religious groups, reformist politics to middle income groups, and nationalism to the members of a given state or ethnic group. In each case, the appeal to some group is shortsighted in that it splits and divides those groups from the allies essential if they are to win even their own demands; it is usually a diversion away from egalitarianism, and it usually appeals to procapitalists from the subordinated group who aim to carve out territory for themselves as new capitalists or junior partners to majority group capitalists.

After a revolution, the danger of opportunism may be more intense. As early as 1903, long before most people thought the Bolshevik Revolution could possibly occur, Lenin prophetically wrote that holding power after a revolution and building egalitarian consciousness—defeating procapitalist ideas—would be ten times harder than defeating the old capitalist ruling class itself. After the capitalist class has lost its dominant position and privileges, that group's drive to reestablish itself is increased tenfold, while it is no longer easily identified as a particular set of people. Among the resources of that group are residual habits and ideologies from that past, such as racism, sexism, elitism, cynicism, and a desire to own things as a way to feel good psychologically.

In the Soviet Union, in China, and in every other case where the working class has been able to gain power, we think power was retrieved by capitalists (now "managers," "bureaucrats," "experts," or new "elites") in the following generation. The fundamental elements of abolition of wages and abolition of the state were not maintained. Why? It is too simplistic to say that a few corrupt individuals sneak into power to restore capitalism. Every elite group, in all of the various pieces of the social structure, was trained and oriented to the old system that was elitist. The social forces striving for privileges succeed partly because of theoretical errors on the part of their opponents. It is just as simplistic to say that opportunism is merely a mistake, an error, the abandonment of a Marxist truth. We think that under concrete circumstances, powerful dynamics combine the social and political forces leading to the abandonment of the heart of Marxism. Neither in the Soviet Union nor anywhere else was this abandonment made in the quiet of some preserve outside the rough and tumble of dealing with urgent, immediate problems. History grants no quiet preserves. It seemed that appeals to nationalism, use of inequality to promote production, or use of old elite groups was essential to beat back the violent, deadly attack from Hitler or from some other quarter. Those decisions may now be seen as shortsighted, but we have the benefit of hindsight. Within the middle of the hurricane of class struggle, we can understand the terrific pressure to give concessions and to succumb to short-term policies. But when this short-sightedness becomes institutionalized, Marxism has given way to another variety of capitalism. Marx developed a materialist social science fundamentally concerned with improving the material well-being, but he was always concerned with understanding, clarifying, and winning people to communist world view. *Anything which confuses, distorts, or otherwise damages that process is fundamentally opposed to the essence of Marxism and destroys the only victory, increased consciousness, unity, and organization, that oppressed people can truly sustain whether living under capitalism or building egalitarianism in a postrevolutionary society.*

In all of this, the role of leadership of those people at the forefront of struggle who are trying self-consciously to create an egalitarian world is decisive. The forces pushing toward abandonment of crucial positions are constant, but the response is not. If leaders make fundamental concessions of principle to capitalism, how can anyone be surprised that many others will tolerate or even embrace capitalist policies? If the *spokespersons for Marxism* say that unequal wages, sexism, nationalism, and other forms of inegalitarianism can and should be relied upon, then many others will gravitate to procapitalist thought. If they say that patriotism is good, the patriotism they are building will sabotage the internationalist consciousness they are also trying to build. If they argue that one should unite under the leadership of capitalists, even temporarily, they undermine their ability to organize a struggle against those capitalists later. If they assert that improving the standard of living in their own country is more important than aiding the worldwide proletariat, they create the theoretical basis for continuation of the nationalist exploitative system. If they argue that some people are "worth more" and should live better than others, they are creating social arrangements in fundamental contradiction to Marxism as a whole.

Reality is contradictory. Some compromise is unavoidable. So the essential, dialectical question is: *which compromises are realistic and which ones lead to abandoning the movement toward egalitarianism?* The question is difficult because the people and policies which lead to reversing the whole thrust of movement will not announce themselves as such. It is not even a question of finding out what they "really want" in the sense of giving them truth serum to find out their true, inner motives. The people whose policies led to reversing the whole movement often did not realize that that is what they were doing. We think that the essential, logical, theoretical basis of concessions of principle is the conception of the process of change in terms of fixed stages. To retreat is not always a betrayal of principle. But to make retreat into a strategy—to declare that inequality, nationalism, elitism, sexism, and selfishness are acceptable or desirable at a certain stage—has led to the defeat of past Marxist movements. It is one thing to admit to being too weak to overcome certain aspects of capitalism, but it is another to conclude that the time is not yet ripe even to mount some kind of struggle against those policies.

Exercise 3.10: What Kind of Action and Organization Does It Take To Win a War of Ideas?

1. Imagine that a workers' movement has become a serious threat to capitalists, and they are smart enough to know it.
2. Write down your initial guess about the ensuing struggle. What will happen with and without a revolutionary vanguard party? What are some of the things that the capitalists will do to beat back the threat?
3. Now branch your speculative history into two scenarios, one with and one without a disciplined, revolutionary, working class-led party. (That is, the previous exercise has begun to explore an idea which Marxists usually discuss in terms of the dialectical relation between theory and practice: the structure of groups leads to people doing different things which leads to their having different experiences which further changes what they do. A "scenario," a speculative construction of what kinds of actions and reactions people might take, is the natural way to explore this.)
4. Try to write down how, practically, you might find out if you are correct. How would you improve your answer?

Is it possible to achieve egalitarianism by voting, based upon numerical superiority? Suppose that one were convinced that capitalism was a bad system which should be replaced by an egalitarian system, communism in Marx's sense. What kinds of action and organization would it take to bring about the abolition of capitalism?

In exercise 3.7, we considered some of the value issues concerned with democracy and abiding by majority rule. But serious arguments about such types of organizations depend on causal issues, as well as value issues. Some Marxists who agree with the standpoint of Lenin on this believe that the only way that a party ever becomes a serious threat to capitalism is by a disciplined form of organization. They believe that without that kind of party, one always slides into a position of accommodation with the system rather than trying to change it. What kinds of party can stand under government attack and what kinds can become a force for change are empirical questions? Neither of these issues are mainly value issues. For example, Stinchcombe (who certainly isn't a Marxist, let alone Leninist) poses the main problem as follows:

> The problem Lenin posed was that in order to win, the working class had to consider its collective interest rather than its individual interests, or its "trade union consciousness." . . . The notion is that like the vanguard party, the capitalist class collectively so organizes itself to give in easily on the particular, disaggregated interests of individual capitalists, but becomes increasingly hard to deal with as the collective interests of capitalism as a system are threatened. The result is that they easily tolerate proclamations over the dialectic or the crisis of Western sociology, or Social Democratic speeches about the rights of the working man, but are careful that the ideology actually operating in work relations, in collective bargaining, in the curricular organization of the university or in foreign policy, is a bourgeois ideology. That is, the hypothesis is that the capitalist class, by being a ruling class, have naturally the advantages that the proletariat can only achieve by a vanguard party. This inequality means that compromise on the workers' side, that is Social Democracy, is almost always compromise of basic principles for concrete advantages, while capitalist compromise is almost always an expedient to save the basic features of the system by bargaining away some concrete advantages. ("Marxist Theories of Power and Empirical Research," in Coser and Larsen, *The Uses of Controversy in Sociology* [Free Press, 1976])

Getting to the point where there is a real threat to capitalism often means taking direct action in real situations. In neighborhoods, factories, schools, and other arenas, issues are being fought. In all of those arenas, anti-capitalists must be able to take direct action. If people were able, without organization, to come to a consensus on the actions which would win egalitarianism, then there would be no need for a revolutionary organization. But if that were true, then there would not be capitalism in the first place.

Does struggle without a revolutionary party mean that one constantly gives way on principle for the sake of transitory benefits? Does the attempt to work within the political system mean that one constantly gives way on principle in return for concrete advantages that vanish in the long run? It is on these difficult questions that communist and socialist parties split. They are fundamental questions for any **practical** attempt to get rid of capitalism. In the last analysis, you will have to decide for yourself. This thought-experiment helps you work through the issues.

How would one decide the question? What is decisive evidence? Is it evidence which one accumulates for oneself in the library? Is it evidence which has to be acquired directly and collectively?

There are obviously many kinds of evidence that you can acquire in the library. You will find that the library has a bias in favor of history and theory written from a liberal and from a gradualist, social democratic point of view. But certainly you would want to become acquainted with the history of leftist movements. It is possible to learn from the work of others, testing theory against historical evidence. We agree with Stinchcombe's argument that however the evidence is acquired, it has to conform to the same logic as evidence with regard to any other theory. Since it is an argument about what happens as a function of the degree of organization of the working class and the degree of organization of the ruling class, one ought to look across groups, societies, and historical periods at times when there have been significant differences in how organized each is. They may not vary much, but there is some variation in each.

If the analysis developed by Lenin and his contemporaries is correct, then the more that the ruling class is organized, and the less the working class is organized into a disciplined revolutionary party, the more there are dynamics of concession of principles. *The struggle for egalitarianism needs principled, anti-opportunist, organized leadership.* Moreover, it also follows that the dynamics, if unchecked, always lead to the erosion and failure of the movement as a whole. Further, the Leninist conception of Marxism implies that whenever the anti-capitalist movement grows, the state changes the rules, making the anti-capitalist activity illegal, so that if the movement has not organized in such a way as to be able to resist outside the law, the whole process of gaining a parliamentary majority merely leads to massive repression. Related questions concern how to consolidate changes made by genuine grassroots revolution. If there is strong leadership, there is danger of elitism. But is the solution weak leadership? That will usually just enable some other group to take power. Or is the solution strong leadership, combined with incessant struggle to challenge elitist tendencies within that leadership?

Obviously the historical and political data relevant to this question are complex. Matched against their aims, all movements—socialist, communist, liberal, whatever—have failed. But all the evidence isn't in. Many gains and setbacks have occurred. Social Democrats see the failure of the Soviet Union as a result of a vanguard party. They believe that if the CPSU had been more like the Democratic or Republican party, it would not have been corrupted by power. But their revolutionary opponents do not see the leaders of the Democratic, Republican, religious, nationalist, or Socialist parties as having been notably successful in avoiding corruption. And they do not see the main problem as one of corruption. They would say that if the main political thrust of a movement is correct, and if it has the conscious support and participation of major sections of the population, it will be better able to resist corruption; and if it is not, it does not matter. What resources does your experience or the library give you for judging these successes and failures? Probably, in the last analysis, life experience will determine how you interpret the academic evidence.

Direct relationships with members of various groups can give you different angles and arguments relevant to formal hypothesis-testing. In many ways, the most powerful evidence comes from direct personal experience. Knowing people and working together against common problems can do more to answer questions about whether people are trustworthy and whether collective struggle will lead to new exploitation and destruction of individual freedom than will any theoretical dissertation.

In the last analysis, any evaluation of modern "social democracy" and its strategies of nonviolence, parliamentarianism, patriotism, nationalism, and opposition to organized, collective leadership is bound up with many of the other questions we have looked at. Are nationalism and patriotism good? Under what circumstances would you consider the use of violence against the state? If you lived in Nazi Germany or in contemporary North Korea, Myanmar, or Iran, would you consider violence to overthrow a regime based on violence and repression? Under what circumstances would you consider it so important as to be worth the risks? We think that there is one major set of developments which shows the existing nation-states to be malignant, and which shows the entire social system of capitalism, in all its forms, to be an insane dead end: namely, the development of war and fascism. The nation-state is a sled to annihilation. The nation-state is the handmaiden of war. Unfortunately, further trial and error is not the best way to find out whether this is true. In the United States we are told that voting is the key to change, that our right to vote is the clear evidence that we live in a free society. Visit the prisons, the courts, the battlefields, the factories, the inner city slums, the crack houses, the depopulated small towns, and the methamphetamine factories, the clusters of homeless, the increasingly destitute elderly. We think that you will not find much freedom there, and this lack of freedom will extend to more and more people.

Suggestions for Further Reading

These issues of political sociology are among the most difficult and important in Marxism. Over the history of the last century, one finds a large number of positions and strategies pursued by millions of people. But history cannot answer questions until theoretical questions are asked. Readings already cited, such as those by Lenin, Bettelheim, Chase-Dunn, and Przeworski, help to ask the key questions. Since the systems involved are ones where people not only take action within given rules of the game, but also their actions change the rules of the game and even change themselves, complex issues of method and value are involved, usually discussed in terms of "dialectic." For examples of some of these issues, to be discussed in the next chapter, see R. Unger, *Social Theory* (Cambridge, 1987).

SUMMARY AND CONCLUSIONS: MARXIST POLITICAL THEORY

Now, we can discuss the next six points of our summary:

13. **Even Liberal Capitalism Does Not Mean Real Freedom, the Capitalist State Generally Serves the Capitalist Class** Most of the "Western democracies" have liberal governments because they are relatively prosperous, and neither economic collapse nor revolutionary upsurge is imminent. The prosperity is due largely to imperialist investments, which means supporting fascist regimes abroad. Furthermore, at home the major institutions are dominated by the capitalist class. Political parties, the media, educational institutions, and major labor unions (to name but four of the institutions that many people believe are what diffuses power away from the capitalist class) are, in fact, concentrated and carefully controlled. Even during liberal periods, the capitalist class and their allied politicians have the ability to send thousands of troops into any American city or to use Raptor Missiles from predator drones, anywhere in the world. It imprisoned tens of thousands almost overnight during the Palmer Raids following World War I and interned thousands of Japanese-Americans during World War II. Besides these well-known limits to political freedom, people are not free when their lives are destroyed by poverty, disease, and air, water, and food pollution. People are not free when they cannot influence the institutions around them. People are not free when they are not able to do the things they need to do to realize their potential. But, when the capitalists must resort to fascism, things get much worse.
14. **In Severe Crisis, Liberal Capitalism Turns into Fascism.** Some individual liberals flee from fascism or try to soften its effects, but to little

avail. Other liberal politicians actively aid fascists in suppressing and jailing Marxists and others who resist these new, terrible circumstances. Fascism is not merely repressive government. It is the capitalist state in severe political crisis in the era of monopoly capitalism. Political crisis accompanies economic crisis, and the capitalist class needs more and more direct control to maintain its rate of profit and political stability. It embraces fascism out of necessity not individual choice. There occurs a merger of some sections of capital with government, accentuating racism, taking sides in intercapitalist rivalry, and squeezing the working class economically. Fascism maintains tight control over the population and helps militarize the society to prepare it for war. Accompanying increased racism is an increase in sexism, nationalism, and other forms of super-exploitation, as well as social, political, and ideological justifications for the neglect and brutality. When members of the "tea party protest movement" show up at public meetings carrying automatic weapons and expressing racist, sexist, and even mystical conspiratorial fantasies, we see visible signs of a culture of dehumanization promoted to win some middle strata people to support facism. But fascism is not a question of either stupidity or sheer sadism on the part of the capitalist class. They either utilize the state to crush opposition or they fall from power.

15. **The Danger of Fascism Can Be Defeated Only by Eliminating Capitalism.** Various milder forms of repression have risen and receded without capitalism being eliminated. But where monopoly capitalism in crisis was forced to develop fascism, only warfare against fascism could truly smash it. And if the warfare does not destroy the capitalist foundation of fascism, the return of fascism remains a constant possibility. Also, fascism is not so extraordinary. Liberal capitalism, such as exists in the United States or Canada, is actually the exceptional form of capitalism today. Most of the world lives under one or another variety of fascism or semi-fascism.

16. **The USSR Initially Defeated Capitalism but then Moved from Marxist Socialism Back to a Kind of State Capitalism.** The Russian Revolution was the first successful overthrow of capitalism. Socialism was established there and soon encompassed a third of the world's population. If so, how did the USSR and China move from socialism back to capitalism? Many explanations have been offered, including that the USSR was too poor, that it was too overpowered by outside economic and political forces, that Marxism has to fail because it is against human nature, or that the existence of a disciplined revolutionary party always produces a new bureaucratic elite. In our opinion, it was mainly political mistakes, especially opportunism, that

led to the development of state capitalism. In a situation of sharp struggle, Marxists in those societies tried to maintain and justify an unequal wage system and nationalism. Nevertheless, if the objective circumstances are that most people would benefit by the replacement of capitalism with genuine communism, then the issue is one of putting that forward even if many people do not yet agree.

17. **Opportunism Has Severely Weakened Marxist Movements.** Both before and after a shift of political power, the most important danger is opportunism—ideologically winning people to some form of anti-Marxist, anti-communist policy by compromising on principle, especially on issues concerning internationalism and egalitarianism. It is not easy to avoid opportunism, because people who compromise often do so under life-and-death circumstances. Nevertheless, if this is the problem, then it is fatal to appeal to procapitalist aspects of people's consciousness. While there is no infallible way of preventing the kind of rollback that occurred in the Soviet Union, the best strategy is clearly to fight uncompromisingly for the truth, trusting that a combination of people's direct experiences and a straightforward presentation of Marxist explanation will win people over.

18. **The Struggle for Egalitarianism Needs Principled, Anti-opportunist, Organized Leadership.** To achieve this requires organization. *Extremely serious care must be taken to avoid organizations that either compromise on issues of principle, or which treat their own leaders in a privileged way.* The danger that revolutions can be reversed is very high, and the quality of the political leadership of revolutions is crucial. But just as Marxists reject the idea that division of labor and social organization inevitably lead to bureaucracy and elitism, so too ought Marxists question whether well organized, revolutionary political leadership will automatically give rise to elitism. In fact, in today's world, to reject the possibility of strong, focused leadership committed to revolutionary egalitarianism will actually guarantee that corrupt leadership will dominate the movement. Is it possible to combine strong leadership with the only real guarantee that egalitarianism can have—a population highly trained and highly sensitive to elitism and corruption? Such a population will need the consciousness to never hesitate to fight against all forms of class exploitation, privilege, and oppression, within the movement, as well as outside it.

4

Applying Dialectics

Some Issues in the Philosophy of Science

INTRODUCTION: DIALECTICS—A WAY OF LOOKING
AT THE WORLD, OR THE WAY THE WORLD WORKS?

In the first three chapters of the book, we discussed how Marxism approaches important questions of history, social change, economics, and politics. **Dialectics,** the methodology of Marxist social science of change, is at the heart of Marxist approaches to all these questions. For some people, dialectics is the most difficult and abstruse part of Marxism. It need not be. Dialectics is a method of investigation, based on some simple concepts that everyone learns to apply in everyday life. If people did not apply them, we would not be able to function at all. However, even though we are generally quite capable of looking at most aspects of the physical world around us in reasonably accurate ways, we are generally not aware of our methods of evaluation. As a result, we often lapse into unscientific ways of thinking because of habit, prejudice, miseducation, one-sidedness, wishful thinking, or other forms of subjective thinking. This is especially true when we try to understand the social world, the world of people, of politics, economics, history, sociology, and even of our personal relationships.

Simply put, dialectics recognizes the reality that everything changes—that everything has an aging process that is primarily the result of internal forces, tensions, or **contradictions** within it. And those changes eventually cause qualitative, irreversible transformations. Furthermore, everything in the universe is connected and therefore, when change occurs in one part, it can sometimes have very powerful effects somewhere else. This is in contrast to many common views of social structure. Some views do not see change

279

occurring, or they exempt certain institutions from the laws of change, or they say that change is primarily external—that things do not have an aging process, but rather change because other things bump into them. Chapter 1 discussed how structures like classes or states differ historically. It is an important issue of method whether to define concepts and causal processes in terms of what all societies have in common or in terms of differences. In Chapter 2 we saw that there is an important issue about how much economic processes depend on social institutions and vice versa.

At the most general level, some people assert that change is only quantitative in amount and never fundamentally irreversible. Some approaches to social structure make it difficult to see the strengths of interconnections or to understand what far-reaching effects a change in one social structure might have. This view might acknowledge change, but it often makes change out to be completely unpredictable when, in fact, events in the world are somewhat predictable. Opposing the view of total determinism does not have to mean asserting a view of total incomprehensibility of a completely chaotic universe.

Dialectics is a way of looking at reality, not as a complex of ready-made "things," but as a set of processes. The dialectical approach examines the ways that everything changes. A dialectical approach asks: how do things change? How do they connect to the rest of the world? This concern with change and interrelation implies that dialectical analyses are usually historical. Some things about classes, parties, war, or human relationships are true for all recorded history. But most things about human relations and social structure are only true within a more defined historical framework, in a more conditional way. Focusing on what is true within a set of historical and social conditions helps the dialectical standpoint concentrate on real or essential structures underlying appearances. By focusing on concepts such as the limits within which a process occurs or the turning points at which qualitative changes begin to produce qualitative results, dialectics is especially sensitive to sudden, abrupt qualitative changes which result from long quantitative processes. For example, when the last straw goes onto the camel's back—CRAAACK—a sudden, abrupt, qualitative, irreversible change occurs. Taking the straw back does not undo it. Dialectics is sensitive to such processes. Such an analysis is obviously important to revolutionary theory. But what is its relevance to sociology? What is its relation to science? Does Marxism have a special philosophical method, called "dialectics"? If so, what is it? Or is dialectics merely the method of the sciences in general?

Some social theorists regard Marx's dialectics as opposed to science. For example, there have been theorists who regarded themselves as "socialist" but who rejected the revolutionary aspects of Marx's analysis. They were oriented toward building a party rather like the Democratic Party in the

United States or the British Labour Party, and they rejected dialectics. Revolution seemed to them an unscientific business, founded on a philosophy of dialectics, which they saw as a speculative, unscientific part of Marx's analysis. They believed that gradual, quantitative change could lead to a world of peace and abundance without need for the qualitative change of a social revolution. Other theorists, some of whom are called "critical theorists," also argue that dialectics is opposed to science, but that is what they like about it. They think that science is a narrow, bad, manipulative way of looking at the world, and so they believe that dialectical ways of looking at the world liberate one from the "narrowness" of science.

In contrast to such positions, we think that most Marxists have been correct to view dialectics as the method of the sciences. The dialectical method is a universal solvent that dissolves the illusory unchangingness of things, concepts, relationships, and points of view. Marxists argue that this dissolution is essential for science and especially for social science. They argue that, without dialectics, the study of humankind cannot be scientific because it gets trapped in false and partial standpoints with respect to humankind and history. Certainly Marx and Engels wanted to construct a science and they regarded dialectics as a tool for doing so.

One of the difficulties in discussing dialectics is that there are several different kinds of doctrines which are sometimes taken to be the core of dialectics. In particular, dialectics is sometimes taken to be a view of our *knowledge* about the world, and sometimes it is taken to be a view of the *world*, itself. In Hegel's philosophy, there is the dialectic of the forms of consciousness in *The Phenomenology of Spirit* and there is the dialectic of concepts in *The Logic*. Moreover, Hegel's more concrete analyses of law, religion, art, and history used those to trace several kinds of dialectical paths and transitions that have been important for Marxists and central to Marxist analysis of culture. An important and paradoxical dynamic occurs when our needs, wants, and abilities are, at least partly, a product of our actions, our resources, and our situation, but our actions, resources, and situation are also a product of our needs, wants, and abilities. For example, suppose that Jennifer's ability and desire to be an engineer is a function of her actions and educational experiences, but that those actions and experiences are also influenced by her abilities and desires. This is, of course, the typical situation, and it is a dialectical loop, which, with many players, will have the dynamic of games of Monopoly and Risk: inequalities will be generated and the game as a whole will have the unstable, discontinuous, partly unpredictable dynamic of games of Monopoly. Moreover, many crucial processes concerning the development of knowledge, the development of human capacities, and the development of human freedom have this dynamic.

Dialectics can help us avoid dilemmas which arise when one asks the "wrong" questions about social structure. To ask whether Jennifer (in the abstract) has the ability (in the abstract) to be an engineer may ignore all of the relevant aspects of her choices and situation. Consider the following questions. What is human nature? Is human society and history a part of nature? If so, is the most scientific way to understand it in terms of biology? Is it an independent realm? If so, should it be understood in terms of human meanings and intentions? Is it possible to have a "deterministic" science of society? Or do human beings' "free will," consciousness, or involvement with questions of value require a fundamentally different kind of method from the natural sciences? How can social science be objective? Should sociology attempt to be politically neutral and value-neutral? Are class, the state, racism, and war universal? Questions of this kind are always involved in explanations of social structure.

In this book, we have often stressed the problems that come from asking a "bad" question in *general*—when there is no answer in *general*. Is inequality "necessary" or "unnecessary"? A better question would be whether certain kinds of inequality (such as slavery) are necessary, given other essential social arrangements. That is an example of how Marxist dialectics is different from nondialectical analyses. In contrast to **mechanical** standpoints, one key to a dialectical way of looking at things is to recognize that anything may be looked at from a number of different standpoints. These different standpoints are partly true in that they have limited validity. They are absolutely false when stretched beyond those limits.

Any social theory involves asking certain kinds of questions. Without a question, empirical evidence can give you no answers. But how can you prove the truth or the accuracy of a *question?* The very kind of theory of society one is trying to build will raise issues which cannot easily be answered empirically: questions of freedom versus determinism, the humanities versus the natural sciences, or fact versus value. Sociologists do not spend a great deal of their time discussing such questions in general. This seems sensible. The questions will be solved in practice or not at all. In practice, sociologists take positions on them. To attempt to resolve these questions dialectically, we have to get beyond the oppositions on which they are based. This fourth chapter raises and attempts to dispose of ten such dilemmas. Only when we can integrate the standpoints from which we know about society can we approach social structure in terms of its changes. Only then can we come to terms with the sudden changes, levels, and twists with which reality presents us.

Ontologically, dialectics is the view that everything in the universe is interconnected with everything else, and that everything is in a process of change. This view implies and it makes us sensitive to interconnections and changes of social arrangements. Dialectics requires viewing reality as a process. As a process, everything changes, and connects to other things. The changes and interrelations between things are central to a dialectical view of them. The opposite of a dialectical standpoint is a **mechanical** standpoint, which is any treatment of things as fixed and isolated from each other. A mechanical viewpoint says that everything is only what it is. A **mechanical** viewpoint treats change as inessential. It sees change as coming from outside the thing being examined. The most characteristic mechanistic view is the universe, made up of hard little billiard balls, governed by a small number of absolutely general, unconditional laws.

There are two common mistakes that many people make—both supporters and opponents of Marxism. The first is to think that dialectics is a mysterious, mystical philosophy that uses big words and weird concepts in utterly different ways from all other kinds of social theory. This is simply not true. Marx and Engels developed their ideas using existing bodies of social science. The second common mistake is to be one-sided in the opposite way: to say that dialectics and Marxism are just plain old common sense, which adds nothing new to traditional science because Marxism asserts that facts are primary, just as regular scientists do. Actually, dialectical Marxism is *very* different from other ways of looking at the world, but it is not *totally* different. Most readers of this book will find a great deal that makes sense from other standpoints. At the same time, there are sharp differences between Marxism and the ways most people have been taught to view things. The dialectical viewpoint highlights the fact that everything changes everything is interrelated, which in turn affects these processes of change.

Most social science models have a view of causes leading to effects with no interactions with other variables and no systemic feedbacks to the causes. In technical terms, most social science models are "linear" and "recursive." These were probably necessary simplifying assumptions during the twentieth century; you have to walk before you can run; but they are not adequate for twenty-first century social theory. At the present time there is a rapid growth of analysis of nonlinear and nonrecursive dynamics in the natural sciences, and we believe that the linkage of such methods to dialectical models in the social sciences establishes some of the main challenges to twenty-first century social theory.

An elaborate philosophical contemporary treatment of dialectics is Roy Bhaskar's dialectical critical realism. Bhaskar and the other theorists associated with the institute for critical realism, have developed a form of dialectics based on the philosophy of scientific realism. The central idea is that our concepts are never totally adequate to the reality. Bhaskar treats dialectics, in part as the family of intellectual and practical responses to the discrepancy between our concepts, particularly our scientific concepts, and our practice, particularly our social practice. To say that there are contradictions in things is partly to say that many dynamical systems have alternate possibilities. This is one of the fundamental insights of the contemporary analysis of complex nonlinear systems. Bhaskar's dialectical critical realism generalizes that issue or problem in a way reminiscent of Sartre, formulating the viewpoint that existing philosophies have been concerned with "presence" to the exclusion of "absence."

We do not regard dialectics as a theory, but as a language, a conceptual scheme, a way of looking at the world. Anything that you can say in one language can also be said in other languages though often not nearly as accurately, as well, or as easily. Nobody can solve concrete, substantive, empirical problems entirely on the basis of dialectics, without data. But we believe that the dialectical approach is the most useful way of looking at things to accurately uncover their interrelatedness and change. Dialectics provides a method of analysis indispensable to getting history, economics, politics, and sociology connected with each other. In turn, we believe that a fertile sociology is only possible at this intersection of the disciplines.

Suggestions for Further Reading

A standard contemporary introduction to the epistemological aspect of dialectics is J. Zeleny, *The Logic of Marx* (Rowman & Littlefield, 1980). An excellent book that illustrates how the dialectical method of analysis fits in with modern physics theories is *Causality and Chance in Modern Physics* by David Bohm (Routledge, 1984). A good general introduction to ontological dialectics from within the analytic tradition is R. Norman and S. Sayers, *Hegel, Marx, and Dialectic* (Humanities, 1976). Closer to the Marxist mainstream is I. Gollobin, *Dialectical Materialism* (Petras Press, 1986). The resolutions to many of the sociological dilemmas which we present are very close to those in P. Sztompka, *Sociological Dilemmas* (Academic, 1980). For a view that dismisses the dialectical method, see C. Wright Mills, *The Marxists* (Dell, 1962). B. Ollman, in *Dialectical Investigations* (Routledge, 1992), *The Dance of the Dialectic* (University of Illinois Press, 2003), and the special issue of *Science and Society* (1998) co-edited with R. Levins, give important, general treatments. A general introduction to critical realism is *Dialectics: The Pulse of Freedom* (Verso, 1993). However, R. Bhaskar's work, *From East to West*, appears to move his dialectics from the sphere of philosophy of science to that of new-age theology, and argues that the key to a liberating social theory is to recognize that everyone is God. In addition to *Valences of the Dialectic* (Verso, 2010), F. Jameson has important forthcoming works on Hegel's and on Marx's dialectic. There is even a clever Internet website called "Dialectic for Kids" that offers a basic discussion: http://home.igc.org/~venceremos/index.htm.

SECTION 4.1: IS A SCIENCE OF SOCIETY POSSIBLE?

We usually do a satisfactory job understanding how the world works when it comes to studying material objects and processes. Even when a car, a disease, or a volcano behaves in puzzling and unpredictable ways we do not suppose that it is impossible to understand it. Rather, we usually suppose that we don't understand it *yet*. We believe that we shall eventually understand it when we have a more powerful theory or more information. However, when it comes to understanding people, some philosophers argue that the sphere of human behavior is a special realm—a spiritual realm—set apart from nature and definite laws. These philosophers argue that if you subject a piece of chalk to a force, it invariably behaves in a predictable way; but if you subject a person to a force, the result is not determined. Some people feel that it is an attack on human dignity even to treat human behavior as following any patterns or laws or to investigate it empirically.

For Marx, human behavior and social behavior display new properties, not visible in prehuman or presocial realms. But Marx rejected any separation of a human realm of spirit from a realm of nature, as a form of **idealism**. When Marx says that he is adopting a **materialist** standpoint, the main thing that he means is that he is adopting a scientific standpoint, according to which the world of people is just as objective as the world of nature. This philosophical definition of the word **materialism** is different from the hedonistic or self-gratifying meaning of materialism associated with *Playboy* magazine or "Lifestyles of the Rich and Famous," that is, wanting to make a lot of money and to acquire a lot of material things. Plenty of professors of fine arts, poets, princes of the church, and idealist philosophers are materialists in this latter sense.

Social structure consists of relationships. Relationships can be as real as a rock. Marx's conception of practice placed great emphasis on doing things, and on what makes it possible or impossible to do something. A situation which has to be changed if something is to happen is a material obstacle to that something. If someone is locked in a jail cell, the cell is a material obstacle to going to McDonald's. Unless the bars are broken or the door is unlocked, the person can't go. Now this should be distinguished from a situation where someone is in an *imaginary* cell. Imagine a prisoner in a circle painted on the ground, afraid to cross the circle because of a belief that a demon will grab anyone who crosses the circle. The obstacle to going to McDonald's is just a belief. Some people believe that all obstacles to change—all cells—are in people's minds and all people have to do is to think differently and they will be free. Marx called that view **idealism** and he thought it was badly mistaken. He poked fun at the German philosophers' arguments:

> Once upon a time a valiant fellow had the idea that men were drowned in water only because they were possessed with the idea of gravity. If they were to get this notion out of their heads, say by avowing it to be a superstitious, religious concept, they would be sublimely proof against any danger from water. His whole life long he fought against the illusion of gravity, of whose harmful

consequences all statistics brought him new and manifold evidence. This val-
iant fellow was the type of the new revolutionary philosophers in Germany.
(*German Ideology*, CW V, p. 24)

On the other hand, not all the real, "material" parts of social structure are
physical objects which could be piled in a room like bars. Neither is gravity.
For example, Marx said that ideas can become a material force when they
are grasped by the masses. What does this mean? One interpretation is that
Marx believed that ideas become real forces when they are embodied in
relationships. Relationships can be as real as a rock. Marx spent most of his
life building a working class party, and he was aware how real that is. Ideas
have a dialectical relationship to actions and relationships. A relationship
is real and material in that it is a function of actual, objective history. *What
have you said to someone? What have they said to you?* One might *imagine* that
one had a friendship with someone, but be mistaken because it all happened in one's own head.

Well, what if the prisoner is surrounded by a circle of people who will
stone him if he crosses the circle because *they* believe in a demon? Is the
obstacle real? It depends. The stones preventing him from going to McDonald's are real enough, but he might be able to talk his way out of the circle.
Possibly. But if you are absolutely (metaphysically) convinced that since
the obstacle is the belief of the circle of people, and one can always change
it by talk, then sometime you should try to talk your way out of a prison.

We have seen that in trying to study society scientifically, Marx agrees
with other theorists in sociology, Durkheim and Weber. Where he disagrees
with them is in his belief about what is the objective basis of social behavior, not whether social structure should be studied empirically. For Marx,
materialism meant that history, economics, and society should be studied
scientifically, in terms of objective consequences. If something is going
wrong in the garden, you don't preach to the asparagus or pray to the gods.
If you want something to stop, you must do something, you must change
something. You must add some fertilizer, lime, weed killer, or water, or
cut down some trees for sun. The same is true if racism, sexism, war, or
other weeds are growing in the society. Poverty, human trafficking, unemployment, toxic wastes, violence, racism, urban decay, alcoholism, war, or
selfishness are objective consequences of other things. Actually, it is a way
of *not* changing them to deplore them without changing their causes. Marx
was not opposed to ideals. But idealism often involves the *denial of cause
and effect in the social realm*. In practice, idealism often justifies deploring
the consequences of social arrangements, while being unwilling to go to the
work of changing them.

The stress on doing something—on finding the objective, empirical consequences of things—is one basis of Marx's concept of practice. At the base of

Marx's philosophy is the idea that the truth of a statement is not something that can mainly be decided in the realm of ideas. It is a practical question.

> The question whether objective truth can be attributed to human thinking is not a question of theory but a *practical* question. In practice man must prove the truth, that is the reality and power, the this-sidedness of his thinking. The dispute over the reality or non reality of thinking which is isolated from practice is a purely *scholastic* question. (Marx, "Thesis 2 on Feuerbach," SW, p. 28)

One of the things "practice" means is that a good theory will yield good predictions and a bad theory will yield bad predictions or none at all. If someone tells you that they have a terrific theory of social class, but they are not able to make correct predictions about social class, we suppose that they are all talk. Another thing practice means is action. If someone tells you they are against poverty, but they refuse to do anything about it, we suppose they are all talk. The job of professors, preachers, politicians, and other professionals is to deal with words, and they often overestimate the importance of talk. Academics often have a persistent tendency to idealism. But it is not possible to gain new knowledge mainly by shuffling words in one's head. One must also look at empirical evidence concerning the objective causes and consequences of things in the real world. Often that involves doing as well as seeing.

Marx agrees with other sociological perspectives that social behavior has an objective basis, but he disagrees with them about *what that basis is*. In looking at the sources of racism, sexism, war, poverty, human trafficking, substance abuse, or any other social structure, Marx denies that they can be explained solely or mainly on the basis of ideas, intentions, norms, values, culture, or beliefs. Of course ideas are very important forces in the world. Marx, after all, thought them important enough to write over fifty books worth of ideas. But Marxists do not believe that ideas are "unmoved movers." Ideas are developed, nurtured, suppressed, accepted, or rejected based largely on people's social experience. Marx denies that social structure can be changed mainly or solely by talk addressed to changing ideas, intentions, norms, values, culture, or beliefs. Marx asserts that "it is not the consciousness of men that determines their social being but, on the contrary, their social being that determines their consciousness (SW, p. 182). What does this mean? What positions is Marx arguing against?

For Durkheim and the functionalists, the fundamental and ultimate basis of society is norms, values, conventions, and culture. For Weber, the fundamental and ultimate basis of society is the meanings, intentions, and beliefs of social actors—both the subjective intentions of individual actors and the institutionalized legitimations, rules, and systematic beliefs of courts, associations, and political or religious groups. Both norms and meanings are mental events in people's heads. In this sense, Marxists regard both

Durkheim's and Weber's theories as idealist and essentially wrong. Non-dialectical forms of Marxism are often forced to choose between **economic reductionism**, in which every idea is explained by economic relations, or alternately a very weak form of common sense that says economic relations often have "some" intellectual consequences, as do other things as well. From a dialectical standpoint, the question whether ideas, in general, are independent of economic and social relations is a bad question. The most important patterns of social relations cannot be explained and they cannot be changed simply by changes in ideas. Indeed, the most important patterns of ideas cannot be changed *merely* by putting forth other ideas. Ideas have to serve some purpose or they will eventually be discarded, even if they are accurate in ways that people do not realize. Beyond that, there is little that can be said *in general* about the relation of ideas to economic and political structures. The question requires substantive historical, political, and social theories, not philosophical debate.

For a long time it appeared that the rigidity of pro-Soviet regimes in Eastern Europe disproved Marx—that ideologies or powerful political groups, backed by the power of the state, could freeze society, regardless of economic forces, interests, developments, or classes. But, whatever else the complex developments of the 1990s show, they seem to show that economic and class forces may exert pressures powerful enough to burst restrictive ideological or political bonds.

Exercise 4.1: Theory and Values in Analysis of Social Problems

Take a social problem of some interest to you (possibly from exercise 1.2). Briefly show how that problem might be analyzed in terms of: (1) inequality and alienation; (2) values and weakening of values; and (3) bureaucracy. Do the three analyses imply different solutions?

No questions have been more problematic for the social sciences than questions about the relation of judgments of fact and judgments of value. In chapter 1, we saw one of the reasons for this. If things are tied together in package deals, then the way that they are tied together affects how one evaluates them. Most social scientists would agree that one cannot ever demonstrate an "ought" statement based merely on statements about what "is." But this is very far from showing that there are no connections at all between "ought" statements and "is" statements. If one sees capitalism as the cause of unnecessary malnutrition and unemployment both in New York and in Brazil, then one will evaluate it differently than one will if one believes the malnutrition and unemployment come from other things, and capitalism has reduced them. Cause and effect judgments affect one's evaluations; one's evaluations affect what cause and effect judgments one is predisposed to believe.

There is not much variation in people's evaluation of poverty, unemployment, hunger, starvation, war, violence, racism, sexism, pollution, cruelty, etc. Almost everyone evaluates them as bad. The Marxist analysis sees the mode of production, capitalism, as the root cause today of those problems. In contrast to Marx's analysis, which sees production and classes as the basis of social structure, other analyses make either cultural values or governments and bureaucracy as basic, and they analyze such social problems in a different way.

Moreover, there is an even more direct way that the main views of social structure have determined our diagnoses of social problems. The three dominant conceptions of the problem of the modern world follow directly from the main conceptions of the structure of society. Marx, Durkheim, and Weber all put forward a vision of what is wrong with society as part of a vision of how society works. The main diagnoses of social problems and the main conceptions of package deals we face turn out to be related to the main sociological paradigms.

For example, Durkheim believed that the basis of social structure was social integration, and especially that integration based upon common norms and values. Thus he diagnosed the main problem of the modern world as the breakdown, weakening, or absence of norms, a state which he called **anomie**. In the modern world, Durkheim said, people are often rootless— they are less connected to their traditions, families, and communities, and there is rapid social change undermining values. All of these tend to dissolve the underlying cultural-normative basis of the society, creating **anomie**. Many people say that the country is going to the dogs because people lack traditions and basic values. Some people who say this often want to beef up the religious and other normative structures in the society. They want to enforce laws more strictly and to make teaching values, especially religion, compulsory in education. This is a popular form of Durkheim's diagnosis and prescription.

Weber believed that structures of authority and the systematic common meanings they produce—law, religion, science, politics, ethics, economics—are the basis of social structure. He regarded the overgrowth of these structures, bureaucratization, as the fundamental problem of the modern world. He saw the proliferation of such formal structures as creating an "iron cage" within which modern life was increasingly confined. Some people view the growth of government and especially of red tape as the main problem of the modern world. Bureaucratization is seen as strangling individuality and individual initiative and producing a rigid, unresponsive structure. This is a popular form of Weber's diagnosis and prescription.

Marx believed that labor and the mode of production are the basis of the social structure. The fundamental problem of the modern world is alienation—powerlessness. People cannot control what they do, and especially what they do at work. In section 1.8, we noted that alienation can be the basis of an analysis of many different inequalities of power and life chances and of other divisions between people. An alienated society is one where money does not just talk, but shouts. It is a society where everything is up for sale, where everyone is out for "number one," where divisive "me first" ideologies (my race first, my nation first, my sex first, my religion first, etc.) dominate social relations. Marx argued that capitalism is such a social structure of alienation. He argued that it leads to some owning and controlling the work and lives of millions of others. He argued that a society where millions go hungry while others spend millions on debutante balls is a society of conflict, division, and alienated social relationships.

Some people say that the modern world is one where the rich get richer, the poor get poorer, or that "you can't fight city hall." This is one simplified expression of part of Marx's analysis. Marx obviously does not say that you can't fight, but he does suggest that without a particular kind of fight, you can't win. More generally, Marx argues that problems like poverty, war, selfishness, and racism are consequences of working people's powerlessness and lack of control over the social structures they have created. This powerlessness is alienation; it creates the feeling of alienation.

Are these three diagnoses consistent with each other? Are they even different from each other? Or do they, perhaps, express the same thing in different words? Consider the example of different views of parking permits, which we discussed in section 1.2. Three people say, "The problem is alienation; the permits are a cheat and rip-off," or "The problem is anomie; there is not enough respect for authority," or "The problem is bureaucracy; the administration is insensitive to students." What, if anything, do the three people disagree about? Which diagnosis is most accurate? What determines which diagnosis one believes? Take a social problem of concern to you, and very briefly write down how it is related to Durkheimian norms and values, to Weber's structures of organization, and to Marxist inequality and alienation. Probably you see one of these analyses as mainly correct and the others as mainly wrong. But the fact of the matter is that other people almost certainly view the problem differently, and so they will act at cross purposes to you. Usually you can formulate these differences in terms of anomie (breakdown of values), the iron cage (stifling of individuals), or alienation (powerlessness). Do these three diagnoses say the same thing in different words? Are there fundamental disagreements concerning the nature of most social problems? If there are, then how might they be resolved? Briefly sketch your answers to these questions.

We believe that you will find these diagnoses are importantly different, as there are profound contradictions between them. One way to see this is to consider what the effects are for bureaucratization and alienation of most ways of dealing with anomie. If you beef up normative structures (rules, law, religion, authority), you are almost certainly going to increase many of the things Weber regarded as problems. Moreover, those normative structures are usually controlled by dominant groups, so strengthening them will increase alienation and powerlessness as well.

Similarly, what are the effects on anomie and alienation of attacking bureaucratization? If you tear down centralized structures, you will almost certainly increase both anomie and alienation. The government steps out of the business of norm-enforcement, regulation, employment, health care, provision of education, or whatever. Those centralized structures were some of the main bulwarks of social norms. Durkheim would say that you have increased anomie. Moreover, who does that leave in charge? Usually it leaves private groups, such as corporations, in charge. If work, schools, food, housing, etc., were hard for the majority to control when they were run by the government, especially when there are power differences, they often become *impossible* to control when they are private property. Marx would say that you have increased people's powerlessness.

What are the consequences for anomie and bureaucratization of treating powerlessness as the main problem? The only way to deal with powerlessness will ordinarily be to organize people, especially those now poor, exploited, or powerless. If you organize the unorganized, you get more class struggle (that is what Durkheim objected to about Marxism) and you are organizing people, which is what Weber saw as the problem.

What this exercise illustrates is the real contradictions, binds, and trade-offs in social action. It is rarely possible to get the best of all possible worlds. While anyone can sit down with a piece of paper and design solutions that have the best of all possible worlds, that piece of paper does nothing to resolve the real, practical disagreements and contradictions between different people and groups.

Suggestions for Further Reading

On science and materialism: a large literature argues that Marx is not or should not have been a materialist in the sense we describe. Usually the motivation is to combine Marx with ordinary religion or with liberal, reformist politics. P. Sztompka, *Sociological Dilemmas* (Academic, 1980), treats dialectics as the way to avoid a series of false choices in the social sciences. It is another false dilemma to pose the choices of pragmatic positivism versus moral philosophy. Virtually the whole literature of anti-materialist Marxism is well described by P. Anderson as "Western Marxism," which he describes as the creation of academic philosophers isolated both from political practice and from social science. See *Considerations on Western Marxism* (New Left Books, 1976) and *In the Tracks of Historical Materialism* (University of Chicago, 1984). R. Miller, *Analyzing Marx* (Princeton, 1984), argues that Marx is not an economic reductionist or technological deter-minist, but that he did hold a theory distinct from common sense.

SECTION 4.2: WHAT ARE THE MAIN
SOURCES OF ERROR IN SOCIAL THEORY?

The issues we have just discussed have been looked at in different ways by different theorists, Marxist and anti-Marxist alike. Often they are discussed in terms of four oppositions: idealism versus materialism; naturalism (scientism or positivism) versus antinaturalism (antiscientism or antiposi-tivism); fact versus value; and necessity (determinism or structure) versus contingency (freedom or agency). We think that the oppositions are often bad, especially when they are posed in mutually exclusive ways. While it is important to have conceptual maps and signposts, these are often maps which lead us astray. There are other such bad signposts.

The idea that judgments of value and judgments of fact are bound up with each other makes many people uncomfortable. The notion that social theory is often tied into social practice also makes many people uncom-fortable. They fear that this will make it difficult to keep our biases and commitments from influencing our theories. To avoid rigidity, they argue for skepticism, flexibility, and the acceptance of many points of view. But this seems to others to throw us into the trap of relativism. If one doubts everything, they say, one is left no starting point at all, or often, one is left with a *hidden bias* toward the status quo.

We can get a new angle on the process of developing better theories if we consider the main ways that our social theories may go wrong. In statistical inference, we learn of two main ways of going wrong. These can be related to two fundamental positions in philosophy. The process of investigation is always dialectically related to each of them.

The first common error is the unwillingness to give up a mistaken theo-ry—we are often told in college courses that the error of **dogmatism** is an error in scientific investigation. Marxist social scientists agree. Dogmatism means seeing things very one-sidedly. While no one wishes to see things in a one-sided way, we are often limited by our own experiences. To the extent that the experiences of the people around us are all similar, to the extent that we have gone to schools which are segregated by race, religion, and class, to the extent that the systems in other times and places are unfamiliar and stereotyped, we have to struggle not to be narrow-minded. The limits of our own experience are always limits to our knowledge, and such limits can be especially serious in a class in sociology. While we can learn from books, those are filtered and limited just like experience, and it is often difficult for us to take books as seriously as our own experience. Thus, one type of narrow-mindedness, deeply opposed to Marxism, is the view that the particular ways that things have been in the past in our own society is the only way that things can ever be. This is the illusion that things never change. When it involves taking the particular norms, roles, and attitudes in our own ethnic or cultural group and projecting them onto human nature, it is called **ethnocentrism**. One of the reasons that this is a problem is that all of us have deeply held values which can lead us to feel threatened and angry at anyone who holds other beliefs and values. This opposition and antagonism to anyone different from ourselves is usually called **bigotry**. Despite the lip service Americans pay to open-mindedness, bigotry has assumed virulent forms in the United States, and has always been an especially serious problem.

The second common error is rejecting a correct theory. One can refuse to believe that the sun shines or that cats meow, even when there is perfectly good evidence for them. In order to avoid the error of dogmatism and bigotry, some people go to opposite positions of **extreme skepticism** and **extreme relativism**. **Relativist** thinking says that there are no right or wrong answers to anything. In an extreme form, relativism says that there are not even better or worse explanations—that everything is just a matter of opinion. This issue might be seen in the relationship between the **relative** and the **absolute**. It is one core of dialectics. On the one hand, if you look at the relation of any belief to the rest of our beliefs, it is evident that every belief is relative, temporary, correctable. And we can be quite sure that every single one of our theories will eventually have to be changed, at least somewhat. Any scientific statement is fallible. On the other hand, it seems equally clear that some beliefs are more fallible than others. We know many things. The Earth is round; a pot of water at sea level boils at 212 degrees Fahrenheit, regardless of whether it is being watched or not; under capitalism, the self-employed portion of the population shrinks. There is concrete truth.

Over the past few decades, we have seen the development of another intellectual trend that seeks to challenge if not completely supplant Marxism as the dominant framework for criticizing society and the powers that control it. This trend, referred to as "postmodernism," is generally not considered a "theory," since it generally does not attempt to explain the sources of stability and change in society. In fact, it often poses as a kind of "anti-theory," asserting in its most extreme versions that there is no possibility of progress, that there is no way to explain anything, and that the way we experience reality is the only reality. The loose cluster of ideas that swirl around postmodernism are often associated with the perspective that the most profound critiques of society are those who supposedly critique "everything" and not just the powerful institutions and class interest groups that Marxism critiques. It often claims to be more thorough and therefore even more "radical" than Marxism, which is sometimes critiqued as being "old-fashioned" and just like all the other philosophies that are unwilling to critique everything and are therefore supposedly tied to "dogmas," unable to critique themselves.

Marxists reject that assertion on two counts. First, the dialectical underpinnings of Marxist analysis allow it to examine all of its assumptions, taking into account changes that develop over time. It is true that Marxism does assert that certain premises about society are not likely to change "for now," much the way that astronomers might say that the sun is not likely to burn out in the next hundred years. But Marxism rejects the false dichotomy between "the real world" and "morality" that claims that "being realistic" means rejecting the idea that humans can live cooperatively and, conversely, that accepting the idea that humans can live cooperatively requires that one be an unrealistic idealist who distorts reality in order to satisfy one's own ideology. So while Marxism is "biased" on behalf of the working class, Marxism at its core does not believe that it serves the interests of the working class, or humanity in general, to falsify or distort reality.

Postmodernist thought and its various corollaries are themselves reflections of various class biases, despite their claim to being detached. The twin philosophies of "despair that nothing can change" and "frivolous playfulness that says that since nothing can change, we might as well all just enjoy the sensations and have a good time" both reflect the despair of some in the capitalist class, in the middle income groups, and of some intellectuals who have given up the idea that there can be human progress. Because capitalism is the only world that they know, and because they have no confidence that humanity in general and the working class in particular is smart enough to create a better world, therefore, when they see capitalism stagnating or even disintegrating, they believe that the whole world is stagnating or disintegrating—just going around in small circles without any hope for progress. Versions of this philosophy have been around for many centuries, but it is worth noting that they tend to become stronger in society during periods of social crisis, when people can either try to develop a deeper understanding of what is causing the crisis or they can just give in to their sense of alienation and isolation and give up.

Interestingly, despite its claim to being "the most revolutionary" way of experiencing the world, much of postmodernist thought really is just ordinary "pluralism" or mainstream procapitalist ideology that dilutes and diffuses its notion of social processes and therefore does not really challenge the core of capitalist power. And in some versions, it can actually take an extremely conservative stand, basically asserting that since nothing is better or worse than anything else, we might as well just go with the flow and accept the way the world is, rather than trying to make it different. While it is certainly true that very oppressed people can embrace despair or reach out to escapism, it is especially easy for upper middle income intellectuals to embrace the "nothing can change so why bother?" philosophy in the comfort of their own relatively affluent lives.

Various branches of social theory have embraced aspects of this perspective, claiming to make the most radical critique of racism, for example, by saying that "everyone is racist (or at least, all 'white' people)" and/or that "convincing people to accept diversity" is the solution to oppression, rather than taking into account how the capitalist class profits from racism. (Marxism, however, believes that stopping racist oppression is not a matter of instituting a new sounding "diversity" policy that is really just a warmed-over version of the tokenism of the past, where a few representatives are given some resources, power, or visibility. Stopping racist oppression means thoroughly opposing racist oppression and ideas, but that it *fundamentally* means opposing capitalism. See chapters 2 and 3.)

Some recent critiques of sexism and even "speciesism" follow similar lines of discussion, claiming to be "more revolutionary than Marxism," as does the notion that all oppressions are equally profound. But seeing race, gender, and class as parallel and occasionally intersecting also reinforces liberal, pluralist views of society rather than grasping where the core form which these oppressions emanate—the exploitation/control of some people's labor/human activity by others.

Many social scientists who embrace aspects of postmodernism, including some of the ideas mentioned above, have made important, insightful analyses of aspects of society. But postmodernism, as a general set of ideas, is proudly ahistorical but actually blind to the processes of change and development in society, and despite its pseudo-revolutionary guise, it accepts and reinforces many traditional, mainstream, procapitalist ideological notions.

We have seen that the dominant intellectual perspective in the United States has been classical liberalism. In a classic statement of liberalism, John Stuart Mill calls for the free competition of ideas, allowing anyone to say whatever they want to say as long as they do not interfere with anyone else's right to say whatever they want. The chief liberal virtue is tolerance: allowing everyone to do their own thing. Unfortunately, we argued, free competition does not always guarantee the truth. In any case, you do not even have competition if people are so "tolerant" that they do not even argue their own positions. While there are often many sides to any question and many possible explanations for any phenomenon, it is not true that all explanations are equally valid. Some points of view do not give a very accurate explanation, and it makes sense to say that they are simply wrong. In an effort to be fair (or to seem "fair-minded") many people embrace relativism. They feel hesitant to disagree with anyone, especially about social issues. They may restrict their statements to those which are vague, middle-of-the-road, and noncontroversial. They may feel reluctant to put forward any definite position. For example, introductory textbooks are often bland. We do not think that is how people learn. It is not even how to learn tolerance. Bigotry and tolerance seem like opposites. But it is perfectly possible that societies with more of one have more of the other. It is even possible to have a bigoted kind of tolerance. One may refuse to listen to anyone who has strong opinions and beliefs, or who talks about them, or acts on them.

In the world of people as in the rest of the world, some explanations are better; they give a more accurate explanation of the situation than others. The real world is seldom vague, although our understanding of it often is. Either the Earth is larger than the sun or it is smaller—the correct answer is not "somewhere in between." Sometimes a middle-of-the-road position is right; sometimes it is wrong. But it is not automatically correct just because it is middle-of-the-road. If a middle-of-the-road position is the best one in a particular situation, it is because it is the most accurate for that situation, not because it is best to simply mix together portions of all viewpoints. The Earth seems flat. For some purposes it makes sense to treat the world as though it were flat. But, in fact, the world is round. Very often in the past different groups of scientists have disagreed about one or another matter. Sometimes one of the opposed positions was correct. Sometimes both groups have been wrong. Sometimes certain parts of each of the opposed positions have been correct. Even then, scientists didn't tolerate the opposed generalizations but rather figured out what was right and what was wrong about each. A mix of black and white marbles in a jar is not the same as a jar full of gray marbles. The group of people who own stock is either large or middling or small. There may be complexities about what constitutes "ownership" or about how to measure the distribution. Even if these were solved, it might be that the United States does not collect the data. And even if you had the data, you might never be able to get everyone to agree about it. But you cannot get everyone to agree that the world is round either. What is, in fact, true is not a matter of our wishes or of most people's opinion or of government statistics. It is deadly for a sociology class and it is deadly for science if every discussion operates on the premise that it is impolite to disagree with anyone else and, anyhow, that isn't how people operate in the real world.

It is not necessarily being narrow-minded or dogmatic to take a strong stand. Having a middle-of-the-road position and not backing it up with facts and arguments, although it poses as being very open minded, is actually *very dogmatic*. One is under no obligation to say that opposing arguments are as valid as one's own conclusion, although one is often under the obligation to know what the opposing arguments are and to analyze them. As you read this book, or examine other books, current events, or explanations put forward by people you know, keep these two types of errors in mind, and use this understanding to help evaluate the accuracy of those opinions.

Thus, in addition to the oppositions rejected in section 4.1, it is important to see other false dilemmas: the opposition between dogmatism and skepticism, the relative and the absolute, and knowing nothing versus knowing anything with absolute certainty.

Exercise 4.2: The Class Structure

Take some particular person whom you know personally. Consider the possibility that their views and experiences are affected by their class situation. Start by writing down everything that you know about their class situation which might have an influence on their views and experiences. Now consider some of the processes that bring you to know that person. Write down some of the aspects of their and of your class situation that brought you into contact.

Most of our social knowledge is based on social experience. By reading books, by taking sociology courses, by getting to know new people, and by many other means we can enlarge our partial or potential experience. But whatever we do, it is still limited.

This means that we have to be especially sensitive to the possibility that people from different positions in the social structure will have different experiences and standpoints and what differences those different experiences and standpoints might make. Someone winning a game of Monopoly may have a very different outlook on the game than someone who is losing, and if someone had been given a raw deal from the start, they might have a different outlook still. Of course, in Monopoly, someone who owns a hotel on Park Place does not move to another room; they continue to sit across the board. In real world Monopoly, class difference produces physical separation. Marxists are concerned with the possibility that people from different classes may importantly live in different social worlds. It is important to pay attention to different elements, components, or measures of class.

In this thought-experiment, you need not limit yourself to the things we have already looked at such as wealth, income, relationship to means of production, blue collar/white collar, etc. Nor do you have to limit yourself to the things that have an "automatic," direct effect. It might be that one's situation or relationships at work bring one into contact with others or with opportunities which then produce further change. You do not have to *know* for a fact that the things you mention have an effect. We are looking for *testable hypotheses.* Just think concretely about what is likely to have some effects and write them down. After you have done so, write a brief summary of what aspects of their views and experiences might have been influenced by class, and in what ways.

Of course, this thought-experiment was something of a trick. Writing down *everything* about someone's class experience, which might affect their views, is a very long task indeed. An enormous body of sociological and social data has only been able to scratch the surface of the question. If you look back over sections 1.3, 1.10, 2.7 or exercises such as 1.4, 1.5, or 2.5, you will find some of the evidence that the effects of social position and class are massive and pervasive. Often, if you do not find differences, it is because your comparison is too narrow, and if you made a broader comparison (e.g., asking how this person is different from a feudal titled aristocrat), you find clear, strong differences.

Almost certainly you started by writing down some things about the person's wealth, income, and job. Everyone knows that millionaires don't have the same experiences as the homeless and that bankers often think about things differently from assembly line workers.

Almost certainly you continued by writing down things about the background, relatives, and spouse (if any) of the person you chose. Everyone knows that people often adopt views and empathize with people who were or are close to them. And you probably noticed that there was a correlation between many of these items and the previous ones, so that they reinforce each other. Often different forces pull one in the same direction. But sometimes they contradict each other, and you probably noticed some contradictions.

Both one's job and one's family background also put one into *relationships* of many different kinds with many different people: friends and neighbors; co-hobbyists and co-religionists; lovers and enemies. These relationships are not random. Usually many aspects of the pattern of these relationships can be pretty well predicted from knowing about someone's job and family. But the relationships are of many different kinds and they have many different effects. If you began to describe the relationships of the person you chose, then your story became fairly long and complicated—at least if it was a true story.

For example, the resources produced by a job and by the relationships which are enabled by the job then create various powers and opportunities. Not everyone uses powers, influence, or opportunities the same way. But you can't use what you don't have. And what you do use has further effects. This means that the story you tell becomes something of a history.

And these relationships also involved history and the history of relationships and conflicts of these groups. Your chosen person may be or know members of various groups such as blacks, Irish Catholics, mineworkers, Jehovah's Witnesses, or other groups, and members of those groups tend to share distinctive ideas. These ideas stem from distinctive experiences and relations with other groups. Describing this involves describing something fairly complex. There are almost certainly contradictory pulls and forces involved.

We will pursue a number of these issues as we go along. For the moment we will just say this: Marx argued that the simplest story involves whether the person is a worker, a boss, or in-between. That simple story is an important part of the whole story, and it usually has a powerful effect. It is not a story about nothing. But usually the story had to become more complicated to involve the bulk of the ideas and experiences of the person. Much of the expansion of the story may have involved just spelling out the implications of the simple story. Almost certainly, most of the expanded, complicated story had some relation to the simple story.

Suggestions for Further Reading

Issues of liberalism and especially the bigoted kind of tolerance based on a conventional view of the world are discussed, among other places, in C. Caudwell, *Studies in a Dying Culture* (Monthly Review, 1974) and H. Marcuse, R. P. Wolff, and B. Moore, *A Critique of Pure Tolerance* (Verso, 1969). On postmodernism: David Harvey, *The Condition of Post-Modernity* (Blackwell, 1990); Alex Callinicos, *Against Post-Modernism* (Palgrave Mac-Millan, 1990).

SECTION 4.3: ARE ATTEMPTS AT NEUTRALITY A GUARANTEE OF OBJECTIVITY?

One of the things that distinguished Marx's theory from those of Durkheim and Weber is that Marx claimed that his theory was both an objective science and also that it was partisan to the interests of the working class. Some people see these two claims as inconsistent. How can something be both objective and partisan? Isn't partisanship the main obstacle to objectivity? The partisanship of Marx's theory is related to the *practical* orientation of his theory. Correct practice is not produced by neutrality. In section 4.2 we saw that commitment to a bad theory may prevent us from getting a better theory. But the *feeling* of being indifferent or neutral does not reduce that problem, which stems from the fact that our social existence is prestructured by our experience, our commitments, and the categories we bring to it.

   In the social sciences many kinds of commitments are theoretically relevant. At the very least, one must be committed to finding the correct theory. Can a more partisan theory be more objective than one which claims neutrality? Some standpoints allow one to see more than others. Some people may have more to hide. In every society, the point of view of those people who benefit most from existing arrangements is often highly educated and literate, and it is dominant in the society. At the same time, those are the very people who have the greatest interest in concealing the seamy aspects of the social structure and promoting myths and illusions about it. In a court of law, testimony by someone who has something to gain from the testimony is less "credible" than testimony of someone who does not. Slave owners are not credible witnesses about slavery, aristocrats are not credible witnesses about feudalism, and businessmen or economists hired by them are not necessarily credible witnesses about capitalism. Moreover, if a particular bias permeates the society, then whenever one averages or summarizes the thinking in the society—giving equal time to all positions—what one will obtain will reflect that bias. For example, to the extent that the viewpoint of slaveowners permeates a slave society, only someone consciously opposed to slavery—an antislave partisan—may be able to shake free of those viewpoints. If the conventional, average viewpoint is mistaken, what one needs to do for objectivity is to filter it out, not average it in. It often takes an organization and a stance of self-conscious opposition to do that.

The attempt to be entirely neutral is often an illusion. The view that the most objective person is the most neutral is sometimes connected to the views we call **positivist**—that objectivity comes from looking directly at "facts" without any theory at all. But facts are dialectically related to theories. A fact is always in part an answer to a question. What one observes and how one interprets those observations is largely governed by the theory or theories which one is considering. The attempt to be above commitments often produces a pseudo-neutrality in which theorists evade discussion of practical implications. For example, even "facts" that one remembers out of one's own experience about race are often indirect, and they turn out to be influenced by one's network of connections: "A friend of mine. . . ." More importantly, even when they are direct, personal experiences, they are often shaped by the dominant ideology. Joe Feagin, in *Racist America* (Routledge, 2000), argues that in the United States, because of structural racism, any white or Anglo person will have ready-made racist perceptions and reactions to the "facts" of their experience. It is possible to bracket that racist reaction, to doubt it, or even to substitute an anti-racist one, but that must be an active, not a passive response, because the racist interpretation is always there, as pervasive as the air we breathe. Political disputes are wrapped in layer after layer of abstraction and disguised as purely theoretical disputes. Fortunately or unfortunately it is not possible to fail to act on one's beliefs, because failure to act has consequences and therefore an effect in the world. The same is true of thinking. Try very hard not to think of a round apple. To try not to think about it is to still think about it! Complete neutrality is impossible. Even saying, "I don't know" in different contexts can have an effect in the world—either strengthening the status quo or weakening it by creating skepticism.

Our experience is heavily pre-structured by the categories which we bring to it. People often perceive a statement which fits into their expectations and preconceptions as "objective." In an academic environment, this means that statements which are vague about the distinctive empirical predictions or political practice which they imply, but which do not conflict with any of the myths and sacred cows of the society, will often be perceived as objective. People may be perceived as objective precisely when they avoid offending anyone or stirring up problems. This is not the most objective social theory but the most conventional. Often it is the *least* objective social theory.

Some of the practice that is relevant to testing a theory may be practice which one can do for oneself—looking up a certain fact in a book, or checking whether a certain relation exists or does not exist, for example. Partisanship may be very relevant to these kinds of practice. But there are other kinds of practice for which partisanship is crucial. Often the key difference between political and social theories would only be evident by trying them out. Trying out a social theory isn't something an isolated individual can very well do. It is something that requires organization, because often only thousands or millions of people can try out a social theory. Unless one has some kind of connection to those thousands or millions of people, there is no way that one can gain the practice key to testing or improving one's theory. This is one of the reasons that Marx said, "The philosophers have only *interpreted* the world in various ways; the point, however, is to change it" ("Thesis 11 on Feuerbach," SW, p. 30). Fundamental theoretical issues almost always have practical implications. In social theory, partisanship may be absolutely crucial to testing a theory because often the only way that a social theory can be tested is if it is tried out in practice, and we do not live in a world governed by philosopher kings. If the attempt to maintain neutrality prevents us from doing that, it prevents us from doing the only thing which would really decisively improve our theories.

Thus, the opposition between neutrality and commitment, between objectivity and subjectivity, can become involved in the oppositions discussed previously in a number of different ways. Within the body of Marxist theory, this set of issues is usually discussed in terms of the overall opposition between theory versus practice, although, as we shall see, that involves several further issues. Part of the reason that practice is a difficult issue is that there is both the individual practice by which one isolated person may come to decisions and the collective practice by which a group may try out something to come to a decision.

Exercise 4.3: Pseudo-Neutrality and Pseudo-Objectivity

Some people say, "Intelligence is biologically inherited, and black and Hispanic people have less of it." What is a neutral, objective statement on this issue? Can you decide what is objective independently of what is true?

When you are explicit about your values, biases, and commitments, at least people can take them into account. Many sociologists believe that everyone has some commitments and biases about society, so that it is merely dishonest to pretend to be neutral. But if that is true, then a very large number of textbooks and theorists are sometimes dishonest—either with themselves or with others.

Many students and some teachers are very distressed by a textbook that argues that partisanship is inevitable and good. If there is no such thing as an entirely neutral standpoint, why should one believe such a text? Is it giving all sides? And sometimes the most effective way of promoting a particular position is to give the appearance of presenting both sides, letting the evidence and arguments "speak for themselves." We think that the process of learning what the issues are often requires that a text "give both sides." The structure of each section of this book presumes that the main way to locate a major issue is to find arguments among different standpoints. But the fact of the matter is that if one could agree what the issue is—what the sides are—one would already have resolved most disagreements.

Consider, for example, the disagreement which has appeared within the fields of psychology and sociology concerning the relationship between IQ test scores, intelligence, and race. It is an observable fact that in the United States, white children on average score higher on IQ tests than black children. Many explanations have been offered for this: (1) The tests are biased. (2) Certain children are more comfortable taking pencil and paper tests. (3) Certain children are better prepared to deal with certain kinds of questions. (4) Certain environments help to sharpen certain kinds of abilities, etc. One explanation that has provoked the most controversy asserts that on average, black people are biologically, genetically less intelligent and inferior to white people. Needless to say, the reaction against this has been very strong, and no major academic organization of biologists, sociologists, psychologists, or anthropologists has endorsed this view.

Critics of this view have responded with a number of arguments raising some of the points mentioned above. They have also made other kinds of arguments. For example, they have argued that the entire concern with genetic intelligence has always been part of a racist ideology, which has always been a part of capitalism. And they have argued that "race," "intelligence," and "inherited" are misleading concepts in that literature. It is virtually impossible to accurately use "race" as a biological variable, since we have common biological origins and most people have joint ancestry in ways that cannot be measured. Many people argue that the tests do not measure "intelligence," whatever that is. And the debate treats the "social" and "environmental" as the remainder, after what is "inherited" has been subtracted, so that in a slave society where slave status is perfectly correlated with skin color, slavery is treated as a biogenetic, inherited trait.

There are different issues involved. The following is a hypothetical statement similar to those widely quoted and reprinted in various psychology and sociology textbooks. These textbooks are all trying to examine the question of why minority children on the average score lower on IQ tests than white children. Students reading those texts try to get an idea of what the issue is. Usually those textbooks discuss many arguments centering on both sides of issues, and then they finish off with a quote such as the one below. You must develop your ability to see what a text is arguing and why. Assume that you have just read several pages of a textbook that discusses the various arguments on whether black people are born, on the average, with less intellectual potential than white people. At the end of the discussion, imagine that the section concludes with a quote like this (with a journal quote within the textbook quote):

> Not much is known about the link between genes and intelligence among individuals, and less is known about the relationship between intelligence and biology among races. Most social scientists would probably agree with Wilson, Watson, and Weston, who wrote that the evidence justifies conclusions no stronger than these:
> "The observed average differences in scores on intellectual ability tests (IQ tests) which are obtained by members of different racial groups probably reflect, to some degree, biases and inaccuracies in the tests, as well as differences in the social and environmental backgrounds of the groups and genetic differences among them. We wish to emphasize that these three factors are not necessarily independent and may interact. . . . in any case, however much weight one might wish to give each of these three factors, it is generally assumed that the differences among individuals within these groups significantly exceeds the average differences between the groups." (A. Wilson, B. Watson, and C. Weston, *Journal of Obfuscated Partisanship* 10:7 [July 1974], pp. 11–26.)

What position is this hypothetical textbook taking?

1. That black people, on average, are biologically inferior, that they are born with less intellectual potential, on average, than white people.
2. That black people, on average, are not biologically inferior, but rather that problems with the tests and the environment are what cause the differences in the scores.
3. A middle position that really does not take sides on the debate, but is rather trying to be objective and see both sides.

What is the basis of your conclusion about what the textbook is asserting? What are the main messages most students will take away from this quote? What will they remember two months or two years from the time they read it?

It is useful to become sensitive to the presentation of an "issue," including the presentation of issues by the text you are now reading. Many students feel that position 3 best describes the issues in the text—that the text is neutral because it presents issues and counterissues, because it says that its conclusions are not strong ones, and because it gives the level of agreement/disagreement among "most social scientists." We think that the plain fact is that the text takes a position on the issue. The text cites another work as a neutral and balanced authority. We think that most students reading the passage will mainly get the message that the issue is what that authority says the issue is. The quote is not neutral; it takes a position.

Many students feel that position 2 reflects the position that the quote and the text are taking, that problems with tests cause the differences in the scores. After all, the quote says that there are biases in the test and little is known about what is going on. But if you react this way, you should notice that the quote says, as plain as day, that differences in IQ scores "probably reflect, to some degree . . . genetic differences" among the groups.

Thus, we agree with those who say that position 1 reflects the position that the quote and the book are taking, that underneath the pseudo-neutrality and qualification of the quote is the racial supremacist position. The claim is put forward that there are "probably" racial differences in intelligence, due to genetic inheritance. The text claims that the issue is whether they account for much or little of the difference in scores. It is analogous to a debate as to whether "Henry" is a crook who stole $10,000. A third person listens to the debate and then enters the discussion saying: "Let me give you a neutral, balanced, moderate, objective compromise. Henry did not steal $10,000; he only stole $5,000!" But what is the message? The message is that Henry *stole money*. And if there is no evidence that Henry stole any money, there is no basis to try to slip in this untrue charge against him for the sake of giving pseudo-neutral support to "both sides."

What the text says is technically correct. Since most anthropologists and sociologists reject any claim for genetic, racial differences in intelligence, they certainly accept claims "no stronger than" the claims in the quote. Indeed, they hold positions which reject the issue as it is posed here. The text *conveys a message* about what the issue is and what the answer is on that issue.

Here, as often, the most important thing is not what position a text takes on the issues, but what issues are presented. The questions asked are more important than the answers given. The fact of the matter is that neither a textbook nor any other book can deal with all possible issues. What it can do is to pose important issues clearly and sharply. Often teachers and textbooks that appear to be neutral and objective are precisely evading and avoiding sharp ways of posing questions.

The positions of theorists such as Jensen and Herrnstein underwent a revival in the 1990s with the publication of Herrnstein and Murray's *The*

Bell Curve (Basic, 1994) and Jensen's *The g Factor* (Praeger, 1998). Both exhibit a mixture of overt arguments of genetic inferiority often disguised by techniques of pseudo-neutrality. The central policy commitment of these analyses was the elimination of social policies such as welfare or affirmative action, designed to equalize opportunities. One can most easily justify the elimination of such policies if one can argue that the huge racial inequalities, visible in any American city, result from biological difference. However, there are known social sources of racial differences in wealth, income, occupation, test scores, or life chances. Therefore, Herrnstein and Murray employ the peculiarly weak form of argument that "some fraction" of the racial differences in academic performance, test scores, etc., is due to biological differences. It is as though one used the empty truism that somewhere between zero and 100 percent of humans can walk on water to argue that therefore some humans probably can walk on water. Some religious arguments, some conspiracy theorists, some global warming deniers, some evolution deniers, and those who spread the lie that Iraq had weapons of mass destruction to use against the United States, have used a similar style of reasoning—saying that since we can't know something 100 percent, that therefore there is a good chance that their particular explanation could be correct. Understanding how to see through the cloud of pseudo-open-mindedness and learning to demand evidence is not just an exercise in a book. It has important relevance to many life and death social and political questions.

Suggestions for Further Reading

There is an immense literature on problems of value-relevance and objectivity in the social sciences and an even larger literature on methods and procedures of hypothesis testing. The standard liberal position starts from Weber, *The Methodology of the Social Sciences* (Free Press, 1949). Brown and Keeley, *Asking the Right Questions* (Pearson-Prentice Hall, 2009) addresses obstacles to critical thinking without using the language of dialectic. R. Herrnstein and C. Murray's *The Bell Curve* (1995) is a good example of the (mis)use of pseudo-neutrality, claiming that blacks are inferior. It is discussed by the essays in S. Fraser, *The Bell Curve Wars* (Basic, 1995) and Jacoby and Glauberman, *The Bell Curve Debates* (Times Books, 1995). Fischer, et al., *Inequality by Design* (Princeton University Press, 1995) noted that in all societies where there is a lower status group, such as Indian untouchables, Burakumin, or Korean immigrants in Japan, that status is associated with academic failure, criminality, and other traits that Jensen claims are racial. But when Burakumin or Korean Japanese migrate to the United States or any other place where the status no longer applies, then the association vanishes. S. Rosenthal gives an excellent account of the funding sources of much of the racist psychology "Pioneer Fund: Financer of Racist Research," *American*

Behavioral Scientist 39:44–61. Knapp, et al., *The Assault on Equality* (Praeger, 1996) showed that claims by *The Bell Curve* that childhood IQ had powerful effects, independent of childhood social class, were a methodological arti- fact. *The Bell Curve* had measured childhood social class by mother's educa- tion, which was usually completed when the respondents were very young. It measured IQ by the Armed Forces Qualifications Test performance when respondents were between 14 and 22 years old. But since social class as they measured it had usually been fixed many years before this, their measures introduce a bias. When IQ is measured at the same time as social class, its net effect vanishes (see proceedings of the symposium, Knapp and Kohn, et al., in *Contemporary Sociology*, vol. 26, 1999).

SECTION 4.4: CRISIS AND CHANGE

Everything changes, both in our ideas and in the material world. Some changes happen gradually, but often the most important changes are not gradual but discontinuous or jerky. In such cases, change, when it is slow, seems so slow that the structure appears immobile, fixed, and eternal. But such periods of stability often alternate with periods of crisis and change. In a crisis, a turbulent turning point is followed by a cascade of changes. Marx- ian theory highlights such processes of structural change when a gradual process of development leads to a crisis and to sharp, qualitative breaks. We have seen such crises in historical processes, such as wars, in epochal transformations of social structure, in economic processes, such as the great financial meltdown of 2008, and in political processes, such as political realignments or the rise of fascism.

Explaining such crises, turning points, and discontinuous patterns of change has posed major problems for twenty-first century social science and social theory. They were also a principal concern of Marxian theory, which developed distinctive approaches to them. Marx analyzed such changes in terms of dialectical concepts such as contradictions, the transi- tion from quality into quantity, negation, crises, limits, and other related concepts derived from Hegel.

Some people feel that it is always necessarily idealist to analyze social, economic, ecological or military processes in terms of **contradictions**. They believe that, while it can be useful to talk about contradiction between dif- ferent theories or views or human aims, it does not make sense to speak of contradictions between social or material processes. In contrast to such views, we have seen that Marx described his dialectical method as the analy- sis of general laws of motion and of the transformation of social forms, from one historical period to another, and he also described it as an analysis of the contradictions of social forms. Some social theorists deny that any such general laws of motion can exist. They deny that there is any general approach to change and they would say that while we can analyze the dynamics of any particular structure, the dynamics of every structure is different, and so there are no general laws of motion. Different structures are driven by different dynamics, and they have different patterns of change. The idea that changes of many different kinds are driven by "contradictions" obviously requires a distinctive, broad, and inclusive concept of "contradiction."

For most Marxian theorists, the concept of a dialectical contradiction is a central tool for analyzing how structures change, both in the natural world, in the social world, and in the intellectual world of our thinking. We have argued that for Marx, the central process is that our practice exposes limits and contradictions in our theories. However, logical or conceptual analysis is never a substitute for scientific or political practice. In exercise 4.6 we shall see that Marx takes the Newtonian derivation of elliptical orbits from the laws of motion as an example of a dialectical contradiction. By this, he does not mean to suggest that some kind of logical or philosophical analysis of concepts can substitute for or solve problems of scientific analysis. But the scientific analysis has to resolve the fact that it is a contradiction to conceive of an object as both orbiting around another and simultaneously as falling toward the other. Marx takes Newton's derivation of elliptical orbit from the laws of motion as the resolution of that contradiction.

It will be useful to sketch out some ways that the simple mechanical motion of projectiles and planets can be viewed as a contradiction, leading to the transition of quantity to quality. That will help us to see the same issues in biological, social, and economic change. Partly, analysis and theory have to resolve two different kinds of practical experiences of motion. If we throw most objects upward, they will follow the maxim "what goes up comes down." The upward movement is gradually overcome by gravity (and friction) until the object reaches a turning point, after which the object falls back down until, usually, it hits the ground—splat! But we now know that even in the simple case of a projectile, there are conditions and limits to this kind of motion. We now know that if an object could be thrown upward with enough force (i.e., if it could reach "escape velocity"), it would not fall back down. It could either travel away from the Earth indefinitely, or it could orbit the Earth elliptically, as many satellites now do. Objects at escape velocity seem to follow a very different kind of maxim: "around and around and around it goes." For thousands of years, those two kinds of motion were known, but they were analyzed as distinct and unrelated.

A transition from one to another is possible: far enough from the Earth's surface, there is so little trace of atmosphere that friction is negligible. But some satellites orbit the Earth closely enough so that they may orbit the Earth for a time, but touch the outer traces of the atmosphere. In those cases, the satellite will go into a death spiral. The slower it goes, the lower it gets; the lower it gets, the more it slows; the more it slows, the lower it gets, until it spirals, crashes, and burns. There is no particular instant when the satellite is captured by the Earth, like a butterfly in a net. But the dynamic of friction and falling, leading to a crash, becomes the main dynamic that governs the behavior of the satellite.

In social, political, historical, and economic theory there are many times when several processes are operating. In the human sciences, it is relatively unusual to find isolated systems. Contradiction between different dynamics often involves contradictions between different conceptions, different rules, and even different values. In social behavior contradictions between different views of what is normal, what is possible, and what is desirable are common. That also means that when there is a change like a satellite's being captured by the atmosphere, there are often also many other changes in people's thinking, as well. As we know, there are processes other than those of satellites being captured by the atmosphere that can lead to "crash and burn" dynamics. Any process of accumulation or alienation tends to hit limits, and we have seen many examples in which such processes lead to health, educational, welfare, economic, or military catastrophes that could be described as a "death spiral." Games of Monopoly have provided a model for many of these "crash and burn" dynamics. The great financial melt-down of the economy, many of the dynamics of "wars on terror," the creation of "mega-slums," and many of the relations between humankind and the natural environment, such as those that led to the loss of the Arctic ice cap or the destruction of the Gulf coast in 2010, involve both accumulation and tensions between contradictory forces, which lead to turning points and to discontinuous patterns of development and change. Concepts such as contradictions, crises, limits, or negations can be useful in analyzing the transformations that result.

Any dynamic process operates within conditions which must be specified, but which can never be exhaustively specified. Marx's description of the circuit of capital in the production and sale of commodities first led to the transition in which the employer, in order to manufacture commodities, participates in the buying and selling of labor power. If a self-employed farmer or storeowner hires help, he or she does not suddenly become a capitalist (poof!) but there is a threshold. At some point, the income, the outlook, and the work of an employer comes to depend mainly on extracting work from others rather than on their own labor. At some point, the dynamic of employment tends to govern the development of the society. That purchase generates further changes that bring about the transformation of the production process, from handcrafts to factory labor, and it ultimately involves the whole social structure of wages, hours, government power, and laws. For example, in exercise 2.3 we saw the qualitative transformation of relations and dynamics as the merchant buyer and seller enter the factory and become capitalist boss and wage-laborer. The same property rules produce a qualitatively different set of relationships and social dynamics. But even after concentrated capital has centralized the productive process in economic enterprises, separate from families, further transformations (the subject of *Capital*, vols. II and III) involve the creation of capital goods industries and financial instruments and a world market. As is well known, *Capital* was left unfinished by Marx's death, and in any case, the processes that he describe did not reach a fixed resting point, any more than the process of biological evolution led to the fixed, final resting point in the age of the dinosaurs. It led to a structure of some dynamic stability, but that was only a temporary resting point.

During the twentieth century, several different kinds of models were developed of such qualitative, structural changes, both in the natural sciences and in the social sciences. Some of these models go by the names of "catastrophe theory," "complexity theory," "chaotic dynamics," "nonlinear dynamics," and other, somewhat faddish, research projects. We noted that Marx compared his own project in *Capital* to Darwin's *Origin of Species*, and here we will overview two contemporary research projects: Stephen Jay Gould's punctuated equilibrium model in evolutionary biology and Paul Krugman's analyses of technological change and urban spatial self-organization. Both are theories of crisis. Both can be viewed as a structural contradiction in which a quantitative accumulation of change produces a qualitative, structural transformation.

The evolutionary biologist, Stephen Gould, developed the concept of a "punctuated equilibrium" to describe and analyze the jerky process of evolutionary change, and specifically to explain the fossil record of biological speciation. He argued that the most evident fact of the geological record is that there is an alternation of long periods of near stasis, punctuated by short episodes of cascading, proliferating change. Some of those periods of change, such as the end of the age of the dinosaurs, were probably occasioned by catastrophic external events, such as a great meteor strike, but other great evolutionary extinctions were not. Moreover, even cases of extinctions that did involve an external event raise questions of why that event caused a massive cascade of further changes. Gould showed that known processes of Darwinian evolution ("allopatric speciation"), when transposed to the archeological time scale and level of analysis, produce a discontinuous pattern of change in which change in the fossil record occurs in fits and starts rather than in a steady process of slow change, and he analyzed implications of that process.

What appears in the fossil record is not just a record of a single organism, but of whole ecosystems. The ecological interdependence of species has been taken as a model as the inspiration of social phenomena, such as models of neighborhoods in a city or institutions in a society. However, the relationships between members of an ecosystem are complex. Gould stresses the fact that biological evolution consists of the accumulation of different kinds of change at different levels of analysis on different time scales. One change in an organism may make other changes adaptive. A change in one organism may encourage other changes in other organisms. Even if all of these changes are gradual, in the sense that they occur over hundreds of generations, they may be instantaneous on a geological time scale in which adjacent layers of rock are separated by tens of thousands of years. Such processes may develop new species in a sub-population, such as the population on an island, but when that species is reintroduced into the main population (on the mainland), it can generate a cascade of changes. If the voracious Asian carp established itself in Lake Michigan, the entire ecosystem of that lake will rapidly and profoundly change. The resulting change processes of competing dominant organisms will appear discontinuous and jerky.

In economics, giant works based on the importance of such discontinuous, jerky processes are the new trade theory, the spatial economics, and the new economic geography of Paul Krugman. We shall focus on Krugman's use of models of technological choice to clarify processes of spatial organization of cities in *The Self-Organized Economy* (1999). Krugman's analyses of technological choice to explain choices of spatial location in urban economics illustrate the dynamics which occurs when there are increasing returns. Sociological processes such as imitation or complementarity can produce an advantage of dominance.

Specifically, Krugman analyzes the particular case of the choice between tapes (for VCRs) and laser disks (for DVD players). Suppose that some people will prefer VCRs regardless of their availability; and others will prefer DVD players, regardless of availability; but most people's preferences are influenced by the relative dominance of the two technologies. The technology that is in common use affects its desirability because it affects availability, choice, how current is the selection, how easy it is to get services, familiarity, fads, etc. Therefore, the demand and supply curves of the two technologies, as a function of the other, may cross several times, and there will usually be both a tape-dominant and a disk-dominant equilibrium. (There will also usually be an unstable middle equilibrium, from which the system will rapidly move to an equilibrium in which one or the other technology dominates, if there is any disturbance.) Krugman shows that if there is a shift between the two technologies, it will be extremely discontinuous. There will be a point at which the market for the previously dominant technology will collapse.

Moreover, the phenomenon is extremely general. While the switch from tape-based to disk-based technology might seem like a peculiar and idiosyncratic process, similar dynamics operate in many other cases. Most technologies will have a self-reinforcing character in the sense that a dominant technology will have an advantage because the very fact that it is in use makes it familiar, better developed, and easier to use.

Music on demand is another example. Live music was around for millennia. It was replaced to a large degree by vinyl records (and limited radio) for about fifty years. Eight-track and then cassette tapes replaced most vinyl records for about twenty years, then CDs (much cheaper to produce) became dominant for about ten years, were in turn replaced by mp3 and other digital technologies, and presently direct downloading of music over the Internet is common. Each of these stages was shorter than the last. There were periods of stabilization, plateaus during these developments. The point is that there are stages, which are not equal in length, and each of them was the result of the dominance of a technique. And each was ended by the collapse of that dominance.

Nor are such dominance effects restricted to technology. Krugman applies a similar model to analyze the dynamics that produce the growth, specialization, and development of some areas of cities and the collapse of the support system and of jobs or of public order in others. A great deal of sociological research focuses on the nature of neighborhoods and of their composition and institutions. Many of them show dominance effects and discontinuous change via crises. More generally, because we are social beings, we act with others. We create identities, rules, and institutions with those with whom we act. These identities, rules, and institutions come into conflict with each other, and their change often involves turning points, crises, and discontinuities. Processes of alienation, accumulation, spatial segregation, and power produce further discontinuities. Analysis of the turning points and discontinuous changes generated by accumulation, alienation, and local spillover effects has become exceptionally important to twenty-first century sociological theory. Without an understanding of how these quantitative changes can lead to sudden, profound change, the same people who dismissed the possibilities of change as being "mystical" will often, themselves, embrace extreme mystical explanations of these changes because they haven't examined the processes of change in a scientific, dialectical way. Some liberals and positivists who deny the possibility of a major crisis as being "nonscientific" will themselves embrace bizarre, unscientific explanations, such as racism or conspiracies when a serious crisis does happen. That's how many seemingly placid people come to embrace fanaticism and even fascism.

Sociologists have studied many mechanisms that generate discontinuous tipping points similar to the loss of dominance of a technology. Small group processes, network formation, imitation, conformity, accumulation, poverty traps, power phenomena, and ethnic, racial, gender, or religious segregation and conflict are only some of the processes that produce dynamic situations with multiple equilibria and discontinuous transitions between them. While some changes in attitudes or social structures or politics are gradual and continuous, many are not. Sometimes there seems to be a turning point or watershed between different periods or dynamics. The investigation of these kinds of transition dynamics is a central problem in contemporary social theory.

The concepts of dialectics are useful in the analysis of crises of this kind partly because such processes of dominance effects and the collapse of dominance require an analysis that emphasizes historical process. Marxist theory has analyzed many examples of such changes. What produced our past gains often strangles our future progress. In the analysis of processes of alienation and the accumulation of wealth, power, and prestige, as well as the patterns of crisis and change to which they lead, Marxian theorists have built up a stock of case studies of the contradictory dynamics of change. We saw that the ability of a particular person to follow a career ("Jennifer's" "ability" to become an "engineer") depends upon an accumulation of an identity, skills, supports, and resources required to become an engineer. The same is true of many large-scale historical and global changes such as wars, realignments, race relations, political movements, or ecological tipping points. Dialectical analysis explores those processes.

Suggestions for Further Reading

There is a large, growing literature on complex systems. A highly readable account of the pervasiveness of contradictory dynamics, producing patterns of jerky change is Per Bak, *How Nature Works* (1996). Steven J. Gould's *Punctuated Equilibrium* (2007) summarizes the arguments and debates he originated about biological speciation. These arguments are now important in fields such as management, political science, and sociology, as well as in evolutionary biology. Marxists have traditionally analyzed issues central to complex systems in terms of dialectic and thus they have explored many of the most historically important examples of such processes. About questions such as the extinctions of the dinosaurs, *Science Daily* summarizes news and refers readers to primary sources. For example, www.sciencedaily.com. A methodology for the qualitative analysis of complex system is outlined in Puccia and Levins, *Qualitative Modeling of Complex Systems* (1985) and by Levins and Lewontin in *Biology Under the Influence* (2005). Paul Krugman's analysis in *The Self Organized Economy* (2006) summarizes arguments about international and urban growth areas and poverty traps.

Exercise 4.4: Crucial Experiments

Choose any (observed) relationship between two or more variables in which you are interested. Invent at least three theories, not now known to be false, which might explain these relations. Choosing appropriate indicators, derive at least three different empirical consequences from each theory, such that the factual consequences distinguish among the theories.

Take as your observed relation something you have observed or seen on the news. As your alternate theories, try to construct at least one Marxist and one non-Marxist explanation of that fact.

What is the practice and evidence which is fundamental for the decision between two theories? Often opposed theories say the same thing about most things. But most philosophers of science and virtually all sociologists believe that if the theories really are different, then they can't say the same thing about everything. There must be some situations where they produce different expectations, or they would not really be different. We may not have any data about the situations where they would make different predictions, but there must be some. What is key for deciding between two theories are the points where the theories **contradict** each other. Hence, it seems reasonable to say that finding contradictions between theories is the key to developing better theories.

Some people think that the task of finding where theories contradict each other is easy—that you just have to *see* where they say something different. Unfortunately, it is not that easy. Often theories say the same thing in different words, or they are talking about totally different problems. Other people think that finding out where two theories contradict each other is always impossible—that different theories put people into two different worlds so that even when they appear to be talking about the same thing, they never are. But while our theories may take us into "different worlds," our practice brings us into the one world. We think there are usually contradictions between theories, but it often takes considerable work to find them.

For example, between Newton's and Einstein's mechanics, there were massive differences. If Einstein was right, matter and energy could be turned into each other, making possible the atomic bomb. And a spaceship traveling from here to a star at half the speed of light and one traveling from there to here at half the speed of light would not pass each other at the speed of light but at about four-fifths of that speed, because time and space would be altered by the motion. And there were indefinitely many other differences between the theories. But you could not merely look and see which of the theories was true, as choosing between them was very complex. None of these differences were any use in finding out which theory was true. To build an atomic bomb, you had to devote massive resources. And we still can't build those spaceships in order to see which theory is more accurate.

World War II was the result of the rise and triumph of fascist movements in one country after another. Different Marxists had different, opposed theories of the rise of fascism and of how to fight it. These different theories had diametrically opposed recommendations about what to do, just as contemporary Marxist and liberal theories disagree about how to deal with the resurgence of racist and neo-Nazi movements. Many people, and most liberal groups, see the rise of these groups as deeply opposed to the main development of liberal politics. They recommend ignoring it when Klan spokesmen are asked to speak on TV or joining in a debate when a neo-Nazi party becomes an organized presence. They recommend "cooling it," relying on the courts and the law, and avoiding "extremism." By contrast, some Marxists believe that these racist groups are a natural development out of normal liberal capitalist politics. They have the passive or active support of key upper class groups, and they thrive when they are ignored by those who understand the threat they represent. Accordingly, some of them have forcibly prevented the Klan and the Nazis from operating in many places. Thus, among all the various tactical, strategic, and value questions concerning the use of force, there is an important practical question. Is it the use of force or the failure to use force which most promotes the growth of such movements? What works is a factual, empirical question, but one can't possibly decide on the basis of a long period of trial and error, because the costs of making a mistake are prohibitive. Besides, there are side effects and other forces promoting growth and decline. So the theoretical/research task of sorting out the causes of growth and the practical effects of different responses is a serious task.

In both cases, the theories predicted the same thing in most situations, especially those we could observe easily. There are observable places where the theories predicted different things, but often they are small discrepancies. The key theoretical training that one needs is the ability to clarify where theories disagree. Stinchcombe correctly makes this task the basis of theory construction. The above exercise is a task he gives theory students in *Constructing Social Theory* (Harcourt, 1968, p. 13). It is a useful exercise.

How can one choose between theories on the basis of their empirical consequences? Is it possible at all? There is much dispute about these questions in the philosophy of science. One problem is that different theories not only give different answers to the same empirical questions, but they also ask different questions. A key part of virtually every article in sociology or in any of the other social sciences is the presentation of data or evidence relevant to an hypothesis. But another key part is a "review" of the literature, which shows that some set of facts is an answer to an important question raised by others' work. The facts do not speak for themselves.

Theories do not speak for themselves either. A theory neither has empirical predictions nor practical implications irrespective of everything else. One must combine a theory with other assumptions and theories about what other forces are at work before it yields predictions. Often this does not matter, so you must merely make reasonable assumptions which both you and opponents of the theory would accept.

Stinchcombe's approach centers on the idea of crucial experiments which decide between alternate theories. A crucial experiment in this sense need not be a laboratory experiment. It is just a situation where alternate theories have different predictions. Any theory has several kinds of alternate theories. One very general alternate theory is random chance. One needs a theory to predict a number of tendencies which would not have come about by chance, and one can use statistical tests to test these alternate theories. But even the tendencies which are unlikely by chance always permit several alternate explanations. **When a theory predicts many different tendencies of many different kinds, all unlikely by chance, then it is harder to construct alternate explanations of them, and they are better theories.**

The three main paradigms of modern sociology almost always allow you to construct alternate explanations. No matter what you are looking at—prostitution, famine, racism, war, or terrorism—one can try to construct alternate explanations by supposing (hypothesizing) in turn: (1) what is going on is a consequence of class struggle, (2) what is going on is a consequence of values and social integration, and (3) what is going on is a consequence of organizational developments. This will not, by itself, develop full theoretical accounts. But with a little ingenuity and brainstorming, you should be able to see at least two different, alternate explanations. Now the task is to find a crucial experiment between them.

For example, consider some of the main explanations for the problems of education in the United States. One possibility is that the class structure, the level of inequality, and the high levels of poverty in many schools is the main source of the problem. Another possibility is that the breakdown of the family and community is the main source of problem. A third possibility is that the bureaucratic structure of administration and its lack of accountability to parents and students is the main problem. Each of these theories has, at various times, been a source of major diagnoses and policy prescriptions about education in the United States.

If each theory predicts the thing you started from, then that cannot be a test between them, because they predict the same thing there. All three theories predict that education will have major problems in the United States. So in order to test between them, one would need to think of (or to construct) a situation where they contradict each other.

In general, any test between theories will always want, at the least, to control the process hypothesized by the other theory. A rough and ready way to find situations which, in principle, decide between two theories is the following. Suppose that one theory says that something mainly results from X and another theory says that it is mainly the result of Y. Then situations characterized by both X and Y will not help decide between the two theories. In those situations, both theories predict the same thing. And the same is true of situations characterized by neither X nor Y. But situations characterized by X and not Y or by Y and not X will help one to decide between the theories because in those situations the theories predict different things. There is variation between different schools, different communities, different states, different societies, and different periods of time about characteristics such as inequality, family, and bureaucracy. Research methods are a way of comparing school performance across schools, communities, societies, or time, to find out what affects school performance. Often this requires generalizing from a particular set of issues about education in a particular context to a broader set of issues.

Deciding between theories will never be a simple, mechanical, automatic process which you can turn over to a computer program. There are many ways that you could have constructed the original theories; there are many ways that you could have generalized them. But the findings one would obtain on those cases where alternate theories disagree are critical for seeing where the theories are different, not only in their words but in the reality they conceive. And such findings are critical for changing and developing the theories and for rejecting some and preferring others.

Whenever any theory seems to predict incorrectly, one can figure out a possible explanation that repairs rather than eliminates the theory. But there are profound practical, theoretical, and empirical differences between Marxist and liberal theories. Whether in the case of racism and fascism or law and religion, their fundamental accounts are different. This book has reviewed many cases where alternate theories have been developed to the point where they are testable. That work is far from mechanical and it is far from finished. We hope you can contribute to it.

Suggestions for Further Reading

Theories and paradigms: one approach to the substantive differences between paradigms is summarized in P. Knapp, "The Empirical Basis of Sociological Paradigms," *International Review of Modern Sociology* 12:129 (1982). Hegel's dialectic is organized in a circle which has many starting points, but the classical beginning is the section of the *Phenomenology of Spirit* (Oxford, 1977, p. 58–79), where sense-certainty knows that what is in front of it is, but without theory cannot say what it is that is in front of it. The classical Marxist argument that positivism is idealist is found in Lenin, *Materialism and Empirio-Criticism* (Progress Publishers, 1970). A simple summary of the Marxist conception of theories arising from experience/data is *On Practice* by Mao, available at www.marxists.org. On hypothesis testing: A. Stinchcombe has outlined his approach to testing social theories in *Constructing Social Theories* (Harcourt, 1968); his *The Logic of Social Research* (Chicago, 2005) summarizes the multiplicity of research methods important in practical theorizing. P. Knapp, "Domains of Applicability of Social Scientific Theories," *Journal for the Theory of Social Behavior* 4:25 (1984) argues that absolutely general theories are neither necessary nor possible. On education: Diane Ravitch, former assistant secretary of education, and once a strong supporter of the No Child Left Behind Act describes why she was forced to reverse her position. Her *Life and Death of the Great American School System* (Basic, 2010) describes why greater testing and school choice, instead of improving education by promoting accountability, has undermined education as a whole.

SECTION 4.5: CAN SOCIAL SCIENCE BE VALUE-NEUTRAL? SHOULD IT BE?

Disagreements of fact are hard to resolve if we don't have the necessary facts. Disagreements of theory are even harder to resolve. They may have powerful practical implications involving deeply rooted prejudices. When we get to issues of **values**, disagreements often are very intense indeed. People often feel that it is pointless to argue about religion or politics because beliefs are so deeply felt that they can never convince others to change their minds on these issues. It is true that values are often deeply entwined with the ways people live, with their expectations, and with their relations with others. If you have a difference of opinion about facts with someone, that usually does not make it difficult to live with them. Theoretical disagreements about what causes what create more difficulty. Fundamental disagreement on the level of values creates still more difficulty.

For example, disagreeing with somebody about whether members of a minority group have higher death rates would be a debate over **facts**, data. Another factual question, which also involves some theory, is whether black people receive worse medical care on average than whites. Even if one agreed there, about whether the lack of medical care causes the deaths and what it would take to change it, this could still involve many disagreements of **theory**. A disagreement about whether one should care whether black people live or die would be a disagreement over **values**. When the values stay at the level of lip service and don't involve anyone's doing anything, such disagreements are often papered over. But imagine that someone is a member of the Ku Klux Klan, and imagine that his roommate believes that the Klan is a threat to the life and the well-being of millions of people, so that he is willing to risk bodily harm and prison to prevent the Klan from operating. The roommates disagree in their beliefs about the causes of various problems, they disagree in their feelings toward various groups, and they disagree in their beliefs about the future. If the Klan member is right, the growth of the Klan would be the main hope. But if the roommate is right, the growth of the Klan would lead to the same kind of disaster as Hitler's Germany. Both people might be wrong, but if either is right, it would probably be undesirable to paper over the disagreement. In any case, it is not likely that it is possible to gloss it over. This is one of the reasons that political disagreements may become quite violent.

What are the relationships between our judgments of matters of fact and our judgments of ethics and values? What are Marx's moral or ethical beliefs? Are the main disagreements between Marxists and anti-Marxists in values?

Some people argue that judgments of fact and judgments of value are totally separate; other people argue that they are inseparable. The people who believe in the absolute separation of fact and value argue that it is never possible to derive a value conclusion from an argument that does not have value premises. Many sociologists are motivated to avoid issues of values because they feel that, since people will always disagree about values, those values should be treated as arbitrary. Thus they are led to seek a scientific theory which is entirely distinct from value judgments. *In practice this may be used to justify having value premises which they do not care to admit.* (Often it is precisely the people doing highly practical and value-charged research who are the first to talk about objective social science. For example, someone doing highly applied counterinsurgency research under contract from the military will argue that it is an entirely objective, abstract, theoretical investigation, which can be used by anyone.)

Another false debate can ensue. The people arguing the separation of fact and value are often led to deny value issues when they are in front of them. The people arguing that issues of fact and value are intertwined are sometimes led to deny facts, and they may be led to the position that all one can do is to chose positions which correspond to one's own prejudices. No doubt an argument with a value conclusion has a value premise. But that does not mean that one cannot argue issues of values, and it does not mean that disagreements about the conclusion usually stem from disagreements about values.

Can one argue values? How and with what effect? In one sense, it might seem impossible to argue with someone who has completely different values. How can you argue with someone who believes that it is okay to kill for fun? It is almost as if there are totally different kinds of people. But exercise 1.1 on package deals suggested that many important evaluations are connected to views about cause and effect, and *even values are ultimately based on one's life experiences,* including indirect experiences of those with whom one has social relationships. There are reasons why people have certain values, and these reasons are based on knowledge of different kinds—evidence, information, life experiences, etc.—which can be debated and discussed. The fact that they are unlikely to be changed by a few arguments does not mean that they are fixed for all time.

Consider "patriotism." Some people think that it is a desirable value for people to have. An intensely patriotic person might say that patriotism is a basic human value, that it is not debatable. That person might become very angry with someone who rejected patriotism—almost to the point of thinking that a nonpatriotic person is a lower creature for not believing in patriotism. Yet even patriotism is ultimately based on how one sees the data, and patriotism should not be immune from debate. Presidents say that patriotism is a good thing. But would a president say that since patriotism is good, then he hopes the youth of say, North Korea, or some other government hostile to the U.S. government, will remain patriotic to their government? Probably not, since he would argue that the **facts** indicate that people should not be loyal to that kind of government. In other words, even patriotic people agree that under certain circumstances, depending on specific facts, patriotism could be a bad thing.

We have seen that important disagreements between Marx and other social theorists concern governments, nations, and states. The disagreement is not, as it is sometimes portrayed in the United States, that liberals value freedom while Marx loved bureaucracy and wished to expand the government. In fact, the main disagreement between Marx and any of the other founders of sociology was precisely that Marx detested bureaucracy and government. Marx believed that governments can and will be abolished. But even this is not mainly an issue of values. Whatever value questions are involved are deeply intertwined with questions such as: were there always governments in the past? What kinds of arrangements are possible without states? What are the consequences of trying to abolish states? For example, do you get worse states? What are the consequences of *not* abolishing states? For example, do you always get war? Very often, the *value premises* of Marxism are identical to those voiced by others who do not consider themselves Marxist, even those who believe that they should oppose Marxism. What is *different* is the causal, theoretical analysis concerning what is possible and concerning the causes and the effects of various social arrangements.

Often we look for **patterns** as a way of understanding cause and consequence, as a way of understanding what is happening and what will happen. This is what science is all about. However, there are two things about patterns which are important to keep in mind. *The first is that it is often very hard to see patterns which are there; the second is that it is often very hard not to see illusory patterns, those which are not really there.* When we stare at a random bunch of dots, we usually see organized constellations. One way of seeing constellations prevents us from seeing others. Often the main obstacle to finding a true theory is having a theory which fits some of the facts. Whenever there is a pattern, several possibilities will fit it with some exceptions. The scientist's pattern, theory, or explanation must accurately fit and explain the facts. What we have found in any body of knowledge which shows real scientific development is that some theories ultimately fit the facts much better than others.

Exercise 4.5: The Game of Eleusis

We can illustrate many of these ideas with a deck of playing cards. Take a deck of cards. Consider the very simple patterns which can be made out of the cards. For instance, suppose that you were laying down the cards in a pattern "odd-even-odd-even . . ." discarding any cards which came up which did not fit the pattern. You might get pattern (1): 10 of spades, 3 of diamonds, 8 of clubs, ace of spades, queen of hearts. Or more briefly: 10S, 3D, 8C, AS, QH. Do you think that you would be able to guess the pattern if you just saw it, without being told that it was "odd-even-odd-even"?

Practice finding patterns by looking for the following five:
pattern (2): 4S, 10D, QS, 9D, 6C, 6H, 4C
pattern (3): 3S, SH, AS, 10C, 3H, 6D, 5D
pattern (4): KD, 10D, KC, 5C, QH, 9S, JD
pattern (5): 6S, QS, AC, 9D, 4D, 9S, 4H
pattern (6): 7H, 6C, JH, IOH, 3S, 6D, 5S

Could you find a pattern like odd-even-odd-even? Quite possibly you could. After all, this is a relatively simple kind of pattern, and playing cards have a relatively small number of variables which characterize them: number which can be higher or lower, odd or even, etc.; suit which can be red or black, higher or lower, etc.; whether they are face cards; etc. People and social structures are much more complicated—they are characterized by many more variables than number, suit, color, being a face card, etc. Patterns are everywhere. Try to fix a deck of cards so that there are no patterns within it: no pairs; no three of a kind; no sequences 4, 5, 6; no sequences 3, 6, 9. Random shuffling won't produce it, and even with careful, nonrandom planning, you will find that it is most difficult. And if it takes careful planning to produce a situation of total disorder, then, of course, there is considerable *order* underlying that situation!

But the fact of the matter is that most people find it extraordinarily hard to find even very simple patterns *unless they know what they are looking for.* Almost every scientific discovery looks obvious once it is made.

Of course, a small number of cards may fit several different patterns. For instance, you may have noticed that the first five cards of pattern (1) fit a number of different patterns as well as "odd-even." They also form the pattern of "every fifth card a face card" or "divisible by 2, divisible by 3, divisible by 4, divisible by 1, divisible by 2. . . ." We didn't plan this, it was a "coincidence," and so if we had given a longer sequence, it would have stopped being true. Thus, a *small number of cases is not good evidence that a general pattern exists.* Most sociologists correctly distrust "anecdotal" evidence, stories, based on limited experiences. Moreover, if one allows patterns that are very complicated, or if one allows patterns which the cards almost fit, with some exceptions, there are any number of patterns for any set of cards. Let's limit ourselves to patterns which fit perfectly and which can be stated in ten words or less.

Let's distinguish patterns of different kinds. Let's call a pattern which only involves one variable a **simple** pattern. For instance, pattern (1) is a simple pattern because it just involves the evenness or oddness of the card. Patterns (2), (3), and (4) are also simple patterns. In order to see those patterns, it is only necessary to see what about a card is relevant. Is it the fact that the ace of spades is the first card in the suit, that it is a prime number, that it is a spade, that it is a black card, or what? Unfortunately, almost no patterns which are of interest in society are simple patterns in this sense. Most of them involve at least two variables.

Let's call patterns that involve two variables **compound** patterns. For example, the rule "odd after face card; even after nonface card" is a **compound** pattern. Most cause-and-effect patterns will be compound, and they are not nearly as easy to see as simple patterns. Pattern (5) is a compound pattern, and they are quite a bit harder to see than simple ones. Knowing that, can you see the patterns in (2), (3), (4), and (5)?

For most people, pattern (5) is much harder to see than pattern (2), (3), or (4). Pattern (2) is red, black, red. Pattern (3) is odd, even, odd. Pattern (4) is face card, nonface card, face card. Pattern (5) involves two variables, color and number. It is red follows odd, black follows even. If most of the patterns we are looking for in society involve at least two variables, then we are going to need a systematic method and some practice to find them. But even pattern (5) is very easy compared to the kind of pattern in (6), which we will call a **compound-complex** pattern. One thing about a card determines another pattern which holds for a while. Can you see pattern (6)?

Compound-complex patterns result when a pattern between two variables is affected by a third variable. They involve two "levels." Pattern (6) is red, black except that a face card changes the pattern and produces three odd, even cards. A very large number of different compound-complex patterns will fit any set of seven cards. Without considerably more than seven cases, you will never be able to distinguish the real one. If social structure were simpler than this, we might be able to ignore history and construct a one-level theory. Then, it would not be crucial to think dialectically about social structure. But what people call "human nature" is not based on a single, unchanging trait in each of us. People learn from each other. And, in social structure, what we actually find are patterns which involve many things and which depend on still other things.

Unfortunately, compound-complex patterns like (6) are often crucial to social structure. Most causal processes in society are conditional upon or affected by institutional structures. They are not always the same, in all times and places, and part of the reason is that they are bound up with views and norms and values that are not the same in all times and places. Compound-complex patterns are the rule, which is unfortunate because most people find it quite impossible to find them without some kind of a theory to tell them what to look for. (More technically, compound-complex patterns are nonlinear relations that result when the effect of one variable on another is affected either by its previous amount or by some other variable that has a "statistical interaction" with the first.) They are markers for the fact that not only does everything change, but even the process of change changes.

This kind of pattern is common; arguably the kind of linear pattern we often assume is only a rare, simplifying assumption; and that kind of pattern is also so complicated that many different patterns would fit a small number of cards (ten or fewer). Sometimes it seems that if compound-complex patterns are allowed, one will never be able to find patterns. There are any number of things which might cause (and affect) any number of things. Major parts of Marx's analysis are compound-complex. They involve ways the mode of production causes other institutional structures and patterns of patterns of cause and effect in the society. Some anti-Marxist sociologists say that this is an improper form of argument, a "historicist" form of argument. They say that you have to have absolutely general patterns in society (in which human nature, political power, education, incentives, or whatever always has the same effects, in all times and places) or you are not doing science. But we believe that the real patterns in society often are compound-complex. If you only look for "absolutely general" patterns, you cannot see the compound-complex ones.

The fundamental thing that finding patterns of cards shows is the enormous difference between hunting for a pattern when you know what the pattern is and hunting for an unknown pattern. For most people, it takes a long time even to find patterns which seem trivially obvious when they are pointed out. Why does it take so long? Often people look for patterns that are much more complex than the one which is there. They overlook a simple possibility. Sometimes people look for patterns which are simpler than the one which is there. They overlook the possibility that the pattern is more complex. When you do science, you are always threatened on both sides. First, you must always keep it simple. But second, if you try to make it too simple, you fool yourself or you decide there is no pattern at all, when one is staring you in the face. When you do social science, both problems are even more severe. When you look at poverty, human trafficking, unemployment, toxic wastes, violence, racism, urban decay, alcoholism, war, or selfishness, it is easy to mistakenly see patterns which are not there. And it's easy to overlook patterns which *are* there. That is one reason social theorists often disagree. Some analysts have suggested that some patterns are genuinely ambiguous or "bifurcating." For a time there are two different patterns, *both* of which fit. But eventually there comes a fork in the road. The system is pulled both ways and has to go one way or the other. Such patterns are often well-described as contradictions.

You can practice finding patterns of playing cards by playing a card game called Eleusis. A simplified set of rules is as follows: players take turns being "dealer," who writes down a rule such as "odd-even." This rule is a "law of nature," kept secret from the other players. A deck of cards is distributed to the nondealer players, and by turn they attempt to place one of their cards on a "truth" pile which the dealer starts. For each try, if the card fits the pattern, the dealer says "right," and the player submitting it gets a point. If a proposed card does not fit the pattern, the dealer says "wrong," and the proposed card is not added to the truth sequence, but discarded, and the player submitting it does not get a point. A round is over when some player gets rid of all his or her cards or when no other cards can be played. The dealer gets the difference between the high score and the low score on any round, to give him or her an incentive to pick a rule easy enough so that someone will see it, but hard enough so that not everyone will.

We learn several things from the game of Eleusis. We learn the enormous difference between looking for a known and an unknown pattern. All of our existence—social and natural—is intensely prestructured through the series of patterns and categories we are used to finding. This does not mean that reality involves merely the categories we take to it. It does mean that most of the "facts" we see are interpreted facts. Another thing we learn from Eleusis is that practice makes perfect. People get much better at finding patterns when they have found a few. This is the fundamental justification for becoming familiar with data and with many patterns in data before theorizing about it.

Suggestions for Further Reading

There is a large literature on whether, in general, findings and theories of the social sciences can or should be value-neutral. It is of limited usefulness in practical, particular cases. There is a debate on whether Marx has an ethical theory. See N. Geras, *Marx and Human Nature: Refutation of a Legend* (Verso, 1983) and "The Controversy about Marx and Justice," *New Left Review* (1984); A. Gilbert, "Social Theory and Revolutionary Activity in Marx," *American Political Science Review* 73:521–537 (1979). R. Miller, *Analyzing Marx* (Princeton, 1984) argues that Marx's moral arguments are fundamentally different from other moral arguments in a way that shows how those other moral arguments must be changed. On patterns: the perception of patterns involves problems of concept formation or induction. Central to phenomenology and dialectics, these are largely unknown continents. A towering work, H. Simon, *Patterns of Inquiry* (Boston, 1981), has shown that our practical facility at a conceptual scheme such as a language or chess playing involves recognition of some 10,000 "friends" or kinds of patterns. Eleusis is described in M. Gardner, *Mathematical Circus* (Knopf, 1979, pp. 45–55).

SECTION 4.6: IS SOCIETY BASED ON
THE THOUGHTS OF ITS MEMBERS?

Many issues in the philosophy of the social sciences have come to be clustered under the opposition between idealism and materialism within Marxism. We have already noted some. One of the most important of those issues is the ways in which social structure or social change is affected by the thinking and understandings of the members of society. This has produced the single largest opposition within the philosophy of the social sciences: the opposition between **explanation** and **understanding**. Some sociologists believe that understanding of the social world must be in terms of the thoughts and feelings of its members, like the understanding of a poem or play. Those understandings are usually of unique instances rather than regular patterns, and they cannot be independent of the values of the social theorist. We think that the entire opposition between the natural and the social world is largely a misunderstanding, which has to be dialectically dissolved.

Philosophers who split the realm of the social and natural sciences believe that the effect of force on a piece of chalk does not depend on what the chalk thinks, but the effect of using force on a person depends on what the person thinks of that force. From this, some philosophers conclude that understanding the mental world of meanings is fundamentally different from explaining physical events. They suppose a split between the process of **explanation** of the material world and the **understanding** of human meanings. One explains the trajectory of a bullet by reducing it to what it has in common with all other projectiles, they say, but one understands the actions of an individual just as one understands the works of Plato or Shakespeare by entering into the meaning of their actions and of their works as unique individuals. One explains the trajectory of the bullet by understanding the causes which operate on it, another understands the behavior of men and women by understanding the reasons behind it. While Marx, Weber, and Durkheim all agree on science, there is a fundamental disagreement between Marx and Durkheim on the one hand, and Weber on the other concerning the importance of understanding meanings. Weber defines this as the center of sociology as a discipline. Because Weber recognizes many traps and illusions of entering into the meaning of someone else, this means that he develops a complex and controversial account of how one constructs simplified representations of those meanings.

Because we are human and because we are social, all of us understand meanings and motives. Why did the chicken cross the road? To get to the other side. Why did Bill go to McDonald's? Because he was hungry. Why does GM speed up workers? To make money. We all make interpretations of this kind. They are the main conventional patterns which we are trained to see. But how important are they to sociological analysis? Some standpoints in sociology make the interpretation of the motives and intentions of human actions the beginning and the end of sociological analysis. At the present time there is a rapid rise in approaches to the study of society which resurrect this old opposition between the methods appropriate to the natural world and to the human, social world. Weber's stress on the social meanings of social behavior has been further extended by action theory, symbolic interactionism, and other approaches.

There is not too much one can usefully say about the importance of motives and meanings in general for explaining social behavior. We have seen that motives, wants, needs, and abilities are usually bound up with social structures of resources, contacts, and opportunities in complex self-reinforcing ways. Therefore, treating motives, wants, needs, or abilities as unmoved movers is usually deceptive. Interpretation of motives cannot be the sole or principal basis of explanation because people often are not sure of their motives, or are mistaken about them, or the same behavior is produced by many different kinds of motives. Consider the position of a plant supervisor. In times of unemployment, plant supervisors speed people up, forcing people to work faster. One may speed people up because he or she likes to see people sweat. Another may speed people up out of fear of being retired before his or her pension. Another may speed people up because he or she identifies with the general manager, or thinks stockholders are all "widows and orphans." It doesn't matter. Given capitalism, any supervisor will speed people up. If they don't, they won't stay supervisors for long. We have seen that the phenomena of racism and prejudice are good examples of this, that systemic and institutional processes of power and privilege are always bound up with the attitudes, and that the attitudes cannot be understood or changed unless we take account of the whole dynamic.

For Marx, motives and understandings are important, but they are never ultimate. Marxists look at the structures which produce those motives and understandings. These structures are tangible and objective. Marxists have maintained that the social realm, though complex, follows certain laws. Social arrangements and social processes have consequences independent of the will of participants. The effects of a rise in unemployment are as real as a rock. While it is true that what people do about unemployment is influenced by what they think about it, it is also true that a 10 percent unemployment rate has objective causes and definite consequences on things like alcoholism, suicide, infant mortality, divorce, or child abuse. People may modify these consequences by modifying the causes. But these consequences are just as objective as the causes and consequences of hurling a projectile into the air.

Sometimes we can approach the explanation of aspects of social behavior via the understandings of the persons in the society. To some extent we have all become sociologists in this sense because we have all spent our lives learning patterns of social behaviors. Common sense consists of a very large number of generalizations, but many of these are both mechanical (over-generalized) and weak. But if we limit ourselves to common sense and to the motives and understandings of participants, we always end up sharing in the illusions of an age. The understandings of citizens and party officials in Eastern Europe and the Soviet Union in the 1970s and 1980s would not have revealed the massive change which was about to occur. But that would not show that the changes were unpredictable or stemmed from the unfathomable personality of Gorbachev.

Suppose in the previous speed-up example that the conventional explanation involves the "widows and orphans." Suppose that any time you ask any supervisor why he or she is making you overwork, he or she dutifully tells you about the widows and orphans. Suppose that the workers tell you the same thing (somewhat tongue in cheek). Any sociologist who laboriously surveys these attitudes and who takes them seriously as causal explanations would conclude that if only people could be convinced that stockholders are not all widows and orphans, the speed up would stop. That conclusion would be wrong. The attitudes are a decoration on the structure, not the structure itself.

You will find that whenever you try to change a structure, it is work. Putting forward a certain idea, by itself, rarely changes anything. You will find that philosophical idealism is one of the things that helps social structures resist being changed. Whenever you start to change anything, many people will say, "No, you can't do that. Until you change people's hearts and minds, until you change people's values, until people are in therapy groups or until the teaching or preaching or culture changes, nothing will have any effect." Changing anything important often involves changing many other things, including attitudes *about* many things. It is very important to know what causes what, because otherwise one is always trying to make it rain by washing the car or opening an umbrella. One is reduced to trying to abolish capitalism by having long, serious discussions about whether stockholders are widows and orphans.

Exercise 4.6: What Are the Contradictions in a Table?

To get used to the idea that things have contradictions which cause change, let's take something much simpler than a society, such as a plain, wooden table, about which it seems that one can make perfectly noncontradictory statements. If we see why someone might say that it and all statements about it are contradictory, then we will be in a better position to understand statements about contradictions in the society or in classes. Look at the table in front of you. Are there important senses in which it is not what it is? Do the best you can to list five senses in which it is not what it is. Perhaps the simplest way to begin is to write down five simple, noncontroversial, true statements about the table. Then see if there are *important* senses in which the *opposites* of those statements are also true.

We have noted that the core ideas of Marxist philosophy are the ideas that everything is related to everything else; that everything contains contradictions, and that everything changes eventually, in qualitative ways, because of those contradictions. The interconnection and change in our ideas is a function of interrelation and change of things. Marxists believe that one can better analyze the interconnections and changes in society within a philosophical framework which sees the interrelation and change of everything.

Against this, some philosophers say that it makes no sense whatsoever to say that there are contradictions in anything—let alone in everything. They say that once you grant contradictory premises, you can prove anything whatsoever. We think that the idea that everything—rocks, society, individuals, chairs, tables—contains contradictions is often a useful way of looking at things. It is a way that takes some getting used to. Of all of the central terms and ideas of dialectics, none is used so often by Marx, and none gives beginners and experienced investigators alike more trouble than the idea of **contradictions**. Many books have been written arguing that it is a nonsensical idea. Even some sympathetic readers find themselves confused by it. It is an idea which can be misused to produce verbal garbage, but we will also find that it is a powerful idea, able to do a fair amount of work if we can make it behave.

Some people say that "there can only be contradictions between ideas; only an idealist thinks there can be contradictions between *things*." Is this true? Can there be a contradiction in a rock, a table, or an armadillo? The opposite of dialectic, the "law of noncontradiction" is often formulated as "everything is what it is; it is not other than it is." Is this true, and is this the only way to look at the world? Is everything really just what it is? Against this, Lenin has said that the central insight of all dialectics is that everything contains contradictions. Everything is not only what it is, it is also other than what it is. That fact is basic to explaining the dynamism and motion of things.

It is reasonably familiar to most people what it means to say that there is a contradiction between two statements. It is much less clear what are the contradictions within a simple true statement like "the cat is on the mat;" "the table is flat;" or "the leaves on the tree are green." It is still less clear, for many people, what it means to say that there are contradictions in a person or a political system. And it seems absolutely mystifying to some philosophers to say that there are contradictions in a table or a rock. But if everything is always in a state of change, and if those changes are not just the result of "bumping into other things" but also come about by a kind of "aging," the development and maturation of internal factors,

internal stresses, then the importance of understanding those internal
stresses and how they affect each other (and are affected by outside factors) becomes more obvious.

One can look at contradictions in anything, and it is often useful to do
so. Remember the analysis of contradictions we looked at in chapter 2. In
Capital, analyzing the relationship between the exchange of goods (commodities) and money, Marx says,

> The differentiation of commodities into commodities and money does not
> sweep away these inconsistencies, but develops a *modus vivendi*, a form in
> which they can exist side by side. This is generally the way in which real contra-
> dictions are reconciled. For instance, it is a contradiction to depict one body as
> constantly falling towards another, and as, at the same time, constantly flying
> away from it. The ellipse is a form of motion which, while allowing the contra-
> diction to go on, at the same time reconciles it. (CAP I, pp. 103–4)

Do not worry about the contradictions ("inconsistencies") in a commodity. In chapter 2 we saw that your table is a commodity, since it was made to
be sold. It is a use value and not a use value, a particular and a component
of general value. As a commodity, your table's **value** embodies a complex
relation to *history* and to *economic* agents. But for the moment, ignore that.
Marx says that when people didn't know what would happen out in space,
they had to build up the idea of an orbit out of two other ideas which were
inconsistent and incompatible with each other. **Before** we know about orbits, all we have to work with, in understanding the motion of the moon,
is "falling" and "flying away." Can something both fall toward the Earth
and fly away from the Earth at the same time? Well, it obviously depends
on what we mean by "fall toward" or "fly away from." But certainly as they
are conceived by common sense, something can't do both at the same time.
That is why common sense is often limited in solving problems in celestial
mechanics (and social theory).

Your table is probably flat, hard, solid, brown, stationary, wooden, and
useful for putting a beer on. Most tables are. What is contradictory about
that? Well, is your table unconditionally and entirely "flat," "wooden,"
"stationary," "useful to put a beer on," etc.? Aren't there some senses and
viewpoints from which it is *not* each of these? Concentrate on the idea that
an orbit is a contradiction. The science of mechanics tells us that an orbiting object really is doing two things which are inconsistent with each other.
Because of that contradiction, the orbiting object is doing a third thing,
different from either. Now apply that insight to the table.

Your table is probably flat, hard, stationary, etc. It would seem like folly
to argue about any of those characteristics. But consider the simple statement, "the table is flat." One of the things that it says is that the table is
flat, that something called a "table" bears some kind of similarity to all the

other things one terms "flat." Is there any sense in which the statement also says that the table is not flat? Is there a sense in which the table has some unlikeness, some differences, with the other things that one calls flat? You bet it does! A statement without any unlikeness, any difference at all would not convey any information at all. You would be limited to saying "the table is the table" and "the flat thing is a flat thing." It is because the table is *not only* flat that it conveys information to say that it is, among other things, flat. From one standpoint, it is only because the statement contains contradictions that it is meaningful! If every meaningful statement of likeness implies difference, it will not be difficult to find contradictions to any statement you may make about the table.

Not only does any meaningful statement about the table contain contradictions, the flatness of the table depends on one's standpoint. If you get closer to the table, modern science tells you that the flatness disappears. If you get close enough, the table is more mountainous than the Alps. It is less substantial than a cloud of bees. Is it a smooth, solid surface? It is porous and mountainous, covered with a liquid which is still flowing and which is chemically changing. Is the table just sitting there? Its parts are not even stationary but moving. Every molecule is in violent and unpredictable motion. Its subatomic particles are whirls. Is it just sitting there? Isn't it spinning around the Earth's axis at a thousand miles an hour? Isn't it spinning around the sun at thousands of miles per hour? The table is "pushing down" with all its weight, or it would fly off into space. To say that it is flat—or anything else—also depends on one's time frame. The table is not what it is because it is changing. There was a time when the table did not exist, and there will be a time when it will cease to exist. Nor is it merely sitting there, waiting for itself to vanish. It is disintegrating in front of your very eyes, but like the hour hand of a clock, too slowly for you to perceive it.

Thus, there are perfectly real senses in which your table is not what it is, or is not only what it is. At the very least, it is not only what it appears. Many philosophers speak of there being "two tables." There is the ordinary flat, brown, stationary table of common sense. And then there is the strange, vibrating, colorless, decaying, probabilistic table in constant motion, of science, physics, or chemistry. And the problem is that these two tables are the *same* table. And from other standpoints there are still others. We have seen that contradictory dynamics often involve contradictory views, definitions, rules, or values of participants. For example, a table is a product. It has uses. It has value. Much of its value depends how others regard it. Under these circumstances, the analysis of contradictions can become quite complex.

Not only are meaningful statements about the table contradictory, but the characteristics themselves involve contradictory and conflicting processes and points of view. To insist that the flatness, hardness, solidness, etc., of the table are all contradictory underlines the fact that *those characteristics are not unconditional.* The table is flat for some purposes and from some points of view. There are many processes going on in that table and there are many standpoints from which it can be considered. In nondialectical language, one would say that a statement like "the table is flat" only holds within a certain theoretical frame, and it only holds under certain empirical conditions. It involves the combination of different dynamic processes. The importance of this frame, those conditions, and those dynamic combinations are mainly hard methodological lessons that quantitative sociology has had to learn in the last generation.

When you say, quite rightly, that the table is flat, solid, sitting there, and useful to put a beer on, you are saying a good deal more than you mean. You are adopting a conventional theoretical framework about the table under particular empirical, historical conditions. That frame and those conditions are fine as far as they go. Maybe everyone knows just what the conventional theoretical and empirical frameworks are which stand behind such statements about the table. (We have found that everyone often disagrees about such frameworks concerning theories of social structure, and we have to be aware of them.) Maybe you don't need to know very much about the mechanics, the chemistry, or the cell structure of the table. Maybe your interaction with it is limited to the part of the world where those conditions and that theoretical frame hold well. But the whole of modern science has pushed back the limitations of those conventional views. If you had to say how the table would respond to stress, or how it would respond at a molecular level, or how it would look in a different society or how it will look in fifty years, then you would do well to relax those conventional assumptions. You would do well to analyze the contradictions in the table.

Your life does not depend on that table, and the future of the human race does not depend upon that table. Probably the table is not going to blow up in your face. Certainly it is not going to turn into a monster and begin eating you and your children. Whether the table lasts for ten years or fifty is no great matter. Conventional concepts and viewpoints on the table are probably quite sufficient. But they are also limited, and if your life did depend on them, you would want to expand them. And when the topic moves to the society or the world economy, we are not so secure that things will always be the way they now seem. Remember that some people now living saw the Great Depression, World War II, and the Vietnam War. Society seems to involve a somewhat more volatile set of contradictions than your table. When there are sudden, volatile, unpredicted changes, it is always useful to look for the conflicts, contradictions, and tensions which had been accumulating in the old society.

Dialectics can dissolve the apparent simplicity and unchangingness of the "flatness," "hardness," "goodness," etc., of the table. For some purposes, these characteristics are unproblematical. But for other purposes even a plain wooden table is dynamic, mystical, enigmatical, and it "evolves out of its wooden brain, grotesque ideas" (CAP I, p. 71). Marx's claim that an elliptical orbit *is* a contradiction does not try to substitute logical-dialectical manipulation of concepts for the whole process of scientific investigation that established the laws of mechanics. Marx and Engels are very clear that *dialectical analysis does not substitute for empirical analysis and scientific method.* But if we do not know about elliptical orbits, but we know about falling and throwing, we see that there are two things going on, and they contradict each other. A third development, *entirely different from either of them*, is the expression and resolution of that conflict or contradiction.

Suggestions for Further Reading

On explanation versus understanding, there is a voluminous literature arguing whether social explanations ought or ought not to be based on the understandings of actors. Most of that literature is *a priori* argumentation by philosophers. Among the arguments that both sides have an inadequate conception of science are R. Bhaskar, *A Realist Theory of Science* (Humanities, 1978) and *The Possibility of Naturalism* (Humanities, 1979). Most sociologists properly regard the matter as a practical contest as to which kind of explanation can explain the most facts, most generally, and most simply. On contradictions: although difficult to read, Hegel is the natural opening to dialectic. His *Logic* (Humanities, 1969) also has a short form within his encyclopedia (Oxford, 1873). Within the Marxist tradition, Lenin's *Conspectus of Hegel's Logic* has been the origin of much later work. For example, R. Routley and R. Meyer, "Dialectical Logic, Classical Logic, and the Consistency of the World," *Studies of Soviet Thought* 16:1–25. A recent overview of dialectic is F. Jameson, *Valences of Dialectic* (Verso, 2010). The analytic tradition, to which we shall return, is much less useful. For example, J. Elster, *Making Sense of Marx* (Cambridge, 1985).

SECTION 4.7: WHAT ARE IDEOLOGIES?

In chapter 1, we saw that an important disagreement between Marx and other sociologists is that Marx regards many ideas in law, politics, and religion to be "ideologies." He found people earnestly constructing arguments about truth, justice, or brotherhood in cases where people's actions were really determined by their interests. He found people constructing theories of social change in which the intrinsic development of philosophy, religion, law, or science were supposed to drive history, when in fact it seemed clear that other social and economic forces were causing the developments. We have suggested that the relationship between ideas and actions is complex. If social ideas reflect the distribution of power and influence in the society, and also reflect something about reality, analysis of ideas can be complicated. What makes it very complicated is that anyone doing the analysis is part of social structure, too, and so they have their own biases, interests, and standpoint.

The central Marxist concept referring to the social bases of our ideas is the concept of **ideology**. An ideology is a set of ideas that serves the interests of a group, particularly the class dominant in a society. Obviously, ideological statements can be false ideas used to justify a group's privileges. On the other hand, just because a statement is ideological does not mean that it is false. Just as the proslavery position that slaves were inferior to other human beings was clearly an ideological position, so too was the position of the abolitionists that slaves were human. In other words, understanding that a statement is ideological deals with the social functions and uses of an idea. Biases or outright lies may serve the interests of a group, but so might true statements. Ultimately, a statement is accurate or inaccurate depending on the facts. It is ideological depending on who can use it for what purposes.

Marx believed that the uses of ideas largely determine their availability and their transmission through society. No matter how sensible an idea seems to people at the bottom of the social structure, if it is threatening to leaders of schools, newspapers, parties, etc., then they will not transmit it accurately, and they will try to counteract it. Conversely, no matter how distasteful an idea seems to people at the bottom of the social structure, if it is useful to leaders of those organizations, then they will promote it and try to make it more palatable. Thus, many ideas become commonplace because they legitimize existing social arrangements. The likelihood that an idea will be put forward in a newspaper, a political speech, or a pulpit is a function of whether the idea supports the interests of the person who owns the newspaper, politician, or pulpit. This does not mean that it is impossible for other ideas to come into existence. It only means that those ideas will not take root if they do not serve the interests of a sizable group of people. Furthermore, if ideas seriously threaten the interests of the ruling group, they will be discouraged or suppressed. Even then, though, the history of humankind is often the history of how such unpopular ideas eventually came to be the prevalent ideas, as more and more people found them useful.

Part of the analysis of ideology involves analyzing how we form ideas, concepts, and beliefs. But this is very complex. In exercise 4.5 we saw that "just seeing" even a very simple pattern can be difficult. We see what we have learned to see and what we have been primed to see. We often see very complex patterns in society. Those patterns appear to be just *there*, with no intervention on our part, and in an obvious sense, we see them just by ourselves. Every idea is something that goes on inside our heads. We think for ourselves. But, on the other hand, our social experience is prestructured. A whole history, involving many people other than oneself, is involved in seeing even very simple patterns. In the United States, **individualism** is a very prevalent attitude. The conventional viewpoint is that one should form one's own opinions. This sometimes makes it difficult for us to see that every thought, feeling, or action has a social basis. Most thoughts take the form of words; thus, they are shaped by thousands of years of development of language. But besides language, there are many other ways that our thinking is influenced by our relationships, and by our position in the social structure.

For one thing, our every idea is partly adopted because it is available. If we lived in a feudal society, dominated by a feudal aristocracy, we would have different ideas because different ideas would be available for us to adopt. Schools, newspapers, televisions, political parties, churches, clubs, and gatherings all transmit ideas. But they do not transmit all ideas equally well. Certain ideas are filtered out and other ideas promoted depending on the control of those schools, newspapers, parties, etc. In this society, such organizations are usually owned by a board of trustees consisting mainly of businessmen. Besides such organizations, ideas can be transmitted by social friendships and personal contacts. But the patterns of those friendships and contacts also filter and limit what ideas are available. Not everyone in the society has an equal say as to which ideas become dominant in the society. To the extent that some people have predominant influence in schools, newspapers, etc., the ideas that are dominant in the society will be the ideas that reflect their standpoint and interests. Marx expresses this by saying that the ruling ideas of any age are the ideas of its ruling class.

As a young man, Marx was an editor, reporting and analyzing parliamentary debates concerning the rights of peasants to gather wood and laws concerning the relation of poor vine growers to richer landowners. In these debates, people spoke of nothing except truth, justice, and the logic of law. But the landholders who didn't want peasants to collect dead wood off their land did not really have a different set of philosophical views than the peasants. Or rather they did, but the reason they did was that they were in a different social position. People presented logic-chopping arguments about when a piece of dead wood ceases to be part of a tree or the land, but the fact of the matter was that landowners didn't want a bunch of poor people coming on their land and they wanted to be able to sell the wood. What was really going on was not disagreements about the logic of law. A sharper logic could not resolve the disagreements. *What was going on was that different groups had different interests and they legitimized and rationalized those interests in terms of truth, justice, and law.* And when Marx wrote about such issues, backers withdrew their support for the magazines for which he wrote.

A similar situation exists today in the world of corporate law. Many big corporations complain that it is too easy for them to be sued by dissatisfied customers. Or they complain about antitrust lawsuits against them saying, "It violates the spirit of competition; it interferes with efficient production." Yet these same corporations sue each other constantly. Or consider the battle going in the United States today over the right to record television shows, or to watch scrambled television signals that enter your house or to download music that, after all, is just a collection of electrical impulses traveling across the Internet. Both sides have brought up arguments from past court cases as obscure as whether someone who stands outside a bakery sniffing the sweet aroma of fresh baked pie is stealing from the bakery. Actually, both sides are developing their arguments on the basis of trying to protect their interests. Conservative politicians complain about government regulation of oil companies and then complain that the government did not prevent the 2010 catastrophic undersea leak caused by British Petroleum's drilling. Big pharmacy companies take different opinions on patent cases, depending on whether they want to copy someone else's drug, or someone is trying to copy theirs! It is common for executives and lawyers to even switch sides if the other company offers them more money, and then they spend their time developing high-sounding philosophical arguments against the positions they were defending just weeks before!

Sometimes ideological battles take place with hired spokesmen who debate for pay. Other times, ideological battles are conducted by people who really believe what they say. But in either case, people's own interests and their class position affect what they believe and what they hear. As in the case of the debates on the theft of wood, people's conceptions of what is right or what follows logically from law is influenced by their interests and by the beliefs of those people they know! And, of course, who they know and what the interests of those people were is influenced by their class position. Their resources for exerting political and intellectual influence are also influenced by their class position! All legal and political arguments and conflicts are ideological in this sense, and it is at least possible that that determines the ultimate fate of legal, political, or ethical arguments. The Marxist analysis of ideology uses this insight to develop a general theory relating people's ideas to the power and interests of different groups in the society. This kind of consideration convinced Marx that developing a philosophical system or making particularly clever arguments is not the fundamental source of social change.

The reason this is important is that the central concepts of sociology necessarily deal with topics which may have ideological uses. Certainly the central concepts of Marxism deal with such topics. Consider the question, "Is capitalism based on exploitation?" Marxism says it is, but liberalism says it is not. This looks like a disagreement in philosophy or *values*. Consider the disagreement in how to define class. Marxists define class in terms of relations to means of production and liberals define class in terms of occupational status.

This looks like a disagreement in *concepts*. Marx argued that political coercion and states were produced by the process of exploitation and the need of ruling classes to hold down subordinate classes. Alongside the procapitalist position, this looks like a disagreement of *theory*. Or consider, "Is the U.S. an affluent, middle class society?" Marxism says it is not. Liberals say that it is. They say that Marx misunderstood the modern class structure and the trends within it. And since the analysis of class and class struggle is very important to Marx, no criticism would be more damaging if it were true. This looks like a disagreement in facts or *data*. But all of these various issues of values, concepts, theory, or data really derive, Marxists believe, from ideological sources. And all these disagreements are clearly tangled up with each other. Whenever anyone argues anything, it is always possible to direct your attention away from what they say to their reason for saying it: their values, interests, standpoints, experiences, etc. Of course, they can always concentrate on your values or standpoint, too, and so the argument might get nowhere. The notion of "dialectic" partly involves the very large number of different ways that issues of various kinds may be involved with each other.

To begin to disentangle them, we shall examine one of the most pervasive ideological debates in U.S. sociology—the nature of class in U.S. society. Different conceptions of class serve the interests of different groups in different ways. Whether conscious members of the capitalist class, the working class, or those (like many sociology and political science professors) who consider "class" an inaccurate term, all these groups will have their real, or perceived, interests served by one or another set of answers to questions about who is on top, who is on the bottom, and why. Yet, as Marxists committed to a materialist understanding of the world, we understand that the answers are not hopelessly unknowable just because everyone has different standpoints. While no explanations can be completely true, some explanations can be much more accurate than others.

Marx viewed capitalism as based upon relations of production in which some people work and others benefit. Marx saw capitalism as based upon an objective relation of exploitation. Is this true? Is capitalism based on exploitation? What kind of statement is this? Is it a statement of facts, of theory, of paradigm, or of value? Terms like "exploitation" are sometimes used in an emotional, diffuse way so that they only mean that the thing so labeled is nasty and the person using the word doesn't like the thing. Marx does not use the term this way. In chapters 1 and 2 we saw that an exploitative society means something quite specific for Marx.

The picture of the United States as a middle class society is an ideological picture. It is a social product. No one walks around making a mental note of the bank accounts of the various people they see. Rather, a certain conception is developed by social institutions. Often there have been sharp battles over which conceptions are accurate or useful. Our present views are the outcome of those previous battles. The conflicts in sociology have not been identical to those in other disciplines, but those in academic disciplines have not been identical to those in the movies. But in all cases, the conceptions which become dominant are partly the result of the social forces and the social interests they represent.

Exercise 4.7: Where Does the View of the United States as a Middle Class Society Come From?

Sample several mass media: movies, magazines, TV, etc. How do they portray society? How do they portray production relations? How do they portray the poor?

Why? What determines which picture of a society becomes dominant?

So what? What difference does it make which aspects of class one concentrates on or what the facts of class are in America? What practical difference does it make?

We have argued that many facts about the class structure of the United States are grossly inconsistent with the common picture of the United States as affluent middle class society which has eliminated the extremes. If means of production are inexorably becoming more concentrated, if the income distribution is an Eiffel Tower in which most people are within a yard of the ground, then what accounts for the common view? If there are tens of millions of people below the poverty line, most of them malnourished, if you can see people sleeping in the streets of any American city, why do many people believe that extremes of poverty have been eliminated? If everyone knows that there are dozens of billionaires, why do most people have a view of the distribution and trends of wealth, income, and means of production which is incorrect? Did someone engineer the mistaken view? Did it just happen? How do people adopt a general model of the society? What determines which image of the society is dominant in the media and in the minds of most people in the society? What determines which image of the society is dominant in sociology?

The issue of class and stratification is complex. It is complex in Marx and it is complex in reality. Most of the arguments against Marx are really addressed against a distorted, oversimplified, nondialectical caricature of Marx. But there certainly is a very basic message in Marx: class society is oppressive, and it can be changed. We think that whenever substantial numbers of people have grasped this message—and that has happened repeatedly in history—enormous resources have been mobilized by the capitalist class to counteract the message.

Perhaps the easiest question to answer is what difference it makes. Practically, it makes all the difference in the world for changing the society. If the society is such that the great majority are pretty well off, then it is hard to see how one is going to convince anyone to change the society, and it is hard to see why anyone would want to try. Not only that, but built into the different concepts of class are very different implications concerning whether it is possible to abolish class. If classes are *defined* by different relations to production, then classes can be abolished by eliminating different relations of production, and that is the only way that they can be abolished. If, on the other hand, you follow Weber in defining classes and strata by many different variables—including income, status, and control, especially supposed political control—then abolishing different relations to means of production won't abolish classes. It won't even help and, according to Weber, it may make classes more unequal. According to that definition, there is no single way that one might go about abolishing classes and probably it could not be done at all.

You can define a word like "class" in many ways. But the disagreement between Marx and Weber is obviously not mainly a disagreement concerning the *meaning of words*. Concentrating on class or status, concentrating on relations of production or lifestyle is the result of a general theory about how class inequalities are generated. Marx thought that production relations generate other inequalities. He did not think that those inequalities would disappear simply by abolishing private ownership of production, but he did believe that as long as control of production was privately owned and inherited, abolition of those inequalities would be blocked.

The question of what picture is dominant in the media is also fairly easily answered. We think that you will find what other studies have found: enormous stereotyping and uniformity in the pictures of class and classes in newspapers, magazines, TV, and movies (especially movies made after many radical and pro-working class actors and authors were banned from the media—"blacklisted" during the McCarthyite period of the 1950s). In general, production relations are not pictured at all; only consumption relations are pictured. On TV, almost nobody works but the bosses (and cops and physicians)! The poor are invisible. The higher in the class structure you are, the more likely you are to appear in movies, in the news, or on TV. When workers or poor people are portrayed at all, they are stereotyped. Most sociologists' conception that the society was classless, affluent, and middle class did not precede but followed the picture in the media.

Common opinions about the affluent nature of U.S. society are often based on ideology rather than data. Looking at the class structure of U.S. society, why do you suppose that such a system would encourage the idea that the United States is a middle class society? The image of a middle class society is partly a media event and it is partly a function of exclusive concern with social prestige. Liberals believe that people think the United States is a middle class society because it is a middle class society. Marxists believe that people think the United States is a middle class society precisely because the high degree of concentration of wealth and resources allows a distorted picture to become dominant.

We do not think that the inaccurate picture came to dominate the media because it reflects everyone's experience. When people watch television, they don't always get what they want. Rather, we think that almost any picture of class is going to offend some people and to ring false to some people. The picture of blue-collar workers as virtually nonexistent or as stupid offends and/or rings false to some people. But when the people who are offended are relatively powerless, it is fairly easy for producers, directors, writers, and advertisers to ignore them. On the other hand, when the people who are offended are influential, very powerful pressures build up to change the picture which is offensive and to produce counterbalancing pictures. Moreover, producers, directors, writers, and advertisers have biases of their own.

Thus, the question of what the process is that determines which picture becomes dominant is complex. Sometimes the natural domination of the media, education, religion, and the written word by middle class people leads to a middle class picture. Capitalists have a decisive role, and sometimes they have a veto, and this can reinforce the middle class picture. But even with this, there are times when opposed pictures of the society intrude. At those times, more conscious efforts to promote certain views as desirable and to crush others as dangerous, subversive, and un-American have occurred. And the residue of such battles is that certain views are uncontroversial because we are used to them, while others strike us as biased because they are unusual.

Suggestions for Further Reading

The concept of ideology is one which is surrounded by submerged reefs. Many sociologists use the concept, and so do historians and philosophers, but different people include very different elements in it. Two useful contemporary treatments are N. Abercrombie, et al., *The Dominant Ideology Thesis* (G. Allen Unwin, 1980) and G. Therborn, *The Power of Ideology and the Ideology of Power* (NLB, 1980). The concept of ideology (and the converse ideal of a situation where views and discussion are not distorted by inequality and power) is the basis of the influential philosophy of J. Habermas. For example, *Theory of Communicative Competence*, two volumes (Beacon, 1981, 1989). Useful broad discussions of Weber and status are in G. Therborn, *Science, Class and Society* (NLB, 1976) and E. Wright, *Class, Crisis, and the State* (NLB, 1978). Wright correctly describes Weber as the "Lenin of the Bourgeoisie," ibid., pp. 181–204. Weber and Lenin were contemporaries, with large experience and concern with actual parties and states, and with intense political commitments. They were on opposite sides. Two introductory treatments of the distribution of wealth, income, and status (both written from functionalist standpoints) are J. Turner and Starnes, *Inequality, Privilege, and Poverty in the United States* (Goodyear, 1976) and D. Gilbert and J. Kahl, *The American Class Structure* (Dorsey, 1982).

SECTION 4.8: WHAT CONTRADICTIONS EXIST IN SOCIETY?

Marx and later Marxists often speak of "contradictions" in society. It is one of the most characteristic and distinctive elements of Marxist analysis. Up to this point, we have used the term **contradiction** to refer to a variety of different tensions, conflicts, or opposed principles or processes. For example, in chapter 1 we looked at the contradiction between the forces of production and the relations of production—times when the very social arrangements crucial to the development of personal, social, and technical forces are also responsible for strangling, frustrating, and inhibiting them. In chapter 2, we saw that Marx views a number of different contradictions as linked: socialized production versus private appropriation; workers versus capitalists; organization and monopoly within firms versus competition and anarchy between firms; and the mode of production versus the mode of exchange. Marxists view these contradictions as overlapping and reinforcing each other. And in chapter 3, we saw that different political principles and different social forces come into conflict with each other, and we argued that these conflicts or contradictions constitute the dynamics of the system as a whole.

In exercise 4.6 it was said that there is a reasonable sense in which *absolutely everything* contains contradictions. And so we are now in a better position to understand the idea of social contradictions. Part of what Marxists mean when they speak of contradictions in a society is the same as what they mean when speaking of the contradictions in a rock, a chair, or a table. The things that are true of the society are not true unconditionally or eternally, but only for a certain period. In the same way that a table both is and is not flat, is and is not stationary, is and is not useful, so important characteristics of a society are only conditionally applicable. Defining the limits of those conditions gives a clearer idea of what we do know and what we do not know. By itself, this is no small insight. One of the main reasons that Marxism stresses process, change, interconnection, and conflict in the whole universe is to make us sensitive to process, change, interrelation, and conflict in society. Sometimes it is particularly hard to see process and change in the society. No one supposes that a chair or a table or a rock will last forever. Usually we are lucky if a chair lasts for twenty years, and it is quite extraordinary for one to last eighty years. But when it comes to social structure, sometimes we are powerfully tempted to suppose that what we see is what has always been and what will always be. If we see prisons, slums, banks, armies, racism, sexism, classes, war, and states, we suppose that even primitive tribal societies must have had them. We suppose that they are eternal, that they are built into human nature. We may even believe that one has not defined a social scientific concept unless it refers to something which is general to all societies and historical periods.

Study of history helps break down this illusion. A conceptual scheme that highlights the dynamics, the conditionality, and the limits of social structure also helps break it down. This is one of the reasons that Marxists say (and anti-Marxists deny) that all social structure contains contradictions. It is partly a way of saying that there is pervasive change and conditionality about social structure.

But social structures do not only have the kinds of contradictions that a table or a rock has. Societies are more complex than rocks, and they have other kinds of contradictions as well. We can further understand why Marx speaks of contradictions in everything if we think of examples when we say that the behavior of a person is self-contradictory. Imagine a man who deeply believes that it is important not to lose his temper, but he always puts himself in situations where he can't keep from losing his temper, and he is not willing to go through the process of change which gives him control over his temper. We feel comfortable saying that his position—indeed, that his whole way of life—is self-contradictory. He may say that he supports the end (not losing his temper) but he is not willing to support the means necessary to that end. The person is frustrating himself and living a life which is inconsistent with his own wishes and values. He is living a contradiction.

In addition to the simple contradictions in chairs or tables, societies and people also have contradictions in this sense. Societies create certain kinds of needs, values, and aspirations. Sometimes a society systematically frustrates the realization of the central values which it creates. Indeed, from a Marxist standpoint, part of the dynamics of human history is that all societies create needs and values which are necessarily frustrated within that society. And that is a motor of history, a basis of change. Specifically, capitalism, in opposition to feudalism, created a *philosophy* in which work is valued, people are regarded as equal, and a leisure class is regarded as parasitic. But, at the same time, it created a social *reality* of enormous inequalities and great top-heavy bureaucracies headed by a leisure class.

Not only that, but also one's ideas are influenced by one's position in the society. The analysis of ideology suggests that all ideas which one finds in the society have their origin in the life situation of specific groups in the society. This means that most of the opposed groups and conflicting processes in the society will be associated with opposed ideas and beliefs of different persons—beliefs and ideas which contradict each other.

Exercise 4.8: Networks and Basebuilding

What is social structure? If it has both "ideal" and "material" components, what distinguishes them? As an example of a "material" component, consider the people that you *know*, that you see, that you talk to. How close are you to a capitalist? To a politician? To a homeless person? To a Latin American guerilla? How do you *know* what they are like?

We have already looked at some issues that often get posed in terms of the opposition between idealism and materialism. But there are more. One of the most important issues concerns relationships. Marxists usually maintain that class positions have to be defined in terms of relationships. It is because of their relationships to nonworkers that workers are workers. It is because of their relationships to nonbosses that bosses are bosses. This stress on relationships rather than those characteristics that are true of individuals *per se* turns out to link Marxism to one of the most important and rapidly growing fields of sociology—the analysis of networks of relationships rather than categorical attributes.

The analysis of relationships is also particularly important for issues concerning ideology, since relationships are often the principal way that people acquire information about or wants concerning the social structure. Aside from books, schools, and newspapers, where does our knowledge of social structure come from? Consider the relationship of being friends with or having chains of friends which connect you to various kinds of people.

Consider the five categories of persons listed in table 4.1. Do you know any "black workers"? (A blue-collar worker is intended, but let's not worry about the definitions of the five categories. Give each a reasonable interpretation.) That is, are there any black workers to whom you could say, "Hello, Constance," and they would be able to answer "Oh, hello, Fred." (Thus by friendship, we don't mean anything very intimate. Is there someone in that category whom you know by name and they know you by name?) If you do, put his or her name down under "Name," and under "Length of chain" put a one (1). If you do not know a person in that category, under "Name," put the name of someone you do know who you think is more likely to know one. If you think she personally knows a black worker, then it would take a chain of two links to connect you to that person. Under "Length of chain" put a two (2). If you think she does not, but that she knows someone who does, then it would take a chain of three acquaintances to connect to the worker, and so you would put down a three (3), and so on. Thus "Length of chain" gives measures of how socially separated you think you are from the categories of people in the table. Fill in the whole table before proceeding. (It is logically possible that there are some categories of persons to whom you cannot connect with any chain of acquaintances, no matter how long. If you think that that is the case for any of these, put "999" under "Length of chain.")

Table 4.1   Chains of Acquaintances

Category	Acquaintance	Length of Chain
Black worker		
Hispanic worker		
Capitalist		
Communist		
Latin American guerilla		
Politician		
Al Qaeda terrorist		

This exercise concerns patterns of relationships. A simple illustration of a relationship is being "friends." It is the basis of a powerful contemporary school of sociology. Patterns of friendships seem unimportant and easily changed, but they turn out to be more powerful and more difficult to change than one might think. Patterns of acquaintanceship reach far. Very often when you meet someone for the first time, you can ask him or her a few background questions and then ask, "Do you know so-and-so?" Often, you find a common acquaintance the first time! This is the "small world" phenomenon.

To illustrate the power of networks of acquaintances, a sociologist named Stanley Milgram gave letters to people in Wichita, Kansas. They were asked to send the letters to personal acquaintances who might be more likely to know the target person, the wife of a divinity school student in Cambridge. All the intermediaries put their names on the letters, so that one could find out how long the chains had to be, as well as some other things about them. Although no one knew the target person, some people knew someone who knew her; many people knew someone who knew someone who knew her. *On average, the letters took less than six jumps to complete their journey.* Why? Most of us know about 500 people by name, when you add relatives, friends, coworkers, neighbors, former schoolmates, fellow members of the glee club, and so forth. Most of these people do not know each other. Your Aunt Sally does not know your coworker Bob. To the extent this is true, you know 500 people directly; you share a common acquaintance with 500 × 500 (or 250,000) people; you know 500 × 500 × 500 (or 125,000,000) people by a chain of three links; by four links you connect to more people than exist on the face of the Earth (although barriers and overlaps will make the chain longer).

What this implies about the table you filled in a little while back is that you almost certainly overestimated the actual length of the chains. Networks (often in the form of "grapevines") are very powerful for getting information and for mobilizing people to do anything. A number of studies have shown that the degree of power, or ability to be mobilized, and the distinctive beliefs of different people result from the patterns of who they know. It also implies that we are both more connected and more separated than is usually apparent. There may well have been "a connection" between the Baath Party of Saddam Hussein and the Islamic fundamentalist, Osama bin Laden, despite their being absolute polar enemies of each other, because networks create connections between virtually every person on the face of the planet.

Check on the pieces of your own network you described in table 4.1. Ask each of the persons you wrote down under "Name" whether they do, in fact, know a person of the type specified. If so, ask who the person is and what they are like. If not, it may be that one of your other acquaintances does; it also may be that your personal network gives a highly filtered, ideological view of that category of person. To the extent that this is true, you should think about what kind of evidence you would need to find out what they are "really like."

Not only do chains of acquaintanceship reach far, but they have distinct patterns. Differences of race, religion, occupation, sex, region, etc., create barriers. While these barriers are never insuperable, they distort one's picture of the world. Various tensions and contradictions in your thinking result from the different messages passing to you along chains of friendship as well as the different messages you read in the newspapers. Your ability to check on or act on those messages depends on those patterns. Activist political organizations have long known this. For example, some Marxist groups have argued that "basebuilding" is fundamental basis for political activity. If you wish to help mobilize a group, you must have a "base" among that group. A base is a circle of people whom you know, who know you, and with whom you spend time. One can get a set of people to change the pattern of their friendships, just as one can get them to pick up and move a pile of rocks if they believe it is important to do so. But it is no easier to change the pattern of your acquaintanceships than to move a pile of rocks. It takes work.

When a solid network of acquaintances exists, and *when* a large group of people has the potential to be moved, it is literally possible for one person to move 500, who move 250,000, who move 125,000,000. This is as easily done as Fred's calling Joe, who calls Mary, who calls Bill. A spark can light a prairie fire, but the basis of this is the structure of the spark and the prairie.

Suggestions for Further Reading

A very large number of works have attempted to analyze the concept of class or social contradictions in Marx. There is no innocent account, and no account can be evaluated independently of its substantive theory. Among the most important works from within the Marxist tradition are L.

Althusser, *For Marx* (NLB, 1970) and M. Godelier "Structure and Contradiction in Capital, " in R. Blackburn, *Ideology in Social Science* (Random House,
1973). An important contribution from within the analytic tradition, arguing against the position taken here, that the term "contradiction" is only
useful in cases like that when a society creates wants which it frustrates, is
J. Eister, *Logic and Society* (Wiley, 1978).

   On networks: the Milgram experiment is described in *Psychology Today*,
1 (1967). Two useful introductions to structural network analysis are: S.
Berkowitz, *Introduction to Structural Analysis* (University of Toronoto, 1982)
and B. Wellman and S. Berkowitz, *Social Structures: A Network Approach*
(Cambridge University Press, 1988). An example of an activist discussion of
basebuilding is "Build a Base in the Working Class" reprinted in *Revolution
Today* by the Progressive Labor Party (Exposition Press, 1974) and available
at www.plp.org. Many of the writings of Mao Zedong, especially his early
writings, are sharply focused on the need for organizers to have deep ties
with the people they are working with.

SECTION 4.9: CAN ONE FIND LAWS OF CHANGE IN HISTORY?

One of the principal sources of sociology in the nineteenth century was philosophies of history. This is not only true of Marxism, but also of the liberal
sociologies of Durkheim and Weber. In the nineteenth century, history was
often the main body of empirical evidence about development and interrelation of social structures. Political developments like the French Revolution which seemed abrupt, discontinuous, and unpredictable when the
actions of "great men" were considered by themselves, were often analyzed
as the manifestation of powerful, predictable, underlying processes. We
have argued that history shows the interconnection and choice and change
of social structure. Historians had developed many ideas and insights about
those changes, and philosophers of history had attempted to organize and
develop those theories and insights.

   Most philosophies of history and most historians had argued that histories were more like a rope than like a pile of sand. At any point in history,
if you cut through the events and relationships of people's lives, you find
something that has an intelligible structure. And if you cut longitudinally,
looking at some components of that structure over the course of time, you
also find an intelligible structure. And history is about how these weave
together. Except for the fact that they looked at the past rather than the
present, much of the data, the theories, and topics in histories were what
sociologists would study today. Some historians concentrated on statesmen
and "great men"; others concentrated on unique individual events rather
than on aspects of events that were lawful or recurrent. But history and the

philosophy of history were major sources of sociology. When historical sociology or Marxist theory is criticized as being only a "philosophy of history," it is important to clarify what the criticism is, because sometimes the criticism is nothing but name-calling.

Philosophies of history had to answer the question: is there any pattern to the course of history? It is obvious that some events are more patterned than others. A common image for the course of history is the course of rivulets, streams, and great rivers. The *particular* course of a river is not completely determined, because it can be changed fairly easily. But its *general* course is very hard to change. Water flows down to the sea, no matter how you divert it. Build a dam; one river moves a little, but the overall system doesn't change. It is possible for there to be large-scale order even when details are turbulent and chaotic.

But other kinds of actions seem to make a great deal of difference. They seem to cumulate rather than wash out. "For want of a nail, a shoe was lost. For want of a shoe, a horse went lame. For want of a horse, a man was lost. For want of a man, a battle was lost. From loss of a battle a kingdom was lost. . . ." The nursery rhyme gives a different picture of historical change than of streams running into rivers, running into the sea. People with these different views are likely to approach the analysis of social change, history, and the relation of sociology to history in very different ways. Are human actions like the stream? Are human actions like the "want of a nail," supposedly changing the course of human history? We think it is quite evident that human actions, *in general*, are neither like one nor the other. Some are like one and some like the other. *A priori* arguments for or against determinism in the large are equally mistaken. In the eighteenth century, at the time of the French Revolution, the German philosopher Immanuel Kant gave an image of historical determination with which we can start:

> Since the free will of man has obvious influence upon marriages, births, and deaths, they seem to be subject to no rule by which the number of them could be reckoned in advance. Yet the annual tables of them in the major countries prove that they occur according to laws as stable as the unstable weather, which we likewise cannot determine in advance but which, in the large, maintain the growth of plants, the flow of rivers, and other natural events in an unbroken, uniform course. (*On History*, 1784 [1963], p. 11)

In Kant's metaphor, the wind and weather stand for individual actions. They are each variable and "undetermined by any rule." The river results from the sum of those individual actions; it is regular, predictable, and determined. The wind and the river represent the lawfulness of an overall development behind the random, accidental components of that development. The wind and the river are images of **contingency** and **necessity**.

This view is now basic to virtually all sociology, although it was popularized in sociology by Durkheim rather than Kant. At the time that Kant wrote, it was not clear why a sum of random events would be predictable. Nor were there very good statistics on marriages, births, deaths, or the economy. By the twentieth century, there were fairly good statistics. Durkheim could show that even phenomena like suicide, which look very random and unpredictable, follow a regular pattern which can be explained by fairly simple laws. At the present time the whole discipline of statistics is founded on the central limit theorem which predicts the (necessary, lawful) distribution of large numbers of random (accidental, unpredictable) events. Most sociological models involve probabilistic processes. Whole bodies of sociology deal with the highly uniform character of births, marriages, suicides, and depressions. While an insurance company obviously does not know when you, in particular, will die—no one knows that—they can calculate the probability that you will die in the next year to five or six decimal places, and they would go out of business if they couldn't.

Many of the main changes in human social structure and history are more like the river than the nail. They have a pattern and dynamics which are very resistant to change. For example, it was discussed that the decline of feudalism and the overthrow of the French monarchy by the French Revolution was relatively determined. The stupidities of a particular king could make it happen sooner rather than later, the particular actions of leaders could make it happen one way rather than another. Perhaps very unlikely circumstances might even have postponed it from happening in France at all throughout the nineteenth century. But we think France would then have become a backwater. The armies tearing down feudal regimes would have come from somewhere else. And even in France, overwhelming pressure would have built up by the twentieth century to get rid of those institutions, one way or another.

In 2004, there was a sarcastic bumper sticker that read: KERRY FOR PRESIDENT. WE'LL GO BACKWARD LESS FAST. Whether one agrees with the sarcasm or not, the philosophy behind it captures this concept. On the one hand, it was predicting that with Bush as president of the United States, the U.S. economy and the standing of U.S. political and economic power in the world would deteriorate more rapidly, but on the other hand, the decline was going to happen no matter who was president. The same debates occur over questions about whether World War II "had to happen" because of the huge build up of economic and political pressures or whether it was caused by the so-called "madman" Hitler.

Thus, with regard to the question whether history has laws or patterns, we think that not everything is determined, but the broader outlines of the biggest and most important changes generally are. One of the tasks of sociology is to look at them. The law of large numbers says that often when one takes a longer or larger view and looks at more people, an analysis may become simpler and the causal forces operating become clearer.

Exercise 4.9: Why Are People Unemployed?

Even before the melt-down of the world financial system, and the resulting worldwide recession, in the United States, according to official definitions, more than 10 million people were unemployed. Some alternate definitions and estimates of unemployment would place the rate of unemployment about twice as high. Why are these people unemployed? List several sources of unemployment. Does unemployment result mainly from individual or social causes?

In explaining poverty, unemployment, and other social problems, some explanations focus on the attributes of individuals. Other theorists regard those explanations as a way of blaming the victim. It is always possible to construct a victim-blaming explanation. If a woman is raped, it is always possible to say that if she had been somewhere else or had done something else, she would not have been raped. But the idea that women always rape themselves, or want to get raped, or are at fault if they are raped is a crazy and sexist idea.

Focusing either on poverty or on unemployment, construct at least two explanations, one of which concentrates on the *individual* level of analysis—relating people's unemployment to their personal characteristics. Your other explanation should concentrate on the *structural* level of analysis—relating the unemployment to characteristics of the society.

Most American students find the individual kind of explanation much easier to construct. We have looked at some of the political and social forces which affect the unemployment rate. But in case you have difficulty constructing a structural explanation, here is a preliminary exercise which may help you. Think of the grade you are getting in one of your other classes. Are there some aspects of yourself which would help explain it? Are there some aspects of the school which would help explain it? List each.

An apparently simple question like, "Why did Janet get an F in physics?" actually conceals a host of different questions. Two very important kinds of questions operate at the individual and the structural or collective level of analysis. There are probably all kinds of reasons peculiar to Janet as to why she got the F; maybe she wrote a terrible exam, because maybe she is working nights; or maybe she was partying before the exam, because maybe all her friends party; or maybe she went to a poor high school, because maybe she lived in a poor neighborhood. You could make a list of reasons of this kind as long as you like. *No matter how long you made the list*, it would still not get at another set of things. For example: what is the distribution of grades? Is there a grade curve in physics? What is the curve?

Let us suppose that physics grades are curved—they usually are—and that the curve allows 10 percent As and 20 percent Fs. All kinds of social forces determine the distribution. The curve results from the schooling and attitudes of the teacher. Maybe a dean is worried about grade inflation and sent around a memo, because maybe there are only so many slots in law school and the dean is worried about the standing of the school. Or maybe the physics department is concerned about the standings of its graduates relative to other schools and departments, etc. You could make a list of reasons of this kind as long as you wanted.

In much of our social life, we take these structural forces for granted. But in fact there usually are structural forces operating. If one is a teacher, one is more aware of forces affecting the curve. But even that is not always true. It may be that one semester you give too many As or Fs and disagreeable consequences happen. After that, you may avoid making that mistake again without even being aware of the process. Certainly a student, while aware that there is a curve of some kind, usually pays attention to what determines his or her place on the curve rather than the curve itself. Students may even come to assume that there is a law of nature producing As and Fs.

There are explanations for unemployment at both individual and structural levels. At the structural level of analysis, some sociologists think the main reason that people are unemployed is that there are more people than jobs which pay a living wage. To the extent this is true, any pressure (or help) which you give the particular unemployed persons will not change the unemployment rate much. It will move the unemployment around but it will not change the total number of people and the total number of jobs. If you apply coercion to the unemployed to make them work, they will undercut the wages of those at the bottom of the job market. If you give them a little help, then they may fit in a little higher up. But if there are more people than jobs, they will move into jobs which other people will have to vacate. The amount of unemployment will stay essentially the same.

By contrast, at the individual level of analysis other sociologists take the neoconservative view that the main reason for unemployment is the characteristics of the people who are unemployed, especially the view that they are lazy and expect a free ride. If that theory is true, then attempts to increase the number of jobs will not change those people and their expectations. Indeed, if the problem is that too many people want a free ride, the worst thing to do is to attempt a collective solution, which will merely convince more people that they deserve something from the government. That will make matters worse.

These two explanations contradict each other. The practical conflict between the two theoretical analyses is very sharp. To the extent that one analysis is right, following the prescriptions of the other analysis not only will not make things better, it will make things worse.

In the case of the grade curve, both answers could be true, operating at different levels. But in the case of overall unemployment, both of the answers cannot be true. They give opposite predictions as to what will happen under various circumstances. The reason for this is that there is not only a question about the processes at the individual and the structural level, there is also a question of a different kind as to which of these aspects of the situation is the *main aspect*. Once again, we can live in any number of different worlds, theoretically, but practically, there is only one world.

Is there a structural mechanism which determines the level of unemployment? Could all the unemployed find work if they had the will to do so, and would that eliminate high unemployment? If not, why not? What other mechanisms might exist? Does some structural mechanism determine the distribution of means of production? The distribution of income? Could everyone make $50,000 per year? If not, why not? Could everyone become a physician? If not, why not?

For Marx, the relations of production are the key structure underlying the distribution of unemployment as well as income, wealth, social status, and other social goodies. Not everyone can become a boss, even in theory, because it takes many workers to make a boss a boss. In the abstract, everyone could have equal income, or wealth, or social status, and everyone could have a decent job. Those concepts are not logically inconsistent. But according to Marx, they are actually inconsistent with the functioning of capitalism. In practice, great inequalities in wealth, income, and social status have proved absolutely intractable under capitalism, and there are theoretical reasons to suppose that as long as capitalism survives, they will continue. Specifically, with regard to unemployment, unless there are fewer jobs than people who need them—millions fewer—then wages will rise and capitalism will not remain profitable. When capitalism is not profitable, it grinds to a halt. When it grinds to a halt, unemployment is "spontaneously" produced.

Moreover, it generates a powerful political force working toward less than full employment. Historically, there have been enormous battles over the labor market. In Marx's day, battles about land and enclosures, the length of the working day, colonies, and welfare ultimately boiled down to pushing millions onto the labor market or pulling them out of the labor market. This may not have been how they were talked about, but it was the most powerful way that they affected others—both profits and wages. And the same is true about somewhat different political policies today, including manipulation of immigration policies, etc. Both individual capitalists and any government devoted to making capitalism work must ensure that there are "sufficient" people looking for work. Both politically and individually, every device, every policy, and every process which dries up the pool of people looking for work is a terrible threat of rising wages and declining profits and they look for ways to counteract it, even though too much unemployment can become a source of serious social instability, as well. Every device or process which adds to millions unable to find work relieves a terrible problem, namely the threat of full employment. By a variety of means, a massive pool of unemployment is maintained.

At the same time, it is convenient to have explanations of unemployment which blame the people who are unemployed. The process of coercing the presently unemployed into the job market, undercutting the wages of those now there, is precisely what increases profitability. It is money in the bank. Thus, one has the ironic outcome that the leisure class—the class of people whose income stems from ownership and property—creates unemployment. They point the finger at the millions of people desperately looking for work, saying, "You lazy bums. Why, if you would only be willing to work cheap enough, I would hire you to shine my shoes and to undercut the wages of my present workers. Your unemployment is your own fault."

Suggestions for Further Reading

On the varieties of collective subjects, see M. Hannan, *Aggregation and Disaggregation in Sociology* (Lexington Books, 1971). It can be argued that the concept of a collective subject is the central one for the existence of sociology as a discipline. There is an elaborate philosophical literature on methodological Individualism, mostly of questionable usefulness to practicing social theorists. For sources, see J. O'Neill, *Modes of Individualism and Collectivism* (Heineman, 1973). One contemporary line of analysis is P. Knapp, "The Revival of Macro-Sociology," *Sociological Forum* 5:545–67. On unemployment: simple and reasonable estimates of real unemployment as being twice the official unemployment rate (adding involuntary part-time unemployment, discouraged workers, and disguised unemployment) appear in H. Sherman, *Stagflation* (Harper & Row, 1976, pp. 8–19). R. Boddy and J. Crotty, "Class Conflict and Macro Policy," *Review of Radical Political Economy*, 7:1–19, discusses wage pressure on profits and unemployment. The respects in which an apparently simple question like "Why did Janet get an F in physics?" conceals a host of different questions has been clarified by A. Garfinkel, *Forms of Explanation* (Yale, 1981).

SECTION 4.10: WHAT POSSIBILITIES ARE OPEN TO HUMAN SOCIETY?

At the beginning of this chapter, we said that dialectics says that everything changes. Dialectics is a way of seeing things in their development and their change. If we are to see things in their development, we have to synthesize the various standpoints from which they can be considered and we have to deal with the contradictions between those standpoints. Each standpoint is limited. Dialectics is a way of avoiding the limitations of one-sided standpoints, a way of avoiding being impaled on the horns of false dichotomies. Each of the sections and exercises in this chapter can be interpreted as a central structure of dialectics. Dialectics involves the relation of ideas and reality, explanation and understanding, the relative and the absolute, theory and practice, the general and the particular, fact and value, the necessary and the contingent, the individual and the collective, and more. Many sociologists feel that they are beyond such "speculative philosophical issues." Often, this merely means that they are not aware of the issue, but the issue is no less troublesome for all that.

There is no abstract, conceptual, philosophical method for solving these problems. Dialectics in Marxism is not something which is entirely separate from substantive conceptions of social structure, history, politics, economics, etc. Usually avoiding a one-sided standpoint requires a specific, substantive multileveled theory concerning how various processes combine. One's language or concepts cannot solve such problems alone. They cannot provide the needed theory or data. But they can make it easier to solve them and to be aware of them. Anything that you can say in one conceptual scheme or in one language, you can also say in another. But often you cannot say it nearly as well or nearly as easily. Many laws and insights of physics which are clear and simple in mathematical language are very difficult to say accurately in words, without using math. Of course, if one does not know mathematics, then one will have to be satisfied with an unclear or an inaccurate version. The same is true of dialectics and Marx's theories.

Dialectics says that everything has relationships to everything else. But often one has to know what are the most important, particular relationships in order to say anything about how something will behave. Dialectics says that everything changes as a result of its internal contradictions. But often one has to know just what are the *principal* contradictions in something to know how it will change. Marxists say that capitalism has fundamental contradictions such that it will eventually be replaced by egalitarian communism. These contradictions involve opposed processes, principles, and groups of many different kinds. But they all come together in class conflicts.

We noted that the distribution of wealth and income forms elongated towers—upwards of 950 miles high, in the case of assets—and most people in the world are just a few inches off the ground. If you concentrate on people's perceptions of income and wealth, you get a very different picture from the one you get if you concentrate on the objective distribution of wealth. In people's perceptions, middle class status, race, religion, ethnicity, nation, and many other groupings are at least as real as class.

Are they real? Or are they merely ideological illusions? Or are all social structures just a product of what people think they are? No scientific or materialist perspective can say that society is just what people think, without asking why people think that way. From a dialectical perspective, nothing is unconditionally real: not a society and not a piece of granite. But things have consequences. One would be well advised not to eat the granite, believing that it is only an illusion. Many of the relations in which we are involved have consequences—including consequences for class struggle—of which we may be unaware. They are more real than we think. Many of the relations in which we are involved appear unproblematical, eternal, and built into human nature; but they turn out to be temporary, historical, and transitory. They are less real than we think. Marxists believe that classes are more real, and nations and races are less real, than popular perceptions allow. But even with respect to classes, it is important not to slide into a mechanical viewpoint.

Classes exist as patterns. Thus, if one measures differences in attitudes and behaviors, one may well find differences of which most members of the society are unaware. But, in addition, classes exist as objective possibilities. They are like the lines of fracture within a crystal, invisible to the naked eye. But if you look at the crystal with special instruments, you can detect chemical and physical flaws. Does their invisibility to the naked eye mean that the lines of fracture don't *really* exist, that they are metaphysical, that they are merely the fantasies of jewelers? Of course not. The fact that they are not easily visible means that it is easier to be mistaken about them, but the chemical, physical, and practical existence of those lines of fracture do not depend on their being visible. They depend on flaws in the crystal and on the structure of the crystal as a whole. They determine how the crystal will, in fact, break.

Classes exist as patterns, and they exist as patterns of patterns—as compound-complex patterns. For Marx, classes and mode of production are not only important because they affect people strongly; they are important because they powerfully affect how other things affect people. The state or individual wealth or greed or selfless ideals do not always have the same effect. And the organization of production has a powerful effect on how other things affect people's lives:

> I seize this opportunity of shortly answering an objection taken by a German paper in America, to my work. . . . In the estimation of that paper, my view . . . that the mode of production determines the character of the social, political, and intellectual life generally, all this is very true for our own times, in which material interests predominate, but not for the middle ages in which Catholicism, nor for Athens and Rome, where politics, reigned supreme. In the first place, it strikes one as an odd thing for anyone to suppose that the well-worn phrases about the middle ages and the ancient world are unknown

to anyone else. This much, however, is clear, that the middle ages could not live on Catholicism, nor the ancient world on politics. On the contrary, it is the mode in which they gained their livelihood that explains why here politics and there Catholicism, played the chief part. For the rest, it requires but slight acquaintance with the history of the Roman republic, for example, to be aware that its secret history is the history of its landed property. (CAP I, p. 82)

What Marx argues is not so much that economic and class structures always determine human behavior but rather that they determine which structures do dominate human behavior. There is a tendency to collapse the analysis down to the one-dimensional economic determinist view. Understanding Marx's historical approach and dialectical method is crucial if one is to avoid this tendency. To avoid that tendency is essential if Marxism is to open up the new possibilities for the human race.

Exercise 4.10: The Dialectic of Class Structure, Struggle, and Formation

We have suggested that an important aspect of dialectics, for Marx, concerned the circular relation between capacities and opportunities, between our needs and our actions, between culture and social structure. As the French say, "Appetite comes with eating." If and to the degree that we think that an ethnic group or gender is incapable of responsibility, we will deprive them of the positions that allow them to develop and show that capacity, and that, in turn, will lead to a set of people who benefit from the exclusion and promote the ideas of incapacity. If and to the degree that we believe that reasons of war or of the choice of what to produce are too difficult to be understood by ordinary people, we will end up supporting structures and policies which require an elite and elite support. If and to the degree that people are too dumb to create a better world, we will support a world that makes people numb and dumb. What you want and what you are able to do obviously affects what you do. What you do equally affects what you want and what you are able to do. It is an often vicious cycle, and Marx always argued that it is class struggle and class consciousness that gets us out of the cycle and that educates the mass of the population about dead ends such as nationalism, racism, and sexism. Dialectical dynamics often hinge on the self-reinforcing and self-developing character of human capacities, needs, and wants. In Marxist theory, production and class struggle are the process by which people develop capacities, and particularly the capacity to take a wider standpoint than their own, narrow self-interests.

The possibilities open to the society often depend upon the situation and the oppression of those at the bottom or base of the society. If in "spaceship Earth," millions of people are sleeping in the street, so that an elite can have 100,000-square-foot mansions, then virtually all other arrangements in the society will be affected by that fact. And, Marx suggests, in the last analysis, the way the human race grows up is by the process of changing the society and dealing with the massive structures of privilege and the dynamics of war and racism generated by class privilege. If that is true, how do you suppose that it works? Erik Wright proposes that the core of Marxian dialectical theory centers on the relationship between class structure (inequality), class struggle (i.e., the conflicts between classes about the direction for the society), and what he calls "class formation" (i.e., structures of organization and solidarity). Before we examine his theory, what do you think the relationship is between these three structures?

Wright argues that the class struggle not only reflects and affects the class structure, but also transforms it. The class formation not only reflects and affects the class struggle, but also it selects which of several different kinds of class struggle will take place. He investigates these relations in terms of survey research about political attitudes, mobility, and friendship and marriage patterns in the United States, Sweden, and Japan. How do you imagine that the attitudes and the relationships differ in the three countries? What, if anything, can these differences tell us about the global processes of social change and human development that are the central concerns of Marxian theory?

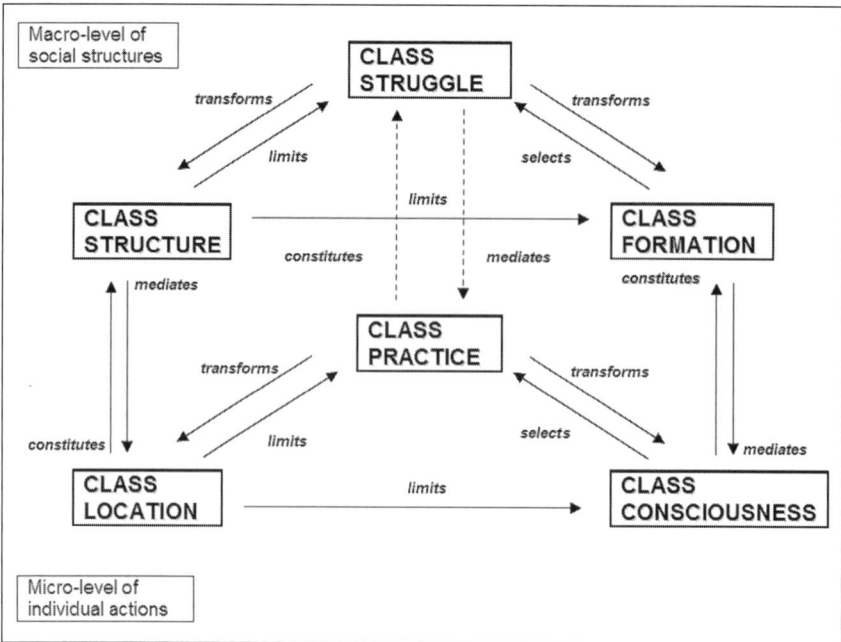

Figure 4.1 Wright's Model of Class and Class Struggle

Earlier, in chapter 1.3, we looked at Wright's parable of the Shmoo, the imaginary beast that lifts the floor of the society, eliminating "the whip of hunger." Wright argued that different groups have different interests about Shmoos. They may be more or less conscious of their interests, and they may disguise them, but capitalists' self-interest is to kill Shmoos, unless they can keep them only for themselves. They benefit from the existence of poor and vulnerable groups. In contrast, Wright argues, the self-interest of workers is that Shmoos be distributed as widely as possible; they benefit from raising the floor and eliminating vulnerable groups. This does not mean that all workers are altruistic and all employers are selfish, though many are. It means that the self-interest of employers is bound up with maintaining pools of poverty and vulnerability, while the self-interest of workers is bound up with eliminating them. The actual, historical organizations, sense of solidarity, and mass ideas that determine how these interests are worked out is the subject of considerable Marxist theory and research.

We have noted the body of Marxist scholarship called "analytical Marxism" that attempted to dispense with dialectics in favor of the methods and assumptions more congruent with mainstream quantitative research. Theorists such as Cohen, Elster, Prejeworski, Roemer, and Wright have attempted to conduct research inspired by the Marxist tradition but detached from dialectics. The problem that they faced is that the kinds of polarizing and discontinuous development which, as we have stressed, are pervasive in society and which Marxists analyze dialectically do not lend themselves to the methods in common use in the social sciences. Therefore, each of the analytical Marxists was forced, in one way or another, to reinvent the light bulb—or rather to reinvent different pieces of the light bulb which, separately, do not give much light. Thus, Cohen used functionalist analysis, arguing that historical materialism is based on the thesis that the relations of production are functionally related to the forces of production. Jon Elster developed a form of methodological individualism in which society is just the actions and intentions of individuals. But since the actions of individuals often interfere with each other, so that no one's intentions get realized, Elster developed frameworks for analyzing times when, in the absence of organization, the actions of separated individuals conflict with the intensions or needs of each individual. John Roemer rejected the labor theory of value in favor of a much looser conception of exploitation, according to which lenders can exploit creditors, or workers can exploit managers, if they would be worse off without them. Wright argued that many Marxist analyses are an attempt to deal with structures of causality that are more complex than those dominant in the empirical social sciences. Wright has tried to develop more complex kinds of causality and more sophisticated concepts of the relation between individual action and social structure. Figure 4.1 represents the results of that analysis. Wright's model is based on what he calls the dialectic of structure and practice—the view that social structures are the product of our actions, our practice, and that our practice is the product of social structure. Thus, each of the analytical Marxists, having rejected dialectics, has gone about reinventing elements of dialectical analysis, using concepts such as game theory or functionalist analysis. The pieces may, in some sense, be "clearer" than the dialectic of classical Marxism, and the pieces of a watch are clearer when they are laid out on a table, than when they are inside a watch. But like the pieces of a watch laid out on a table, they do not work very well.

Any science makes some simplifying assumptions; but the question is whether the assumptions clarify or obscure the essential, important features of the thing being studied. Most of the analytical Marxists have assumed that causal influences can be analyzed into its parts. Many, such as Elster and Roemer, further believe that social structure should be analyzed as a product of individual choices. Most empirical social science models are based on what is called a "linear" model, in which more of the cause produces more of the effect, invariably, regardless of other conditions. It is recognized that this model is a simplification and that a great deal of causality in the real world is what we call "nonlinear." For example, the amount of gasoline in a car has a linear effect on the distance it will go (but not regardless of whether there are roads), but not on the speed it will go. With respect to speed, gasoline has an effect; a car will not go at all unless there is some gasoline in it, but how fast it will go has nothing to do with how much gasoline it has in it. Similarly, the effects of having gasoline in the tank and having an electric charge in the battery are not additive and linear; they depend on each other. If either one of them goes to zero, then the car will not start, and the other one has no effect at all. Nonlinear dynamics are immensely more difficult to deal with than linear dynamics, and they are currently undergoing explosive development in the natural sciences.

Wright's model consists of three kinds of nonlinear relationships concerning the class structure, which he called "transformation," "limitation," and "selection." His analysis of income in *Class Structure and Income Determination* (1978) had showed that the effects of education on income are not independent of one's relation to means of production. For the bourgeoisie, there is a very large effect of education on income, for managers and the petty bourgeoisie, the effect is much smaller, and for workers, the effect of education on income is almost negligible. It appeared that education promotes higher income only when it is combined with social relationships that give one control over other's labor.

Wright's books, *Class Counts* (Cambridge University Press, 1996) and *Interrogating Inequality* (Verso, 1994), developed these ideas. They show both the importance of complex, nonlinear forms of causality and the difficulty of analyzing such relationships without a dialectical framework. What the top of Figure 4.1 says is that at the macro level (at the level of analysis of the whole society and the comparison of different societies) the nature of the class struggle transforms both the class structure (i.e., what economic slots exist) and the class formation (i.e., what forms of organization and forms of class solidarity exist). But the class struggle does not drop out of the sky. Only when the organizational and mass consciousness have been built can certain forms of class struggle appear (class formation selects forms of class struggle) and only in certain kinds of class structure can certain forms of class struggle appear (class structure limits form of class struggle). Thus, for example, comparing the United States to Sweden and Japan, the fact that the Swedish Socialist party has governed Sweden for most of the period since World War II is partly the result of the fact that Swedes are much more likely to agree with an attitude item such as, "corporations benefit owners at the expense of workers and consumers." Respondents in Japan were the least likely to agree, and respondents in the United States were somewhere in between. And Wright also found that there was the greatest difference between employers and workers in Sweden, the smallest difference in Japan, with the United States somewhere in between. Employers always get their position articulated; the strength of the counter position depends on the organization and struggles of workers.

At the bottom of Figure 4.1 Wright argues that similar relationships exist between class consciousness, class location and class practices. Wright argues that the level and nature of class practices transforms both class consciousness and class location; that class location limits class practices and class consciousness; and that class consciousness selects which of several possible class practices occurs. Although Wright is not a methodological individualist, the element of his analysis that most closely corresponds to the methodological individualism of the analytical Marxists is that each of the micro-variables describing individual behaviors "constitutes" the macro-variables; class structures, struggles and formations are the sum of what individuals do as class location, practices, and consciousness. Wright also assumes that the large scale structures "mediate" the individual behaviors.

Figure 4.1 looks complicated, and in one sense it is. The set of nonlinear relationships and feedbacks between even as few as 6 variables (or complexes of variables) that are pictured there are at the very limit of our ability to analyze. However, in another sense, the figure is obviously oversimplified and much too neat. For example, the symmetry by which the relationships between the micro-variables at the individual level are exactly the same as the relationships between the macro variables is not very plausible. The fact that the outcome of class struggle is a transformation of the class structure does not imply that the outcome of one's class practices will be a change in one's class location. An individual who engages in action to reduce inequality is not, thereby, himself or herself upwardly mobile. Indeed, individuals sometimes obtain upward mobility precisely by abandoning or betraying their co-workers.

Wright's books have only investigated a fraction of these relationships, and he would be the last person to claim that he has fully investigated the relationships modeled in the figure. He notes that "at first glance it may seem that the empirical studies in this book have little to do with such grand visions [i.e., aspirations for an egalitarian, democratic society and analysis of the conflicts and struggles that it would take to get there]" (*Class Counts*, p. 519), and many Marxists would say, and have said, that it is not news that measures of class consciousness, friendship patterns, and marriage patterns are affected by ownership, authority, and skill. Nor is it news that they are affected by ownership the most and by authority the least and that they are most affected in a country like Sweden and least affected in a country like Japan. However, demonstrating in detail that something is true is different from supposing that it is probably true, and one of the differences between them is that once an empirical finding has been laid out in detail, it can be built upon in a way that an abstract thesis never can. Wright notes that most of the relationships which are pictured in figure 4.1 are not well operationalized in terms of survey research and that it is important not to overestimate the usefulness of survey research methods in testing Marxist theories. Wright's analysis of survey data answers some questions about the nature of the class struggle in these countries and it raises further questions about the nonlinear relationships involved, that will keep researchers busy for decades. However, they have lost touch with some of the motivating questions about the dialectical process of the development of human capacities.

While it is important not to overestimate the usefulness of survey research methods in testing Marxist theories, it is important not to underestimate it either. While there are many times when dialectical modes of thought can run far beyond our ability to test or to operationalize, the connection of theories to empirical research data is one of the kinds of practice crucial to Marxist theory.

Suggestions for Further Reading

Wright is notable in the degree to which he has engaged his critics in works such as *The Debates on Classes* (Verso, 1994). Examples of criticisms of Wright's analysis include P. Kamolnick, *Classes: A Marxist Critique* (General Hall, 1988) and Gubbay, Review of *Classes* in *Historical Materialism*, vol. 5 (1999).

SUMMARY AND CONCLUSIONS:
CONTRADICTIONS, DIALECTICS, AND SCIENCE

We have now very briefly discussed ten topics concerning Marx's dialectical method. As one can see from what we have written, much of what we discuss as the Marxist dialectical method does overlap with other mainstream methodologies to some degree. But there are some fundamental differences, distinctive aspects to Marxist methodology that allow for a fuller, more dynamic explanation of social institutions, social processes, and social change. By way of summary, let's go back to the guideposts that we offered in the Preface, to expand them in order to cover some of the points we have just discussed:

19. **The World Exists Outside of Our Consciousness**. Marx believed that there is a material reality which exists outside the total control of willpower and consciousness. Our consciousness is part of the reality of the world, and therefore our consciousness is capable of acting on the reality of the world, in accordance with its laws. Indeed, it is in the course of acting upon the world, in practice, that one expands one's knowledge of the world. Others' consciousnesses and others' actions are a major part of the reality of the social world. One form of acting on the world involves talking, arguing, and discussing with others. This has tempted some talkers to think that the social world is nothing but consciousness and that it can be changed by pure talk. But what we have, who we know, and how we relate to others is not just mental. There is a real world, and the social realm is part of it. This set of ideas is woven through many sections of chapter 4. Sections 4.1 and 4.8 developed the idea of the objective reality of relationships and understandings. The concepts of ideology and practice also concern the material reality of ideas.

20. **Everything Changes in Qualitative, Irreversible Ways**. Materialism asserts the objectivity of the world, and dialectics asserts that it is not inert. Everything is in constant, dynamic flux. Rocks change. Ideas change. Social structures change. Even the process of change changes. This simple, basic idea is at the core of Marx's method. It is easy to say, but working out what it implies about the analysis of particular theoretical issues is far from easy or simple. Many things appear unchanging. Many changes appear gradual and reversible. But Marxism says that ultimately every process experiences qualitative, irreversible changes. This set of ideas, too, is woven throughout the chapter. It is fundamental to Marxist attempts—and all genuine attempts—to do social science because science is not simply concerned with measuring and counting. Science is concerned with understanding processes and

patterns of change. These patterns are often complex. In an abstract way, we illustrated this change in the pattern of change by crises, turning points, and the kinds of patterns which we called compound-complex patterns. What happens if you try to impose a pattern which is not dialectical, which is not compound-complex, on a reality which is? You may falsify or misperceive the pattern; you may find yourself forced to construct a very weak theory that asserts some pattern but only probabilistically or for a relatively short period, without being able to see any larger patterns of which the pattern is a part. Finally, you may simply give up the task of finding the relevant pattern, asserting that there is no pattern at all—that all patterns are illusions. To a considerable extent, non-Marxist sociology has been forced to adopt each of these strategies. Nevertheless, we have suggested that kinds of complex patterns, like those in neighborhoods or ecological systems, with turning points and discontinuities, are the topic of a many twenty-first century social science theories, and Marx's dialectic, the understanding that everything changes, can help us avoid false, weak options and build those theories.

21. **There Are No Absolute Truths, but There Are Concrete Truths**. To reject either of these ideas would destroy any reason to do science. Absolute truth implies that there is absolute authority to impose it. In that case, there is no need for scientific investigation in as much as none of the essential parts of the universe are subject to change. On the other hand, if there were no order, no pattern, no concrete truth, there would be no basis for science. There is order and regularity in the world, including the social world. But this order is not prior to the changing universe. *It is implicit in the patterns of change themselves.* We know much, even when we know that every item of our knowledge will be shown partial, incorrect, and in need of qualifications. In line with this, Marxism rejects all theories of total determinism, whether of a mystical/religious/fatalistic or a mechanical/pseudo-scientific variety. But conversely, Marxism rejects both idealist and relativist theories of total nondetermination. We saw that it would take a concerted effort to create a situation of absolute disorder. Asserting a position of absolute disorder to avoid dogmatism is making absolutist assertions. It is making a very dogmatic error.

22. **Humans Change. There Is No Fixed Human Nature**. From the fact that everything changes, it follows that humans change. From the absence of absolute truth it follows that humans are neither inherently good nor inherently evil. Humans change. Humans are capable of thought and of passing on what they have learned to other people in the form of science, technology, culture, etc. But what ideas people have are the result of their experiences, mediated by their relations

to others. It is a false stereotype that Marxist theory denigrates the individual as a helpless pawn of broad historical forces, or worse, as a kind of rat in a psychology experiment, helplessly dependent on external stimuli. Because we can learn, we can change the world. Social structure is the outcome of historical struggles. The outcome of these is a set of relationships which are real. They affect consciousness and the rest of the world. Human consciousness, with greater or lesser understanding, can react back upon the social world as also the natural world. Ideas and ideology are important for sociology in two ways. Sociology involves the science of ideology, the study of the ways that social structure conditions ideas. But sociology must also be sensitive to the ideology of science, to the fact that all our ways of looking at the social world are saturated with ideology. This is relevant not merely to the particular studies of ideology, but to the general connection between Marxism, values, partisanship, and practice.

23. **Social Structure and History Can Be Studied Scientifically**. Cause and effect is just as pervasive in the social realm as in the material world, and just as objective, because the social realm is part of the material world. Social relationships such as social networks are still quite real. Social reality is part of material reality, and it effects changes in the rest of the material world. Your friendship with someone can be the crucial fact in getting your automobile started in the morning. Even elusive concepts such as "morality" can be explained and understood. While rejecting dogmatic notions of a morality fixed for all time, Marxism rejects the relativist notion that what is best for people is a matter of taste. Assuming agreement on some fundamental needs, it is always possible to consider what structures objectively meet those needs. Needs change, and one can also discuss the importance of various needs. In all this, the situation is not materially different from what it is in any other theoretical disagreement. We may not fully understand everything, but this does not make all opinions equally valid. Theories, paradigms, and even values, the most general principles people use to guide their lives, are formed. They are formed by one's experience in the world, by the information one absorbs from personal experiences and experiences of others, by data about the social world, and by general theories about how the world works.

24. **One Must Examine the Contradictory Forces, the Contradictions that Lie Within Everything, Especially Social Phenomena**. For some people, this is the most perplexing idea in Marx. It need not be. Take any statement about any characteristic of anything whatsoever. It turns out, in fact, that that characteristic is not unconditional and eternal. It is true, given certain meanings, assumptions, and temporal

limits. The statement turns out, in fact, to hold only within certain empirical limits. Pushed beyond those limits, the statement is not true, but false. Why is this important? For one thing, to fail to know the limits of a true theory is to fail to know its truth. For another, social processes also occur within conditions and limits. Beyond those limits, crises and turning points often occur. All science grows by focusing on the limits to the truth of its statements. In the social realm particularly, the historical process of change and the social conflict of different groups push processes and structures beyond their limits. What was true becomes false. What was good becomes bad. What conformed to one model conforms to another. Without some conceptual means for looking at the opposed objective tendencies in things, the process of historical change tempts some to a relativism that denies all objectivity. It tempts others to a mechanism that denies all change. The idea of contradictions is no more mysterious than to say that everything is in a state of constant development, of aging. External events can and do impact on this development, but it is crucial to understand the process of change going on within a thing, or a process, or a society. Thus, for Marx, the importance of studying classes is not just to draw an elaborate chart specifying where each person fits. It is important because class contradictions are the main driving dynamics of historical change.

Index

absolute, 293
absolute surplus value, 120
absolute truth, 360
accomplishments, 242
accumulation, 24, 61–62, 71, 81, 92, 96–97, 113, 118–19, 124–25, 134, 155, 187–88, 190, 200–1, 218, 262, 267, 308–12
acquaintance, chains of, 342
activism, contradiction between determinism and, 194
Aid to Families with Dependent Children (AFDC), 98
Alexander the Great, 40
alienation, 19, 32–33, 84–91, 204, 289–91; economic, 86–87, 107; empirical analysis of, 90–92; ideas, 90; individualism, 90; institutions, 90; kinds of, 88–90, 204–5; means of production, 21, 25, 29, 88, 204; political system, 88, 204; process, 88; product, 88–90; surplus value, 89; value, 89
al Qaeda, 342
American Civil Liberties Union, 55
American Civil War, 73, 223
American Dream: achievement of, 163, 225; as a reality, 163–68

American Nazi Party, 55
American Revolution, 73
anarchism, 268
anomie, 32, 288–91
anti-communism, 228–29, 235
Anti Duhring (Engels), 111
antielitists, 250
anti-Marxist theorists, 108
antinaturalism, 292
antipositivism, 292
antiscientism, 292
antiwar movement and the Vietnam War, 248
a priori arguments, 192, 301, 331, 345
Aristotle, 39–41
Asiatic empires, 26–28

bads, 22–24
basebuilding, 340–44
Berlin Wall, destruction of, xi
Bernstein, E., 253
BETA, 99
Bettelheim, C., 260
bias, 300
bigotry, 293
blacks, concentration of in the working class, 224
Blumberg, L., 59, 65

Bohemian Grove, 207
borrowing, over-reliance on, 190–91
bourgeoisie, 21, 52, 56, 203–6, 245, 338, 356
Brown, John, 74–78
bubble, 62, 170–4, 179, 190–1, 213–15
bureaucracy, iron cage of, 32, 289
bureaucratization, 289–91
business cycle, 128, 217

capitalism: contradictions within, 108–10; dynamics of, 109; and education, 166; and exploitation, 334–36; and freedom, 275; importance of profit in, 119–20, 122, 129, 209; Marxist critique of, 34; political resources under, 203–11; productivity of, 120, 200; return to in Soviet Union, 213, 223, 246; strangling tendencies in, 80, 105, 110, 169, 312, 339; two class system in, 28, 48; world development of, 80–84
capitalist class, 89, 90, 93, 105, 144–45, 171, 200, 203, 206–9, 211, 216
capitalist production, 89, 123, 126, 127, 129; contradictory tendencies in, 115, 195, 205
Capital (Marx), 5, 13, 107
cause and effect relationships, 194, 286, 381
Chavez, Caesar, 232
China: agrarian bureaucracy in, 27, 74; Cultural Revolution in, 262; lessons of, 264–67; split with the Soviet Union in, 254; unemployment in, 262
circulation mobility, 166
civil society, 21
Civil War, origins of, 5, 73, 75–78, 223
class: abolition of, 251; as basis of social structure, 13–16, 26, 36–37; changes in, 27, 36–37; definition of, 42, 44; elimination of, 1–2; exploitation of, in U. S., 92–101; and stratification, 46–49
class contradictions, 86, 107, 110, 155, 246, 362
class-for-itself, 159–61

classical liberalism, 54, 107, 197–98, 295; see also pluralism; conservative, 54, 99, 194
class-in-itself, 159-61
class societies and accumulation, 201–9
class structure in the United States, 46–49, 62, 62, 289
class struggle, 2, 8, 44–46, 66–68, 104, 145, 193, 195, 199
Cloward, R., 98–102
Committee on Economic Development (CED), 207
commodities, 83; definition of, 112; exchange value of, 115–17, 122–23, 131; production of, 114–15, 118, 123–28, 328; use value of, 115–17, 122–23, 131; value of, 8, 112, 120, 189
common sense, 283, 288, 292, 326, 328–29
communism, 2, 27, 99, 140, 197; comparison of, with fascism, 226; opposition of, to fascism, 227, 238; and socialism, 227, 246–47, 250–51
Communist Manifesto, 3, 4, 67, 247
communist societies, contemporary survival of, 251, 261, 264, 277
comparative historical research, 16
competition, 54–57, 123–26, 130, 144, 183
compound-complex patterns, 321–22, 352
compound patterns, 320
conceptual issues, 35, 43
concrete truth, 9, 293, 360
consciousness, existence of world outside of, 9, 30, 281–82
contemporary historical sociology, 16–17
contingency, 292, 345
contradictions, 9, 20, 44, 68, 77, 104, 108–10, 122–27, 131, 135, 162, 170, 225, 234, 244, 283, 290, 306–8, 322; class, 44, 86, 107, 111; existence of, in society, 65, 72, 77, 80, 111–12, 154, 160, 339; of forces and relations of production, 31, 80, 172; in a table, 326–31

convergence, 59–60
corporate elite, 178, 207
 corporate state, 199, 233, 269
Coughlin, Father, 227
Council on Foreign Relations (CFR),
    207
critical theorists, xii, 281
Critique of Political Economy (Marx),
    5, 89, 107
crucial experiments, 312–15
culture: analysis of, 9, 18, 56, 103, 353;
    as a basis of social structure/change,
    21, 25, 108, 162, 227, 326

data, 38, 51, 86, 139, 241, 284,
    296–98, 314, 335, 358, 362
democracy: formal, 56, 210; and
    freedom, 54, 197, 244–45, 247; and
    private ownership, 200, 272; sub-
    stantive, 210; in the United States,
    197–99
democratic socialists, 199
dependency theory, 184
dependent development, 183–88
determinism, 9, 72, 108, 193, 265, 267,
    280, 282, 292, 345, 360;
    technological determinism, 259
Devine, J., 175–80
dialectical approach 279–84; to change,
    196; to freedom, 196
dialectical contradictions, 108, 213,
    306
dialectical method, 108–9, 194
dialectics, 2, 279–361; in analysis of
    social problems, 80; and change,
    234, 265, 280, 351; and crisis, 125,
    201, 280, 312; and crucial experi-
    ments, 312–16, 331; definition of,
    275, 279–80, 306; game of Eleusis
    in, 320–23, 360; ideologies, 69–70,
    143, 222, 228–29, 331–38; as a
    language, 109, 125; and laws of
    change in history, 27, 109–10; and
    networks in basebuilding, 341–42;
    and neutrality, 271; ontological,
    282, 284; and pseudo-neutrality,
    300–6; relationship of facts to theo-
    ries, 281–83, 300, 331; and science,

7, 108–9, 311; and self-reinforcing
    processes, 128–29, 281–83, 353–57
dictatorship of the proletariat, 197,
    243–51
dictatorship of the bourgeoisie, 203
discrimination: racial, 145–54, 223,
    239; sexual, 239
dogmatism, 269, 292–93, 297, 360
Domhoff, W., 206–7, 212
Durkheim, Emile, 18, 21, 32–34, 82,
    132, 199, 246, 286–91, 346

Eastern Europe, re-establishment of
    capitalism in, 169, 191, 244, 261,
    288, 326
economic alienation, 88, 170, 188, 204
economic contradictions, 29
economic crisis 23, 167, 183, 192, 216,
    276
economic cycles 216–20
economic determinism 25, 105, 154,
    193–94
economic reductionism 108, 288
economism, 268–69
education 166–68, 178
Edwards, R. 153, 219
egalitarianism, 238–39, 250, 256–57
Eiffel Tower of Wealth, 154
Einstein, A., 313
Eleusis, game of, 320–23
elitism, 145, 197–200, 250, 259, 269,
    273, 277
empirical issues, 35
Employment Act (1946), 213–14
Engels, Friedrich, 4, 5, 11, 25, 31, 11, 244
Enlightenment philosophers, 16, 18
epistemological dialectic, 284
equality of opportunity, 162–63, 166,
    169, 244
ethics, 28, 39, 291, 318
ethnocentrism 293
Evans, P., 185–87
exchange value, 115, 122–23, 131, 170
expropriation, 61, 81, 88, 166

factory, life in the, 116–18, 127
Fascism, 73–74, 77, 105, 200, 216,
    222–30, 234, 240

feudalism, 28, 45, 52–53, 300, 340, 346
forced-draft industrialization, 260
forces of production, 27, 31, 34, 80,
    169, 237, 259–60, 339, 355
Ford Motor Company, 126, 181, 184,
    187
Ford, Henry, 137
foreign investments, effects of, 175,
    181–89
foreign workers, wages of, 121
formal democracy, 210
France, socialist party in, 74, 252
freedom, 16, 85, 117, 156, 229,
    244–45, 274–75, 281, 319; theories
    of, 105, 128–29, 189, 196–99, 284
free society, basis of a truly, 195–200
French Revolution, 3, 15, 18, 39,
    71–78, 344–46
Friedman, Milton, 55, 65, 123, 169, 199
functionalist theory, 18, 20, 25, 36, 43,
    49, 51, 65, 254, 287, 339, 355

Gamson, William, 241–43
generalizations, 110, 296, 326
General Motors, 260
genocide, 23, 222–24, 231, 235
Genovese, E., 75, 78
Germany, 3–5, 18, 72–74, 86, 195,
    216, 223, 226, 229, 235–38, 249,
    274, 317
Glorious Revolution (Great Britain,
    1688), 72
Google Earth, 47, 81, 84, 116, 155, 233
Gorbachev, Mikhail, 263, 326
great financial crisis of 2008, 62, 108,
    167, 170, 180, 215, 306, 308
Griffin, L., 102, 175–80
Grundrisse (Marx), 5, 107, 127

Hegel, G. F. W., 4, 5, 17–25, 35, 42, 52,
    84, 87, 160, 246, 281, 284
Hicks, A., 99–102
Hispanics, 167, 183, 222, 224, 301, 342
historical materialism, 5, 25, 26, 34, 80,
    154, 291, 355
human nature, 25, 28, 39, 110, 144,
    195, 265, 276, 282, 293, 321–23,
    340, 352, 360

hypothesis testing, 92, 274, 305, 316

idealism, 5, 194, 196, 285–87, 292,
    324, 326, 341
ideology, 4, 21, 54, 56, 68–69, 86,
    90–92, 145, 153, 159, 161–63, 205,
    228, 236, 256, 272, 286, 294, 300,
    302, 332, 334, 338, 340–41, 359–61
imperialism, 82–83, 179–81, 191, 237,
    239, 257
income distribution, 86, 94, 336
individualism, 54–56, 90, 123, 144,
    161, 333, 341
industrial reserve army, 136, 155
inequality, 2, 32, 43–44, 46, 54, 57–59,
    63–65, 80, 92–97, 122, 124, 158,
    162–63, 169, 173, 185–88, 201–2,
    214–15, 255, 260, 264–66, 282,
    338, 354; effect of segregation on,
    70, 146–53, 224–26
inflation, 157, 170–74, 176–78, 218
institutions, 2, 13, 39, 71–72, 90,
    104–5, 135, 203–9, 215, 240, 359
instrumentalist, 206–12
invisible hand, 20
IQ, 302–6
iron cage of bureaucracy, 32, 289–90

Japan, 73, 182, 216, 226, 305, 354,
    357–58
Japanese-American, internment of,
    223–24, 227, 275
Jim Crow laws, 151, 223

Kant, Immanuel, 17–18, 345–46
Katrina, hurricane, xii, 156
Keynesian militarism, 174–80
Keynesian macroeconomic policies, 8,
    169, 172–74, 190
Kondratieff cycles, 217–18
Krugman, P., 180, 189, 214–19, 291,
    309–12
Ku Klux Klan, 55, 70, 74, 223, 317

labor, 5–6, 10, 52; alienation of labor,
    87, 204, 289; sale of labor power,
    38, 54, 61, 103–5, 118, 128, 136,
    308; sexist division of, 132, 143–49;

segmented labor market, 120–22, 132–33, 148–53;

labor power, price of, 65, 118–20, 189; labor theory of value, 2, 81, 89, 93, 112–17, 204, 253, 355; labor unions, 70, 176, 179, 213, 234, 268; Latin America, 10, 23, 68, 105, 191, 227

law, 39, 42, 52, 65, 196, 225, 255

legal and political superstructure, 29–30

Lenin, V., 11, 24, 180, 200, 248, 251–56, 272, 316, 327, 331

Leninism, 82, 180, 200, 251, 272–73

liberalism, 52–65, 107, 295; and fascism, 226–30, 275

liberal theory, 54–57, 177

majority rule, 247–49, 272

Mao Zedong, 211, 262, 344

Marxism, 1, 2–5, 7, 10; definition of, 5–6, 11, 34; on dialectics, 279–358; on economics, 107–92; varieties of, 251–55

material incentives, 257

materialism, 2, 5, 194, 203, 285–86, 291, 324

McCarren Act (195), 214

McCarthyite period, 337

means of production, 27, 31, 88, 127, 139, 190, 198–99, 227, 244, 246, 251, 258; class defined by relationship to, 44, 46, 66, 334, 337, 356; concentration of ownership of, 48, 51, 59–63, 93–94, 123, 154, 166, 204, 336; mechanical standpoint, 189, 193–95, 282–83, 307, 326, 352, 360

Medicaid, 98

metaphysical standpoint, 25, 196, 286, 352

Metternich, 244

Mexico, 116, 156

Michels, R., 198

middle class society, United States as a, 49, 86, 214, 335–38

Milgram, Stanley, 342, 344

military Keynesianism, 174–80

military spending, 172–80

Mill, J. S., 55, 295

Miller, R., 34, 291, 323

misery in the United States, 62, 81, 83, 154–62

mobility, social, 93, 162–69

mode of production, 26, 28–31, 44–46, 68, 107, 11, 159, 172, 289, 322, 339, 352

modernization theory, 81–83, 184, 187

modern society, diagnosing problems of, 22, 31–35, 103, 155, 289–90

modern world, dynamics of, 65, 78–80, 84, 28–90

money as a claim on labor, 89, 112–14

Monopoly, game of, 61, 128–34, 150–52, 171, 187–88, 200–3, 217, 281

Moore, B., 71–74, 299

nationalism, 35, 57, 68–71, 145, 161, 228, 236, 253–54, 260, 263, 268–71

National Labor Relations Board, 213

national socialism, 227

naturalism, 292, 331

necessity, 35, 109, 104, 292, 345

neocolony, 182

neoconservative, 65, 137, 189, 348

network, 116, 208, 216, 341–44

neutrality, 299–306; pseudo, 301–6

New Deal, 59, 63, 101–2, 173, 179, 201, 213–16, 221, 225

Newton, I., 307, 313

nonviolent movements, 240–43

norms, as basis of social structure, 18, 25, 32–33, 287–93

Obama, B., xii, 99, 178, 191, 200, 213, 220, 223–26, 233

objectification, 19

objectivity, attempts at neutrality as the basis of, 299–306, 359, 362

occupation, 51, 138–43, 154, 305, 342

occupational mobility, 163–68

occupational prestige, 51, 154

occupational status, and class, 48, 334

ontological dialectic, 282, 284

OPEC, 130, 182, 216, 238

opportunism, 9, 253, 268–70, 277

Orshansky, M., 156–57
overproduction, 8, 11, 122–27

pacifism, 255, 268
package deals, 22–25, 32, 70, 288–89, 318
Palmer Raids, 223, 275
paradigms, 112, 361; in sociology, 17, 35, 289, 315–16
Paris Commune, 3, 5, 245, 251
parliamentarianism, 252, 268, 274
partisanship, 175, 299–303, 361
particularistic bonds and relationships, 82, 132
patriotism, 28, 35, 175, 228, 231, 270, 274, 318–19
patterns, 142, 194, 222, 285, 288, 306–12, 319–23
Philippines, 184
philosophies of history, 16–17, 39, 65, 344–45
Piven, F. 99, 180,
pluralism, 54–56, 123, 194, 294. See also classical liberalism
Poland, 266
polarization, 49, 60–62, 125, 129, 132–33, 150–51, 156, 187–88, 201–4, 217, 230, 267
political action, economic change and, 159–62, 167, 193
political changes, crucial to modern world, 212–17, 253
political conflicts, 29, 133, 243
political economy, 5, 20–21, 75, 78, 89, 107–8, 110–17, 189, 218, 243, 256, 350
political left, 221, 230, 233, 238–39, 247, 255–57
political power, 159, 198, 204–5, 212, 256, 268, 277, 322
political resources, 102, 203–11
political sociology, 195, 198, 211, 220, 251, 275
political theories of a free society, 195–200
popular will, effect on U.S. government, 58
pork barrel spending, 177

positivism, 291–92, 300, 316
Poulantzas, N., 212, 235
poverty line, 59, 98, 155–58, 336
power, measuring, 206–9
powerlessness, 19, 32–33, 85–91, 110, 149, 154, 210, 289–91
practice, 9, 17, 40, 70, 196, 200, 234, 252, 271, 292, 299, 301, 307, 313, 316, 349, 351, 356–59
preliterate societies, 14, 36
primitive accumulation, 118–19
primitive communism, 27
private ownership, 27, 43, 124, 127, 154, 199, 227, 244, 251, 258, 337
product, alienation of, 88–89, 203–6
production: forces of, 31, 34, 169, 237, 259–60, 339, 355; means of, 27, 43, 46, 48, 51, 59, 61–63, 80, 88, 93, 103–5, 139, 154, 166, 199, 204, 244–46, 251, 258, 297, 334, 336, 338; mode of, 26–27, 44, 46, 67–68, 78–80, 84, 104, 111, 159, 172, 189, 289, 322, 352; relations of, 26–27, 31, 34, 46, 48–9, 53, 61, 80, 103–5, 110, 159, 202, 237, 258, 335, 338, 349, 355
profit, 58, 78–81, 93–94, 108, 112, 119, 122–26, 129–31, 137, 143, 149, 170–72, 189–92, 206–9, 266, 276
proletarian, 48, 93–94, 111, 131, 149, 170, 195, 197, 243–51, 272
proletariat, 48, 93–94, 111, 131, 149, 170, 195, 197, 243–51, 272
property income, 43, 47, 94, 96, 112–14, 118, 124, 128, 133, 244, 256
Protestant Reformation, 53, 55, 211, 224
pseudo-neutrality, 300–5
public ownership, 198–200, 258

race, relationship of IQ scores to, 301–6
racial conflict, 66, 223–24; and discrimination, 145–46, 150, 153–54, 223, 239; and genocide, 23, 222–24, 231, 235
racism, 35, 77, 90, 92, 143–50, 161, 179, 195, 205, 216, 232, 240, 257, 269; causes of, 32–33, 57, 86, 90,

150–54, 188, 286–87, 290, 300, 315; and class conflict, 32–33, 68–71, 104, 143–54, 190, 216, 353–54; and genocide, 222–24, 231; relationship of fascism to, 222–29, 276, 316; struggle against, 195, 249, 295, 200, 353–54

Reagan, R. 63, 97, 167, 173–74, 178–79, 191, 212, 216, 220–21

realism, 283–84

realignment, 220–22, 226

reductionism, 108, 288

Reich, M., 146–47, 153, 219

relations of production, 26–27, 31, 34, 46, 48–49, 53, 61, 80, 103–5, 110, 159, 202, 237, 258, 335, 338, 349, 355

relative, 293, 297

relative surplus value, 120

relativism, 292–95, 362

religion, 129, 132, 143, 190, 205, 236, 281, 289, 331

religious fundamentalists, 40, 238, 343

revisionism, 253

revolutionary Marxism, 200

Robinson, R., 166, 169

Roots, 117

ruling class, 21, 27–28, 30, 63, 104, 144–45, 159, 175, 206–12, 245, 247, 253, 269, 272–73, 333, 335

Russia, agrarian bureaucracy in, 39, 74

Ste. Croix, G. E. M. de, 42, 44, 52, 162

science of society, possibility of, 102, 282–88

scientific analysis, 110, 307

scientism, 292

Second International, 253

segmentation of the labor market, 145, 148, 153, 170, 192, 229

segregation, 146–47, 150–52, 170, 188, 222, 238, 311, 331

self-employment, 14, 44, 48, 63, 89, 93–94, 123, 126, 139, 152, 166, 308

serfs, 27–28, 52, 67, 86, 119

sexism, 32, 57, 68, 90–91, 104, 122, 143–50, 205, 224, 228, 255, 270–71, 295, 340, 353

sexist division of labor, 148–49

sick societies, 34, 92

Silicon Valley, 137

skepticism, 292, 297, 300; extreme, 293–97

slavery, 1, 14, 18–19, 28, 39–45, 52, 60–61, 64, 75–78, 81, 83, 104, 121, 144–45, 151, 153, 155–58, 300

Smith, A., 20, 58, 112

social behavior, 51, 66, 285–87, 308, 325–26

social change, 24–25, 41, 45, 65–68, 69, 71, 107, 132, 159, 167, 194, 240, 255, 259, 279, 289, 324, 331, 345, 359

social consciousness, 26, 28, 30

social democrats, 199–200, 232, 274

social fascist, 230–35

social formation, 27–29

social history, 13, 21

social institutions, 2, 13, 18, 46, 80, 104, 113, 240, 280, 335, 359

socialism, 2, 9, 25, 35, 73–74, 84, 189, 197–99, 226–27, 240, 243–44, 246, 250–54, 256–568, 276

social movements, 65–71, 76, 200, 241–43

social positions, 47–49, 298, 333

social problems, 32–33, 40, 97, 180, 194, 238, 288, 289, 347

social revolutions, 65–67, 71, 104

social science, 7, 10, 15, 17, 34, 85, 135, 180, 188, 222, 237, 270, 279, 282–83, 291, 299, 306, 309, 314, 317–19, 323, 324, 355–56

Social Security Act, 100, 102, 213

social structure, 2, 13, 15, 32, 67, 71, 87, 103, 135, 270, 287, 289, 306, 321, 330, 332, 339, 351, 359, 361

social system, 31, 40, 41, 52–54, 68, 72, 87, 89, 90, 96, 127, 189, 229, 274

social theory, 23–25, 31, 34, 107, 125, 175, 275, 282–84, 292, 295, 301, 306, 312, 314, 323, 328

society: contradictions in, 13–15, 26, 211, 339–44; thoughts of members as the basis of, 17–18, 323–30

sociology: link between history and, 1–2, 13–17, 65–68; paradigms in, 289–316; philosophies of history as a source of, 17–22
South Vietnam, fascism in, 235
Soviet Union: Bolsheviks in, 248; communism in, 244, 246; elitism in, 248–52; nationalism in, 223; transition to capitalism, 213; split with China, 246, 251–54
species being, 19, 87
spirit, Hegel's concept of, 18–21, 25, 281, 285, 316
stagnation, 56, 60–64, 172–73, 191
stagflation, 111, 170
Stalin, J., 253, 258, 266
state capitalism, 9, 226, 244, 247, 257–58
states, 13–14, 27, 35–39
status: relationship to class, 49–52, 94; status inconsistency, 51
Stinchcombe, A., 129, 272–73
stratification, 36–38, 43, 46–51, 58–60, 142–43, 154, 336
structuralist, analysis of power, 206–12
structural mobility, 163–67
success, distinguishing different kinds of social movements, 240–43
super-exploitation, 68, 120–22, 144, 276
superstructure, 26–30, 89, 156
surplus, value, 2, 27, 38, 44, 89, 92, 104, 112, 118, 120, 122, 124, 200, 203; absolute, 120; definition of, 38, 114; relative surplus value, 120
Swank, D., 99–102
Sweden, social Democracy in, 354, 357–58

Taft-Hartley Act (1947), 101, 214
technology, 17, 31, 32, 37–41, 110, 135, 137, 185, 203, 260, 310–11, 360
television, 57, 63, 261, 333–34, 338
tertiary sector, 185–89
Theories of Surplus Value (Marx), 5, 107
Third (Communist) International, 232, 233, 253

Tilly, C., 17, 39, 42, 66–67, 71, 122, 151–53, 226
Timberlake, M., 185, 187
Tocqueville, A. de, 168–69
totalitarianism, 226
Trotsky, L., 253, 266
truth, absolute v. concrete, 293, 360
Tubman, H., 76

unemployment, 135–37, 155–57, 170, 176–78, 180, 288–89, 325, 347–50
Uneven Tides, 65,
United Farm Workers of America, 232
United States, 74, 77, 121, 179; class exploitation in, 62–64, 83–86, 92–97, 213; class stratification in, 1, 29–30, 46–47, 58, 62–64; as a middle class society, 49–50; mobility in, 162–66; misery in, 154–61; role of popular will in controlling, 134, 206–8, 213
unproductive workers, 89
use value, 115, 122, 131, 135, 169, 328
U.S.S.R. See Soviet Union
utilitarianism, 55, 123, 128
utopianism, 168

Vanguard Party, 251–54, 271–74
veil of money, 116–18
Vietnam, 10, 224, 235–38, 248–49
violence, 118, 231, 240–43, 254, 268, 274
voluntaristic analysis, 75, 193
voluntarism, 265

Wagner Act (1935), 213
Wallace, M., 175–80
Wallerstein, I., 17, 81–84, 117–18
war on poverty, 224
wealth: accumulation of, 6, 24; see Monopoly; distribution of, 37, 47–48, 93–96; wealthy capitalists, power of, 203–9
Weber, M., 18–19, 21, 25, 32, 34, 35, 42, 48, 49, 50, 52, 82, 93, 132, 198, 246, 263, 286–91, 305, 324–25, 327, 337–38, 344
welfare state, 54, 78, 97–102, 157–58, 199

women, oppression of, 121, 145, 148–50, 152, 211, 228, 240
workers, labor power of, 54, 61, 103, 105, 119
working class, 10, 28, 38, 49, 61–62, 68–70, 77, 111, 121, 137–38, 142, 148, 153–56, 181–82, 192, 196, 198, 200, 207, 210–12, 224–26, 229, 231, 233, 235, 244, 246–48, 253, 256, 258, 262, 264, 266, 269, 270, 272
world-systems theory, 81, 84, 184
Wright, E. O., 34, 41–42, 202–3, 212, 338, 354–58

About the Authors

Peter Knapp is a professor of sociology at Villanova University and the author of *One World-Many Worlds: Contemporary Sociological Theory* and *The Assault on Equality* as well as articles on Hegel, path dependency, and sociological theory. He is currently working on the use of geographic information systems such as Google Earth for sociological teaching and research

Alan Spector was a full-time traveling organizer for Students for a Democratic Society (SDS) for three years before completing his Ph.D. in sociology from Northwestern University. A professor of sociology at Purdue University Calumet, his publications include "Marxist Sociology and Humanist Sociology: Diversity, Intersections, and Convergence" in *The American Sociologist* and "Globalization or Imperialism? Neoliberal Globalization in the Age of Capitalist Imperialism" in *International Review of Modern Sociology*. He has served as chair of the Section on Marxist Sociology in the American Sociological Association and is an active member of the Society for the Study of Social Problems, the International Sociological Association, and Sociologists without Borders. He is the current vice president for publications of the Association for Humanist Sociology. He remains active in campus and community groups working against racism, imperialism, and for working class rights.